www.wadsworth.com

www.wadsworth.com is the World Wide Web site for Thomson Wadsworth and is your direct source to dozens of online resources.

At *www.wadsworth.com* you can find out about supplements, demonstration software, and student resources. You can also send email to many of our authors and preview new publications and exciting new technologies.

www.wadsworth.com
Changing the way the world learns®

FOURTH EDITION

Judicial Process and Judicial Policymaking

G. ALAN TARR
Rutgers University–Camden

THOMSON
WADSWORTH

Australia • Canada • Mexico • Singapore • Spain • United Kingdom • United States

Publisher: Clark Baxter
Executive Editor: David Tatom
Assistant Editor: Anne Gittinger
Editorial Assistant: Cheryl Lee
Technology Project Manager: Michelle Vardeman
Marketing Manager: Janise Fry
Marketing Assistant: Teresa Jessen
Advertising Project Manager: Kelley McAllister
Project Manager, Editorial Production: Megan E. Hansen
Art Director: Maria Epes

Print/Media Buyer: Rebecca Cross
Permissions Editor: Joohee Lee
Production Service and Compositor: Kathy Glidden,
    Stratford Publishing Services, Inc.
Compositor: Cadmus
Cover Designer: Jeanette Barber
Copy Editor: Sally Townsend
Cover Image: © CORBIS
Printer: Malloy Incorporated

For more information about our products,
contact us at:
Thomson Learning Academic Resource Center
1-800-423-0563

For permission to use material from this text
or product, submit a request online at
http://www.thomsonrights.com.

Any additional questions about permissions can be
submitted by email to
thomsonrights@thomson.com.

Library of Congress Control Number: 2005922297

ISBN 0-534-60243-6

Thomson Higher Education
10 Davis Drive
Belmont, CA 94002-3098
USA

Asia (including India)
Thomson Learning
5 Shenton Way
#01-01 UIC Building
Singapore 068808

Australia/New Zealand
Thomson Learning Australia
102 Dodds Street
Southbank, Victoria 3006
Australia

Canada
Thomson Nelson
1120 Birchmount Road
Toronto, Ontario M1K 5G4
Canada

UK/Europe/Middle East/Africa
Thomson Learning
High Holborn House
50–51 Bedford Row
London WC1R 4LR
United Kingdom

Latin America
Thomson Learning
Seneca, 53
Colonia Polanco
11560 Mexico
D.F. Mexico

Spain (including Portugal)
Thomson Paraninfo
Calle Magallanes, 25
28015 Madrid, Spain

For Bob and Andy

Contents

Preface   xv

Chapter 1

Courts and Law   1

Legal Systems   3
  The Common-Law Legal Family   3
  The Civil-Law (Romano-Germanic) Legal Family   7
  Civil Law versus Common Law   8

Law   9
  Private Law and Public Law   9
  Criminal Law and Civil Law   11
  Substantive Law and Procedural Law   12
  Law and Equity   12

Common Misconceptions about Law and Courts   13
  Law and Uncertainty   13
  Courts, Law, and Public Policy   15

Conclusions   17
Notes   18

Part One

STRUCTURES AND PARTICIPANTS IN THE JUDICIAL PROCESS   23

Chapter 2

The Federal and State Court Systems   25

The Federal Court System   28
  Structure   28

The Development of the Federal Judicial System   28
Federal Jurisdiction   31

The Federal Courts Today   36
The District Courts   36
The Courts of Appeals   39
The United States Supreme Court   41

State Courts   41
The Structure of State Court Systems   43
The Development of State Court Systems   46

Conclusions   48

Notes   49

Chapter 3

Judges   53

What Sort of Judges Do We Want?   56
Judicial Independence versus Accountability   56
Representativeness   57

Judicial Selection in the States   57
Modes of Judicial Selection   57
The Politics of Judicial Elections   61
The Politics of Merit Selection   65
What Effect Do Judicial Selection Systems Have?   68

Who Are the State Judges?   69

The Selection of Federal Judges   71
The Size of the Federal Judiciary   71
The Selection of District Court and Appeals Court Judges   72
Selection of Lower Court Judges from Carter to George W. Bush   74

The Selection of Supreme Court Justices   79
Criteria for Selection   80
Obstacles to Presidential Influence   84

What Do Judges Do?   86
From Advocate to Arbiter   86
The Work of the Trial Judge   88
The Work of the Appellate Judge   90

Conclusions   92

Notes   93

Chapter 4

Lawyers   97

The Trouble with Lawyers   99

The Legal Profession   102
    Becoming a Lawyer   102
    A Portrait of the Legal Profession   107
    The Organization of the Legal Profession   111

Practicing Law   112
    An Overview of Legal Practice   112
    Current Types of Legal Practice   113
    The Divided Legal Profession   117

Access to Legal Services   117
    Criminal Justice   118
    Civil Law   119

Lawyers and Clients   124

The Transformation of the American Legal Profession   127

Notes   128

Part Two

JUDICIAL PROCESS AND JUDICIAL DECISION MAKING   133

Chapter 5

Trials and Appeals   135

An Overview of the Chapter   138

Trials   138
    Disputes and Fact-Finding   138
    The Diversity of Trials   140
    Rights at Trial   140
    The Trial Process   142

The Jury in the United States   150
    The Changing Jury   150
    Jury Size and Jury Decision Making   151
    Evaluating the Jury   152

Appeals   155
    The Appellate Process   155
    The U.S. Supreme Court   156
    Other Appellate Courts   166

Beyond Trials and Appeals   168
Notes   168

Chapter 6
Criminal Justice and the Courts   172

Prosecutors and Defense Attorneys   173
    Prosecutors   173
    Defense Attorneys   174
The Process of Criminal Justice   175
    Crime and Arrest   175
    Charges and Dismissals   178
    Bail and Pretrial Release   180
    Preliminary Hearings and Grand Juries   181
Plea Bargaining   183
    The Process of Plea Bargaining   183
    Why Plea Bargaining Occurs   187
    Attacks on Plea Bargaining   189
    Evaluating Plea Bargaining   191
Policy Issues in Criminal Justice   192
    The Exclusionary Rule   193
    The Insanity Defense   197
    Crime and Punishment: Sentencing   201
    Crime and Punishment: Drug Courts   205
Conclusions   208
Notes   210

Chapter 7
Civil Justice and the Courts   216

How Cases Arise   219
    Injuries and Grievances   219
    Responses   221
Rules and Processes   223
    Rules   223
    The Process of Civil Litigation   223
Civil Cases and Their Outcomes   227
    The Universe of Cases   227
    Outcomes of Civil Cases   231

A Litigation Crisis?   233
   The Indictment   233
   Is the United States a Litigious Society?   233
Is There a Better Way?   237
   Alternatives in Dispute Resolution   238
   Does ADR Work?   240
Conclusions   *242*
Notes   *243*

Chapter 8

Judicial Decision Making   247

The Legal Perspective   248
   The Phases of Judicial Decision Making   248
   The Tools of Judicial Decision Making   249
   Legal Reasoning as Deductive Reasoning   253
   Legal Reasoning as Reasoning by Example   255
   Implications   259
The Political Perspective   260
   Attitudes   262
   Judicial Role Orientations   265
   Institutional Factors   267
Analyzing the Two Perspectives   270
Notes   *271*

Part Three

JUDICIAL POLICYMAKING   275

Chapter 9

Judicial Policymaking: An Introduction   277

The Occasions of Judicial Policymaking   278
   Judicial Review and Constitutional Policymaking   278
   Remedial Policymaking   282
   Statutory Interpretation and Judicial Policymaking   283
   Oversight of Administrative Activity and Judicial Policymaking   286
   The Common Law and Judicial Policymaking   287
   Cumulative Policymaking   289

The Incidence of Judicial Policymaking   290
    The Level of Judicial Policymaking   290
    Historical Shifts in Judicial Policymaking   291
    The Agenda of Judicial Policymaking   292

Assessing Judicial Policymaking   293
    Criteria for Evaluation   293
    Judicial Capacity and Policy Effectiveness   293
    Legitimacy   297

Conclusions   *299*

Notes   *300*

Chapter 10

Federal Court Policymaking   304

School Desegregation   304
    The Road to *Brown*   305
    Brown I and *Brown* II   306
    The Response to *Brown*, 1954–1964   308
    School Desegregation, 1964–1971   310
    The Courts and School Desegregation, 1971–2004   312
    The Legacy of *Brown*   315

Abortion   315
    Abortion Becomes a Legal Issue   317
    Roe v. Wade   319
    The Response to *Roe*   321
    The Effects of *Roe*   324

Brown, Roe, and Beyond   325
    The Development of Legal Issues   325
    Policy Change   326
    Legal Obligation   327
    Policy Effectiveness   330

Notes   *331*

Chapter 11

State Court Policymaking   337

School Finance   337
    The Development of School Finance Litigation   338
    The Broader Context of State Constitutional Policymaking   345

The Tort Law Revolution and Products Liability Law   349
    The Changing Face of Products Liability Law   350
    The Consequences of Policy Change   357
    Responses to the Products Liability "Crisis"   362
Conclusions   *363*
Notes   *364*

For Further Reading   371
Index   383

Preface

The fourth edition of *Judicial Process and Judicial Policymaking*, like the three preceding editions, is designed as a basic text for courses on the judicial process, the American legal system, or law and politics. Its approach to these subjects is based on four major premises.

First, courts in the United States have always played an important role in governing, and that role has increased in recent decades. Various factors have been suggested to explain this judicial involvement in governing, including the common-law system imported from England and modified in response to American conditions and beliefs, the institution of judicial review, and the legalistic and litigious orientation of the American populace. Whatever its causes, the phenomenon of judicial participation in governing makes understanding the processes and consequences of judicial policymaking essential for understanding U.S. government.

Second, judicial policymaking is distinctive. Judges develop public policy in the course of resolving disputes. They bring to the task of policymaking a particular training and orientation. The institutional constraints they operate under differ considerably from those on legislators or administrators. Together, these factors affect the way that judges view problems and the policies they develop. They also highlight why understanding the judicial process and the participants in it is crucial for understanding judicial policymaking. Therefore, Chapters 2 through 8 are devoted to examining the processes by which courts operate and the participants in those processes.

Third, courts make policy in a variety of ways. Sometimes, a court announces a landmark decision with national implications. More frequently, however, judicial policymaking occurs through less heralded rulings or series of rulings. At times, this policymaking brings courts into conflict with other branches of government, as when a court strikes down a statute as unconstitutional. But often judicial policymaking complements policymaking by another branch, as when courts choose between competing understandings of the law through statutory interpretation. At other times, judicial policymaking may be altogether independent of the actions of other branches, as when judges elaborate the common law. To provide a sense of this diversity, Chapter 9 surveys the various forms of judicial policymaking, and Chapters 10 and 11 provide detailed case studies of the development and consequences of important judicial policies.

Finally, courts may be the objects of public policy, as well as its creators. Reformers have attacked various features of the administration of justice in the United States, including the insanity defense, the adversarial system, plea bargaining, and the jury system. Sometimes they have succeeded in enacting their reforms into law. Even when they have not, their criticisms require us to consider how effectively the judicial process in the United States promotes justice and what effects the proposed reforms would have on the administration of justice. Throughout the book, therefore, we discuss and assess these various reform proposals. We also survey legal practices and institutions in other nations, so readers can consider how other countries have dealt with common legal problems.

Many people contributed to the completion of this project. At Rutgers University (Camden), Karen McGrath and Sylvia Somers provided needed secretarial assistance with their usual cheerfulness and efficiency. Mary Cornelia Porter read portions of the manuscript and offered excellent suggestions on how to improve it. Many reviewers of this and the previous editions also provided useful comments and rescued me from various errors of fact or interpretation: Lauren Bowen, John Carroll University; John C. Domino, Sam Houston State University; Margaret E. Ellis, James Madison University; Larry Elowitz, Georgia College; Sheldon Goldman, University of Massachusetts; Jona Goldschmidt, Northern Arizona University; A. J. Goubler, Delgado Community College; Roger Handberg, University of Central Florida; Mark Iris, Northwestern University; Christopher L. Markwood, University of Central Oklahoma; Phillip M. Simpson, Cameron University; Ken R. Stockholm, University of Alaska; Richard N. Weldon, Coastal Carolina University; and Gary Young, George Washington University. Henry Glick, Craig Emmert, Sheldon Goldman, Frank Coffin, Barbara Curran, James Eisenstein, Herbert Jacob, Jeffrey Segal, Harold Spaeth, Stephen Halpern, and Charles Lamb all graciously consented to my reprinting material from their research. Any errors that remain are, of course, solely my responsibility. Finally, I would like to thank my wife, Susan, for her loving support and my sons, Bob and Andy, to whom this book is dedicated.

COURTS AND LAW

Today the United States has more than a million lawyers, and the country's law schools annually graduate another 39,000.[1] In 2002, the nation's state and federal courts resolved almost 100 million cases, more than one for every three Americans, and the courts' caseloads increase with each passing year.[2] Striking as these figures are, they do not capture the full impact of law and the courts in the United States. Scan a newspaper, and one is immediately struck by how often Americans call upon judges to resolve important policy disputes. Judicial rulings affect everything from the contents of the Internet to conditions in jails and prisons, from the definition of marriage to the selection of the president.[3] Many judicial decisions, of course, affect only the parties to the dispute. But as the U.S. Supreme Court's rulings on school desegregation and abortion illustrate, other decisions may focus public attention on issues and encourage broad social changes.[4] Thus, courts do not merely resolve large numbers of disputes; they also actively participate in governing.

It is hardly surprising, therefore, that Americans have long had a fascination with law, lawyers, and legal institutions. We closely follow publicized trials— more than 150 million Americans tuned in for the verdict in the O. J. Simpson murder case—and through Court TV and CNN we daily monitor other legal developments. We indulge our interest in the law through bestsellers by John Grisham and Scott Turow, through television programs such as *Law and Order,* and through movies such as *A Few Good Men* and *A Civil Action.*[5] We incorporate legal terms such as "taking the Fifth" and "the right to privacy" into our everyday conversations. We even tend to think about political issues from a legal perspective.[6] Ours is truly a law-permeated society.

Combined with our fascination with the legal order, however, is often a concern about the law and American legal institutions. This concern extends to the ways in which courts operate and to the decisions they render. It underlies the frequent, often biting jokes we tell about lawyers: "What do you have when you have a lawyer buried up to his neck in the sand? Not enough sand." It is reflected more directly in poll data expressing public dissatisfaction with courts and attorneys. A Harris poll conducted in 2000, for example, found that only 12 percent of Americans voiced "a great deal of confidence" in law firms, while a Gallup poll a year earlier revealed that only 13 percent of Americans rated the honesty and ethical standards of lawyers as "very high or high," placing them just above gun salesmen. Fully one-third of the respondents in a Gallup Poll in 2000 voiced little or no confidence in the criminal justice system.[7] Earlier surveys found dissatisfaction with the civil justice system as well. A Louis Harris poll had found that 54 percent of Americans believed that the nation's civil justice imposed unreasonable costs on society, while a poll in California found that 58 percent of Californians felt that politics affected court decisions.[8] The sense that Americans are dissatisfied with their legal system led George W. Bush in his 2004 reelection campaign to charge that lawyers filing "frivolous lawsuits" were driving up the costs of health care and preventing American companies from competing effectively in the global marketplace. Simply put, there is a widespread perception that American legal institutions are not working very well.

Whether this perception is correct is, of course, a matter of dispute.[9] Some commentators deny that there is a crisis in the courts and view such criticisms as exaggerated claims designed to justify fundamental changes in the administration of justice.[10] It is also noteworthy that the attacks on the courts come from widely divergent perspectives and reflect quite different diagnoses of what ails the courts. Many Americans insist that the courts are too lenient in their treatment of criminals; since 1974, more than three-quarters of Americans have taken that position in annual polls.[11] Others contend that courts are not evenhanded in dispensing justice. For example, following the not guilty verdict in the first Rodney King case, the police brutality case that sparked the Los Angeles riots of 1992, critics charged that U.S. courts were guilty of racism.[12] Sometimes the same events can trigger different complaints. A poll conducted after O. J. Simpson was acquitted of murder found that one-third of African American respondents expressed "little confidence" in the judicial system, while one-third of white respondents concluded that the case showed that "there is no justice."[13] Yet although the criticisms may vary, the chorus of complaints raises questions about how effective American courts and legal institutions are in promoting justice.

This volume seeks to provide readers with the information and the range of perspectives they need to arrive at their own assessment of the U.S. legal system. To do so, it first describes the nation's legal structures and the participants— judges, lawyers, and litigants—in the judicial process. Next, it examines the processes by which courts—from trial courts to the U.S. Supreme Court—resolve the cases that come before them and the ways in which judges reach their decisions. Finally, it surveys how courts participate in policymaking and analyzes the consequences of this judicial involvement in governing.

The book provides analyses of various reform proposals, such as eliminating plea-bargaining and permitting the use of illegally seized evidence at trial, so that readers may consider the likely consequences of their adoption. In addition comparisons are drawn with the legal systems of other countries. These comparisons highlight what is distinctive about the American legal system and also show how other countries have dealt with similar legal problems.

Let us begin with an overview of legal systems and of the law and consider certain common misconceptions about law and the courts.

LEGAL SYSTEMS

Legal scholars group the legal systems of the world into "legal families," based on their common origins and on similarities in their law and their legal institutions (see Table 1-1).[14]

The most influential families of legal systems—the common-law and civil-law (or Romano-Germanic) families—originated in Europe. These legal systems have spread their influence throughout the world through colonialism and through the process of modernization in non-European countries. Nevertheless, many countries in Africa and Asia have also retained elements of their indigenous legal systems.

The legal system of the United States belongs to the family of common-law legal systems. So, too, do the legal systems of other former British colonies, such as Australia, Nigeria, and India. Most legal systems on the European continent belong to the civil-law (Romano-Germanic) family, as do the legal systems of most Latin American countries and of the former French and Belgian colonies in Africa and Asia. In some countries—for instance, in Japan—the legal system defies easy categorization into a legal family because it has derived elements from French, German, English, and American law.[15]

The Common-Law Legal Family

Although each country within the common-law legal family has developed its own legal institutions and bodies of law, common-law systems resemble each other in the general organization of their courts, in the rules of evidence and procedure they employ, and in the legal doctrines they developed. Because these features of common-law systems derive from English law and legal practice, an understanding of the historical origins of the common law in England is crucial to understanding common-law systems of other countries including the United States.

The Development of the Common Law[16]   The Norman conquest of England in 1066 under William the Conqueror laid the groundwork for the development of the common law. To extend royal authority over their dominion, King William's successors created permanent courts, staffed by judges

TABLE
1-1

FAMILIES OF LEGAL SYSTEMS

Legal Family	Origins	Geographic Area	Distinguishing Feature
Common Law	England, beginning in the 12th century	England, former English colonies, and other countries with strong political ties to England such as Australia and New Zealand North America: the United States and Canada (with the exception of Quebec) Africa: Nigeria, Kenya, and Uganda, among others Asia: India and Pakistan	Judges decide cases through inductive reasoning, relying heavily on precedent.
Civil Law (Romano-Germanic)	European universities, during the 12th and 13th centuries, which adapted the Code of Justinian to new circumstances	Most countries in continental Europe and in Latin America, as well as former French colonies in North America (Quebec and Louisiana) and the former Belgian and French colonies in Africa (e.g., Rwanda and Burundi). Some other legal systems (e.g., Algeria, Morocco, and Indonesia) contain elements of the civil law and other legal traditions.	Judges decide cases through the application of legal principles, which are often drawn from a legal code.
Socialist Law	The Soviet Union, in the aftermath of the Russian Revolution of 1917	Formerly, all Communist countries in Europe, such as the Soviet Union, Yugoslavia, and Bulgaria; today, with the collapse of European communism, a few countries that continue as communist, such as Cuba and Vietnam.	Its primary objective is to move society toward communism in accordance with Marxist-Leninist theory.

Islamic Law	The founding of Islam in the sixth century	Most Muslim nations in North Africa, the Middle East, and Asia base their law, at least in part, on Islamic law.	Islamic law is religious law, understood by believers as divinely revealed and inseparable from the religion.
Hindu Law	Sacred texts known as the *dharmasastras*, written between 800 B.C. and A.D. 200	While Hindu law imposes obligations on all Hindus, it primarily affects the national law of India.	Hindu law is religious law, regulating virtually all aspects of life for believers.
Far Eastern Law	Traditional Chinese notion of social order, exemplified by writings of Confucius (551–479 B.C.)	Historically, China, Japan, Korea, and Indochina; today, despite communism in China and Vietnam and changes in Japanese law associated with its economic development, it still influences the law in all those countries.	Far Eastern legal systems encourage the resolution of disputes by compromise, settlement, or other mechanisms rather than by the rule of law.
African Law	Custom within various African tribes	Although some African states (e.g., Senegal and Tanganyika) have sought since independence to collect and codify tribal customs, the influence of those customs on the law of modern African states has been minimal.	Traditional African law stresses custom and tradition as authoritative

Sources: Information for this table is drawn from Rene David and John Brierly, *Major Legal Systems in the World Today*, 2d ed. (London: Stevens & Sons, 1978), and Konrad Zweigert and Hein Kotz, *Introduction to Comparative Law*, 2d ed. (Oxford: Clarendon Press, 1987).

appointed by the king, to administer the law of the realm. From the twelfth century onward, the English monarchs also dispatched "traveling justices" to rule in the king's name in the county courts.[17] By the thirteenth century, the kings had succeeded in establishing a common set of legal procedures and legal standards throughout England.

But what legal procedures were the royal judges to follow in deciding cases, and what legal principles were they to employ? The judges could not rely upon parliamentary enactments for guidance—Parliament's emergence as a legislative body was still several centuries in the future. Nor could the judges rely much on royal edicts, for these did not extend to many of the legal problems confronting the judges. Rather, as William Blackstone observed in his famous treatise on the common law, the judges looked to a body of "unwritten law," the common law, for guidance.[18] In speaking of the common law as "unwritten," Blackstone was emphasizing that the doctrines of the common law, unlike legislative enactments, "are not set down in any written statute or ordinance, but depend merely upon immemorial usage." Common law was thus custom sanctioned by popular acceptance. Judges served as the "depositories of the law," and their decisions served as "the principal and most authoritative evidence that can be given of the existence of such a custom as shall form a part of the common law."[19] Thus, the common law originated in judicial decisions, which enunciated authoritative legal principles, presumably drawn from the customs and practices of the society, in the course of resolving disputes between litigants.

As these judicial decisions accumulated, they comprised a body of law that judges could draw upon to resolve the cases coming before them. Recurrence to precedent—that is, to the judges' own earlier decisions or to those of their predecessors or colleagues—facilitated judicial decision making by giving judges standards that they could rely upon in deciding the cases before them. Initially, "there was merely a tendency to establish a procedure, and perhaps adopt a few substantive principles which, taken together, constituted the custom of the court" and provided a standard for judicial decisions.[20] Over time, however, as the practice of publishing written reports of judicial decisions developed, judges could more easily consult the rulings of other courts. Over time, too, the authority of these precedents increased. This is reflected in the judges' acceptance of the doctrine of *stare decisis et non quieta movere* (to stand by precedents and not to disturb settled points). Common-law judges under this doctrine of *stare decisis* are obliged to conform their decisions to those that earlier judges reached in similar cases.

Despite the proliferation of legislation and administrative regulations over the last two centuries, judge-made law continues to govern important areas of life in common-law countries. Moreover, as Roscoe Pound has observed, the common law provides "a mode of treating legal problems rather than a fixed body of definite rules."[21] Thus, in dealing with statutes and other enactments, judges in common-law systems usually employ the same approaches to decision making, such as reliance on precedent, that they had developed for dealing with the common law. Recent legal developments have therefore not altered the basic character of common-law legal systems.

The Common Law in the United States   During the seventeenth century, most colonists emigrated to North America from England, and they brought the English legal system with them. When the United States declared its independence from England, the new states retained their common-law legal systems. Thus, like their English counterparts, American judges have enunciated legal standards in the absence of legislation to resolve disputes between litigants. This in turn has guaranteed American judges a major role in lawmaking.

U.S. courts have nevertheless modified the body of common law that they received from England in several important respects. In the decades following independence, American judges expunged aspects of the common law that reflected the aristocratic character of English society and were therefore inappropriate for the more democratic society being created in the United States.[22] During the nineteenth century, they also adapted common-law doctrines that originated in an agrarian society to encourage economic development and accommodate industrialization.[23] Finally, although they have generally adhered to precedent, American judges have never viewed precedent as binding to the same extent as have their English counterparts. They therefore have shown greater willingness to overrule earlier decisions and to alter the common law in response to changing circumstances.

The Civil-Law (Romano-Germanic) Legal Family

The other major family of legal systems is the civil-law (or Romano-Germanic) family. Civil-law legal systems are found on the European continent, throughout South America, and in various countries in Africa and Asia. The origins of the civil law, however, can be traced to the rediscovery of Roman law during the Middle Ages in Europe.

The Rediscovery of Roman Law   The creation of civil-law systems began with the intellectual revival during the twelfth and thirteenth centuries in Western Europe.[24] The founding of universities and the spread of learning during this period led to the rediscovery of the highly developed body of law that had governed ancient Rome. Collected in the Emperor Justinian's *Corpus Juris Civilis,* a systematic compilation or code of law dealing with relations between private persons, Roman law became the subject of law studies in major European universities. The study of Roman law promoted the notion that society should be governed by formal law and provided the vocabulary, categories, and concepts needed for the construction of a modern body of law.

This is not to say that European monarchs seized upon Roman law in order to impose it on their subjects. Because of the political fragmentation in Europe, rulers were rarely in a position to impose much law on anyone. In addition, societal changes had rendered parts of the Roman law obsolete—for example, those sections dealing with slavery. Other elements of the Roman law—for example, family law—were already dealt with by the canon law established by the Catholic Church. As a result, the law that came to prevail in Europe reflected local, non-Roman sources. Nevertheless, jurists and practitioners alike drew their conceptions of law, as well as their legal terminology and their approach to legal reasoning, from the tradition of Roman law.

The Napoleonic Code   The influence of Roman law scholars on civil-law systems, especially on their approach to law and on their terminology, continued from the Middle Ages to the nineteenth century.[25] For modern civil-law systems, the decisive event was the formulation of the Napoleonic Code (French civil code, or *Code civil français*) in 1804. This code, developed by legal experts in France with Napoleon's active participation, immediately became the law in France. French conquests in Europe under Napoleon spread the code throughout the continent, and various European countries quickly developed their own codes modeled on Napoleon's, either under pressure from France or out of respect for the country's military prowess. Even after the defeat of Napoleon, his code continued to influence law throughout much of Europe and became the basis for legal codes in Central America and South America.

Developed in the aftermath of the French Revolution, the Napoleonic Code destroyed the remaining vestiges of feudalism and replaced them with a body of modern law. The code recognized the legal equality of all citizens, freed economic enterprise from traditional constraints, and secularized family law. Equally important, it demonstrated the advantages of systematizing the national law and provided a model for other countries.

Civil Law versus Common Law

Civil-law systems differ from their common-law counterparts in more than their historical roots.[26] Some differences involve the structure and operation of legal institutions, such as the role of judge and attorney at trial and the forms of legal procedure. (These differences are discussed in Chapters 3 and 4.) Others involve the characteristic source of law. In common-law systems, it is the judge, enunciating law in the course of resolving disputes. In civil-law systems, it is the legislative authority, announcing governing legal principles or, in the case of the Napoleonic Code, a more or less comprehensive body of law. Perhaps the most important difference, however, relates to what might be called the legal "frame of mind." Legal thinking in common-law systems emphasizes the concrete rather than the general and places its faith in experience rather than in abstractions. In contrast, legal thinking in civil-law systems reasons from principles to particular instances and has an inclination toward systematizing. As one commentator has put it, a civil-law "system differs from a common-law system much as rationalism differs from empiricism or deduction from induction."[27]

LAW

A speed limit is law; so too are wills, regulations established by the Internal Revenue Service, congressional statutes, trial court rulings, and business contracts. The length of the list (and it is hardly comprehensive) illustrates the diversity of law. To make sense of this diversity, practitioners and scholars have devised various ways of categorizing law.

Private Law and Public Law

Legal scholars often distinguish between *private law* and *public law*. This distinction is particularly important in civil-law systems, such as those in France and Argentina. Many civil-law countries have established separate sets of courts that only hear cases involving public law.

Private law is concerned with relations among private citizens, private organizations, or both. Often these private parties enter into legal agreements (contracts) to order their affairs and to prevent disputes from arising. These efforts, however, are not always effective. Disputes between tenants and landlords over the payment of rent, between neighbors over a noisy pet, and between family members over an inheritance are all examples of private law disputes. So too are suits by consumers injured by unsafe products, by patients accusing physicians of medical malpractice, and by retailers claiming that their suppliers failed to deliver merchandise as promised. These disputes may arise out of legal obligations voluntarily assumed by the parties, as in contracts. Or the applicable law may be found in statutes or in judicial decisions. Whatever its source, in the realm of private law "the sole function of the government [is] the recognition and enforcement of private rights."[28] Table 1-2 identifies important fields of private law. Public law, in contrast, involves relations between the government and private citizens or organizations. Thus, public law includes statutes outlawing murder or fraud, setting auto emissions standards, and taxing capital gains. It also encompasses Supreme Court rulings protecting constitutional rights, such as the freedom of speech, and administrative regulations governing airline safety.

Two major branches of public law are *constitutional law* and *administrative law*. Constitutional law is the fundamental law within a political unit, embodied in the Constitution itself and in the decisions of courts and other bodies interpreting that document. The Constitution establishes the government and

| TABLE 1-2 | SOME CATEGORIES OF PRIVATE LAW | |

Type of Law	What Does It Address?	Who Makes It?
Contract law	The enforcement of those promises for the breach of which the law provides a remedy	State law (primarily state courts through the decision of cases at common law)
Tort law	Legal wrongs committed upon a person or property, other than the breach of contract, and the award of damages for such torts	State law, primarily state common law, but more recently legislation as well
Family law	Relationships between husband and wife and between parent and child, with the rights and duties arising from those relationships	Chiefly state legislation; also federal legislation (social welfare and taxation) and judicial rulings (e.g., abortion)
Commercial	Aspects of business, such as the sale of goods, bank deposits and collections, investment services, etc.	State law (especially the Uniform Commercial Code, legislation adopted by almost all legislatures)
Business	The formation and conduct of business enterprises (corporations, partnerships, etc.)	State law primarily (e.g., incorporations), but also congressional enactments

prescribes how the public business shall be conducted. More specifically, it creates the major offices within a government, determines how they shall be filled, distributes governmental power among those offices, defines the procedures by which government shall operate, and establishes limitations on the scope of governmental power. The United States has fifty-one constitutions. The federal Constitution establishes the national government and governs its operations, while state constitutions do the same for the governments of the fifty states.

Courts in the United States, both federal and state, participate in the development of constitutional law through the exercise of judicial review. Because the U.S. Constitution is the "supreme law of the land," actions of the national or state governments that conflict with the Constitution are invalid, and persons affected by those actions can challenge them in court.[29] (Similarly, litigants may challenge state or local actions that they believe violate a state constitution.) When a litigant claims that the government has acted unconstitutionally, the judge must determine whether the government has exceeded its power or violated rights guaranteed by the Constitution. In exercising this judicial review of governmental enactments, the U.S. Supreme Court has struck down more than 140 federal statutes and more than 1,100 state statutes as unconstitutional.[30]

Administrative law is concerned with the powers and procedures of governmental bodies that exercise power delegated to them by the legislature.

Within the U.S. government, these bodies include such government departments as the Department of Agriculture, such administrative agencies as the Environmental Protection Agency, and such independent regulatory commissions as the Securities and Exchange Commission. These institutions establish rules and regulations that have the force of law. They also conduct hearings and adjudicate disputes that arise from such actions as the termination of welfare benefits. In addition, these institutions decide on the award or withdrawal of government grants—one may recall the controversy during the early 1990s over grants from the National Endowment for the Arts to artists whose works were alleged to be obscene. Finally, these institutions control the distribution of other government benefits—for example, the broadcast licenses awarded by the Federal Communications Commission to radio and television stations. Administrative law largely deals with the processes by which public officials discharge their responsibilities and with the oversight of administrative action by the courts.[31]

Criminal Law and Civil Law

Law is also sometimes categorized based on the relationships that it regulates.[32] The *criminal law* establishes which actions are offenses against the political society and prescribes the punishment to be imposed for such conduct. The criminal law thus is a branch of public law. The parties in a criminal case are always the government, which prosecutes the case, and the defendant, who is charged with the criminal violation. Although they may have an interest in the outcome of a prosecution, victims of crime are not parties to the litigation. The criminal offense is understood as a violation of the public order, not as an offense against a particular person. Familiar crimes include murder, arson, fraud, and burglary.

All other law is classified as *civil law*. (Note that this is different from the distinction between common- and civil-law systems discussed earlier.) Civil law, in contrast to criminal law, is concerned with private rights and obligations and with legal remedies when those rights are violated or those obligations unmet. It usually involves legal relationships between private persons, organizations, or both.

Rights and obligations at civil law may arise from voluntary agreements, as in the case of a contract between a borrower and a lender. They may also result from legislation or administrative action. A law establishing tax rates, a statute permitting victims of sex discrimination to sue for damages, a regulation of the Environmental Protection Agency setting auto emission levels—all involve civil law. Finally, rights and obligations at civil law may be established by judicial decisions interpreting the common law. For example, if you are involved in an automobile accident because your car malfunctions, you may sue the manufacturer for damages. The obligation of manufacturers to produce safe and serviceable products—and their legal liability when they fail to do so—is established by the common law.

Substantive Law and Procedural Law

The distinction between substance and procedure, or substantive law and procedural law, cuts across the previous classifications into public law and private law, criminal law and civil law.[33] *Substantive law* creates, defines, and delimits rights, duties, and obligations. *Procedural law,* in contrast, prescribes the processes by which those substantive rights and obligations are enforced by courts or by other public agencies.

For example, suppose you are seriously injured by a reckless driver. The substantive law determines your right to redress—whether you can obtain damages for your hospital costs, for the pain and suffering you endured, and for the loss of income caused by your hospitalization. The procedural law determines in what court you should file your complaint, what evidence can be admitted, whether you are entitled to a jury trial, and whether you have a right to appeal should the trial court rule against you.

Law and Equity

The distinction between law and equity, which is important in common-law legal systems such as that of the United States, dates from the fourteenth century in England.[34] Parties unable to obtain satisfaction in the royal courts, often because of burdensome and inflexible procedural requirements, applied to the king for redress. As petitions for relief outside the normal legal channels multiplied, the responsibility for deciding on them devolved from the monarch to the chancellor, the highest administrative official of the realm. Petitions came to be addressed to the chancellor directly, who would render decisions based on "the equity of the case"—that is, based on his own sense of the justice of the claim.

By the eighteenth century, the process of considering petitions for equitable relief had become institutionalized in a Court of Chancery, separate from the regular law courts and presided over by the chancellor. This court differed from the regular law courts in the flexibility of its procedures, the absence of a jury, and the broad relief it could provide. Over time, however, as volumes of Chancery decisions were published and a system of precedent was established, "the rules of law applied by the Court of Chancery [became] as much fixed by decisions and as much formed into technical legal rules as the rules of the Common Law."[35] As the Court of Chancery became more and more judicial in its decision making, equity emerged as an alternative to—and a rival of—the law propounded by the regular law courts. This dual system of courts operated in England until the late nineteenth century, when the separate courts of equity were abolished. Thus, when the American colonists developed their legal systems, they typically adopted a dual system of courts, as was familiar to them from England. Most American states merged their law and equity courts during the century after independence, although Mississippi, Tennessee, and Arkansas still maintain separate courts for law and equity.[36]

The merger of legal institutions did not eliminate equity from the U.S. legal system; it merely placed law and equity powers in the same set of hands. Thus, in interpreting a statute or awarding monetary damages in a civil case, a judge is exercising law powers. However, when a judge provides a remedy other than monetary damages, issuing, for example, an injunction (a legal order to a defendant to stop or start doing something), the judge is exercising equity powers. Judicial orders that limit picketing by strikers outside a business or that compel local school districts to bus children to desegregate their schools are contemporary examples of how judges employ their equity powers.[37] These examples show that a judge's equity powers today are primarily exercised in devising remedies for violations of the law.

COMMON MISCONCEPTIONS ABOUT LAW AND COURTS

Misconceptions about law and the courts, just as much as lack of information, may prevent a full understanding of the role of courts in the United States. Often these misconceptions are half-truths, capturing part, but only part, of the reality of law and courts. Two common misconceptions are that (1) law is a body of established rules that govern behavior, and that (2) judicial decisions on important policy issues resolve those issues.

Law and Uncertainty

In thinking of "the law," one tends to think in terms of a body of established, authoritative rules. There is considerable truth to this notion. Obviously, most people most of the time understand what the law requires and conform their conduct to its requirements. According to Justice Oliver Wendell Holmes, a famous justice on the U.S. Supreme Court, this applies to bad people as well as good ones. For even the bad man, Holmes suggested, craved certainty about the law, so he could predict how far he could go without running afoul of governmental authorities.[38]

Nevertheless, as Holmes himself recognized, not all law is clear and certain. Consider, for example, the case of *Lee v. Weisman*.[39] Robert Lee, the principal of a public middle school in Providence, Rhode Island, invited Rabbi Leslie Gutterman to give the invocation and benediction at the school's graduation. In extending the invitation, Lee was following the school district's long-standing practice of having local clergy offer prayers as part of the graduation ceremony. In this instance, however, Daniel Weisman, a parent of one of the graduating students, objected to the invitation. He claimed that the practice of prayers at graduation violated the Establishment Clause of the First Amendment, which requires a degree of separation between church and state.[40] Four days before the graduation, Weisman filed suit in federal district court to prevent the prayers at graduation. Although Weisman's suit came too late to block the prayers at his daughter's graduation, the court agreed with his contention that religious ceremonies at public-school graduations violated the Establishment Clause. It therefore issued a permanent injunction prohibiting the Providence school district from including religious ceremonies as part of future graduations. The school district appealed the decision, but both the federal court of appeals and the U.S. Supreme Court upheld the trial court's ruling.

What is striking about *Lee v. Weisman* is the nature of the dispute. Lee and Weisman agreed completely regarding the facts of the case. Both acknowledged that the school had invited Rabbi Gutterman to give the invocation and benediction, that inviting clergy to offer prayers at graduation was an established practice in the district, and that students were not obliged to attend the graduation ceremony. What Lee and Weisman disagreed about was whether the practice of having clergy lead prayers at graduation was legally permissible. More precisely, they disagreed about the meaning of the law (the Establishment Clause of the First Amendment) and about its application to religious ceremonies at public-school graduations. If the meaning of the Establishment Clause were clear and well known, there would have been no dispute and no litigation.

Lee v. Weisman's exclusive focus on legal rather than factual questions is by no means exceptional. Often, in cases ranging from the most highly charged constitutional conflicts to the most mundane private disputes, the issue is solely the meaning of the law and how it applies. Many other cases raise issues of fact and law simultaneously. Yet the view that litigation is aimed at defining the meaning of law is inconsistent with the notion that law is a set of rules, whose meaning is stable and certain. Indeed, much litigation arises precisely because the meaning of the law is not certain.

The law may be uncertain for several reasons. The language of the law may be vague or general, either by design or because of poor draftsmanship. The aims of those who enacted the law may be unclear. The situation in the case may not have been contemplated by those who enacted the law. And so on.[41] But whatever the reason, judges, when called upon, must "say what the law is."[42] And if the litigation arises because the law is unclear, then judges must choose between the competing understandings of the law and how it applies that are offered by the attorneys arguing the case. In making this choice, judges are doing more than merely substituting certainty for uncertainty, clarity for obscurity. They are, in a very real sense, creating the law.

This is not to say, of course, that judges are free to give whatever interpretation they wish to the law, to decide cases however they choose. Judges operate within a set of legal and political constraints. For example, all judges take an oath to decide cases in accordance with the law. Even before their elevation to the bench, they are socialized through years of legal training and experience as to the proper behavior for a judge. Once in the court, they must consider the expectations of colleagues and lawyers. These factors affect the range of discretion that judges exercise and the sorts of constraints that they feel. Ultimately, however, judicial choice is channeled rather than completely eliminated. Because the law may be uncertain or unclear, a judicial commitment to decide cases according to the law does not eliminate the necessity of judicial choice.

Courts, Law, and Public Policy

Courts in the United States often must resolve disputes involving contentious public issues. Indeed, one of the most perceptive observers of American politics, Alexis de Tocqueville, suggested that "there is hardly a political question in the United States which does not sooner or later turn into a judicial one."[43] This transformation of political issues into legal disputes furnishes judges with the opportunity to influence the course of public policy. And judges have sometimes been more than willing to seize the opportunities presented to them.

Because courts regularly decide cases that involve important policy issues, it might seem that they are in a position to dominate policymaking in the United States. But in actuality the relationship between judicial decisions and public policy is quite complex. *Regents of the University of California v. Bakke*, the U.S. Supreme Court's first ruling on affirmative action, reveals some of these complexities.[44]

Ten years after graduating from the University of Minnesota with a degree in engineering, Allan Bakke decided to become a physician.[45] He applied to the medical school of the University of California at Davis in 1973 and again in 1974, but on both occasions he was denied admission. At that time the university had a special admissions program, under which sixteen seats in the entering class were reserved for minority students. This quota system was not established to remedy earlier discrimination by the medical school—there was no evidence that the school had discriminated—but to redress societal discrimination against minority group members. Bakke, who was white, did not qualify for admission under the program. His undergraduate grades and his score on the Medical College Admission Test, however, were substantially higher than those of most students accepted under the special admissions program. Bakke claimed that he was the victim of "reverse discrimination" and sued the university in state court, insisting that his constitutional rights had been violated.

When the U.S. Supreme Court heard Bakke's case on appeal, the justices split sharply. Four justices voted to strike down the university's affirmative action program, insisting that racial preferences in admissions were illegal. But four other justices voted to uphold the university's program and deny Bakke admission. Justice Lewis Powell cast the decisive vote. Powell agreed that the university had violated Bakke's rights by establishing a racial quota and denying him admission on that basis. Yet Powell also concluded that the Constitution did not bar affirmative action admissions programs, as long as there were no fixed quotas, even if race figured in the admissions decisions.

When the Supreme Court announced its decision in *Bakke,* the case was viewed as a landmark ruling. And in one sense it was. For the ruling did more than compel the University of California to admit Allan Bakke to its medical school and to abandon its system of quotas for the admission of minority group members. It also established national policy on affirmative action in college admissions. Thus, other universities that had instituted similar quota programs were likewise obliged to eliminate them in order to comply with the Court's ruling.

Nevertheless, *Bakke* did not resolve the issue of affirmative action. Opponents of affirmative action might hail the invalidation of the University of California's quota system and call upon other universities to abandon their race-conscious admissions programs. But proponents of affirmative action could reply that the Court permitted the use of race as a factor in admissions decisions and urge universities to adopt more aggressive programs of affirmative action consistent with the Court's ruling.[46] Thus, instead of being converted by the Court's ruling, both opponents and proponents of affirmative action used it to buttress their own positions.

Bakke did not eliminate affirmative action admissions programs. In fact, the programs expanded at colleges and universities in the decades after the Court's ruling; the University of California at Davis itself introduced a new affirmative action admissions program.[47] Nor did the decision eliminate conflict over affirmative action. In 1996, California voters approved an initiative (Proposition 209) to terminate affirmative action programs for hiring and admissions at the state's colleges and universities, and proponents of those programs responded by challenging the result in court, which upheld the provision, prompting California's government to revise admission standards for the state's universities in order to ensure diversity within the student population.[48] And in 2003, the Supreme Court revisited the issue of affirmative action in university admissions, striking down one program at the University of Michigan but upholding another.[49] Instead of establishing public policy, the Court's ruling in *Bakke* turned out to be merely one skirmish in an ongoing policy debate.

In this respect, *Bakke* is hardly unique. Although judicial rulings may establish legal obligations, those affected by a ruling may refuse to comply with it. For example, a decade after the Supreme Court in *Brown v. Board of Education* ordered the elimination of dual (racially segregated) school systems, less than 2 percent of black children in the South were attending integrated schools.[50] Rather than endorsing judicial rulings, public officials may ignore them, attack them, or attempt to overturn them. For instance, in the early 1990s, many members of Congress campaigned for a constitutional amendment to override the Supreme Court's ruling that the First Amendment protected the burning of the American flag as a form of symbolic protest.[51] Groups also may reject judicial rulings and organize to oppose them in other political arenas. The most visible example of this during the 1970s and 1980s was the right-to-life movement, which emerged as a national movement in direct response to the Supreme Court's ruling in *Roe v. Wade,* announcing a constitutional right to obtain an abortion.[52] Indeed, the controversy engendered by the Supreme Court's abortion rulings suggests that judicial rulings may at times aggravate rather than resolve policy disputes.

Taken together, these examples indicate that although courts often announce rulings on policy issues, they are seldom in a position to dictate public policy. Rather, whether judicial rulings accomplish their objectives often depends upon—among other things—the political support that they generate and the opposition they encounter.[53] Courts do not operate outside the political process; like other governmental institutions, they are enmeshed in it.

CONCLUSIONS

This chapter has examined law and the U.S. legal system from both legal and political perspectives. From a legal perspective, probably the most important point to note about the American system is that it is a common-law legal system. As such, it shares many features with the legal systems of Great Britain and its other former colonies. From a political perspective, the distinctive aspect of the American legal system is the courts' involvement in policymaking. This involvement stems from the courts' responsibility to say what the law is, even in cases with political ramifications. Thus, while courts in the United States do not dominate policymaking, their responsibilities nonetheless enmesh them in the political process.

This chapter has also briefly examined the character of law. From a legal perspective, what is most striking are the diverse types of law that courts interpret. As we have seen, to make sense of this diversity, scholars and attorneys have categorized law in various ways: public law and private law, criminal law and civil law, law and equity, and so on. From a political perspective, what is most important is the degree of uncertainty in the law. This uncertainty in the law provides the basis for disputes and hence for litigation. It also creates opportunities for judicial discretion in interpreting the law and in deciding cases. The range of discretion that judges exercise—and the uses that they make of it—will be an ongoing theme of this volume. Part 1, however, focuses on the structure of American legal institutions and the judges, lawyers, and litigants who are involved with them.

NOTES

1. Data on the size of the U.S. legal profession and its growth in relation to population are drawn from *Statistical Abstract of the United States* at http://www.census.gov. Data on students graduated from law schools accredited by the American Bar Association are drawn from www.abanet.org/legaled/statistics/Degrees.html.

2. Our estimate of case filings is based on data collected by the National Center for State Courts at www.ncsconline.org, and by the Administrative Office of the United States Courts at www.uscourts.gov.

3. On "indecent" materials on the Internet, see *Reno v. American Civil Liberties Union*, 520 U.S. 1113 (1997); on the "Napster" controversy over copyrighted songs available on the Internet, see *A & M Records, Inc. v. Napster, Inc.*, 2001 U.S. Dist. LEXIS 2186 (N.D. Cal. 2001); on prison conditions, see *Hudson v. McMillan*, 503 U.S. 1 (1992); on same-sex marriage, see *Goodridge v. Massachusetts Department of Public Health*, 798 N.E.2d 941 (2003); and on the presidential election of 2000, see *Bush v. Gore*, 531 U.S. 98 (2000).

4. The U.S. Supreme Court recognized a broad right for women to terminate their pregnancies in the companion cases of *Roe v. Wade*, 410 U.S. 113 (1973), and *Doe v. Bolton*, 410 U.S. 479 (1973). Subsequent rulings have narrowed that right; see, e.g., *Webster v. Reproductive Health Services*, 492 U.S. 490 (1989), and *Planned Parenthood of Southeastern Pennsylvania v. Casey*, 505 U.S. 833 (1992). The Supreme Court's most important ruling on racial discrimination is *Brown v. Board of Education*, 347 U.S. 483 (1954). The Court's rulings on abortion and racial discrimination are discussed in detail in Chapter 10.

5. See, e.g., John Grisham, *The Brethren* (New York: Doubleday, 2000), and Scott Turow, *Personal Injuries* (New York: Farrar, Straus & Giroux, 1999).

6. See the discussion in Mary Ann Glendon, *Rights Talk: The Impoverishment of Political Discourse* (New York: Maxwell Macmillan, 1991).

7. The Gallup Poll, June 22–25, 2000, reported at http://www.gallup.com/poll/indicators/indconfidence.asp; the Harris Poll, January 6–10, 2000, and the Gallup Poll, November 4–7, 1999, both reported at http://pollingreport.com/institut. In 1976 a Gallup Poll found that only 26 percent of Americans rated the honesty and ethical standards of lawyers as "very low" or "low," but two decades later that percentage had climbed to 41 percent. Cited in Robert W. Tobin, *Creating the Judicial Branch: The Unfinished Business* (Williamsburg, VA: National Center for State Courts, 1999), p. 83.

8. In September and October 1986, the Louis Harris polling organization asked 2,008 interviewees whether they agreed or disagreed with the following statement about the civil justice system: "The overall cost of the system to society is reasonable." Fifty-four percent of respondents disagreed with the statement, and another 9 percent answered "not sure." These data are reported in *Public Attitudes Toward the Civil Justice System and Tort Law Reform* (New York: Louis Harris and Associates, 1987), p. 20, table 2-1. The California data are reported in *Report of the Commission on the Future of the California Courts: Justice in the Balance 2020* (1993), cited in Tobin, *Creating the Judicial Branch*, p. 33.

9. For differing interpretations of various reform proposals, see Deborah R. Hensler, "Taking Aim at the American Legal System: The Council on Competitiveness's Agenda for Legal Reform," *Judicature* 75 (February–March 1992): 244–250; Gregory B. Butler and Brian D. Miller, "Fiddling while Rome Burns: A Response to Professor Hensler," *Judicature* 75 (February–March 1992): 251–254; and Stephen Daniels, *Civil Juries and the Politics of Reform* (Evanston, IL: Northwestern University Press, 1995).

10. See, e.g., Christine B. Harrington, *Shadow Justice: The Ideology and Institutionalization of Alternatives to Court* (Westport, CT: Greenwood Press, 1985); Marc Galanter, "Reading the Landscape of Disputes: What We Know and Don't Know (and Think We Know) about Our Allegedly Contentious and Litigious Society," *UCLA Law Review* 31 (1983): 4–71; and Jay Feinman, *Un-making Law: The Conservative Campaign to Roll Back the Common Law* (Boston: Beacon Press, 2004).

11. These data are drawn from the General Social Survey of the National Opinion Research Center, University of Chicago, various years.

12. For a penetrating discussion of racism and the American system of criminal justice, see Randall Kennedy, *Race, Crime, and the Law* (New York: Pantheon, 1997).

13. These data are reported in *U.S. News and World Report,* October 16, 1995, p. 25.

14. Major works analyzing contemporary legal systems include Konrad Zweigert and Hein Kotz, *Introduction to Comparative Law,* 2d rev. ed. (Oxford: Clarendon Press, 1987); and Rene David and John Brierly, *Major Legal Systems of the World Today,* 2d ed. (London: Stevens & Sons, 1978).

15. See Yosiyuki Noda, *Introduction to Japanese Law,* trans. and ed. by Anthony H. Angelo (Tokyo: University of Tokyo Press, 1976).

16. This account of the development of the common law in England relies primarily on Theodore F. T. Plucknett, *A Concise History of the Common Law,* 5th ed. (Boston: Little, Brown, 1956), and Geoffrey R. Y. Radcliffe and Geoffrey N. Cross, *English Legal System,* 6th ed., edited by Geoffrey J. Hand and David J. Bently (London: Butterworths, 1977).

17. Plucknett, *History of the Common Law,* p. 104.

18. William Blackstone, *Commentaries on the Law of England,* vol. 1 (Chicago: University of Chicago Press, 1979), p. 63.

19. Blackstone, *Commentaries,* p. 69.

20. Plucknett, *History of the Common Law,* p. 342.

21. Roscoe Pound, *The Spirit of the Common Law* (Francestown, NH: Marshall Jones, 1921), p. 1.

22. William E. Nelson, *Americanization of the Common Law: The Impact of Legal Change on Massachusetts Society, 1760–1830* (Cambridge, MA: Harvard University Press, 1975).

23. Morton J. Horwitz, *The Transformation of American Law, 1780–1860* (Cambridge, MA: Harvard University Press, 1977).

24. This account of the rediscovery of Roman law relies on Zweigert and Kotz, *Introduction to Comparative Law,* pp. 76–86; David and Brierly, *Major Legal Systems of the World Today,* pp. 33–59; and Alan Watson, *The Making of the Civil Law* (Cambridge, MA: Harvard University Press, 1981), chaps. 1–3.

25. This account of the creation of the Napoleonic Code and its consequences derives from Zweigert and Kotz, *Introduction to Comparative Law,* pp. 82–122, and Watson, *The Making of the Civil Law,* chaps. 8–9.

26. The analysis follows that of Zweigert and Kotz, *Introduction to Comparative Law,* chap. 20.

27. Thomas Mackay Cooper, "The Common Law and the Civil Law—A Scot's View," *Harvard Law Review* 63 (January 1950): 470–471.

28. John H. Merryman, *The Civil Law Tradition* (Stanford, CA: Stanford University Press, 1969), p. 100.

29. U.S. Constitution, art. 6, sec. 2.

30. For a listing of federal and state statutes invalidated by the U.S. Supreme Court, see *The Constitution of the United States of America: Analysis and Interpretation* at www.access.gpo.gov/congress/senate/constitution/98supp.pdf.

31. This account of administrative law relies chiefly on E. Allan Farnsworth, *An Introduction to the Legal System of the United States*, 2d ed. (London: Oceana Publications, 1983), pp. 134–138.

32. The definitions of criminal and civil law are derived from *Black's Law Dictionary: Centennial Edition*, 6th ed. (St. Paul, MN: West, 1990). For a detailed discussion of the distinction between criminal and civil law, see Farnsworth, *Introduction to the Legal System of the United States*, pp. 148–152.

33. The discussion follows that of Edgar Bodenheimer, John Bilyeu Oakley, and Jean C. Love, *An Introduction to the Anglo-American Legal System* (St. Paul, MN: West Publishing, 1980), pp. 10–11, and Farnsworth, *Introduction to the Legal System of the United States*, pp. 84–85.

34. The account of the development of equity relies on Gary L. McDowell, *Equity and the Constitution* (Chicago: University of Chicago Press, 1982), chap. 1; David and Brierly, *Major Legal Systems of the World Today*, pp. 300–306; and Zweigert and Kotz, *Introduction to Comparative Law*, pp. 194–198.

35. Zweigert and Kotz, *Introduction to Comparative Law*, p. 195.

36. Tobin, *Creating the Judicial Branch*, p. 55.

37. See McDowell, *Equity and the Constitution*, especially chap. 1.

38. Oliver Wendell Holmes, "The Path of the Law," *Harvard Law Review* 10 (1897), quoted in Walter F. Murphy and C. Herman Pritchett, eds., *Courts, Judges, and Politics*, 2d ed. (New York: Random House, 1974), p. 21.

39. *Lee v. Weisman*, 505 U.S. 577 (1992).

40. The Establishment Clause states: "Congress shall make no law respecting an establishment of religion." Originally a limitation only on the national government, the Establishment Clause was made applicable to state and local governments through the Due Process Clause of the Fourteenth Amendment in *Everson v. Board of Education*, 330 U.S. 1 (1947).

41. This topic is discussed in greater detail in Chapter 9.

42. The reference to the judicial responsibility to "say what the law is" is drawn from *Marbury v. Madison*, 5 U.S. (1 Cranch) 137, 173 (1803).

43. Alexis de Tocqueville, *Democracy in America*, J. P. Mayer, ed. (Garden City, NY: Doubleday, 1969), p. 270.

44. *Regents of the University of California v. Bakke*, 438 U.S. 265 (1978).

45. For background on the *Bakke* case, see Allan P. Sindler, *Bakke, DeFunis, and Minority Admissions: The Quest for Equal Opportunity* (New York: Longman, 1978), and Bernard Schwartz, *Behind Bakke: Affirmative Action and the Supreme Court* (New York: New York University Press, 1988).

46. Reactions to the *Bakke* ruling are reported in Schwartz, *Behind Bakke*, and in Ron Simmons, *Affirmative Action: Conflict and Change in Higher Education After Bakke* (Cambridge, MA: Schenckman, 1982).

47. For data on the use of affirmative action in admissions, see William G. Bowen and Derek Bok, *The Shape of the River: Long-Term Consequences of Considering Race in College and University Admissions* (Princeton, NJ: Princeton University Press, 1998).

48. A federal court of appeals upheld the constitutionality of Proposition 209 in *Coalition for Economic Equity v. Wilson*, 122 F.3d 718 (9th Cir. 1997).

49. *Gratz v. Bollinger*, 539 U.S. 244 (2003), and *Grutter v. Bollinger*, 539 U.S. 306 (2003).

50. *Brown v. Board of Education*, 347 U.S. 483 (1954). The figures on the response to *Brown* are drawn from Rosenberg, *The Hollow Hope*, p. 50, table 2.1. For further discussion of the response to *Brown*, see Chapter 10.

51. *Texas v. Johnson,* 491 U.S. 397 (1989).

52. *Roe v. Wade,* 410 U.S. 113 (1973). For a detailed discussion of the response to *Roe,* see Chapter 10.

53. This point is emphasized in Rosenberg, *The Hollow Hope,* chap. 1, and documented in the case studies throughout that volume.

STRUCTURES AND PARTICIPANTS IN THE JUDICIAL PROCESS

THE FEDERAL AND STATE COURT SYSTEMS   25

JUDGES   53

LAWYERS   97

THE FEDERAL AND STATE COURT SYSTEMS

On its face, the case seemed routine. Although Clarence Earl Gideon was not a professional criminal, at age fifty-seven he had a history of run-ins with the law and had four times been convicted of minor felonies and imprisoned. Thus, when he was charged with breaking into a poolroom in Bay Harbor, Florida, with intent to commit petty larceny, it seemed like merely another episode in Gideon's rather unsuccessful criminal career.[1]

Gideon was tried before a six-member jury in one of Florida's circuit (trial) courts in August 1961. At the outset of the trial, Gideon requested that a lawyer be appointed to defend him because he was too poor to hire one himself. But the judge refused Gideon's request, maintaining that neither Florida law nor the United States Constitution required that an attorney be provided. The trial thus commenced with Gideon representing himself.

One prosecution witness testified that he had seen Gideon leaving the poolroom carrying a pint of wine at 5:30 A.M. on the morning of the break-in. The eyewitness also claimed that, looking into the poolroom, he could see that someone had removed the front of the cigarette machine and emptied its money box. The operator of the poolroom confirmed that a window had been smashed and the cigarette machine and the jukebox broken into. Gideon's cross-examination of the witnesses was unfocused and ineffectual, and he offered no explanation for why he was outside the poolroom in the early morning. The jury quickly convicted Gideon, and three weeks later Judge Robert McCrary sentenced him to five years in prison.

This, however, did not end the case. Writing from his prison cell, Gideon petitioned the Florida Supreme Court for a *writ of habeas corpus,* a legal order freeing him on the ground that he was illegally imprisoned. The Florida justices denied Gideon's petition, rejecting his claim that the U.S. Constitution guaranteed him a right to an attorney at trial. Gideon then appealed the Florida Supreme Court's decision to the U.S. Supreme Court, requesting that the Court agree to review his case.

The Supreme Court annually receives hundreds of petitions from prisoners who claim that their trials were unfair and that they should be released. Thus, Gideon's petition—four pages painstakingly printed in pencil on lined paper—was hardly unique. Most of these petitions lack substantial legal merit and are dismissed by the Court. In this instance, however, the justices granted Gideon's petition in order to consider whether the Constitution requires states to provide a defense attorney to poor defendants in criminal cases. After receiving legal briefs and hearing oral argument from Florida's assistant attorney general and from Abe Fortas, a prominent Washington attorney appointed by the Court to represent Gideon, the justices unanimously ruled in Gideon's favor. Overruling a twenty-year-old precedent, *Betts v. Brady* (1942), the Court concluded that the Sixth Amendment, which was made applicable to the states by the Fourteenth Amendment, required that the states must provide counsel for indigent defendants in felony cases.[2]

The Supreme Court's decision in *Gideon v. Wainwright*[3] overturned Gideon's conviction, but it did not decide his fate. The state of Florida appointed an attorney to represent Gideon and proceeded to retry him for the break-in. Having an attorney at trial made all the difference for Gideon. Gideon's lawyer deftly undermined the credibility of the prosecution's eyewitness, and after an hour's deliberation the jury returned a verdict of not guilty.

The story of Clarence Gideon illustrates four basic aspects of the structure and operation of courts in the United States.

1. A *dual court system*.   Under American federalism each of the fifty states operates its own judicial system. So, too, does the federal government. Although the state and federal judicial systems are separate, federal and state courts can both rule on the same case. *Gideon v. Wainwright,* for example, began in a Florida state court, was appealed to the U.S. Supreme Court, and eventually was returned to a Florida trial court for resolution.

Gideon's case, however, is atypical. The vast majority of cases remain in the judicial system in which they are initiated. Indeed, this might well have happened in Gideon's case. Had he not appealed the Florida Supreme Court's ruling, his case would have been resolved within the state judicial system; and if the U.S. Supreme Court had refused to review that ruling, the Florida court's decision would have been final.

2. *Separate courts performing distinct functions*.   Gideon's case was considered by two different types of courts, each of which played a distinct role in the resolution of the case. The Florida circuit court served as the trial court, hearing evidence from witnesses about the facts of the case, deciding whether Gideon was innocent or guilty, and imposing sentence following his conviction.

When Gideon appealed his conviction to the Florida Supreme Court and then to the U.S. Supreme Court, the issue changed, and so too did the function of the courts. For these appellate courts (courts that review the rulings of lower courts), the concern was less Gideon's factual guilt or innocence and more the legal correctness of the procedures under which he was convicted. Thus, when the Florida Supreme Court concluded that the trial judge had acted properly in refusing to appoint a lawyer to defend Gideon, it upheld his conviction. When the U.S. Supreme Court ruled that the judge had erred and that Gideon was entitled to a lawyer, it did not decide his guilt or innocence. Rather, it sent the case back for a new trial at which Gideon's right to counsel was honored.

3. *Hierarchies of courts.* Not only are there various types of courts, but also those courts are hierarchically arranged. This means that cases follow a set path when they move from one court to another, proceeding step by step from the lowest court up the various rungs of the judicial ladder. In *Gideon,* for example, the case began in a Florida trial court, moved to the highest court in the state, and then to the nation's highest court, the U.S. Supreme Court. In addition, the hierarchical arrangement of courts reflects the authority exercised by some courts over others. Lower courts are legally obliged to abide by the rulings of higher courts. Thus, once the Supreme Court had ruled in *Gideon* that states must furnish an attorney to indigent defendants, the Florida court retrying Gideon had to comply with the ruling and appoint a lawyer to defend him.

4. *Multiple bodies of law.* Just as both the state and federal governments have their own court systems, so too each has its own body of law. It might seem logical therefore for state courts to decide cases involving state law and federal courts cases involving federal law. In actuality, however, the rules governing the jurisdiction of U.S. courts—that is, the types of cases a federal court is authorized to decide—are not that simple. For one thing, a single case might involve more than one body of law. Gideon, for example, was convicted of violating a Florida criminal statute in a court established by the constitution and laws of Florida. However, he claimed that the U.S. Constitution guaranteed him the right to an attorney. Thus, the Florida courts in Gideon's case had to consider both state law (the criminal statute) and federal law (the constitutional rights guaranteed to defendants in state court).

Now that I've highlighted some of the intricacies of the structure and operation of American courts, let us turn to a more detailed treatment of those courts, beginning with the federal judicial system.

THE FEDERAL COURT SYSTEM

Structure

Although Article III of the federal Constitution establishes only the U.S. Supreme Court, it authorizes "such inferior Courts as the Congress may from time to time ordain and establish."[4] The courts that Congress creates under Article III of the Constitution are known as *constitutional courts* (or Article III courts), and those it creates under Article I are known as *legislative courts* (or Article I courts). Constitutional courts handle the bulk of federal litigation. The independence of their judges is secured by constitutional guarantees that the judges serve during "good behavior" and that their salaries cannot be reduced while they remain in office.[5] By contrast, legislative courts may have administrative and quasi-legislative responsibilities, as well as judicial duties. Congressional statutes determine how long judges on legislative courts shall serve and whether their salaries can be reduced. Because they do not have the Article III guarantees of judicial independence, the Supreme Court ruled in 1982 that judges on legislative courts cannot be assigned the same duties and jurisdiction as judges on constitutional courts.[6] In fact, legislative courts usually have quite specialized jurisdictions. Current legislative courts include, for example, the U.S. Court of Military Appeals, the Tax Court, and the Court of Veterans Appeals.

Figure 2-1 outlines the organization of the federal judicial system. Despite the multiplicity of courts, the structure of the federal judicial system is really quite simple; basically, it is a three-tiered structure. The most important federal courts are the constitutional courts: the district courts, the courts of appeals, and the U.S. Supreme Court. The district courts serve as the primary trial courts of the federal judicial system. Most federal cases originate in the district courts and are resolved by those courts. However, dissatisfied litigants may appeal the district courts' rulings to the courts of appeals, the main first-level appellate courts. The U.S. Supreme Court is the sole second-level appellate court, the court of last resort. It hears some appeals from the courts of appeals, from various specialized federal courts, and, when questions of federal law are involved, from state supreme courts. In some cases, it may also hear appeals directly from federal district courts. Whereas the district courts and the courts of appeals must decide all cases that are properly brought before them, the Supreme Court has broad discretion in choosing what cases it will hear.

The Development of the Federal Judicial System

The Creation of the Federal Judicial System   Political conflict over the structure of the federal judicial system has erupted periodically throughout American history.[7] The conflict began at the Constitutional Convention of

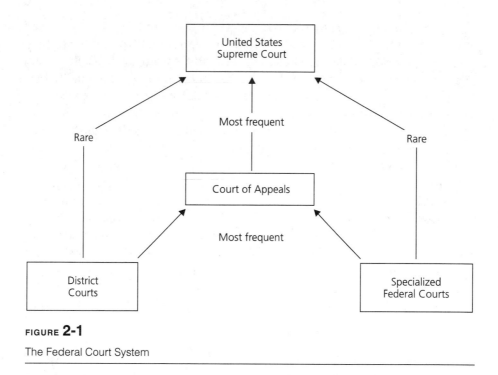

FIGURE **2-1**

The Federal Court System

1787. Although the delegates agreed that a national judiciary should be established, they disagreed over its structure and organization. Some delegates wanted only a single federal court, a supreme court, that would review state court decisions on matters of federal concern. Other delegates, among them James Madison, distrusted state courts and insisted that federal trial courts should also be instituted. Rather than resolving the conflict, the delegates in effect postponed it. Article III of the U.S. Constitution created the U.S. Supreme Court but left the creation of additional courts to Congress.

As its first order of business, Congress enacted the Judiciary Act of 1789, establishing the nation's judicial system. Atop the structure was the Supreme Court, consisting of six justices. The Act also provided for two tiers of federal trial courts. The thirteen district courts were each staffed with a single district judge. Although the number of district courts and judges has increased, this set of federal trial courts, organized along geographic lines that do not overlap state boundaries, has survived to the present day. Less familiar is the second set of trial courts created in 1789, the three circuit courts. These courts initially had no judges of their own. They operated in three-judge panels consisting— at least at the outset—of the district court judge for the district and two Supreme Court justices who "rode circuit" to hear cases.

From the beginning these circuit courts posed problems. The roads and the means of transportation in the new nation were primitive, and the justices found themselves riding circuit almost constantly. As early as 1792, they complained to Congress, arguing that it was "too burdensome" for them "to pass the greater part of their days on the road, and at inns, and at a distance from their families."[8] Advocates of state power, however, opposed the creation of circuit court judges, fearing that increasing the number of federal judges would permit more cases to be routed to federal courts. When Congress finally did create circuit judges in 1801, the partisan fashion in which it proceeded virtually guaranteed that the reform would not last. After having lost the election of 1800, President John Adams and the lame-duck Federalists who controlled Congress pushed through legislation that abolished circuit riding and created judgeships for each circuit. Adams then proceeded to appoint Federalists to all the new positions. According to legend, Adams signed the commissions for these "midnight judges" late into the last night of his presidency. Incoming president Thomas Jefferson and his Democratic-Republican Party were outraged, and in 1802 Congress—now controlled by Jefferson's party—abolished the new judgeships and reinstituted circuit riding.[9]

The Nineteenth and Twentieth Centuries   For most of the nineteenth century, the structure of the federal judicial system remained unchanged. In 1891, Congress added a new set of courts, the circuit courts of appeals, to expand the capacity of the federal courts to hear appeals and to relieve caseload pressures on the Supreme Court. These courts, now simply called the courts of appeals, remain a vital component of the federal judicial system. In 1911, Congress completed the basic structure of the federal judicial system by abolishing the circuit courts and transferring their responsibilities to the district courts.

Since 1911, despite dramatic increases in the caseloads of federal courts, Congress has rejected fundamental changes in the structure of the federal judicial system. It has dealt with caseload problems primarily by creating new district courts and appeals courts and by increasing the number of federal judges. Congress has also added various specialized courts to the federal judicial system. Some of these specialized courts resolve cases arising under particular statutes. For example, the U.S. Tax Court, originally part of the Internal Revenue Service, was established as an independent court in 1969 and charged with deciding taxpayer challenges to income-tax assessments. Other specialized courts deal with cases in a specific area of the law. The U.S. Court of Military Appeals (1950) hears appeals from court-martial convictions, and the Foreign Intelligence Surveillance Court (1978) oversees the issuance of warrants to use electronic surveillance to acquire "foreign" intelligence within the United States. The most recent addition to the roster of specialized courts is

TABLE 2-1	THE FEDERAL JUDICIAL POWER

Article III of the U.S. Constitution defines the federal judicial power. Underlying the specific grants of power are four basic purposes:

1. Vindicating the authority of the federal government
   a. Cases arising under the laws of the United States
   b. Cases arising under the U.S. Constitution
   c. Cases in which the federal government is a party

2. Maintaining the exclusive control of the federal government over foreign relations
   a. Admiralty and maritime cases
   b. Cases arising under treaties
   c. Cases affecting ambassadors or other representatives of foreign countries
   d. Cases between states, or the citizens thereof, and foreign states, citizens, or subjects

3. Umpiring interstate disputes
   a. Controversies between two or more states
   b. Controversies between a state and the citizen of another state

4. Protecting out-of-state litigants from the possible bias of local tribunals
   a. Controversies between citizens of different states

the Alien Terrorist Removal Court, created by the 1996 antiterrorism bill enacted in the wake of the bombing of the federal building in Oklahoma City. This court was established to streamline the deportation of criminal aliens after they have served their sentences.

Federal Jurisdiction

The Law of Federal Jurisdiction   For a court to decide a case, the case must fall within its jurisdiction—that is, the range of cases that it is empowered to rule on by constitutional provision or by statute. Article III of the U.S. Constitution sets the outer reaches of the federal judicial power by specifying the types of cases that federal courts may be empowered to hear.[10] Table 2-1 describes the scope of the federal judicial power and explains why those types of cases were given to the federal courts.

Within these boundaries, the Constitution generally leaves it to Congress to define the jurisdiction of the various federal courts. Congress is not obliged to vest the full federal judicial power in the federal courts.[11] Thus, congressional legislation largely determines the actual division of responsibility between federal and state courts and among federal courts.

The bases for exercising federal jurisdiction are diverse and complex. The subject matter of a case, the identity of the parties to a case, or the citizenship of those parties all may provide the basis for federal courts to hear the case. For example, a job applicant may sue an employer for discrimination in federal court (1) if the statute securing the right against employment discrimination is a federal statute, or (2) if the employer is the federal government or one of its agencies, or (3) if the employer and the job applicant are citizens of different states. If the job applicant sues in a state court, and the employer and job applicant are citizens of different states, the employer can have the case transferred to a federal district court on the basis of diversity of citizenship.

Although the federal judicial power is extensive, it hardly extends to all possible cases. When a person is charged with violating a state criminal statute, the case is heard in state court. Most criminal statutes—for example, those outlawing theft, armed robbery, and rape—are state statutes, and more than 98 percent of criminal prosecutions occur in state courts. State courts also have exclusive jurisdiction when a civil case involves only state law and the parties to the case are each citizens of the same state. Because the vast majority of civil cases have that character, they likewise are heard in state courts. Finally, the U.S. Supreme Court in recent years has held that the doctrine of sovereign immunity restricts Congress's power to authorize suits against state governments without their consent in federal courts.[12]

Congress has not required that all cases arising under the federal judicial power be heard in federal court. Instead, it has allowed state courts to decide some of these cases by granting concurrent, rather than exclusive, jurisdiction to federal courts. What this means is that, with a few exceptions such as criminal cases based on federal statutes, cases that could be filed in federal court can be initiated in state courts as well. Lawyers thus can choose to file a case in the court in which they believe they have the best chance of winning or where they expect the highest awards should they win. Throughout the nation's history, Congress has also limited the jurisdiction of federal courts. One example is federal jurisdiction over "diversity of citizenship" cases. Although the Constitution permits federal courts to be assigned all cases involving a suit by a citizen of one state against the citizen of another state, Congress has restricted federal courts to those cases in which a sizable amount is involved. Currently federal courts can hear "diversity" cases only when at least $75,000 is at stake.

The Politics of Federal Jurisdiction

Federalism and Federal Jurisdiction   Although federal jurisdiction might seem merely a technical concern, it has generated intense, though episodic, political conflict for more than two centuries.[13] During the nation's first century, the conflict over federal jurisdiction centered on questions of federalism. Nationalists in Congress sought to enlarge federal jurisdiction, while champions of states' rights attempted to maintain the prerogatives of state courts, assuming those courts would reflect a more localistic perspective.

The Judiciary Act of 1789 was a partial victory for both nationalists and states' rights advocates. Congress created lower federal courts, as the nationalists wished, but it severely limited their jurisdiction. Federal district courts were vested with jurisdiction only over admiralty cases and petty crimes— those for which punishment could not exceed six months in jail, a fine of $100, or thirty stripes of whipping. Federal circuit courts, the main trial courts, could hear diversity-of-citizenship cases (where more than $500 was at stake), major criminal cases arising under federal law, and appeals from the district courts in admiralty cases. But neither district nor circuit courts were given jurisdiction over all cases arising under federal law ("federal question" cases). Thus, many "federal question" cases were heard in state courts. Not until 1875 were federal trial courts awarded this "federal question" jurisdiction.

The appellate jurisdiction of the Supreme Court was likewise circumscribed under the Judiciary Act of 1789. The Court could not review federal court rulings in criminal cases. Moreover, it could review state rulings involving federal constitutional claims only if state judges rejected the constitutional claim and upheld the challenged state law. Underlying the second limitation was the assumption that, although state judges might be prone to favor state law against federal claims, they would be unlikely to expand federal restrictions on the governing power of the states.

The strength of states' rights forces was also manifest in a controversy that erupted just four years after the passage of the Judiciary Act of 1789. In *Chisholm v. Georgia,* the Supreme Court ruled that the executor of the estate of a South Carolina citizen could sue the state of Georgia in federal court to recover payment for supplies that were sold to the state during the American Revolution.[14] The Court's decision was arguably a faithful reading of Article III of the Constitution, which authorized federal courts to hear disputes "between a state and citizens of another state." However, states rights' advocates were outraged, detecting a threat to state sovereignty in the Court's ruling. The lower house of the Georgia legislature responded by passing a bill to punish by hanging without benefit of clergy any person aiding in the enforcement of the *Chisholm* decision. A more lasting response was the adoption of the Eleventh Amendment, which prohibited the federal courts from hearing suits against a state by a citizen of another state or of a foreign country.[15]

The Impact of the Civil War   After the Civil War, the issue of federal jurisdiction reemerged, but this time a nationalist perspective prevailed. Congress suspected, with good reason, that state courts in the Southern states might be unwilling to vindicate the rights of the newly freed slaves. To ensure that those rights were protected, it expanded the jurisdiction of the federal courts. The Habeas Corpus Act of 1867 enabled all persons in custody "in violation of the constitution, or of any treaty or law of the United States" to seek redress in federal court. This in effect authorized federal courts to oversee state courts in criminal cases to ensure that defendants were not imprisoned in violation of federal law. The Judiciary Act of 1875 conferred on the federal courts jurisdiction in all cases involving questions of federal law and in all diversity cases where more than $500 was at stake. This ensured that those who believed their federal rights had been infringed could get a hearing before a federal judge.

Congress versus the Courts   Since the late nineteenth century, changes in federal jurisdiction have reflected either congressional dissatisfaction with judicial decisions or a concern to relieve the caseload pressures on the federal courts. An example of the former is a law enacted in 1914 that empowered the Supreme Court to review all state rulings that relied on federal law. Congress's action was in response to *Ives v. South Buffalo Railway,* in which New York's supreme court ruled that the state's workmen's compensation act (the first in the nation) violated the federal Constitution.[16] Because most members of Congress favored such legislation and believed it constitutional, they wanted the Supreme Court to be able to overturn constraints placed on state legislatures by state courts. The congressional enactment ensured that state courts could not restrict state power on federal constitutional grounds further than the Supreme Court authorized.

Over the last four decades, conservatives in Congress have responded to controversial judicial rulings by proposing legislation to restrict the power of federal courts to rule on particular issues. During the 1970s and 1980s, conservatives attempted to prevent federal courts from ruling on abortion, school prayer, and school busing, but none of the bills they introduced was enacted. Following the election of Republican majorities in both houses of Congress in 1994, however, less drastic restrictions on the jurisdiction of federal courts were approved. In 1995, Congress enacted the Prison Litigation Reform Act, which reduced the discretion of federal courts in supervising prisons and requiring the early release of prisoners. And it also adopted the Effective Death Penalty Act of 1995, which limited the power of federal courts to consider successive habeas corpus petitions filed by inmates awaiting execution.

Caseloads and Federal Jurisdiction   Concern about caseload pressures on the federal courts emerged after Congress expanded the federal courts' jurisdiction in 1875, as this created a demand for court services that those courts were ill-equipped to handle. Data on pending cases in the circuit and district courts illustrate the heavy caseloads in those courts. In 1873, federal trial courts had 29,013 pending cases. Following the expansion of federal jurisdiction in 1875, however, the number of pending cases jumped to 38,045 by 1880 and 54,194 by 1890. Similar caseload problems plagued the Supreme Court. Its docket rose from 636 cases in 1870 to 1,212 in 1880 to 1,816 cases in 1890.[17]

Congress has alleviated the caseload pressures on the Supreme Court by reducing its mandatory jurisdiction—that is, those cases it is legally obliged to hear. Until 1925, the Court had little control over which cases it decided because Congress had awarded litigants a right of appeal to the Supreme Court. The Judges' Bill of 1925—so named because it was drafted by Chief Justice William Howard Taft and supported by the other justices—dramatically altered the Court's jurisdiction by giving the justices broad discretion in choosing their cases. This reform temporarily relieved case pressures. Since 1925, Congress incrementally eliminated more and more of the Supreme Court's mandatory jurisdiction, so that the Court now has almost total discretion in setting its agenda.

The contraction of the Supreme Court's mandatory jurisdiction, although prompted by caseload concerns, has also affected how the Court views its responsibilities. Relieving the Court of relatively unimportant cases has allowed it to focus its attention on those cases that are crucial to the development of federal law. The justices now deliberately choose cases with that function in mind. Thus, the reform of the Court's jurisdiction has produced effects probably never contemplated by its proponents.

Congress has sought to ease caseload pressures on federal district and appeals courts by increasing the number of courts and judges. For example, the number of federal district court judges has increased from 241 in 1960 to 680 in 2004. Some scholars and jurists—most notably Chief Justice William Rehnquist—have proposed further reducing the caseloads of federal district and appeals courts by eliminating their diversity-of-citizenship jurisdiction.[18] These reformers insist that state courts today treat residents and nonresidents even-handedly, so that the original justification for the diversity jurisdiction (avoiding bias against nonresidents in state courts) no longer exists. Certainly, shifting diversity cases to state courts would have an effect on caseloads. In 2003, diversity-of-citizenship cases accounted for almost one quarter of all civil cases filed in federal district courts.[19] Opposing this change have been the American Bar Association and various trial lawyers' organizations, who argue that federal courts do a better job of dispensing justice than do state courts.[20] Thus far, these groups have blocked all efforts to curtail federal jurisdiction over diversity cases.

Although both proponents and opponents of this reform are concerned about the just and efficient operation of the federal judicial system, this is not all that is involved. Because of the different procedural rules in federal and state courts, attorneys find that their clients may have a better chance of presenting their case or winning it in one forum rather than in another.[21] Some litigants seek to have their cases heard in federal court and others in state court, indicating a perception that where a case is heard makes a difference. Finally, the transfer of diversity cases to state courts would increase the caseloads of those courts.[22] Thus, reforms designed to promote efficiency may have other effects as well.

THE FEDERAL COURTS TODAY

The District Courts

"The people of this district either get justice here with me or they don't get it at all. Here at the trial court—that's where the action is."[23] This comment by a district court judge in Iowa is hardly an exaggeration. Most federal cases begin and end in the district courts, the primary trial courts of the federal judicial system. About 15 percent of district court rulings are appealed, and of these only some 16 percent are reversed. Taken together, the low rates of appeal and reversal mean that less than 4 percent of district court judgments are ultimately overturned.

Congress has established ninety-four district courts, staffed by 680 judges (as of 2004), serving the fifty states, the District of Columbia, and some U.S. territories. As Figure 2-2 indicates, every state has at least one district court, and no district extends beyond the borders of a single state. Larger or more populous states are divided into more than one district, with three states— California, New York, and Texas—each having four district courts.

Every district court has at least two judges. The number of judges assigned to a district court, however, depends on its caseload and thus varies considerably from district to district. The Southern District of New York, which includes Manhattan and the Bronx, is currently the nation's largest with twenty-eight district judges. By federal law, reapportionment cases and voting rights cases must be heard by three-judge panels, comprised of two district court judges and one appeals court judge. But the vast majority of cases in district courts are tried before a single judge. District courts can therefore hear several cases simultaneously at courthouses located throughout the district.

The Cases   District courts exercise no discretion over the cases they hear. Any litigant who satisfies the jurisdictional requirements and follows proper legal procedures can initiate a case in federal district court. However, a federal district court cannot address a legal issue unless a litigant brings it before the court in a bona fide case. Thus, litigant demand determines the business of the district courts.

Over the past few decades, the filings in federal district courts have risen sharply: from 87,421 cases in 1960 to 328,616 in 2002.[24] Civil filings have declined, from a high of 273,670 in 1985 to 265,091 in 2002. They represent 81 percent of filings in district courts. However, the decline in civil filings has been more than offset by a substantial rise in federal criminal cases.[25] Indeed, criminal filings in federal courts are the highest they have been since the repeal of the Prohibition Amendment in 1933.

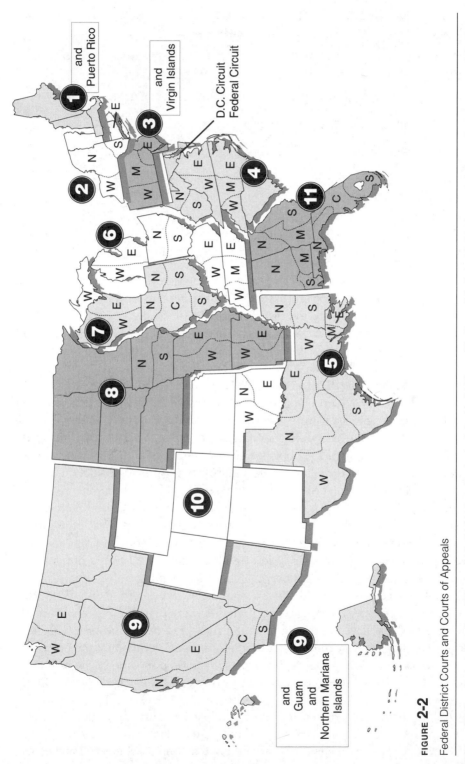

FIGURE 2-2

Federal District Courts and Courts of Appeals

Source: This figure is adapted from Russell Wheeler and Cynthia Harrison, *Creating the Federal Judicial System* (Washington, D.C.: Federal Judicial Center, 1989), figure 4. The letters and boundaries within states refer to federal court districts with states (W = West, C = Central; etc.). The circled numbers refer to federal appellate circuits.

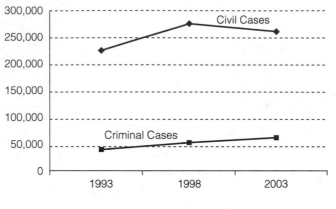

Source: Data drawn from www.uscourts.gov/caseload2003.

FIGURE **2-3**

Civil and Criminal Cases in Federal District Courts

Congressional legislation and executive-branch actions affect the number and type of cases brought before the district courts. In 1960, for example, only 306 civil rights cases were filed in district courts. During the 1960s, Congress adopted major civil rights laws, such as the Civil Rights Act of 1964, the Voting Rights Act of 1965, and the Fair Housing Act of 1968. These laws, together with the expansive judicial interpretation of civil rights laws enacted during Reconstruction, encouraged victims of discrimination to seek redress in the federal courts, and the number of civil rights cases rose accordingly. In 2002, for example, there were 40,549 civil rights cases, accounting for more than 15 percent of all civil cases filed in district courts.[26] Figure 2-3 depicts changes over time in the civil caseload of federal district courts, as well as of state trial courts of general jurisdiction.

A similar pattern can be seen in criminal cases. During the 1980s, concern about the influx of cocaine and other illegal drugs into the United States, led President Ronald Reagan to announce a "war on drugs" to deal with the problem. By devoting more funds and personnel to the interdiction of drugs and the enforcement of drug laws, the federal government increased its number of drug arrests and thus the number of drug cases coming before the district courts. In the course of the decade, the criminal workload of the district courts increased 50 percent, but drug cases increased more than 270 percent. Subsequent presidents have continued to target drug trafficking and use, with the result that drug cases in 2002 constituted more than 28 percent of the criminal cases in district courts.[27] Figure 2-3 depicts changes over time in the criminal caseload of federal district courts and state trial courts of general jurisdiction.

Court Operations   In hearing cases, the district courts may operate as we have come to expect from television and novels. This means that in criminal trials the judge presides, while the prosecutor and defense attorney call witnesses and introduce other evidence designed to prove the guilt or innocence of the defendant. In trials in civil cases, it is the legal rights or obligations of the plaintiff and defendant that are at issue, but the process is much the same. If it is a jury trial—and just under half of the trials in district courts are—the judge instructs the jury about the law following the presentation of evidence and the attorneys' closing arguments, and the jury decides the case. If there is no jury, the judge decides the case and, when the case has a broader legal significance, may write a judicial opinion explaining the reasons for the decision.

More frequently, however, cases follow a quite different pattern. Most criminal cases in federal district courts are resolved by guilty pleas, and most civil cases by a settlement between the parties following pretrial negotiations. When this occurs, no jury is selected, no witnesses are called, and no formal courtroom sessions are held except to ratify the decision reached by the parties in the case.

The Courts of Appeals

The courts of appeals are the first-level appellate courts of the federal judicial system. As Figure 2-2 indicates, these courts are organized regionally, with most "circuits" made up of three or more states. Thus, the Fifth Circuit includes Texas, Louisiana, and Mississippi, and the Seventh Circuit includes Illinois, Indiana, and Wisconsin. The sole exception is the Court of Appeals for the District of Columbia, which reviews large numbers of appeals from administrative agencies and serves as a sort of state supreme court for the District of Columbia.[28] The boundaries of most circuits were established long ago, and as population shifts have occurred, some courts of appeals have experienced disproportionate increases in their caseloads. Congress has responded by adding judges to overburdened circuits, and as a result the number of judges varies considerably among the courts of appeals. The First Circuit, which includes Maine, Vermont, New Hampshire, Massachusetts, and, surprisingly, Puerto Rico, has the fewest appeals court judges (six). The Ninth Circuit, which includes Alaska, Washington, Oregon, California, Nevada, Idaho, and Montana, has the most (twenty-eight).

The Cases   Every litigant in federal court has a right to one appeal. As a result, courts of appeals primarily engage in error correction, overseeing the work of the district courts in cases that are of interest only to the immediate parties.[29] More than three-quarters of their cases come to courts of appeals from district courts within their circuits, with the remainder coming from certain federal administrative agencies and from some specialized courts, such as the Tax Court. The mix of cases varies from circuit to circuit. The Court of Appeals for the Second Circuit, for example, considers large numbers of banking cases because New York City, the hub of the nation's banking, is within its jurisdiction. And because so many federal administrative agencies are located in the District of Columbia, about half the caseload of its court of appeals involves challenges to orders issued by those agencies.[30]

Like the district courts, the courts of appeals have experienced an enormous increase in their caseloads in recent years.[31] Indeed, the figures for the two courts are connected, because an increase in district court rulings means an increase in the number of potential appeals. In 1982, the courts of appeals heard 27,946 cases; by 1992, 44,452; and by 2002, 56,534.[32] Much of this change reflects the increase in criminal cases currently heard in district courts and the greater willingness of defendants to appeal. Still, civil cases make up roughly two-thirds of the caseload of courts of appeals, which is hardly surprising given the composition of the caseloads of federal district courts.

Intercourt Relations   After a court of appeals decides a case, a dissatisfied litigant might appeal to the Supreme Court. However, most litigants accept the appeals court ruling as final, and the Supreme Court generally refuses to hear most appeals. As a result, the courts of appeals have the final say in more than 99 percent of the cases they decide.

Over time, a rough division of labor has developed between the courts of appeals and the Supreme Court. As the Supreme Court has become more involved in resolving constitutional disputes, it has in effect ceded primary responsibility for the interpretation of federal statutes and the supervision of administrative agencies to the courts of appeals. This shift, however, poses the danger that a court of appeals in one circuit might interpret a statute differently from a court of appeals in another circuit. Different interpretations of the same law would thus be authoritative in various regions of the country. What prevents this threat to the uniformity of federal law from posing a serious problem is the tendency of courts of appeals to consider the rulings of sister courts. Even if those rulings are not authoritative, they may well be persuasive. When differences in interpretation do emerge, the Supreme Court can also step in to resolve the conflict. In fact, the rules of the Supreme Court list conflict between the circuits as one of the criteria for deciding to hear cases.[33]

Court Operations   The courts of appeals hear more than 95 percent of their cases in three-judge panels, deciding cases by majority vote. This means that several cases can be heard simultaneously by different three-judge panels, often sitting in various cities throughout the circuit. In some cases the judges decide on the basis of the written record from the lower court and the legal briefs submitted by the attorneys on each side. In particularly important cases, however, counsel for each side may present oral argument as well. When the judges have reached a decision in a case, they may announce their decision in a brief order or a longer written opinion.

Because judges bring different perspectives to the law, the decision that an appeals court renders may depend on the composition of the panel that hears the case.[34] In the past, some chief judges were accused of "stacking" the panels to achieve the results they favored. Today, extraordinary efforts are made to prevent this. Judges are rotated so that the same ones do not sit together constantly. The Eleventh Circuit uses a computer-generated random matrix to set the composition of every panel a year in advance. In addition, each circuit has developed mechanisms for ensuring randomness in the assignment of cases to panels.[35]

Federal statutes also permit courts of appeals to hear cases *en banc*—that is, with the court's entire membership hearing the case together. Courts of appeals use this procedure to resolve intracircuit conflicts, when different panels within a circuit have reached conflicting results in similar cases. They also may sit *en banc* to decide particularly important cases. Each circuit has discretion to determine when an *en banc* panel is warranted.

The United States Supreme Court

The U.S. Supreme Court sits at the apex of the federal judicial system. It hears appeals from the federal courts of appeals, from state supreme courts, and, occasionally, from federal district courts or the Court of Military Appeals. The Constitution also assigns the Supreme Court a very limited original jurisdiction (cases it hears as a trial court), but this rarely involves more than one or two cases per year. Altogether, over the last decade more than 7,000 cases were appealed to the Supreme Court annually, and the Court typically accepted less than 3 percent for review. In fact, the number of cases heard by the Supreme Court in recent years has declined considerably. Whereas in its 1987 term the Court decided 147 cases, from 1997 to 2000 it averaged only 85 decisions, and in its 2003 term it heard only 80.[36] In choosing the cases it will hear, the Court exercises almost total discretion. Because virtually all cases coming to the Court have already been tried and received appellate review, the justices are less concerned with correcting lower court errors than with establishing legal principles or resolving disputes that have national implications. During its 2003–2004 term, roughly half the cases the Court chose to hear raised constitutional issues.

The operations of the Supreme Court are discussed in greater detail in Chapter 5.

STATE COURTS

Justice William Brennan, who served on the New Jersey Supreme Court before his elevation to the U.S. Supreme Court, once observed that "the composite work of the courts in the fifty states probably has greater significance [than that of the U.S. Supreme Court] in measuring how well America attains the ideal of equal justice for all."[37] This is true in part because of the sheer volume of cases

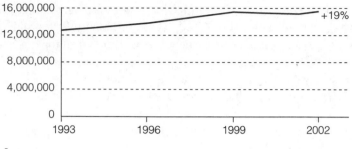

FIGURE **2-4**

Criminal Cases in State Trial Courts

Source: www.ncsconline.org/D_Research/csp/2003_Files/2003_Criminal. Used by permission.

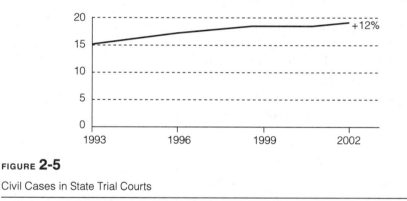

FIGURE **2-5**

Civil Cases in State Trial Courts

Source: www.ncsconline.org/D_Research/csp/2003_Files/2003_Criminal. Used by permission.

that state courts decide annually. The trial courts of California, for example, decided more than 8.1 million cases in 2002, more than twenty-five times the number decided by federal district courts during the same year.[38] Thus, for most Americans, their personal experience with courts—and the ideas they develop about the fairness of the nation's courts—usually involve state courts. (Figures 2-4 and 2-5 show the change over time in the caseloads of state trial courts of general jurisdiction.)

In addition, many decisions that state courts render have a direct and immediate impact on the daily lives of ordinary citizens. The vast majority of criminal cases are state cases, arising under state criminal laws. Familial matters (divorce, child custody, and adoption) and landlord–tenant relations are regulated by state law and addressed in state court. So, too, are traffic violations, creditor–debtor disputes, most personal injury suits, and most commercial transactions. Such issues not only arise in state courts but also are ultimately settled by them. Although some state judicial decisions are subject to review by the federal courts, most fall outside the federal judicial power—that is, they resolve disputes under state law between citizens of the same state. Even when the U.S. Supreme Court might in theory review state rulings, the sheer number of state cases means that only a miniscule percentage actually receive federal judicial scrutiny. Thus, state courts render the final and determinative decision in the vast majority of cases they consider, including most cases that announce major policy initiatives.

The Structure of State Court Systems

State court systems share the following three basic organizational features (see Figure 2-6).

   1. Supreme court.   Forty-eight states vest ultimate appellate authority in a single court, usually designated as the supreme court. (The sole exceptions, Oklahoma and Texas, each have established a Court of Criminal Appeals, which is the court of last resort in criminal cases, and a Supreme Court, which has the final responsibility for appeals in civil cases.) A state supreme court is responsible for the development of state law, and its decisions serve as authoritative precedent within the state court system. Its jurisdiction is defined by the state constitution, state statutes, or both. Usually, it does not enjoy the nearly total discretion over the cases it hears that the U.S. Supreme Court does. The mandatory jurisdiction of the Washington Supreme Court, for example, includes certain criminal, administrative agency, juvenile, and lawyer-discipline cases. Not surprisingly, given the more extensive mandatory jurisdiction, most state supreme courts decide more cases per year than does the U.S. Supreme Court.

   2. Intermediate court of appeals.   Thirty-nine states have also created intermediate courts of appeals—that is, first-level appellate courts below the state supreme court. These courts generally focus on error correction. They review decisions of trial courts to ensure that judges did not make errors in procedure or in the interpretation of the law that would warrant reversal of their decisions. Because all litigants under American law are entitled to one appeal, these courts—like the federal courts of appeals—exercise no discretion over the appeals they hear. If the appeal is properly filed, they must review the lower court's decision. Decisions of an intermediate court of appeals typically can be appealed to the state supreme court, though that court may have some control over what decisions it reviews. In practice, intermediate courts of appeals render the final decision in most cases that come before them.

   Intermediate courts of appeals were initially established in populous states to alleviate caseload pressures on state supreme courts, but in recent years many other states have also created intermediate courts of appeals. There is

SUPREME COURT

A state's court of last resort for appeals in civil and criminal cases: A state may have a single supreme court (48 states) or separate courts for civil and for criminal appeals (Oklahoma and Texas).

Name of court: Supreme Court (46 states), Court of Appeals (Maryland, New York), Supreme Judicial Court (Maine, Massachusetts), Court of Criminal Appeals (Oklahoma, Texas).

Number of justices: Varies from state to state; 3 justices (Oklahoma's Court of Criminal Appeals), 5 justices (18 states), 7 justices (26 states), and 9 justices (6 states).

↑

INTERMEDIATE COURT OF APPEALS

A state's main appellate court, handling routine appeals and subject to review in some cases by the state supreme court (39 states).

Name of court: Varies from state to state; most frequent is Court of Appeals (28 states).

Number of judges: Ranges from 3 (Alabama, Alaska, Hawaii, Idaho) to 88 (California); 27 states have 10 or more judges.

↑

TRIAL COURTS OF GENERAL JURISDICTION

Found in all states, the trial courts for more serious criminal and civil cases; may hear appeals from trial courts of limited jurisdiction.

Name of court: Varies from state to state; most frequent names are Circuit Court (15 states), District Court (16 states), and Superior Court (14 states).

Number of judges: More than 7,500 judges.

Jurisdiction: On the basis of geography (judicial districts) and subject matter (cases not delegated to trial courts of limited jurisdiction).

↑

TRIAL COURTS OF LIMITED JURISDICTION

Found in all but six states, the trial courts for less serious criminal and civil cases; may also handle preliminary matters, such as arraignments and preliminary examinations in more serious cases.

Number of judges: More than 13,000 judges.

Jurisdiction: Usually on the basis of geography (for example, municipal courts), although may also be specialized on the basis of subject matter (for example, traffic court) or the amount involved (for example, small claims court).

FIGURE **2-6**

The Structure of State Court Systems

Source: *Book of the States, 2003* (Lexington, KY: Council of State Governments, 2003).

wide variation in the structure and operation of these courts. Some sparsely populated states—for example, Alaska—have a single court that hears appeals *en banc* (that is, with all the judges sitting on each case). Other states, such as California and Louisiana, have followed the model of the federal courts of appeals, with several courts serving various regions of the state. These courts typically meet in three-judge panels, just like the federal courts of appeals. In contrast, Alabama and Tennessee have created separate courts for appeals in criminal cases and in civil cases.

3. *Trial courts.* Four states—Illinois, Iowa, Minnesota, and South Dakota—have a single set of original jurisdiction (trial) courts. Forty-six states, however, operate two sets of trial courts: courts of limited jurisdiction and courts of general jurisdiction. Courts of limited jurisdiction go under a variety of names: municipal court, county court, district court, justice of the peace court, and so on. They handle less serious criminal cases and civil cases involving relatively small sums of money. For example, North Carolina's trial courts of limited jurisdiction, known as district courts, decide civil cases involving less than $10,000, domestic relations cases, and criminal cases involving juveniles or misdemeanors.[39] Courts of general jurisdiction decide more important civil cases and serious criminal cases. In several states they may also hear appeals, often with a new trial (called a trial *de novo*), from courts of limited jurisdiction. (This new trial is necessary because limited jurisdiction courts do not keep a verbatim record of proceedings.)

Despite these basic uniformities, what is most striking about state court systems is their bewildering organizational diversity. No two state court systems are exactly the same. One important source of variation is found in the organization of state trial courts. Although forty-six states divide original jurisdiction between courts of limited jurisdiction and courts of general jurisdiction, most further subdivide it on the basis of geography, subject matter, or both. Thus, Maryland has a separate Orphans' Court; Colorado, a Water Court; and New York, ten separate sets of trial courts, including special civil and criminal courts for New York City. Figure 2-7, which depicts New York's judicial system, illustrates the complexities that may result.

Another source of variation among state judicial systems involves the assignment of appellate responsibilities. Some states, particularly less populous states, such as Hawaii and South Dakota, route all appeals to their supreme courts. Others, as noted earlier, permit their trial courts of general jurisdiction to hear some appeals. Still others have created intermediate courts of appeals to relieve caseload pressures on their supreme courts.

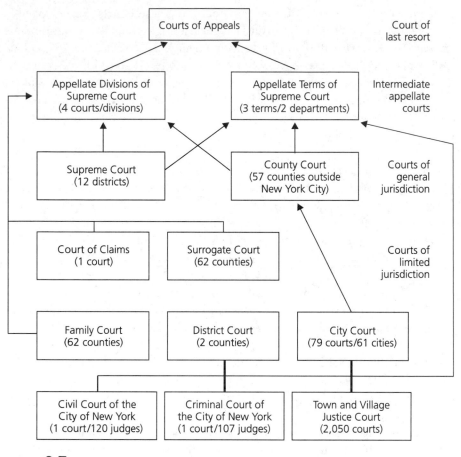

FIGURE **2-7**

The Court System of New York

Source: Adapted from *State Court Structure Charts, 2003* at www.ncsconline.org.

The Development of State Court Systems

Historical factors generally account for the organizational complexity found in state court systems.[40] In creating their court systems, most states designed them to serve a relatively sparse and predominantly rural citizenry. Over time, urbanization and population growth produced new demands for court services. In some states constitutional amendments were adopted to modernize the court system, but these amendments themselves frequently were outpaced by subsequent development, requiring further changes. In other states the legislatures responded not by overhauling the existing court structure but by creating additional trial courts to satisfy those demands. Thus, in contrast to the

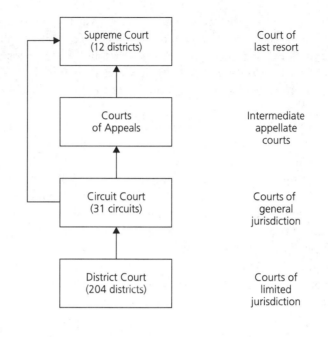

Supreme Court (12 districts)	Court of last resort
Courts of Appeals	Intermediate appellate courts
Circuit Court (31 circuits)	Courts of general jurisdiction
District Court (204 districts)	Courts of limited jurisdiction

FIGURE **2-8**

The Court System of Virginia—A Reformed Court System

Source: Adapted from *State Court Structure Charts, 2003* at www.ncsconline.org.

federal court system, whose basic structure was largely established in 1789, many state court systems reflect the continuing pattern of demand and response that occurred in the state. Typically, the new state trial courts were added with little consideration of their impact on the overall coherence of the judicial system, and the result was a multiplicity of separate courts reflecting no underlying organizational principle.

During the twentieth century, state court reformers introduced important changes in state court systems. One reform campaign led by the American Judicature Society and the American Bar Association focused on streamlining state court systems. According to these reformers, the complexities of state court systems—particularly the myriad specialized trial courts with their overlapping jurisdictions—interfered with the efficient and uniform administration of justice. Litigants often did not know in which court to file suits, and the varying procedural requirements from court to court meant that cases were often dismissed on procedural grounds, without consideration of their merits. To remedy these problems, the reformers proposed a consolidation of state trial courts and a clearer definition of the jurisdictional boundaries among them.[41] (To understand the dramatic structural simplification sought by the reformers, compare New York's unconsolidated trial courts, depicted in Figure 2-7, with Virginia's consolidated courts, shown in Figure 2-8.) During the last half of the twentieth century, the reformers' campaign for trial court consolidation enjoyed considerable success. Once structural changes were adopted in a few states, such as New Jersey in 1947, other states followed their lead and modernized their courts. Although some scholars have questioned the alleged benefits of trial court consolidation, most states today have simplified their systems of trial courts.[42]

Another structural reform, adopted in response to increases in the number of appeals filed in state courts, has been the establishment of intermediate courts of appeals. By itself, this structural change has little effect on caseload problems. The number of appeals tends to increase following the establishment of an intermediate court of appeals; with appeals from that court to the state supreme court, filings in the supreme court may soon approximate earlier levels.[43] When this reform is combined with a limitation on the right to a second appeal, however, it can substantially reduce the caseloads of state supreme courts.[44] Equally important is the effect of the reform on the types of cases coming before the state supreme court and on the role that the court plays in the state. By diverting routine cases to intermediate appellate courts, a state allows its supreme court to devote more attention to cases that raise important policy questions and to assume a position of leadership in the legal development of the state.[45] As discussed in Chapter 11, some state supreme courts have availed themselves of this opportunity to undertake major initiatives in tort law (involving such matters as product liability and personal injury cases) and in constitutional law.

CONCLUSIONS

In choosing federalism, the United States embraced complexity in its governmental structures in general and in its courts in particular. The structure of courts in the United States, however, is complex even in comparison with judicial structures in other federal systems. Both the federal government and each state government operate a full set of trial and appellate courts. Not surprisingly, perhaps, the division of responsibility between national and state courts has remained a contentious issue for most of the nation's history.

The structure of both the federal and state courts has changed over time, largely in response to increases in population and the demand for court services. For the federal courts, the changes have been less dramatic. The Judiciary Act of 1789 created the three-level structure of the federal judicial system that has remained to the present day. During the late nineteenth and early twentieth centuries, however, Congress established an entirely new set of courts, the courts of appeals, and eliminated the circuit courts. More recently, congressional legislation has granted the U.S. Supreme Court the discretion to set its own agenda, thus facilitating its transformation into a court that deals primarily with constitutional issues. Another recent change has been the proliferation of specialized federal courts, though most cases continue to be resolved by the federal district courts and courts of appeals.

The development of state courts has followed a different pattern. For most of the nation's history, the states responded to demands for court services by creating new courts, frequently with limited or specialized jurisdictions. Often these incremental steps provided only temporary relief and were followed by renewed demands and by further piecemeal responses. These changes over time produced unduly complex and incoherent court systems that simply did not function well. Thus, whereas in recent years the number of specialized federal courts has increased, judicial reformers in the states have urged the elimination of specialized courts and a simplified court structure. Many states have adopted the reformers' model, in whole or in part, and state court systems now resemble one another more closely than at any time in the past.

Some reforms—for instance, the creation of the federal courts of appeals—have undoubtedly produced a more efficient administration of justice. The verdict on others, among them state court consolidation, is less clear. What is clear, however, is that structural and jurisdictional changes have had diverse—and at times unanticipated—effects on the role that courts play in governing. As burgeoning caseloads prompt renewed calls for reform, wise reformers will keep in mind the broader effects that their efforts to alleviate caseload pressures might produce.

NOTES

1. The description of this landmark case draws on Anthony Lewis's fascinating account, *Gideon's Trumpet* (New York: Vintage, 1964).

2. "Incorporation" is the name given to the process by which the Supreme Court, relying on the Due Process Clause of the Fourteenth Amendment, has extended federal judicial protection against state violation of rights. For an overview of how the Court has proceeded, incrementally applying various guarantees of the federal Bill of Rights against state governments, see Ronald Mykkeltvedt, *The Selective Incorporation of the Bill of Rights: Fourteenth Amendment Due Process and Procedural Rights* (New York: Kennikat, 1982).

3. *Gideon v. Wainwright,* 372 U.S. 335 (1963).

4. U.S. Constitution, art. 3, sec. 1.

5. Ibid.

6. *Northern Pipeline Construction Co. v. Marathon Pipeline Co.,* 458 U.S. 50 (1982).

7. Standard accounts of the development of the federal judicial system include Edwin C. Surrency, *History of the Federal Courts,* 2nd ed. (Dobbs Ferry, NY: Oceana, 2002), and Howard Ball, *Courts and Politics: The Federal Judicial System,* 2d ed. (Englewood Cliffs, NJ: Prentice Hall, 1987).

8. David M. O'Brien, *Storm Center: The Supreme Court in American Politics,* 5th ed. (New York: Norton, 1999), p. 104.

9. The conflict over the "midnight judges" also led to *Marbury v. Madison,* 5 U.S. (1 Cranch) 137 (1803), the Supreme Court's first exercise of judicial review to strike down a federal statute.

10. The Tenth Amendment to the U.S. Constitution states: "powers not delegated to the United States by the Constitution, nor prohibited by it to the States, are reserved to the States respectively, or to the people." This means that the range of cases not falling within the federal judicial power are to be decided by state courts.

11. The Constitution does specify the original jurisdiction of the U.S. Supreme Court— that is, the range of cases in which the Court rules as a trial court. When Congress in the Judiciary Act of 1789 attempted to expand the Court's original jurisdiction, the Supreme Court struck down that section of the act as unconstitutional in *Marbury v. Madison,* 5 U.S. (1 Cranch) 137 (1803).

12. *Seminole Tribe of Florida v. Florida,* 517 U.S. 44 (1996). The Supreme Court subsequently held that the federal Government also could not subject states to suit in their own courts in *Alden v. Maine,* 527 U.S. 706 (1999).

13. This account relies on Ball, *Courts and Politics,* and Martin H. Redish, *Federal Jurisdiction: Tensions in the Allocation of Judicial Power* (Indianapolis: Michie, 1980).

14. *Chisholm v. Georgia,* 2 Dallas 419 (1793).

15. Although the Eleventh Amendment prohibits suing a state in federal court, it does not preclude suits against state officials. For example, Wainwright in *Gideon v. Wainwright* was the state director of corrections.

16. *Ives v. South Buffalo Railway,* 201 N.Y. 271 (1911).

17. Felix Frankfurter and James M. Landis, *The Business of the United States Supreme Court* (New York: Macmillan, 1927), p. 60.

18. For a discussion of proposals to eliminate the federal courts' diversity jurisdiction, see Thomas D. Rowe, Jr., "Abolishing Diversity Jurisdiction: The Silver Lining," *American Bar Association Journal* 66 (January 1988): 177–180, and Harry Phillips, "Diversity Jurisdiction: Problems and a Possible Solution," *University of Toledo Law Review* 14 (spring 1983): 747–757.

19. These data are drawn from the Web site of the Federal Judiciary, at: www.uscourts. gov/caseload2002.

20. For a summary of arguments against eliminating the federal courts' diversity jurisdiction, see John P. Frank, "An Idea Whose Time Is Still Here," *American Bar Association Journal* 70 (June 1984): 17–18, and Victor E. Flango, "Attorneys' Perspectives on Choice of Forum in Diversity Cases," *Akron Law Review* 25 (summer 1991): 41–122.

21. Flango, "Attorneys' Perspectives on Choice of Forum."

22. For the effect on state court caseloads of eliminating the federal courts' diversity jurisdiction, see Victor Eugene Flango, "How Would the Abolition of Federal Diversity Jurisdiction Affect State Courts?" *Judicature* 74 (June–July 1990): 35–43.

23. Judge Henry N. Graven, quoted in C. K. Rowland and Robert A. Carp, *Politics and Judgment in Federal District Courts* (Lawrence: University Press of Kansas, 1996), p. 1.

24. Data are drawn from www.uscourts.gov/caseload2002.

25. Data are drawn from table 5, *Report of the Proceedings of the Judicial Conference of the United States* (September 22, 1992), pp. 51–52; and the Web site of the judicial branch at www.uscourts.gov/judbus2000.

26. Data are drawn from the Web site of the federal judiciary at www.uscourts.gov/ judbus2000.

27. Ibid.

28. Of course, the rulings of the Court of Appeals for the District of Columbia can be appealed to the U.S. Supreme Court.

29. See J. Woodford Howard Jr., *Courts of Appeals in the Federal Judicial System* (Princeton, NJ: Princeton University Press, 1981); Donald R. Songer, "The Circuit Courts of Appeals," in *The American Courts: A Critical Assessment,* eds. John B. Gates and Charles A. Johnson (Washington, DC: CQ Press, 1991); and Christopher P. Banks, *Judicial Politics in the D.C. Circuit Court* (Baltimore: Johns Hopkins University Press, 1999).

30. See the Web site of the federal judiciary at www.uscourts.gov/caseload2002.

31. For short-term changes, see ibid. For a historical account of changes, see Lawrence Baum, Sheldon Goldman, and Austin Sarat, "The Evolution of Litigation in the Federal Courts of Appeals, 1895–1975," *Law & Society Review* 16 (1981–1982): 291–309, and Richard A. Posner, *The Federal Courts: Challenge and Reform* (Cambridge, MA: Harvard University Press, 1996), part 2.

32. *Annual Report of the Director of the Administrative Office of the United States Courts, 1990,* p. 3, table 1; *Report of the Proceedings of the Judicial Conference of the United States* (September 22, 1992), p. 51; and www.uscourts.gov/caseload2002.

33. Although Rule 10 lists conflict between the circuits as one criterion for granting review, the Court is not obliged to grant review even when such conflicts exist. See H. W. Perry Jr., *Deciding to Decide: Agenda Setting in the United States Supreme Court* (Cambridge, MA: Harvard University Press, 1991), pp. 246–252.

34. See Howard, *Courts of Appeals in the Federal Judicial System,* chapter 7.

35. Ibid., pp. 241–247.

36. For a discussion of this phenomenon, see Arthur D. Hellman, "The Shrunken Docket of the Rehnquist Court," *The Supreme Court Review* 1996, pp. 403–438.

37. William J. Brennan, Jr., "State Supreme Court Judge versus United States Supreme Court Justice: A Change in Function and Perspective," *University of Florida Law Review* 19 (1966): 236.

38. The data for California's trial courts are taken from the Web site of the California judiciary: www.courtinfo.ca.gov/reference/documents/ar2001-2.pdf.

39. *State Court Organization, 1998,* reproduced at www.ojp.udoj.gov/.

40. This account draws on Larry Berkson and Susan Carbon, *Court Unification: History, Politics, and Implementation* (Washington, DC: National Institute of Law Enforcement and Criminal Justice, 1978); and Robert W. Tobin, *Creating the Judicial Branch: The Unfinished Revolution* (Williamsburg, VA: National Center for State Courts, 1999).

41. The reformers also favored (1) centralized management of the court system by the state chief justice, (2) centralized rulemaking for the courts by the state supreme court, (3) a unitary budget for the judiciary prepared by a judicial budget office, and (4) state financing of all courts, rather than the system of shared state and local finance found in most states.

42. For analyses critical of the reformers' claims, see Carl Baar and Thomas Henderson, "Alternative Models for the Organization of State-Court Systems," in *The Analysis of Judicial Reform,* ed. Philip Dubois (Lexington, MA: Lexington Books, 1982); G. Alan Tarr, "The Effects of Court Unification on Court Performance: A Preliminary Assessment," *Judicature* 64 (March 1981): 356–368; and Geoff Gallas, "The Conventional Wisdom of State Court Administration: A Critical Assessment and an Alternative Approach," *Justice System Journal* 2 (spring 1976): 35–56.

43. Victor Eugene Flango and Nora F. Blair, "Creating an Intermediate Appellate Court: Does It Reduce the Caseload of a State's Highest Court?" *Judicature* 64 (August 1980): 74–84.

44. For examples, see Roger D. Groot, "The Effects of an Intermediate Appellate Court on the Supreme Court Work Product: The North Carolina Experience," *Wake Forest Law Review* 7 (1971): 548–572, and John M. Scheb and John M. Scheb II, "Making Intermediate Appellate Courts Final: Assessing Jurisdictional Change in Florida's Appellate Courts," *Judicature* 67 (May 1984): 474–485.

45. See Paul D. Carrington, Daniel J. Meador, and Maurice Rosenberg, *Justice on Appeal* (St. Paul, MN: West, 1976), p. 150, and Groot, "Effects of an Intermediate Appellate Court."

JUDGES

When Justice Lewis Powell announced his retirement in June 1987, President Ronald Reagan viewed it as a unique opportunity to influence the future direction of the Supreme Court.[1] The Court was closely divided on several constitutional issues—including affirmative action, abortion, and the rights of defendants—about which the president felt strongly, and Justice Powell had often cast the decisive vote. Replacing Powell with a conservative justice could tip the balance on the Court and dramatically shift its orientation. At a press conference six days after Powell's announcement, President Reagan nominated Robert H. Bork, a member of the Court of Appeals for the District of Columbia, to fill the vacant seat.

The president's three previous nominees for the Supreme Court had all been confirmed, and Bork himself had easily won Senate approval in 1982 when he was appointed to the court of appeals. However, the Bork nomination pitted a lame-duck Republican president, weakened politically by allegations of executive branch wrongdoing, against a Democratic-controlled Senate just one year before a presidential election. Political observers in Washington expected a bitter battle over confirmation, and they were not disappointed.

Liberals also knew how crucial Powell's successor could be to the future direction of the Supreme Court, and Reagan's nomination of Bork confirmed their worst fears. As a law professor at Yale University, Bork had sharply criticized rulings of the Supreme Court that gave a broad reading to rights claims. After his appointment to the bench, his rulings solidified his reputation as a leading judicial conservative. Senator Ted Kennedy of Massachusetts, who was to lead the fight against Bork, forecast a catalog of horrors if the Senate should confirm him:

> Robert Bork's America is a land in which women would be forced into back-alley abortions, blacks would sit at segregated lunch counters, rogue police would break down citizens' doors in midnight raids . . . and the doors of the Federal courts would be shut on the fingers of millions of citizens for whom the judiciary is often the only protector of the individual rights that are the heart of our democracy.[2]

Although Kennedy's statement exaggerated and distorted Bork's views, as Kennedy himself later acknowledged, it did signal the intensity of the opposition to the nomination and the determination of liberals to block it in the Senate.

Senator Joseph Biden of Delaware, chairman of the Senate Judiciary Committee, scheduled the committee hearings for eleven weeks after the nomination, allowing the anti-Bork forces plenty of time to mobilize. Groups such as People for the American Way, the NAACP, and the National Abortion Rights League spearheaded a massive lobbying and media campaign against Bork; seldom, if ever, had a Court nominee generated such intense opposition. In radio and television ads, these groups portrayed Bork as a dangerous radical, outside the legal mainstream. Their claim received a boost when the American Bar Association's Select Committee on the Federal Judiciary split sharply on the nomination, with four members rating Bork "not qualified" for the Court. Pro-Bork forces denounced what they termed the politicization of the selection process but, unsure of what strategy to follow, failed to mount an effective counteroffensive. By the time the committee hearings commenced, public opinion had coalesced against Bork, and the nomination was in serious trouble.

Although scores of witnesses testified for or against Bork, it was his five days of testimony that proved decisive. Under questioning from committee members, Judge Bork repeated his earlier criticism of the Supreme Court's recognition of an unenumerated constitutional right to privacy (the basis for the Court's rulings striking down statutes banning abortion and contraception). However, he did seek to distance himself from positions he had espoused in law review and periodical articles written before he ascended the bench, prompting accusations that he was experiencing a "confirmation conversion." Whatever the truth of the accusation, many senators remained convinced that, if elevated to the Court, Bork would seek to reshape constitutional law in fundamental ways. By a 9–5 vote, with Republican Senator Arlen Specter of Pennsylvania joining all the Democratic members, the Judiciary Committee voted against confirmation.

Faced with an adverse vote in committee, a nominee usually withdraws from consideration. Bork, however, vowed to combat what he termed the "public campaigns of distortions" by carrying the fight to the floor of the Senate. Continuation of the process allowed Bork's supporters to make his case before the full Senate, but without changing many minds. The Senate rejected the nomination by a 58–42 vote.

The monumental battle over the Bork nomination seemed to exhaust both sides. President Reagan next announced plans to nominate Douglas Ginsburg, a forty-one-year-old appeals court judge, to fill Justice Powell's seat. But, shortly after the announcement, reports surfaced that Ginsburg had smoked marijuana at parties while a faculty member at Harvard Law School. This revelation led some conservatives within the Reagan administration to oppose the nomination, and Ginsburg was forced to withdraw from consideration. With his third nominee, Judge Anthony Kennedy, President Reagan enjoyed better luck. Of all the groups that had opposed Bork, only the National Organization for Women also opposed Kennedy. His testimony before the Judiciary Committee convinced the Senate of his moderation and judicial temperament, and he easily won confirmation.

The conflict over Justice Powell's successor illustrates three important themes that will guide the discussion of judges and judicial selection.

1. The political character of judicial selection. Though political conflict over judgeships is rarely as visible and intense as during the Bork nomination, it is never totally absent. Judges in the United States may be appointed or elected, chosen by political officials, by "merit selection," or by popular vote. But no selection system altogether banishes political or ideological considerations. Different selection systems may affect who exercises political influence, but not whether it will be exercised.

2. The importance of who the judges are. Though they agreed on little else, both proponents and opponents of the Bork nomination assumed that his appointment would affect the Court's decisions. This was not because they feared—or hoped—that Bork would cynically ignore his oath of office and use the position to advance his own policy views. Rather, partisans on both sides recognized that even judges who seek to banish personal predilections and decide in accord with the law may arrive at quite different conclusions. These differences among judges may occur (1) because judges' views and values inevitably influence their judgment, (2) because the exercise of judgment necessarily involves an element of discretion, or (3) for a variety of other reasons. But whatever the reason, the possibility that judges may have different perspectives on the same legal question underlines the importance of who judges.

3. Ambiguity about judicial qualifications. When President Reagan announced his choice for the Supreme Court, he stressed Judge Bork's legal qualifications. However, opponents of the nomination focused on Bork's constitutional views, insisting that his views placed him outside the mainstream of American legal thought. Responding to the charge that they were attempting to politicize the selection process, anti-Bork forces responded that the president himself had considered Bork's views before nominating him. Because judicial decisions have important consequences, they contended, senators too should assess how a nominee will decide cases before voting to confirm.

The debate between the pro- and anti-Bork forces reflects a more general ambiguity in Americans' expectations about judges. On the one hand, we want judges to be independent and impartial. On the other hand, we want all officials who exercise power to be responsive to public sentiment and accountable for their actions. Over the course of the nation's history, Americans have alternated between these two perspectives, and changes in the mode of selecting state judges have reflected this alternation. It is to these competing perspectives and their effect on judicial selection that the discussion now turns.

WHAT SORT OF JUDGES DO WE WANT?

Judicial Independence versus Accountability

Basic to our understanding of a fair trial are the notions of judicial impartiality and neutrality; we believe that rulings should be unaffected by political considerations or the identity of the litigants. Yet not all legal systems share this expectation. In some legal systems judges are expected to decide politically sensitive cases so as to further the ends of the regime. Even in systems that proclaim their commitment to "equal justice under law," such as the United States, officials sometimes attempt to influence judicial decisions, and judges occasionally succumb to political pressures.[3] Moreover, even in the absence of overt efforts to influence decisions, judges are certainly aware of the stakes in politically sensitive cases like *Bush v. Gore*, which involved the vote count in Florida in the aftermath of the 2000 presidential election. Thus, if judges are to act impartially, they must be freed from pressures to act otherwise. This freedom from external pressures is known as *judicial independence*.

Historically, the pressures on judges usually involved threats to a judge's salary or position. For example, the Declaration of Independence accused George III of having made "judges dependent upon his will alone for the tenure of their offices and the amount and payment of their salaries." To prevent similar pressures on federal judges, Article III of the United States Constitution guarantees that judges "shall hold their Offices during good Behaviour, and shall, at stated Times, receive for their Services a Compensation which shall not be diminished during their Continuance in Office." Although most states do not safeguard judicial independence to quite that extent, they award longer terms of office to judges than to most other officials.

The American concern for judicial independence, however, is in tension with another deeply held American value: the *accountability* of governmental officials. In democratic systems citizens select those who wield power and hold them accountable for its exercise. This ensures that the government's decisions reflect the values and perspectives of the community. Advocates of judicial accountability maintain that because judges, like legislators, make decisions that have broad societal effects, they too should be answerable for their decisions. The federal Constitution establishes a degree of accountability by providing for the impeachment of judges. Although Thomas Jefferson dismissed this check as a "mere scarecrow," in the 1980s two district court judges were impeached.[4] The states, however, have gone considerably further. Some fill judgeships by popular election and require judges to run for reelection. Most limit judges' terms of office and require that they periodically seek reappointment or public approval of their performance in office.

Representativeness

In recent decades some Americans have also voiced concern about the representativeness of the judiciary—that is, the extent to which the judiciary reflects—or fails to reflect—the demographic makeup of the populace. Underlying this concern is the belief that a demographically homogeneous judiciary cannot adequately take into account the perspectives and interests of excluded groups.

Demographic considerations have influenced the selection of judges throughout American history: Political parties have sought to "balance the ticket" in judicial elections, and presidents and governors have considered religion and ethnicity in appointing judges. Indeed, during the early twentieth century there were identifiable Catholic and Jewish seats on the Supreme Court.[5] However, the recent pressure for a more representative judiciary has become entangled in the larger societal debate over diversity and affirmative action. Women's organizations and civil rights groups, noting the discrepancy between the proportion of group members in the population and their representation on the bench, have called for concerted action to remedy the disparity. Those opposing affirmative action in judicial selection insist that, because judges function not as representatives but as neutral arbiters, they should be selected on the basis of merit rather than group membership.

The debate over representativeness, like the tension between judicial independence and accountability, reflects the competing views Americans have about judges and judging. We want judges who are impartial, yet we also want them to be mindful of community sentiment. We want a legal system free of racial and gender bias, but disagree about whether efforts to achieve demographic representativeness promote or jeopardize equal justice for all. As Box 3-1 suggests, we also differ among ourselves about the attributes and qualities that judges should have. The sections that follow examine how the states and the federal government have attempted to balance these conflicting concerns for independence, accountability, and representativeness in their systems of judicial selection.

JUDICIAL SELECTION IN THE STATES

Modes of Judicial Selection

Each state establishes its own mode of judicial selection by constitutional provision or by statute. As Table 3-1 indicates, states currently employ five methods in selecting judges.

Judicial Qualifications: A Sampling of Views

"All persons selected as judges should be of good moral character, emotionally stable and mature, physically able to discharge the duties of office, patient, courteous, and capable of deliberation and decisiveness when required to act on their own reasoned judgment." (American Bar Association)

"Judges ought to be more learned than witty, more reverend than plausible, and more advised than confident." (Francis Bacon, English philosopher)

"The trial judge ought to be neutral, detached, kindly, benign, reasonably learned in the law, firm but fair, wise, knowledgeable about human behavior, and in lesser respects as well, somewhat superhuman." (Judge Marvin Frankel)

"The more relevant things about an appointee are his breadth of vision, his imagination, his capacity for disinterested judgment, his power to discover and to suppress his prejudices." (Justice Felix Frankfurter)

"It is as important to a judge called upon to pass on a question of constitutional law, to have at least a bowing acquaintance with Acton and Maitland, with Thucydides, Gibbon, and Carlyle, with Homer, Dante, Shakespeare and Milton, with Machiavelli, Montaigne and Rabelais, with Plato, Bacon, Hume and Kant, as with the books which have been specifically written on the subject." (Judge Learned Hand)

"In the long run, there is no guarantee of justice except the personality of the judge." (Justice Benjamin Cardozo)

Sources: American Bar Association, *Standards Relating to Court Organization* (1990 ed.), sec. 1.21; Francis Bacon, "Of Judicature," in *Bacon's Essays*, ed. Michael J. Hawkins (London: J. M. Dent & Sons, 1972), p. 162; Marvin Frankel, "The Adversary Judge: The Experience of a Trial Judge," in *Views from the Bench*, ed. Mark W. Cannon and David M. O'Brien (Chatham, NJ: Chatham House, 1985), p. 47; Felix Frankfurter and Learned Hand, quoted in David O'Brien, *Judicial Roulette* (New York: Priority Press, 1988), p. 5; and Benjamin Cardozo, *The Nature of the Judicial Process* (New Haven, CT: Yale University Press, 1921), p. 149.

<table>
<tr><td>TABLE
3-1</td><td colspan="5">JUDICIAL SELECTION IN THE STATES*</td></tr>
</table>

Merit Section	Appointment by Governor	Election by Legis- lature	Non- partisan Election	Partisan Election
Alaska	California (A)	South Carolina	Arizona (T)	Alabama
Arizona (M)	Maine	Virginia	California (T)	Arkansas
Colorado	New Hampshire		Florida (T)	Illinois
Connecticut	New Jersey		Georgia	Indiana (T)
Delaware			Idaho	Louisiana
Florida (A)			Kentucky	New York (ICA)
Hawaii			Maryland (T)	North Carolina
Indiana (T)			Michigan	Pennsylvania
Iowa			Minnesota	Tennessee (T)
Kansas			Mississippi	Texas
Maryland (A)			Montana	West Virginia
Massachusetts			Nevada	
Missouri (M)			North Dakota	
Nebraska			Ohio	
New Mexico			Oklahoma (T)	
New York (SC)			Oregon	
Oklahoma (A)			South Dakota (T)	
Rhode Island			Washington	
South Dakota (A)			Wisconsin	
Tennessee (A)				
Utah				
Vermont				
Wyoming				

*Listings do not include trial courts of limited jurisdiction. All listings are for initial selection, not for retention or for filling vacancies occurring during a judicial term.

Key for symbols following the names of states: A: appellate judges only; ICA: judges of intermediate court of appeals only; M: most judges, but with idiosyncratic variations; SC: supreme court justices only; T: trial court judges only.

Source: *Book of the States, 2000–01* (Lexington, KY: Council of State Governments, 2000), pp. 137–139, table 4.4

1. Merit selection. This system is also called the Missouri Plan after the state in which it was first adopted. Designed to remove politics from the selection process, it emphasizes judicial independence rather than judicial accountability. The key feature of merit selection is a judicial nominating commission, composed of lawyers selected by the state bar and nonlawyers typically appointed by the governor. When a judicial vacancy occurs, the commission nominates three—or in some states as many as six—qualified persons to fill the position. The governor then selects the judge from that list. After a short period of service on the bench, the judge runs in an uncontested retention election, which allows voters to decide whether the judge should remain in office. Twenty-three states currently employ some version of merit selection.

2. *Election by the legislature.* In Virginia and South Carolina the legislature elects state judges. This system favors the judicial candidacies of former legislators—more than three-quarters of supreme court justices in these states had served in the state legislature.[6]

3. *Appointment by the governor.* Although governors appoint judges in four states, in most states another body—usually the state senate—must confirm the appointees. Judges appointed by the governor typically serve for a set term of office. In New Jersey, for example, judges serve for seven years, after which, if reappointed by the governor and confirmed by the senate, they hold office until the retirement age of seventy. In California, judges run in a retention election at the general election after their appointment and serve twelve-year terms thereafter.

4. *Partisan election.* This system, now the main mode of selection in eleven states, emphasizes judicial accountability. Political parties nominate candidates for judicial office, and they run with party labels in the general election. Once elected, they serve for terms that range from two years for Arkansas's justice courts (trial courts of limited jurisdiction) to fourteen years for New York's trial courts of general jurisdiction. The judges usually must seek reelection in a partisan election, although Illinois and Pennsylvania hold retention elections for incumbent judges.

5. *Nonpartisan elections.* Nineteen states conduct judicial elections with no party affiliation indicated on the ballot. Typically, the top two candidates in a nonpartisan primary qualify for the general election. In most states judges elected in nonpartisan elections run for reelection in retention elections.

No listing of modes of selection, however, can do justice to the incredible interstate and intrastate diversity. Some states have adopted different modes of selection for judges on various courts. South Dakota, for example, uses merit selection to choose its appellate judges and nonpartisan election for trial court judges. In addition, many states permit local political authorities to select judges for some trial courts of limited jurisdiction. Some also use a different system for filling interim vacancies (those occurring during a judicial term because of death or resignation) than for the initial selection of judges. This can altogether transform the system of judicial selection in a state, if most judges are initially appointed by the governor to fill judicial vacancies and run for election as incumbents. Finally, some states that elect their judges have introduced distinctive elements to the process. For example, although Michigan and Ohio elect their judges in nonpartisan elections, they nominate judicial candidates in party primaries.[7]

What accounts for the differences in how states select their judges? In part, the interstate variation follows a regional pattern. Gubernatorial appointment is most common in the Northeast, partisan election in the South, nonpartisan election in the northern tier of states from Michigan to the Pacific Northwest, and merit selection in the West. Thus, shared political values within regions of the country and the tendency to emulate the laws and institutions of neighboring states provide part of the answer.

Interstate diversity also reflects the waves of political reform that have periodically swept the nation.[8] At the time the U.S. Constitution was ratified, all thirteen states selected their judges either by gubernatorial appointment (the system used in the colonies before independence) or by legislative election. States whose legislatures now elect judges have retained that system since the late eighteenth century, and three states in which the governor appoints judges had adopted that system before 1800. During the Jacksonian era, many states underwent a democratizing process, removing property-holding requirements for voting and providing for popular election of most governmental officials, including judges, to secure greater accountability. By the Civil War, twenty-four of the thirty-four states had instituted popular (partisan) election of judges, and every new state from Iowa in 1846 to Arizona in 1912 provided for an elective judiciary. Most states that currently elect judges in partisan elections initially adopted this mode of selection during the nineteenth century. During the Progressive era, when reformers sought to improve government by restricting the influence of partisan politics, several states established nonpartisan elections for judges. Merit selection—first adopted in 1940 in Missouri—has replaced nonpartisan elections as the preferred means to eliminate partisan influences from judicial recruitment and attract highly qualified persons to the bench. From 1960 to 2004, twelve states instituted merit selection, although the pace of change has slowed considerably since the 1980s. When a state changes its mode of selection it, of course, changes the politics of judicial selection in the state. Let us consider two main modes of judicial selection, elections and merit selection, and the politics associated with each.

The Politics of Judicial Elections

Those who favor judicial elections insist that they promote judicial accountability, but critics dispute this. They argue that judicial elections are uncompetitive, do not provide the basis for an informed choice by voters, and have little or no effect on judicial behavior in office. Political scientists have conducted numerous studies examining these claims.

Uncompetitive Elections?   Electoral accountability requires that voters be offered a choice between an incumbent and a challenger or between two candidates for office. Yet critics maintain that judicial elections often are uncontested or not seriously contested. Incumbents tend to win lopsided victories and remain in office indefinitely.

Studies of nonpartisan elections confirm many of the critics' charges. Melinda Gann Hall found that from 1980 to 1995, in states with nonpartisan judicial elections, more than half the supreme court justices running for reelection ran unopposed in their first election, and less than 10 percent were defeated.[9] Nonpartisan elections for trial courts were even less competitive. "Judges on the major trial courts of Ohio were opposed only 27 percent of the time, those of Michigan 26 percent of the time, and those of California only 7 percent."[10] For incumbent judges who were challenged, close races were rare, and defeat even rarer.

Partisan elections for the state supreme court promote greater competition. Far fewer justices reach the state high court by appointment, appointed justices who run for election are almost always opposed, and almost 20 percent of incumbent justices were defeated from 1980 to 1995. The margin of victory and the frequency of incumbent defeat are comparable to the figures for incumbent members of the U.S. House of Representatives.[11] However, the greater competitiveness of partisan elections usually does not extend to elections for the trial court bench. These elections instead follow the pattern for other local elections, which is generally one of domination by a single party. For trial court judges, therefore, nomination by the majority party is tantamount to election, and incumbent judges are rarely defeated unless they lose their party support.

An Uninformed Electorate?   Electoral accountability requires that voters have not only a choice but also the information necessary to determine which candidate has the views or other qualifications they desire. Critics charge, however, that judicial elections seldom promote informed choice because the campaigns tend to be low-intensity, low-visibility affairs. Press coverage of judicial races is rare, and financial constraints and ethical norms prevent candidates from communicating their views to the public. As a result, voters either make uninformed choices or, recognizing their ignorance, refrain from voting in judicial elections altogether.

Many of these assertions are accurate. Judicial candidates rarely have sufficient funds to publicize their views. Judicial ethics prohibit them from campaigning like prospective legislators, promising to benefit particular groups or saying how they will vote on particular issues. This may be changing: the U.S. Supreme Court ruled in *Republican Party of Minnesota v. White* (2002) that the First Amendment protects the right of judicial candidates to take public positions on controversial issues.[12] Nevertheless, for the most part, judicial candidates have been limited to pledging to deal impartially with the cases coming before them. When both candidates made the same pledge, voters had little basis for deciding between them.

Not surprisingly, issueless judicial campaigns attract little voter interest and make it difficult to mount a strong challenge to incumbent judges. Often voter knowledge of candidates is woefully inadequate. A survey of voters in one Texas election found that fewer than 5 percent could name a candidate for the trial court of general jurisdiction.[13] Voters deal with this lack of information in various ways. In partisan elections, voters typically take their cues from the party affiliation of the candidates, and thus, the vote for judges tends to reflect the partisan division in the state.[14] In nonpartisan elections, where voters lack even that cue, voting patterns tend to be more diffuse as voters look for something—a familiar name, a newspaper endorsement, or incumbency—to differentiate among the candidates. When judicial elections are not concurrent with elections for other offices, many potential voters do not bother to turn out. When the judicial elections are concurrent, voters still may ignore the judicial races, particularly in nonpartisan systems. According to one study, 90 percent of voters going to the polls voted for judicial candidates in contested partisan elections but only 70 percent in contested nonpartisan elections.[15]

Yet not all judicial elections are ill-financed, issueless endorsements of the incumbent.[16] In fact, the costs of running for judicial office—particularly a seat on a state supreme court—have escalated dramatically in recent years. For example, in Alabama campaign spending in 1986 on two Supreme Court seats was $237,281, but in 2000, candidate spending for four seats had escalated to $13,104,909. In Michigan in 2000, with three incumbent Republicans seeking reelection, candidates spent $7,058,914, and groups interested in the outcome spent another $6,000,000. At times, special interests have blatantly tried to buy influence on a court. While an $11 billion lawsuit by Pennzoil against Texaco was pending before the Texas Supreme Court, Texaco representatives made campaign contributions totaling $72,000 to members of the court, and Pennzoil's lawyers responded by contributing more than $315,000 to the justices. But such blatant efforts to influence judicial votes through contributions are rare. More frequently, groups contribute to the campaigns of judicial candidates that they believe are generally sympathetic to their views or seek to defeat candidates whose views they oppose. Thus, Citizens for a Strong Ohio, affiliated with the Ohio Chamber of Commerce, spent more than $4 million on television ads in 2000 seeking to defeat Justice Alice Resnick, while trial lawyers and union groups spent sizable sums supporting her successful reelection bid.

Allegations of improprieties against a sitting judge may also whet media and voter interest and enable a challenger to upset an incumbent. A case in point is the successful challenge in 1986 to Frank Celebrezze, the controversial Democratic chief justice of Ohio.[17] Since his election in 1978, which had ended the long-standing Republican domination of the Ohio Supreme Court, Celebrezze had presided over a "quiet revolution" in Ohio law. Rulings of the Celebrezze court facilitated suits against employers, doctors, landlords, manufacturers, and the state and its municipalities. The court's decisions earned the approval of labor and consumer groups but the enmity of business interests, which campaigned for Celebrezze's defeat. However, what galvanized popular opposition to Celebrezze were his abrasive personal style and his penchant for unjudicial behavior. He conducted a running feud with the Ohio Bar Association after it rated his brother "not qualified" for a seat on the Ohio Supreme Court and repeatedly clashed publicly with the Republican minority on the court. While on the bench, he actively explored a campaign for the governorship, giving speeches and raising campaign funds. After a decision ordering utility companies to pay refunds to customers, he apparently sought to curry favor by sending out the refund checks over his signature. These actions earned him media notoriety, gave his Republican challenger a ready campaign issue—"restoring the dignity of the court"—and led directly to Celebrezze's defeat.

No Predictable Effect on Judicial Behavior?   Critics claim that judicial elections cannot influence judges' decisions because voters have no way of knowing what cases will arise or how judges will resolve them. Furthermore, judges are bound to decide cases in accord with the law, so elections cannot— and should not—influence their conduct in office. Although (as Chapter 8 will show) judges have some leeway in their interpretation of the law, judges who decide cases on the basis of public opinion or political advantage violate their oath of office.

Yet even if voters in judicial elections do not directly affect the outcome of particular cases, this does not mean that their votes have no effect. The prospect of a forthcoming election may induce judges to consider community sentiments in their decisions. Moreover, voters in judicial elections, like those in congressional elections, can select that candidate whose overall orientation most closely resembles their own. When they do so, they influence the general direction of judicial decisions, even if they do not determine the outcomes in particular cases.

Judicial elections can directly affect judicial decision making only if there are competing candidates and voters can distinguish between their orientations. In nonpartisan elections, these conditions are often not met. In partisan elections, party labels can serve as indicators of general orientation: Republican candidates are more likely to be conservative; Democratic candidates, liberal. Studies of voting behavior on state courts by and large confirm that party affiliation is a fairly good predictor of how judges decide.[18] Kathleen Barber has explained why this happens:

> Direct response to the bidding of a political party is probably rare. . . . Indirect response to needs expressed by groups in the political system with which judges have been and may still be identified is more probable. The deepest and possibly

unconscious level of response reflects consonance of the values of judges and of parties with which they have been affiliated, values which predispose judges both to associate themselves with a given party and to make decisions which favor that party.[19]

The Politics of Merit Selection

Merit selection, developed as an alternative to the political selection of judges, is designed to enhance judicial independence and limit judicial accountability. Instead of party leaders or voters, a commission composed of lawyers (selected by the organized bar) and nonlawyers (usually selected by the governor) nominates prospective candidates. Although governors select judges under merit selection, their range of choice is limited. In contrast to appointive systems, in which a governor exercises complete discretion, merit selection requires the governor to choose the judge from the short list of candidates submitted by the commission. A retention election offers voters an opportunity to approve or reject the governor's choice, but neither party labels nor competing candidates appear on the ballot.

Those who originated merit selection expected that retention elections, while accommodating demands for popular involvement and serving to remove judges who had committed gross abuses, would guarantee long tenure for most judges.[20] Critics have charged that, in practice, retention elections eliminate judicial accountability altogether. Several criticisms leveled against judicial elections in general apply with particular force to retention elections. Not many voters bother to cast ballots in retention elections.[21] Without electoral competition, incumbents have historically enjoyed an immense advantage. From 1980 to 1995, only four state supreme court incumbents were defeated in retention elections—less than 2 percent of all those seeking reelection—and the average vote for incumbents during this period was greater than 70 percent.[22] Often voters lack even rudimentary information about the incumbent judge—for example, more than half the voters in a Wyoming retention election admitted that they knew nothing at all about any of the candidates for retention.[23] Because voters in retention elections typically support incumbents unless they have a basis for opposing them, this lack of information virtually guarantees that judges will be returned to office.

Incumbents have been defeated in retention elections only when confronted by organized opposition from the legal profession, the media, or segments of the general public. In some instances, judges have violated the law or professional norms, prompting campaigns to unseat them. One judge, for example, was defeated after consistently appearing on the bench drunk; another, after repeatedly patronizing or insulting female lawyers and witnesses in his courtroom; and a third, after using his power to assign cases to ensure that the judges deciding politically sensitive cases would be responsive to the Democratic Party.[24]

66   CHAPTER 3

BOX

3-2   *Conflict in California*

Bill Roberts, the leader of one group seeking to unseat Chief Justice Rose Bird, put it bluntly: "There's nothing that's going to save her. She is going to be slam dunked out of business." Retention elections seldom generate such strong feelings. But from the moment Governor Jerry Brown appointed her in 1977 as California's first female chief justice, Rose Bird found herself embroiled in controversy. Although the necessary two members of the Commission on Judicial Appointments voted to confirm her, one member dissented because the forty-year-old secretary of agriculture had no judicial experience. Throughout her tenure as chief justice, Californians remained sharply divided about her qualifications and performance.

Twenty months after her appointment, Chief Justice Bird narrowly avoided defeat in a retention election. The conservative groups campaigning against Bird argued that she and fellow justices had unduly expanded the rights of defendants, allowing criminals to escape punishment because of legal technicalities. They also charged that she had purposely withheld publication of a controversial decision until after the election. Although a state judicial performance commission convened at Bird's request cleared her of the second charge, its investigation revealed a court split by conflicts of personality and judicial philosophy.

After 1978 the California Supreme Court, with Chief Justice Bird in the lead, continued in its liberal course. The court's reliance on the state constitution to expand defendants' rights led California voters to adopt a constitutional amendment, the so-called Victim's Bill of Rights, overturning several of these decisions. When opponents challenged the amendment as a violation of the federal Constitution, the California Supreme Court upheld the measure, but Chief Justice Bird dissented. Even more controversial were the court's rulings in death penalty cases. After California voters ratified a constitutional amendment to reverse a pre-Bird decision invalidating the death penalty, the California court

Public opposition to sitting judges may also emerge because of ideological disagreement with judges' rulings, particularly in cases involving criminal justice and the death penalty. Perhaps the most bitterly fought retention election ever occurred in 1986, when conservative forces spent $5 million to unseat Chief Justice Rose Bird and two associate justices of the California Supreme overturned the death sentences in more than 90 percent of the capital cases that came before it. Bird herself voted to strike down the death sentence in every capital punishment case.

Chief Justice Bird's votes in these cases became the major issue in the 1986 retention election, when conservative groups targeted Bird and two other justices for defeat. Leading the anti-Bird coalition were Crime Victims for Court Reform, whose membership included relatives of the victims in thirty murder cases in which the Bird court had overturned convictions, and Californians to Defeat Rose Bird. Prominent politicians, including Republican Governor George Deukmejian, also urged voters to reject her. The anti-Bird forces spent the previously unheard-of sum of $5.5 million in the campaign, hammering home her opposition to the death penalty with hard-hitting media ads and mass mailings. In response, Bird sought—unsuccessfully—to rally support by raising the banner of judicial independence. Quite early in the campaign, it became evident that she stood no chance of victory, and many Democratic politicians distanced themselves, refusing to support her publicly.

When the votes were counted, California had made political history. Never before had a California chief justice lost a retention election, but Rose Bird was defeated by an extraordinary 66 percent of the votes cast. Never before had California voters removed more than one justice at an election, but the two liberal associate justices running in 1986 also suffered lopsided defeats. In the short term the rejection of the incumbent justices gave Governor Deukmejian the opportunity to appoint three new members of the California Supreme Court. Because of those appointments, the court's orientation has changed dramatically. More broadly, this election demonstrated that groups can defeat justices who make unpopular decisions if opponents have the organization and finances to mount a major campaign to oust them. Thus, the success of the anti-Bird effort paved the way for future campaigns aimed at unseating judges.

Sources: This analysis is based on John H. Culver and John T. Wold, "Rose Bird and the Politics of Judicial Accountability in California," *Judicature* 70 (August–September 1986): 81–89; John T. Wold and John H. Culver, "The Defeat of the California Justices: The Campaign, the Electorate, and the Issue of Judicial Accountability," *Judicature* 70 (April–May 1987): 348–355; and Barry Latzer, "California's Constitutional Counterrevolution," in *Constitutional Politics in the States: Contemporary Controversies and Historical Patterns*, ed. G. Alan Tarr (Westport, CT: Greenwood Press, 1996).

Court because of their apparent opposition to capital punishment (see Box 3-2). Ten years later a vote in a death penalty case cost Justice Penny White her seat on the Tennessee Supreme Court.[25] The prospect of defeat in a retention election, even if unlikely, may lead judges to avoid rulings that could generate opposition. Thus, since the defeat of Chief Justice Bird, the reconstituted

California Supreme Court has upheld the death penalty in more than 95 percent of the capital cases reviewed.[26] And interviews with judges who ran in retention elections from 1986 to 1990 reveal that as the elections approached, 15 percent sought to avoid controversial cases and rulings, while 5 percent became more conservative in sentencing in criminal cases.[27]

Whether or not merit selection guarantees accountability, its proponents maintain that it removes politics from judicial selection. In actuality, however, merit selection merely transforms the politics of judicial selection.[28] Lawyers are placed on the selection commission because they "have daily opportunities to observe the character and professional qualifications of their fellow lawyers seeking judicial appointment . . . and of the judges . . . seeking reappointment."[29] But as Box 3-1 suggests, judicial qualifications are rather nebulous. It is easier to state minimal qualifications than full qualifications, and it is often difficult to determine who possesses the necessary qualifications. Thus, once commission members eliminate obvious incompetents, other factors necessarily come into play. Plaintiffs' attorneys on the commission may favor members of their own group, Republicans or Democrats fellow party members, and so on. Although selection of judges solely on the basis of qualifications may be the aim of merit selection, it is not, and cannot be, the full reality.

At one time, nonlawyer members of the selection commissions were predominantly white businessmen. Now, however, as a result of efforts to secure greater representativeness, selection commissions more accurately reflect the states' demographic diversity.[30] Yet, in one sense, the lay commissioners are not representative of the general populace. Appointed by the governor, they tend to reflect his or her political perspective. In fact, one-third have served in a party office, and one-quarter have held some public post.[31] As one observer in Missouri notes, "some of the laymen are more concerned with politics than anything else, and some of them will do whatever the governor wants them to do when it comes to the selection of panels of nominees."[32]

In addition to appointing lay members of the commission, the governor can also influence the commission's deliberations by letting members know whom he or she favors for a vacant judgeship. The pressure on commission members need not be overt to be effective. Once commissioners know whom the governor wants for a position, they are unlikely to omit that person from the list of candidates unless the person is clearly unqualified.[33] As a result, under merit selection governors may exercise almost as much control as they do under a system of gubernatorial appointment.

What Effect Do Judicial Selection Systems Have?

Underlying the debate between proponents of merit systems and advocates of judicial elections is the assumption that the mode of selection affects the decisions judges render. However, this assumption is questionable. Political scientists have conducted several studies comparing the voting patterns and decisions of judges selected by various methods. Taking similar cases in various states, some studies find no significant relationship between the mode of selection and judicial voting behavior. Studies focusing on how various classes of litigants (e.g., corporations, criminal defendants, and state agencies) have fared before judges selected by various methods likewise conclude that the mode of selection did not affect outcomes.[34] Other studies, however, have found differences. A recent study by Daniel Pinello concludes that appointed judges were more likely to vindicate the rights of defendants in criminal procedure cases, while another recent study found that appointed judges were more likely to uphold sex discrimination claims.[35]

Advocates of merit selection also proclaim that their system produces better-qualified judges. Given the difficulty in determining what qualifications are most important, it is impossible to test this claim directly. Scholars have therefore examined the backgrounds and characteristics of judges chosen through various modes of selection, under the assumption that these factors might serve as indicators of judicial quality. Even if they cannot, they do indicate what sorts of people become state judges under various selection systems.

WHO ARE THE STATE JUDGES?

Altogether, there are more than 1,000 state appellate judges and more than 26,000 state trial judges. Because it would be impossible to collect detailed background information on so many judges, scholars have focused their attention on state supreme court justices. Table 3-2 summarizes their findings.

What is most striking about state supreme court justices are the similarities in their backgrounds. Whatever the mode of selection, the justices have historically tended to be white, male, middle-aged, and middle- to upper-class. To some extent, this reflects the pool of candidates from which judges are chosen. The legal profession itself is hardly representative of the nation's population either demographically or economically. Usually, state supreme court justices are natives of the state in which they serve, have attended law school there, and have been active in state or local politics. Again, this is not surprising. If political considerations cannot be altogether excluded from judicial selection, then prospective judges who develop good contacts within the state and have been politically active will have an advantage. According to one judge, "frequently judgeships become consolation prizes for those who failed in big-time elected politics."[36]

Backgrounds of the justices do vary somewhat from state to state. For example, judges in the West are more likely to be born out of state than their counterparts elsewhere; judges in the South are more likely to be Democrats; and more Catholic and Jewish judges are found in the Northeast.[37] Political scientists have concluded that region, rather than different modes of selection,

TABLE 3-2	CHARACTERISTICS OF STATE SUPREME COURT JUSTICES	
		Percent
Localism		
In-state undergraduate school		60.4
In-state law school		59.9
Race and gender		
Female		20.2
African American		7.6
Asian American		1.8
Hispanic American		1.2
Religious affiliation		
Protestant		58.7
Catholic		29.6
Jewish		5.7
Other		6.0
Political affiliation		
Democrat		56.0
Republican		37.9
Independent or other		6.1
Prior judicial experience		67.6

Source: John B. Wefing, "State Supreme Court Justices—Who Are They?" *New England Law Review* 32 (fall 1997): 89–95.

explains almost all the interstate differences. Thus, at least in terms of judicial backgrounds, merit selection does not produce judges who differ significantly from those selected by other methods.

Table 3-2 summarizes the background of current state supreme court justices. The most striking changes in recent years have involved the demographics of state courts. The first woman appointed to a state supreme court was Florence Allen, who served on the Ohio Supreme Court from 1922 to 1933. No other female justice was appointed until 1958. During the past two decades, however, the number of women serving on state supreme courts has increased dramatically. In 1980, there were ten female justices; by 1996, sixty-six; and by 2000, eighty-eight. The appointment of Judge Sandra Gardebring in 1991 made the Minnesota Supreme Court the first to have a female majority.[38]

The racial composition of state high courts has also changed. In 1980, less than 1 percent of justices were members of racial minorities, but by 1994, the percentage had risen to 8.7 and by 2000 to 11.6 percent. Whereas in 1980, only one African American served on a state supreme court, by 2000 that number had risen to twenty-five.[39] One can expect these changes to continue and perhaps accelerate, because previously excluded groups make up a larger proportion of the legal profession and have become more influential politically.

THE SELECTION OF FEDERAL JUDGES

Article II of the Constitution grants the president the power to appoint federal judges, including Supreme Court justices, with the advice and consent of the Senate. Alexander Hamilton argued in *Federalist No. 76* that this system of shared responsibility has several advantages. The appointment of judges by a single person secures better judgment, imparts a greater sense of responsibility for the choice, and ensures that there will be "fewer personal attachments to gratify" in selecting judges. Senatorial confirmation of appointees serves as "an excellent check upon a spirit of favoritism in the President" and, more generally, encourages the president to appoint only highly qualified persons.[40]

The reality of federal judicial selection is more complex than the constitutional text suggests. Historically, the respective influence of the president and the Senate on selection has differed depending on the level of court, the importance the president attaches to judicial appointments, and whether a single party controls the presidency and the Senate. Members of the Senate have often played the initiating role in selecting lower court judges. When a justice of the Supreme Court is appointed, the president is actively involved. As the hearings on Judge Bork (1989) and Justice Clarence Thomas (1991) show, however, members of the Senate can assume an adversarial stance and conduct their own detailed investigation of the nominee's qualifications and constitutional views. During the presidencies of Bill Clinton and George W. Bush, the Senate has played a key role in reviewing nominees to the courts of appeals as well.[41] Within the executive branch, the group of officials involved in selecting candidates varies according to the level of court and the wishes of the president. Moreover, the criteria used in selecting judges vary from administration to administration.

What does not change from administration to administration is the political character of the process. As a rule, presidents appoint judges who are politically active members of their own party. Merit certainly plays a role in the appointment of federal judges, but competence is a minimum requirement. In choosing among qualified candidates, political considerations necessarily tip the balance.

The Size of the Federal Judiciary

Of course, for the president to appoint a judge, there must be a vacant judgeship. Vacancies can occur because of the death, the retirement, or, in rare cases, the impeachment of a judge. Most federal judges regard their service on the bench as the capstone of their legal careers, and only a few leave the bench before required to do so by age or failing health. Over the last twenty years, the term for Supreme Court justices has averaged about twenty-six years, with lower-court judges serving about twenty years.

Vacancies can also occur when Congress creates new judgeships. Although the Supreme Court has had nine justices since 1869, caseload pressures have forced Congress to increase the number of district court and appeals court judges periodically. In fact, since the late nineteenth century, the number of federal judges has doubled approximately every thirty years.[42] As of 2004, there were 665 district court judges and 179 appeals court judges. Adding large numbers of positions at one time can drastically alter the composition of the federal bench, and so political factors may affect Congress's timing in creating new judgeships. During the 1970s, the Democratic-controlled Congress delayed adding judgeships until there was a Democratic president to appoint the judges. After the election of Jimmy Carter in 1976, Congress passed the Omnibus Judgeship Act of 1978, creating 152 new positions. But there are limits to partisan manipulation of the size of the federal judiciary. The press of judicial business forced Democrats in Congress to expand the federal judiciary during President Ronald Reagan's term of office. This action, together with normal attrition on the federal courts, gave Reagan the opportunity to appoint 290 district court judges and 78 court of appeals judges—almost half of the federal judiciary and more than any previous American president. However, the presidency of Bill Clinton, a Democrat, produced a dramatic shift. By the end of his two terms, Clinton had appointed 357 judges (43 percent of the federal bench), while appointees of his two Republican predecessors filled 40 percent of federal judgeships. With the election of George W. Bush, a Republican, the composition of the federal judiciary shifted again: by September 2004, President Bush had appointed more than 200 federal judges.

The Selection of District Court and Appeals Court Judges

Since at least the 1840s, the selection of district court judges has reversed the constitutional prescription and lodged the primary power in the Senate. More precisely, under the system that developed during the mid-nineteenth century, power rests in the hands of the senators from the president's party in the state in which a judge is to serve. If these senators invoke *senatorial courtesy*, indicating their opposition to a nominee, the Senate almost invariably rejects the president's choice. This does not mean that the Senate frequently rejects nominees. Rather, the prospect of defeat in the Senate creates a powerful incentive for presidents— or, more accurately, for the officials in the Justice Department to whom the president has delegated the responsibility—to confer with the appropriate senators before selecting nominees. Usually senators have their own candidate, or list of candidates, for the vacant seat, and the president typically endorses the senators' recommendation. This means that candidates for judgeships will campaign to win the support of the senators. Some senators dislike the process (according to one, "all you get out of that mess is hundreds of enemies and one ingrate"), but most recognize it as an important opportunity to distribute patronage.[43] Presidents have usually viewed the system as an opportunity to trade judgeships for senatorial support on other matters. Attorney General Robert Kennedy exaggerated only slightly when he described the process as "senatorial appointment with the advice and consent of the Senate."[44]

Senatorial courtesy influences what sort of person is appointed to the district courts. Because these judgeships serve as political patronage for senators, the vast majority of appointees are affiliated with the senator's (and the president's) political party. During the twentieth century, more than 90 percent of all district court judges were members of the appointing president's party.[45] In addition, district court judges usually have "earned" their positions by active party service before their appointment. From the point of view of prospective judges, this establishes a clear career path. As one judge put it, "if I wanted that appointment, [I knew] I had better get back into politics—which I did."[46] Because state party contacts are particularly important in securing support, this political activity has typically involved state or local, rather than national, politics. The judges therefore tend to share the political perspectives dominant in the state. This has at times posed a problem: in the 1950s and 1960s, for instance, many Southern district court judges were reluctant to enforce the Supreme Court's school desegregation decisions.[47]

In selecting judges for courts of appeals, the president's power is enhanced and that of the Senate somewhat diminished. Because of the importance of the positions, the attorney general and other high-ranking officials in the Justice Department participate in identifying and screening potential nominees. Occasionally, the president himself may be involved. Because each appeals court encompasses more than one state, senators from a single state cannot control its membership. Nonetheless, a modified form of senatorial courtesy has developed, extending to the specific seats on the court that have been informally earmarked for each state in the circuit. Still, this extra leverage for the state's senators is balanced by the greater presidential interest in these appointments resulting in a need for negotiation and compromise.

The appeals court judges selected through this process in many ways resemble their counterparts on the district courts—indeed, a sizable minority serve on district courts before being promoted to the court of appeals. Most of the judges were politically active members of the president's party before their appointment, and for much of the nation's history, presidents used appointments to these courts as a form of patronage. A perfect example is former Attorney General Griffin Bell, who served on the Fifth Circuit before resigning to head the Justice Department. In addition to his legal credentials, Bell noted that he had other qualifications for the court of appeals: "I managed John F. Kennedy's presidential campaign in Georgia. Two of my oldest and closest friends were the two senators from Georgia. And I was the campaign manager and special, unpaid counsel for the governor."[48] In more recent years, the emphasis has shifted from patronage to ideology, with presidents nominating on the basis of judicial philosophy and the Senate confirming or failing to confirm nominees on the same basis.

One should note that positions on the courts of appeals are avidly sought, that those who are selected usually have campaigned actively (though discreetly) for the position, lining up a coalition of supporters when a vacancy occurs. One judge candidly stated: "Anybody who thinks judicial office seeks the man is mistaken. There's not a man on the court who didn't do what he thought needed to be done."[49]

A final unofficial participant in the process of selecting federal judges has been the American Bar Association (ABA) through its Standing Committee on Federal Judiciary. Beginning in the Eisenhower administration (1953–1961), presidents submitted the names of prospective judges to the committee, which investigates their professional qualifications. The committee rated nominees from "exceptionally well qualified" to "not qualified," and nominees who received a "not qualified" rating were rarely confirmed. During the Reagan administration, the ABA committee came under fire from political conservatives, who charged that liberals on the ABA committee were allowing their political disagreements with the Reagan administration to color their evaluations of its judicial nominees. They pointed in particular to the fact that four committee members had rated Robert Bork "unqualified" to sit on the Supreme Court. The ABA further earned the ire of conservatives when its House of Delegates voted to endorse reproductive choice, thereby giving the appearance that the organization was taking sides in the public debate over abortion. In response, Senate Judiciary Committee chair Orrin Hatch in 1997 decided to exclude the ABA from a privileged position in testifying on judicial nominees. In 2001, the Bush administration notified the ABA that the president would no longer submit a list of potential nominees for the organization's rating of their professional qualifications, although the president did submit the names of nominees to the ABA at the same time they were submitted to the Senate.

Selection of Lower Court Judges from Carter to George W. Bush

Presidents Jimmy Carter and Ronald Reagan altered the traditional politics of judicial selection through concerted efforts to advance their political agendas through the appointment of district court and appeals court judges. Their success shows that presidents who feel strongly about lower court judgeships can have a real impact, even in an area traditionally dominated by the Senate. To a considerable extent, President George Bush (1989–1993) and George W. Bush followed Reagan's lead in their appointments, and President Bill Clinton followed Carter's.

Judicial Selection under Carter (1977–1981)   President Carter assumed office committed to using affirmative action to increase the demographic representativeness of the federal judiciary by appointing African Americans, women, and other minorities. As he stated, "If I didn't have to get Senate confirmation of appointees, I could tell you flatly that 12 percent of my appointees would be Black and 3 percent would be Spanish-speaking and 40 percent would be women and so forth."[50] To identify qualified candidates for appeals courts who might have been overlooked under the traditional selection system, President Carter established circuit nominating commissions and included women and minority group members on them. Although he did not directly challenge senatorial prerogatives in naming candidates for district judgeships, he convinced some senators to form their own nominating commissions. As a result, Carter was able to name more women and African Americans to the federal bench than had all his predecessors combined. Yet he did not ignore political considerations in his choices. More than 90 percent of the judges he appointed were Democrats, and almost two-thirds had been political activists before their appointment.

Judicial Selection under Reagan and Bush (1981–1993)   President Reagan was concerned less with the demographics of his nominees than with their legal and political views. Early in his administration he announced that he would only appoint judges who embraced the philosophy of judicial restraint— that is, judges who would defer to the popularly elected branches of government and give a presumption of constitutionality to governmental actions. To accomplish this, Reagan devised what one participant called "the most thorough and comprehensive system for recruiting and screening federal judicial candidates of any administration ever."[51] In place of the nominating commissions, he established the Office of Legal Policy, which scrutinized the backgrounds of prospective nominees and conducted rigorous daylong interviews with them. Candidates whose views meshed with the Reagan administration's were put forward, but candidates who failed what critics called an "ideological litmus test" were not. As a result, far more than in previous administrations, President Reagan's nominees reflected a consistent legal and political perspective. (See Tables 3-3 and 3-4.)

Congressional legislation expanding the federal judiciary, along with normal attrition, allowed President Reagan's successor, George H. W. Bush, to appoint almost 200 federal judges. Like Reagan, he sought to guarantee presidential influence over nominations by asking senators for several nominations for each vacancy. He also continued the practice of screening prospective nominees with an eye to judicial restraint. His nominees, like Reagan's, tended to be young, white Republicans, often with previous judicial experience. However, while Bush found few African American Republicans to appoint to the bench, he appointed a higher percentage of women to the federal bench than had any previous president.

Reagan's and Bush's efforts to realign the federal courts largely succeeded. President Reagan's appointees were only half as likely as Carter's to support the

TABLE 3-3   CHARACTERISTICS OF FEDERAL DISTRICT COURT JUDGES

	W. Bush	Clinton	Bush	Reagan
Occupation				
Politics/government	8.4%	11.5%	10.8%	13.4%
Judiciary	48.2	48.2	41.9	36.9
Gender				
Male	79.5	71.5	80.4	91.7
Female	20.5	28.5	19.6	8.3
Ethnicity/race				
White	85.5	75.1	89.2	92.4
African American	7.2	17.4	6.8	2.1
Hispanic American	7.2	5.9	4.0	4.8
Asian American	0.0	1.3	0.0	0.7
Percentage white male	68.7	52.4	73.0	84.8
American Bar Association rating				
Exceptionally/Well Qualified	69.9	59.0	57.4	53.5
Qualified	28.2	40.0	42.6	46.6
Not qualified	1.2	1.0	0.0	0.0
Political affiliation				
Democrat	7.2	87.5	6.1	4.8
Republican	83.1	6.2	88.5	91.7
Independent	9.6	6.2	5.4	3.4
Past party activism	56.6	50.2	64.2	60.3
Average age at appointment	50.3	49.5	48.2	48.6
Total number of appointees	83	305	148	290

Source: Adapted from Sheldon Goldman, Elliot Slotnick, Gerard Gryski, Gary Zuk, and Sara Schiavoni, "W. Bush Remaking the Judiciary: Like Father, Like Son?" *Judicature* 86 (May-June 2003): 304, Table 2. Reprinted by permission of the American Judicature Society.

claims of defendants in criminal cases or plaintiffs with civil liberties claims.[52] They also were far more likely to rule against abortion-rights claims than were federal judges appointed by previous presidents, including Republican presidents.[53] Overall, whereas President Carter's appointees to federal district courts rendered liberal rulings in 53 percent of all cases they decided, Reagan's appointees did so in only 36 percent of their cases, and Bush's in only 33 percent of theirs.[54] These findings confirm that presidents who feel strongly about

TABLE 3-4 CHARACTERISTICS OF FEDERAL APPEALS COURT JUDGES

	W. Bush	Clinton	Bush	Reagan
Occupation				
Politics/government	6.2%	6.6%	10.8%	6.4%
Judiciary	50.0	52.5	59.5	55.1
Gender				
Male	81.2	67.2	81.1	94.9
Female	18.8	32.8	18.9	5.1
Ethnicity/race				
White	81.2	73.8	89.2	97.4
African American	18.8	13.1	5.4	1.3
Hispanic American	0.0	11.5	5.4	1.3
Asian American	0.0	1.6	0.0	0.0
Percentage white male	62.5	49.2	70.3	92.3
American Bar Association rating				
Exceptionally/Well Qualified	68.8	78.7	64.9	59.0
Qualified	31.2	21.3	35.1	41.0
Not qualified	0.0	0.0	0.0	0.0
Political affiliation				
Democrat	12.5	85.2	2.7	0.0
Republican	83.1	6.6	89.2	96.2
Independent	6.2	8.2	8.1	3.8
Past party activism	75.0	54.1	70.3	66.7
Average age at appointment	50.6	51.2	48.7	50.0
Total number of appointees	16	61	37	78

Source: Adapted from Sheldon Goldman, Elliot Slotnick, Gerard Gryski, Gary Zuk, and Sara Schiaroni, "W. Bush Remaking the Judiciary: Like Father, Like Son?" *Judicature* 86 (May-June 2003): 308, Table 4. Reprinted by permission of the American Judicature Society.

lower court judgeships can have a real impact, even in an area that the Senate has traditionally dominated.

Judicial Selection under Clinton (1993–2001) President Clinton appointed 305 district judges and 61 appeals court judges during his two terms. However, he did not view these appointments as a major part of his policy agenda and thus placed less emphasis on appointing ideologically compatible judges than his predecessors did. According to Assistant Attorney General Eleanor Dean Acheson, "The process has been wildly disserved by the idea that this is a huge ideological battle for the courts and [that] there is no middle ground and, somehow, whatever anybody is, they are primarily and most importantly for judicial selection somewhere on this ideological axis."[55] Nevertheless, because more than 90 percent of Clinton's appointees were Democrats, they brought a different perspective to cases than did those judges appointed by Presidents Reagan and Bush.

Complicating the appointment process for President Clinton was the Republican Party's control of the Senate during the last half of his first term and throughout his second term. Divided government typically means that nominees undergo more critical scrutiny. In addition, Republican senators were more than willing to "pay back" Democrats for the harsh treatment given to Robert Bork and Clarence Thomas by the Democratic-controlled Senate when they were nominated for the Supreme Court. Thus, whereas more than 90 percent of Clinton's nominees for the lower federal courts were confirmed in 1993–94, when the Democrats controlled the Senate, only 70 percent were confirmed in 1995–96, 80 percent in 1997–98, and 61 percent in 1999–2000.[56] During 1996, confirmations slowed to a trickle as the Senate refused even to consider Democratic nominees, hoping for a Republican victory in the 1996 presidential race. After the election, conflict between Clinton and Republicans in the Senate continued to stall consideration of judicial nominees, and the process was further slowed during the investigation of President Clinton, his impeachment by the House of Representatives, and his trial in the Senate. With the prospect of a new president, the Senate in 2000 confirmed only 37 nominees, so that that there were 57 vacant seats on federal district courts and 25 on appeals courts when George W. Bush was inaugurated in 2001.

Judicial Selection under George W. Bush (2001–2004)   The composition of the federal judiciary was a prime concern of President Bush when he took office. According to Associate White House Counsel Brett Kavanaugh, the president "has devoted more attention to the issue of judges than any other president."[57] Moreover, circumstances seemed propitious for him to make an impact. Although the Senate was evenly divided between Republicans and Democrats, Vice President Richard Cheney held the decisive tie-breaker vote, and so Republicans controlled the Judiciary Committee and could move nominations along. Beyond that, the judicial vacancies left from the Clinton presidency gave President Bush opportunities to appoint immediately a number of judges.

Yet things did not proceed as the president anticipated. Barely five months into his presidency, Senator Jim Jeffords of Vermont defected from the Republican Party, giving the Democrats control of the Senate and the Judiciary Committee. Liberal interest groups, such as People for the American Way and the National Abortion Rights and Reproductive Action League, mobilized to oppose several Bush nominees to the courts of appeals. Some Democratic senators, recalling Republican opposition to Clinton nominees, slowed the process of confirmation. So did others who objected to what they claimed was the president's attempt to pack the courts with conservative activists. Meanwhile, external events such as 9/11, the anthrax scare on Capitol Hill, and the need to enact anti-terrorism legislation all combined to distract attention from judicial nominations.

When Republicans recaptured the Senate in the 2002 congressional elections, it appeared that this would speed the process of confirmation. However, during 2003 only thirteen of President Bush's thirty-two nominees for appeals courts (40.6 percent) and fifty-five of his eighty-two nominees for district courts (67 percent) were confirmed. Democratic senators used the unlimited debate in the Senate to filibuster several nominations, and Republicans were unable to gather the sixty votes they needed to invoke cloture (limit debate). President Bush responded by giving recess appointments to two controversial nominees (see Box 3-3); following his reelection and Republican gains in the Senate, he indicated his intention to resubmit to the Senate several nominations that previously had been stalled there.

The partisan and ideological disputes over the judicial nominations of Presidents Clinton and Bush reflect the polarization in American politics more generally. Also contributing to the conflict have been the tendency of recent presidents to appoint to the federal bench judges who shared their political perspective, the increasing involvement of ideological interest groups, and the willingness of senators to use confirmation politics to court such groups. Thus, it seems likely that the appointment of federal judges will remain a lightning rod for conflict and controversy.

THE SELECTION OF SUPREME COURT JUSTICES

When Justice William Brennan retired in 1990, he had served more than one-third of a century on the Supreme Court. Appointed by President Dwight Eisenhower in 1956, only two years after the Court's historic ruling in *Brown v. Board of Education*,[58] Brennan remained on the bench through the turmoil of the 1960s, the Watergate scandal of the 1970s, and the Reagan Revolution of the 1980s. Altogether he participated in the decision of almost 5,000 cases, and his opinions defined the Court's position on freedom of religion, flag burning, libel, political patronage systems, and the exclusion of illegally seized evidence.[59] For the last two decades of his service, he was the acknowledged leader of the liberal wing of the Court, sometimes in the majority, but in later years in dissent. Justice Harry Blackmun summed up his colleague's career on Brennan's retirement: "By any measure, Justice Brennan must be regarded as one of the great names among those who have served on the Supreme Court of the United States."[60] President Eisenhower's assessment was less laudatory. Asked whether he had made any mistakes during his presidency, Eisenhower reputedly replied, "Yes, two, and they [Justice Brennan and Chief Justice Warren] are both sitting on the Supreme Court."[61]

BOX
3-3
Appointing Judge Pickering

To his detractors, he was a racially insensitive right-wing ideologue whose "record as a trial judge [was] undistinguished and downright disturbing." To his supporters, he was "a man of personal and professional integrity" committed to "obey[ing] existing law rather than usurp[ing] the legislature's place." About the only thing the two sides could agree on was that their opponents had gravely distorted the record of Charles Pickering, who was nominated for a seat on the Court of Appeals for the Fifth Circuit. The tortuous course of the Pickering nomination illustrates the harsh ideological and partisan politics that over the last decade have characterized the selection of federal appeals court judges.

President George W. Bush nominated Judge Pickering in 2001, eleven years after his father had appointed Pickering to the federal district court in Mississippi. When the Pickering nomination came before the Senate Judiciary Committee, various liberal groups—such as the NAACP and People for the American Way—testified against the nomination and mobilized opposition. In 2002, the Judiciary Committee, on which Democrats held a majority, rejected the nomination in a straight party-line vote. In 2003, after the Republicans had regained control of the Senate, President Bush renominated Pickering, and the reconstituted Judiciary Committee recommended confirmation. But on the floor of the Senate, Democratic senators mounted a filibuster against the nomination, and Republicans lacked the votes to end debate and force a vote. With Congress adjourned, President Bush in January 2004, appointed Judge Pickering to the appeals court as a "recess appointment," meaning

Criteria for Selection

Justice Brennan's career, spanning eight presidencies, shows that Supreme Court appointments can influence the course of the nation, for better or worse, long after a president's term has ended (see Table 3-5). Not surprisingly, then, presidents tend to take an active part in the selection of Supreme Court justices. Those selected characteristically have had distinguished public careers—they include a dozen members of Congress, many cabinet officers, and even a former president—and possess outstanding legal credentials. Many of the justices have served as judges at some time before their selection, though this that the appointment would lapse if the Senate failed to confirm Pickering in 2004. To Tom Daschle, the Senate Democratic leader, the recess appointment showed that "the president has no interest in working in a bipartisan manner to appoint moderate judges who will uphold the law." To the White House, on the other hand, the recess appointment simply prevented a small minority in the Senate from using "unprecedented obstructionist tactics" to block a Senate vote. In fact, the Senate did not confirm Judge Pickering in 2004, creating a vacancy to be filled by President Bush in his second term of office.

The partisan and ideological furor over Judge Pickering and several other Bush nominees reflects the increasing polarization of American politics—Republican senators had opposed some of President Bill Clinton's nominees just as vehemently as Democrats opposed Pickering. The conflict also reveals the increasing importance that advocacy groups on both sides of the political spectrum attach to appeals court nominations and their increasing influence in the selection process. The determination of these groups to block nominees with whom they disagree reflects a recognition of the important role played by the lower federal courts. Courts of appeals render the final decision in more than 95 percent of the cases that come before them, and as Senator Diane Feinstein put it: "Many of the issues that we wrestle with as a nation . . . a woman's right to choose, civil rights, the relationship between church and state . . . are essentially decided by the courts." Moreover, recent presidents have looked to members of those courts in selecting Supreme Court justices. Thus, the battle over Judge Pickering promises to be just one episode in a continuing politicization of the selection process for federal judges.

Sources: *New York Times*, 1/17/04; *Washington Post*, 1/17/04; Free Congress Foundation, at www.judicialselection.org; and Sheldon Goldman, "Unpicking Pickering in 2002: Some Thoughts on the Politics of Lower Federal Court Selection and Confirmation," *U.C. Davis Law Review* 36 (February 2003): 695–719.

is not a requirement, and several outstanding justices have had no judicial experience. Beyond these minimal qualifications, presidents have weighed a variety of factors in making their appointments, with the importance of various factors changing over time and from president to president.

Party Affiliation   Presidents have drawn more than 90 percent of all nominees from the ranks of their own party. If a president does cross party lines, he usually anticipates some political advantage from doing so. Thus, when Republican President Eisenhower appointed Justice Brennan, a New Jersey Democrat and a Catholic, he viewed the appointment as a way to appeal to potential

JUSTICES OF THE U.S. SUPREME COURT, 2005

	Year of Birth	Home State	Position before Appointment	Prior Judicial Experience	Party Affiliation	Year Appointed	Appointing President
William Rehnquist*	1924	Arizona	Associate Justice Assistant Attorney General	No	Republican	1986 (CJ) 1972 (AJ)	Reagan
John Stevens	1920	Illinois	U.S. Court of Appeals	Yes	Republican	1975	Ford
Sandra Day O'Connor	1930	Arizona	State appeals court	Yes	Republican	1981	Reagan
Antonin Scalia	1936	New Jersey	U.S. Court of Appeals	Yes	Republican	1986	Reagan
Anthony Kennedy	1936	California	U.S. Court of Appeals	Yes	Republican	1988	Reagan
David Souter	1939	New Hampshire	U.S. Court of Appeals	Yes	Republican	1990	Bush
Clarence Thomas	1948	Georgia	U.S. Court of Appeals	Yes	Republican	1991	Bush
Ruth Bader Ginsburg	1933	New York	U.S. Court of Appeals	Yes	Democrat	1993	Clinton
Stephen Breyer	1938	California	U.S. Court of Appeals	Yes	Democrat	1994	Clinton

*William Rehnquist was appointed as Associate Justice by Richard Nixon and then elevated to Chief Justice by Ronald Reagan.

Sources: Ralph A. Rossum and G. Alan Tarr, *American Constitutional Law*, 5th ed. (New York: St. Martin's Press, 1999), and Henry J. Abraham, *Justices, Presidents, and Senators: A History of U.S. Supreme Court Appointments from Washington to Clinton*, 4th ed. (Lanham, MD: Rowman & Littlefield, 1999).

crossover voters during an election year and portray his administration as non-political and bipartisan.[62] Presidents typically choose only members of the opposition party with whom they feel ideologically compatible. This is exemplified in President Richard Nixon's selection of Justice Lewis Powell, a conservative Democrat from Virginia, for the Supreme Court.

Region   Well into the twentieth century, region played an important part in appointments to the Supreme Court. Initially, having representation from the various sections of the country bolstered the legitimacy of the Court and the national government. From the founding through 1971, except during Reconstruction, there was a Southern seat on the Court and, until the 1930s, a New England seat as well. Today the concern for regional balance has largely disappeared. For example, President Reagan appointed Arizona Judge Sandra Day O'Connor to the Court, even though Justice William Rehnquist was also an Arizonan.

Demographic Characteristics   If region has declined in importance, demographic characteristics have increased. During the early twentieth century, a concern with religious representation led to identifiable Catholic and Jewish seats on the Court. By the late twentieth century, however, race and gender were the major concerns. In 1967, President Lyndon Johnson appointed Justice Thurgood Marshall, the first African American to serve on the Court. When Marshall retired in 1991, President George Bush took into consideration the concern for black representation on the Court when he named Justice Clarence Thomas as Marshall's replacement. In 1980, while campaigning for the presidency, Ronald Reagan pledged to appoint a woman to the Court, and he fulfilled that promise a year later by naming Justice Sandra Day O'Connor. Bill Clinton also made a woman his first appointee to the Court.

Ethnicity is also important. Justice Antonin Scalia, appointed by President Reagan in 1986, is the first Italian American on the Court, and one expects that in the future there will be efforts to ensure representation for Hispanic and Asian Americans.

Legal–Political Compatibility   Presidents want justices on the Supreme Court who share their views on constitutional issues. As President Theodore Roosevelt put it, "I should hold myself guilty of an irreparable harm to the nation if I should put [on the Court] any man who was not absolutely sane and sound on the national policies for which we stand in public life." Usually, presidents are concerned less with a potential justice's overall jurisprudential approach than with his or her position on certain salient legal issues. Thus, President Franklin Roosevelt appointed judges who shared his broad view of the national government's power to regulate the economy and who would uphold the New Deal programs he had championed. President Richard Nixon, concerned about the

Court's expansion of the rights of defendants, sought to select "strict constructionist" justices who would "strengthen the peace forces as against the criminal forces of the land."[63] President Reagan sought proponents of "judicial restraint" who might reverse the Supreme Court's decisions on abortion, voluntary prayer in the schools, and the rights of defendants, whereas President Clinton announced during his initial run for the White House that he would appoint only jurists committed to safeguarding abortion rights.

Obstacles to Presidential Influence

Presidents do not always succeed in influencing the Court's orientation by their appointments. As President Harry Truman ruefully observed, "packing the Supreme Court simply can't be done. . . . I've tried and it won't work."[64] Once appointed, the justice may not behave on the Court as the president expected. For example, after Theodore Roosevelt appointed Oliver Wendell Holmes to the Court, Holmes wrote opinions in several antitrust cases that so enraged Roosevelt that he complained: "I could carve out of a banana a Judge with more backbone than that!"[65] President Richard Nixon must have felt betrayed when Chief Justice Warren Burger ruled against his claim of executive privilege in *United States v. Nixon,* and President Bush was doubtless disappointed when Justice David Souter aligned himself with the liberal justices on the Supreme Court.[66] In addition, presidents often do not anticipate changes over time in the issues confronting the Court and, therefore, do not probe a nominee's views on unforeseen issues. Thus, although President Nixon appointed Justice Harry Blackmun to the Court, expecting that he would take a conservative position on the rights of defendants, Blackmun is best known for his opinion in *Roe v. Wade* (1973), announcing that the Constitution safeguarded a woman's right to choose to have an abortion.[67] Indeed, in the years since that decision, Blackmun frequently aligned himself with the liberal wing of the Court. In sum, once appointed, a justice's perspective may change. Judicial independence allows justices to shed their partisanship and change their views. When this happens, there is nothing the appointing president can do. As legal scholar Alexander Bickel observes, "You shoot an arrow into a far-distant future when you appoint a Justice and not the man himself can tell you what he will think about some of the problems he will face."[68]

Yet one should not overstate the matter. When justices are appointed, they already have established legal views, and only rarely do those views change dramatically once they are on the Court. Moreover, presidents can minimize "mistakes" by canvassing the views of potential nominees before appointment. For example, President Reagan appointed several potential nominees to appellate judgeships to get some indication of their judicial philosophy and abilities. With the exception of Chief Justice Rehnquist, already serving as an associate justice, and Justice O'Connor, all Reagan's Supreme Court nominees had "auditioned" on a court of appeals. Before appointing Justice O'Connor, Reagan thoroughly investigated her constitutional views. He dispatched an aide to Arizona for a day of interviews with her and others knowledgeable about her background and views. She was then questioned in Washington by the Attorney General, by three senior White House staffers, and by the president himself. Only after this painstaking examination did the president appoint her to the Court. The current orientation of the Supreme Court demonstrates the success of President Reagan's efforts to create a conservative Court.

The Senate can also frustrate presidents' efforts to "pack" the Supreme Court by refusing to confirm their nominees although it has not often done so. Only twelve Supreme Court nominees have been rejected, while sixteen other nominations were either withdrawn from consideration or indefinitely postponed because of opposition in the Senate.[69] From 1968 to 1992, however, the Senate refused to confirm five of sixteen nominees. Moreover, even when the nominees were ultimately confirmed, the questioning during Senate committee hearings could be intense, as the battle over the nomination of Clarence Thomas illustrates.

The recent spate of rejections can be attributed in part to problems with particular nominees, ranging from ethical lapses to lack of judicial stature to allegations of extreme constitutional views. However, the Senate's willingness to confirm presidential choices also depends on political considerations. The Senate is more likely to reject a nominee if the Senate and presidency are controlled by different parties or if the president has been politically weakened by scandal, unpopular policies, or a forthcoming presidential election. Indeed, it has confirmed 90 percent of nominees for the Supreme Court during the first three years of presidential terms, but less than 67 percent during the final year of their terms. The Senate also may reject nominees opposed by powerful interest groups. The influence of these groups has increased during the twentieth century as the process of confirmation has become more public.[70] Before 1913, senators were elected by state legislatures, thus limiting their accountability to the general public. And until the 1920s, Senate deliberations on prospective justices nominees were secret. Nominees did not testify, and they were confirmed or rejected without a roll-call vote, so it was impossible to know how individual senators had voted. Now, however, nominees testify before the Senate Judiciary Committee in public hearings, as do groups and individuals supporting or opposing the nominee. Since 1982, when President Reagan appointed Sandra Day O'Connor to the Court, the hearings and final confirmation votes have been televised. This opening up of the process has made it easier for groups to mobilize opinion for or against nominees, as occurred during the Bork confirmation battle, and to influence votes on confirmation by pledging to hold senators electorally accountable. Yet whether groups do mobilize depends on the character and views of the nominee. President Clinton's appointees to the Supreme Court, Ruth Bader Ginsburg and Stephen Breyer, were uncontroversial and overwhelmingly confirmed by the Senate.

BOX
3-4   *French Judges*

In France, as in other civil law systems, judges are *not* selected from the ranks of practicing attorneys. Prospective judges receive an education designed to prepare them for their professional responsibilities and upon graduation immediately commence their judicial careers.

To become a judge, one must first graduate from a university law school. Except for a few minor exceptions, law graduates opting for a judicial career must take the examination for admission to the École Nationale de la Magistrature (National Judicial College) before their twenty-eighth birthday. The exam is highly competitive. In 1988, more than 1,300 applicants took the exam, but only 186 (77 men and 109 women) were admitted. Those admitted to the École Nationale not only receive professional training in law and the responsibilities of a judge in a civil-law system but also serve a probationary period before graduating.

Upon graduation the new judges are initially assigned to one of the criminal or civil courts at the lower end of the judicial hierarchy. Because most French courts, including trial courts, sit as multijudge courts, the new graduate has the advantage of working with more experienced colleagues. From their initial assignments, judges may, over time, be promoted

---

WHAT DO JUDGES DO?

From Advocate to Arbiter

On assuming office, new judges immediately confront daunting responsibilities. Often they feel themselves unprepared and isolated. In civil-law countries, such as France, a judge attends a specialized school and follows a separate career path from lawyers (see Box 3-4). In contrast, in the United States, prospective judges receive no special preparation. They attend law school like other lawyers and then typically pursue a career in either government or private practice. Once selected for the bench, however, they are expected to shed their identities as advocates and partisans and become impartial arbiters. Not surprisingly, many new judges encounter problems.[71]

First, new judges are frequently unfamiliar with much of the law that they must apply. This may seem strange, because judges are chosen from the ranks

to higher and more important posts within the French judicial system. Advancement in the system depends on seniority and the "notations" a judge receives from senior judges and supervisors. The French judiciary is a career service; that is, judges cannot be removed from office except for a gross abuse of their authority.

The closest American analogy to the French system of selection, training, and promotion is the civil service system. Like the civil service, the French system is designed to create a set of professionals pursuing careers in a specialized field and to eliminate political considerations and personal favoritism in the selection phase through competitive examinations. The promotion process, however, may pose a threat to judicial independence because those determining promotions may reward loyalty and conformism and penalize independence. One factor that reduces pressure toward conformity is the collegial character of most French courts. Because of the practice of announcing decisions without indicating who authored an opinion or whether there were any dissents, all judicial decisions are rendered in the name of the court as a whole, and no individual judge must take responsibility for a decision. Nonetheless, judicial independence remains a fundamental issue in civil-law systems.

Sources: Henry W. Ehrmann, *Comparative Legal Cultures* (Englewood Cliffs, NJ: Prentice Hall, 1976); John H. Merryman, *The Civil Law Tradition* (Stanford, CA: Stanford University Press, 1969); John Bell, "Principles and Methods of Judicial Selection in France," *Southern California Law Review* 61 (September 1983): 1757–1794; and Jacqueline Lucienne Lafon, "The Judicial Career in France: Theory and Practice under the French Republic," *Judicature* 75 (August–September, 1991): 97–106.

of attorneys. However, the lawyers elevated to the bench have often had specialized legal practices. They may have focused on criminal law or, more likely, on civil law; they were plaintiffs' lawyers, defense attorneys, or prosecutors; they were patent attorneys, environmental lawyers, or tax specialists. Judges, in contrast, are generalists; they have jurisdiction over a wide range of conflicts, and most judges must accept whatever cases come before them. Trial judges may preside over a murder case one day and a product liability suit the next. To undertake these diverse responsibilities, they must become knowledgeable in areas of law that they may not have studied since law school.

Second, new judges must change their basic orientation. Lawyers are accustomed to acting as advocates, taking a position and arguing it. In contrast, "the essence of the judicial role, active or passive, is impartiality and detachment, both felt and exhibited."[72] Thus, as Justice Charles Russell of the Virginia Supreme Court indicates, "your skills [as an advocate] are so diametrically opposed to those demanded of a judge that you've got to do a frightful gear shift."[73]

Third, before their selection, judges tend to be actively involved in politics—indeed, political involvement is often a prerequisite for selection. Except in systems with partisan elections, however, judges are expected to avoid partisanship not only in their decisions but also in their behavior off the bench. Many states forbid judges from engaging in any sort of political activity, from endorsing candidates or speaking at political meetings to making political contributions. Some judges take this insulation from politics very seriously indeed. Justice John Marshall Harlan even refused to vote during his service on the U.S. Supreme Court. Others seek to reconcile, often unsuccessfully, their political concerns and their judicial role. Justice Abraham Fortas, for example, was sharply criticized for continuing as an adviser to President Lyndon Johnson even after his appointment to the Supreme Court.[74] For many judges, the transition from politically engaged lawyer to what Justice Felix Frankfurter referred to as "judicial monk" is a difficult one.

A more general isolation also accompanies elevation to the bench. Becoming a judge affects one's social life. Lawyers with whom one associated before selection are reluctant to socialize for fear of being seen as currying favor. Beyond that, trial judges find themselves moving from the collegial context of a law firm to presiding alone over a court, forced to make momentous decisions without the opportunity to confer with others. New judges feel this pressure particularly in sentencing. "This is the hardest part," one judge admits. "You see so many pathetic people and you're never sure of what is a right or fair sentence."[75]

How do judges cope with these problems? Many avail themselves of formal judicial training. The Federal Judicial Center conducts seminars for newly appointed judges and continuing education courses for their more senior colleagues. State trial judges may take courses at the National Judicial College, and appellate judges at the Institute for Judicial Administration. In addition, new judges try to emulate successful colleagues: "Judges learn through role models."[76] Finally, they may seek the counsel of veteran judges to ease the transition from advocate to arbiter.

The Work of the Trial Judge

If asked, many people would probably say that trial court judges preside over jury trials. Scholars have discovered, however, that a trial judge's responsibilities are more diverse than conventional wisdom suggests. In a nationwide survey, more than 3,000 judges in courts of general jurisdiction described the tasks they most commonly perform in the course of a day.[77] The results of this survey are summarized in Table 3-6.

The survey reveals that jury trials are the most time-consuming of judicial activities. Those judges who reported conducting jury trials on their most common workday indicated that they spent almost five hours a day on them. However, less than one-half of the judges reported presiding at a jury trial on their

TABLE
3-6   THE WORKDAY OF THE TRIAL JUDGE

Task	Judges Reporting Task on Their Most Common Workday (%)
Courtroom work	
Conducting jury trials	44.3
Conducting nonjury trials	44.5
Nontrial work	52.0
Waiting time	42.4
Negotiations	
Case-related discussions with attorneys	47.5
Socializing with attorneys	38.9
Settlement discussions	32.0
Plea negotiations	18.9
Legal work	
Reading case files	70.1
Keeping up with the law	68.1
Preparing/writing decisions, judgments, orders	56.2
Administrative work	71.2

Source: Adapted with the permission of The Free Press, a Division of Simon & Schuster, from *American Trial Judges: Their Work Style and Performance,* by John Paul Ryan, Allan Ashman, Bruce D. Sales, and Sandra Shane-DuBow. Copyright © 1979 by The American Judicature Society.

most common workday. Likewise, less than one-half reported presiding over nonjury trials. But on a typical day, more than one-half reported being involved in nontrial courtroom work. This work may involve ruling on pretrial motions, such as whether evidence was illegally seized and should be excluded from trial. Judges may also preside over the resolution of cases without trial, through guilty pleas in criminal cases or default judgments in civil cases. Finally, judges may sentence defendants convicted in criminal cases.

Much of the trial judge's work, however, takes place outside the courtroom. As Chapters 5 and 6 will show, most cases are resolved by some sort of negotiated settlement, and judges promote settlement either by urging negotiations between the parties in a case or by actively participating in them. Although some judges believe it inappropriate to get involved in plea negotiations in criminal cases, many others discuss with prosecutors and defense counsel the evidence in a case, the charges to which a defendant will plead guilty, and the sentence he or she will receive. Judges also meet with opposing counsel in civil cases to encourage the two sides to settle before trial. Effective participation in case negotiations depends not on judges' legal expertise but on other interpersonal skills. It thus underscores the range of talents a successful judge needs.

Judges foster settlements in civil cases and negotiated pleas in criminal cases because settlements expedite the flow of cases. It is less time-consuming to settle a case than to try it. Many of a judge's administrative responsibilities are also associated with managing the flow of cases. Judges must schedule the cases on their dockets, keep up-to-date with the cases assigned to them, and keep track of case files and materials. In addition, a judge may be responsible for hiring law clerks and other court personnel. In trial courts with several judges, usually a senior judge is designated as chief judge and assumes full-time administrative responsibilities for the court.

Finally, trial judges must keep abreast of the legal work associated with their position. Unlike appellate judges, trial judges do not issue written opinions in most cases they decide, so their writing responsibilities are not onerous. However, whether judges are to be involved in negotiations or in trying a case, they must read the files in all the cases assigned to them. In addition, they must inform themselves about pertinent legal developments, such as appellate court decisions that affect their work. Taken altogether, the responsibilities of the trial judge are daunting indeed.

The Work of the Appellate Judge

Appellate courts are multijudge courts whose job is to review the legal correctness of lower court rulings in cases that are appealed to them. The appellate court announces its rulings in judicial opinions that explain the legal bases of its decisions. Because the responsibilities of trial and appellate courts differ, so too do the jobs of trial and appellate judges. Frank Coffin, formerly Chief Judge of the U.S. Court of Appeals for the First Circuit, has identified the various steps in his cycle of work as an appellate judge (see Table 3-7), and his experience is probably quite typical.

Several differences between the work of an appellate judge and that of a trial judge are immediately apparent. First, appellate judges conduct their work in relative isolation from the outside world. Trial judges continually come into contact with members of the general public, who serve as parties, witnesses, or jurors. They also regularly interact with attorneys within the courtroom and in conferences and negotiations outside it. They get to know the "regulars" in their court quite well and tend to socialize with them during the course of the workday. In contrast, appellate judges have no direct contact with the parties or witnesses in the cases they hear, and their communications with lawyers are formal, occurring solely through the submission of legal briefs and through oral argument in court. Because the appellate court draws cases from a much larger geographic area than the trial court, appellate judges are unlikely to develop close ties with the attorneys who argue before them.

TABLE 3-7	THE WORK CYCLE OF THE APPELLATE JUDGE

Although the list may differ in some details from judge to judge, this list identifies the main stages in appellate decision making.

1. I read (or scan) briefs alone, usually at night.

2. I talk over each case with my clerks, one of whom has given particular attention to it. I make notes of our colloquy.

3. I listen to oral argument in court and ask a few questions.

4. I confer with my fellow judges late in the day after the argument.

5. I research, discuss, and draft an opinion in chambers or discuss, edit, and redraft the first draft of a clerk.

6. I circulate my draft to my colleagues and respond to their suggestions; when they circulate their drafts, I propose changes to which they respond.

Source: Reprinted from *On Appeal: Courts, Lawyering and Judging,* by Frank M. Coffin, by permission of W.W. Norton & Company, Inc. Copyright © 1994 by W.W. Norton & Company, Inc.

Second, appellate judges' isolation from the outside world is mitigated by their interaction with other appellate judges and court personnel. Whereas trial courts operate within severe time constraints in processing cases, the pace of work on appellate courts promotes deliberation. Often the chambers of an appellate judge works like an autonomous little "law firm," conducting legal research, discussing cases, and preparing opinions. Judges also discuss cases with colleagues after they are argued, and participate in the continuing interchange necessary to produce decisions that reflect truly collaborative deliberations. The trial judge may be the ruler of his or her courtroom, but the appellate judge acts as part of a team.

Third, in contrast with a trial court, an appellate court issues written opinions in most of the cases it decides. As a result, a large proportion of an appellate judge's time is spent either researching and writing judicial opinions or responding to the draft opinions of colleagues. Typically, the response to a colleague's opinion itself takes the form of a memorandum selectively accepting some aspects of the opinion and constructively critiquing other aspects. When a judge perceives problems with an argument in a colleague's opinion, collegiality demands that the judge should offer an alternative line of argument or a different formulation. Such a detailed critique usually cannot be conveyed orally, and thus, much of the communication among the judges on a case is written. In many instances this interchange enables the court to devise an opinion that all the judges can join. Failing that, the exchange of views may narrow the differences among the judges. Because so much hinges on the opinions issuing from the court, appellate judges need to be good writers.

Finally, in reviewing the rulings of trial courts, appellate judges continually confront complex and difficult legal questions. Resolving these questions tests the judges' knowledge of the law and their analytic capacity. Because they must decide whether the trial court's actions are consistent with authoritative legal precedent, they must continually update themselves on recent legal developments. Because the pertinent precedents often offer guidance without altogether resolving an issue, appellate judges must analyze the issue in the light of logic, precedent, policy, concern for the parties, and a host of other factors, guided by professional norms and the traditions of the law. They then must provide a persuasive justification for the conclusions they reach. These responsibilities can challenge even the most talented and conscientious appellate judge.

CONCLUSIONS

This chapter revealed important differences in the responsibilities of trial court judges and appellate judges. Yet what distinguishes these judges is less important than what unites them: All these judges play an important role in governance. Their decisions help define the law that governs state and nation. Moreover, their rulings reflect—at least to some extent—the legal perspectives of the judges who render them. Not surprisingly, then, the criteria for selecting judges and the processes by which they are selected have aroused controversy throughout U.S. history.

Some have argued that the independence of judges should be safeguarded so that judges can render decisions unaffected by partisan concerns or external pressures. Advocates of this position have championed modes of selection that minimize the influence of political parties, such as merit selection and nonpartisan elections. They also have promoted extended terms of office for judges—or tenure, revocable only for wrongdoing—and have opposed competitive elections for the retention of judges. To some extent their efforts have succeeded, as indicated by the rapid spread of merit selection in the states during the last few decades.

However, other commentators on judicial selection have argued that judges—like other officials whose decisions have political consequences—should be accountable to, perhaps even responsive to, the populace. Proponents of this position have usually promoted partisan judicial elections or the appointment of judges by the executive. Despite the spread of merit selection, there seems to be a resurgence of efforts to hold judges accountable for their views and their judicial decisions. The defeat of Chief Justice Rose Bird and her fellow justices, whose rulings in criminal justice cases angered many Californians, is an example; others are the Senate's rejection of Judge Robert Bork and its close scrutiny of the charges against Justice Clarence Thomas.

Finally, still other commentators have insisted that the state and federal bench should reflect the demographic diversity of the nation. Supporters of a demographically representative judiciary have persuaded the courts that the Voting Rights Act applies to judicial elections and have had some success challenging selection systems that seem to disadvantage minority-group candidates. Even Presidents Reagan and Bush, who announced their opposition to affirmative action, considered demographics in their appointments, for instance, of Sandra Day O'Connor and Clarence Thomas, and President Clinton placed a high priority on ensuring a demographically representative judiciary.

Even as one recognizes the importance of who judges, one must still recognize that judges alone do not determine the political role that courts play. Judges can address the issues that are brought before them, and thus, they depend on lawyers and their clients for their agenda. It is to these equally important actors in the judicial process that the discussion now turns.

NOTES

1. This discussion of the Bork nomination relies on Robert H. Bork, *The Tempting of America* (New York: Free Press, 1990); Ethan Bronner, *Battle for Justice* (New York: Norton, 1989); and Patrick B. McGuigan and Dawn M. Weyrich, *Ninth Justice: The Fight for Bork* (Washington, DC: Free Congress Research and Education Foundation, 1990).

2. Quoted in Bronner, *Battle for Justice,* p. 98.

3. For an example of the political pressures visited on judges and their reactions, see Jack Peltason, *Fifty-Eight Lonely Men* (New York: Harcourt, Brace and World, 1961).

4. Quoted in David O'Brien, *Judicial Roulette* (New York: Priority Press, 1988), p. 16. Altogether, only seven federal judges have been impeached and convicted. See Eleanore Bushnell, *Crimes, Follies, and Misfortunes* (Urbana: University of Illinois Press, 1992), and Mary L. Volcansek, *Judicial Impeachment: None Called for Justice* (Urbana: University of Illinois Press, 1993).

5. See Henry Abraham, *Justices, Presidents, and Senators: A History of the U.S. Supreme Court Appointments from Washington to Clinton* (Lanham, MD: Rowman & Littlefield, 1999), pp. 46–47; and Barbara A. Perry, *A "Representative" Supreme Court?* (Westport, CT: Greenwood Press, 1991).

6. Henry R. Glick and Craig F. Emmert, "Selection Systems and Judicial Characteristics: The Recruitment of State Supreme Court Justices," *Judicature* 70 (December–January 1987): 232.

7. For extensive up-to-date information on judicial selection in the various states, see the Web site of the American Judicature Society: www.ajs.org .

8. Philip L. Dubois, *From Ballot to Bench* (Austin: University of Texas Press, 1980), pp. 1–3, and Kermit L. Hall, "The Judiciary on Trial: Constitutional Reform and the Rise of an Elected Judiciary, 1846–1860," *Historian* 44 (May 1983): 337–54.

9. Melinda Gann Hall, "State Supreme Courts in American Democracy: Probing the Myths of Judicial Reform," *American Political Science Review* 95 (June 2001): 317–319.

10. Lawrence Baum, *American Courts,* 2d ed. (Boston: Houghton Mifflin, 1990), p. 102.

11. Hall, "State Supreme Courts," p. 319. For an analysis of lower court elections within a single state, see L. Douglas Kiel, Carol Funk, and Anthony Champagne, "Two-Party Competition and Trial Court Elections in Texas," *Judicature* 77 (May–June 1994): 290–293.

12. *Republican Party of Minnesota v. White,* 536 U.S. 765 (2002).

13. R. Neal McKnight, Roger Schaefer, and Charles A. Johnson, "Choosing Judges: Do the Voters Know What They're Doing?" *Judicature* 62 (August 1978): 94–99.

14. Dubois, *From Ballot to Bench,* chap. 3.

15. Ibid., chap. 2, and Philip Dubois, "Voter Turnout in State Judicial Elections: An Analysis of the Tail of the Electoral Kite," *Journal of Politics* 41 (August 1979): 865–888.

16. Expenditures in Alabama and Pennsylvania judicial elections are reported in Mark Hansen, "A Run for the Bench," *American Bar Association Journal* (October 1998): 69–70. On contributions seeking to influence the outcome of the Pennzoil lawsuit, see James Alfini and Terrence Brooks, "Ethical Constraints on Judicial Election Campaigns: A Review and Critique of Canon 7," *Kentucky Law Journal* 77 (1988–89): 671. On recent spending increases in Alabama, Michigan, and other states, see Roy A. Schotland, "Financing Judicial Elections," in David B. Magleby, ed., *Financing the 2000 Election* (Washington, D.C.: Brookings Institution Press, 2002).

17. This account relies on G. Alan Tarr and Mary Cornelia Aldis Porter, *State Supreme Courts in Nation and State* (New Haven, CT: Yale University Press, 1988), chap. 5.

18. For an overview of these studies, see Daniel R. Pinello, "Linking Party to Ideology in American Courts: A Meta-Analysis," *Justice System Journal* 20 (1999): 219–254.

19. Kathleen L. Barber, "Partisan Values in the Lower Courts: Reapportionment in Ohio and Michigan," *Case Western Reserve Law Review* 20 (February 1969): 403.

20. Susan B. Carbon, "Judicial Retention Elections: Are They Serving Their Intended Purpose?" *Judicature* 64 (November 1980): 220.

21. William K. Hall and Larry T. Aspin, "What Twenty Years of Judicial Retention Elections Have Told Us," *Judicature* 70 (April–May 1987): 347.

22. Hall, "State Supreme Courts," p. 318, table 2, and p. 319, table 4.

23. Kenyon N. Griffin and Michael J. Horan, "Patterns of Judicial Behavior in Judicial Retention Elections for Supreme Court Justices in Wyoming," *Judicature* 67 (August 1983): 72.

24. Carbon, "Retention Elections," p. 226.

25. Stephen B. Bright, "Political Attacks on the Judiciary," *Judicature* 80 (January–February 1997): 165–173.

26. See Barry Latzer, "California's Constitutional Counterrevolution," *Constitutional Politics in the States,* ed. G. Alan Tarr (Westport, CT: Greenwood Press, 1996), pp. 155–158, and Stephen B. Bright and Patrick J. Keenan, "Judges and the Politics of Death: Deciding between the Bill of Rights and the Next Election in Capital Cases," *Boston University Law Review* 75 (May 1995): 759–835.

27. Larry T. Aspin and William K. Hall, "Retention Elections and Judicial Behavior," *Judicature* 77 (May–June 1994): 312, table 4.

28. The classic account of the politics of merit selection is Richard A. Watson and Rondal G. Downing, *The Politics of the Bench and the Bar: Judicial Selection under the Missouri Non-Partisan Court Plan* (New York: John Wiley & Sons, 1969).

29. Quoted in Martin A. Levin, *Urban Politics and the Criminal Courts* (Chicago: University of Chicago Press, 1977), p. 13.

30. Hall and Aspin, "What Twenty Years of Judicial Retention Elections Have Told Us," pp. 344–345.

31. Ibid., p. 332.

32. Quoted in Watson and Downing, *Politics of Bench and Bar,* p. 186.

33. Baum, *American Courts,* p. 110.

34. Atkins and Glick, "Formal Judicial Recruitment and State Supreme Court Decisions," and Dubois, *From Ballot to Bench,* chap. 5–7.

35. Daniel R. Pinello, *The Impact of Judicial-Selection Method on State Supreme Court Policy: Innovation, Reaction, and Atrophy* (Westport, CT: Greenwood Press, 1995).

36. Richard Neeley, *Why Courts Don't Work* (New York: McGraw-Hill, 1983), pp. 41–42.

37. Henry R. Glick and Craig F. Emmert, "Selection Systems and Judicial Characteristics: The Recruitment of State Supreme Court Judges," *Judicature* 70 (December–January 1987): 233, table 2; Craig F. Emmert and Henry R. Glick, "The Selection of State Supreme Court Justices," *American Politics Quarterly* 16 (October 1988): 445–465; John B. Wefing, "State Supreme Court Justices—Who Are They?" *New England Law Review* 32 (fall 1997): 47–100; and Chris W. Bonneau, "The Composition of State Supreme Courts 2000," *Judicature* 85 (July–August 2001): 26–31.

38. Wefing, "State Supreme Court Justices," pp. 55–62; and Bonneau, "Composition of State Supreme Courts," p. 28.

39. Bonneau, "Composition of State Supreme Courts," p. 28.

40. Alexander Hamilton, James Madison, and John Jay, *The Federalist Papers,* edited by Clinton Rossiter (New York: New American Library, 1961), p. 456.

41. See Sheldon Goldman, "Unpicking Pickering in 2002: Some Thoughts on the Politics of Lower Federal Court Selection and Confirmation," *U.C. Davis Law Review* 36 (February 2003): pp.695–719; Nancy Sherer, "The Judicial Confirmation Process: Mobilizing Elites, Mobilizing Masses," *Judicature* 86 (March–April 2003): 240–250; and Lisa Holmes and Elisha Savchak, "Judicial Appointment Politics in the 107th Congress," *Judicature* 86 (March–April 2003): 232–239.

42. The effects of partisan politics on the periodic expansion of the federal judiciary are analyzed in Deborah J. Barrow, Gary Zuk, and Gerard S. Gryski, *The Federal Judiciary and Institutional Change* (Ann Arbor: University of Michigan Press, 1996).

43. Quoted in Neeley, *Why Courts Don't Work,* p. 37.

44. Quoted in O'Brien, *Judicial Roulette,* p. 33.

45. These data are drawn from Sheldon Goldman, *Picking Federal Judges: Lower Court Selection from Roosevelt through Reagan* (New Haven, CT: Yale University Press, 1997), pp. 349–350, table 9.1; and from Goldman et al., "Clinton's Judges," p.17, table 3.

46. Joseph Samuel Perry, "How I Got to Be a Federal Judge," in *Courts, Judges, and Politics,* ed. Walter F. Murphy and C. Herman Pritchett, 2d ed. (New York: Random House, 1974), p. 169.

47. See Peltason, *Fifty-Eight Lonely Men.*

48. Quoted in J. Woodford Howard Jr., *Courts of Appeals in the Federal Judicial System* (Princeton, NJ: Princeton University Press, 1981), p. 93.

49. Quoted in ibid., p. 101.

50. Quoted in O'Brien, *Judicial Roulette,* p. 58.

51. Ibid., p. 61.

52. C. K. Rowland, "The Federal District Courts," in *The American Courts: A Critical Assessment,* ed. John B. Gates and Charles A. Johnson (Washington, DC: CQ Press, 1991), p. 70, and Ronald Stidham and Ronald Carp, "Judges, Presidents, and Policy Choices: Exploring the Linkage," *Social Science Quarterly* 68 (1987): 395–407.

53. Steve Alumbaugh and C. K. Rowland, "The Links between Platform-Based Appointment Criteria and Trial Judges' Abortion Judgments," *Judicature* 74 (October–November 1990): 153–162.

54. C. K. Rowland and Robert A. Carp, *Politics and Judgment in Federal District Courts* (Lawrence: University Press of Kansas, 1996), p. 48, table 2-9.

55. Quoted in Sheldon Goldman and Elliott Slotnick, "Clinton's First Term Judiciary: Many Bridges to Cross," *Judicature* 82 (May–June 1997): 256.

56. Goldman et al., "Clinton's Judges," p. 4. More generally, see Roger E. Hartley and Lisa M. Holmes, "Increasing Senate Scrutiny of Lower Federal Court Nominees," *Judicature* 80 (May–June 1997): 274–278.

57. Quoted in Sheldon Goldman, Elliot Slotnick, Gerard Gryski, Gary Zuk, and Sara Schiavoni, "W. Bush Remaking the Judiciary: Like Father Like Son?" *Judicature* 86 (May–June 2003): 284. The analysis of the politics of judicial selection under President Bush relies heavily on this article.

58. *Brown v. Board of Education,* 347 U.S. 483 (1954).

59. On freedom of religion, see *Sherbert v. Verner,* 374 U.S. 398 (1963), and *Edwards v. Aguillard,* 482 U.S. 578 (1987); on flag burning, see *Texas v. Johnson,* 491 U.S. 397 (1989); on libel, see *New York Times v. Sullivan,* 376 U.S. 254 (1964); on political patronage, see *Rutan v. Republican Party of Illinois,* 497 U.S. 62 (1990); and on exclusion of illegally seized evidence, see *Mapp v. Ohio,* 367 U.S. 643 (1961).

60. Harry A. Blackmun, "A Tribute to Mr. Justice Brennan," *Harvard Civil Rights Civil Liberties Law Review* 26 (winter 1991): 1.

61. Quoted in Abraham, *Justices, Presidents, and Senators,* p. 200.

62. Abraham, *Justices, Presidents, and Senators,* pp. 199–200.

63. The Roosevelt quotation is from Rehnquist, *The Supreme Court,* pp. 216–217. The Nixon quotation is from Donald Grier Stephenson Jr., *Campaigns and the Court: The U.S. Supreme Court in Presidential Elections* (New York: Columbia University Press, 1999), p. 181.

64. Quoted in Abraham, *Justices, Presidents, and Senators,* p. 51.

65. Quoted in ibid., p. 51.

66. *United States v. Nixon,* 418 U.S. 683 (1974). On President Bush's expectations for Souter, see Tinsely E. Yarbrough, *The Rehnquist Court and the Constitution* (New York: Oxford University Press, 2000), pp. 19–22.

67. *Roe v. Wade,* 410 U.S. 113 (1973).

68. Quoted in Abraham, *Justices, Presidents, and Senators,* pp. 51–52.

69. For a listing of nominees and Senate action on them, see Joan Biskupic and Elder Witt, *The Supreme Court at Work,* 2d ed. (Washington, DC: CQ Press, 1997), pp. 316–319.

70. For discussion of these developments, see John Anthony Maltese, *The Selling of Supreme Court Nominees* (Baltimore: Johns Hopkins University Press, 1995), and Mark Silverstein, *Judicious Choices: The New Politics of Supreme Court Confirmations* (New York: Norton, 1994).

71. The analysis in this section relies on "On Becoming a Judge: Socialization to the Judicial Role," *Judicature* 69 (October–November 1985): 139–146, and Robert Carp and Russell Wheeler, "Sink or Swim: The Socialization of a Federal District Judge," *Journal of Public Law* 21 (1972): 359–394.

72. "On Becoming a Judge," p. 140.

73. Quoted in ibid., p. 141.

74. For discussion of Fortas's activities and the criticism they engendered, see Bruce A. Murphy, *Fortas: The Rise and Ruin of a Supreme Court Justice* (New York: William Morrow, 1988), and Laura Kalman, *Abe Fortas: A Biography* (New Haven: Yale University Press, 1990).

75. Quoted in Carp and Wheeler, "Socialization of a Federal District Judge," p. 373; cf. Donald Dale Jackson, *Judges* (New York: Atheneum, 1974), chap. 10.

76. Quoted in "On Becoming a Judge," p. 141.

77. John Paul Ryan, Allan Ashman, Bruce D. Sales, and Sandra Shane-Dubow, *American Trial Judges* (New York: Free Press, 1980), pp. 150–151.

LAWYERS

This is a tale of two lawyers who pursued very different legal careers before serving together on the United States Supreme Court.[1] Lewis Powell was born in 1907 to a wealthy, "old line" family in southern Virginia (the original Powell landed at Jamestown in 1607). As an undergraduate, Powell excelled at Washington and Lee College, graduating first in his class. Two years later he received his law degree from the same school. After a year at Harvard Law School, where he received a master's degree in 1932, Powell joined one of the most prestigious law firms in Richmond, Virginia. He rose to the rank of senior partner in the firm, which had more than 100 lawyers by the time he was appointed to the Court. In his thirty-five years of private practice, he represented a long roster of important corporate clients, such as the Baltimore and Ohio Railroad, the Prudential Insurance Company, and the Virginia Electric and Power Company. He also served on the board of directors for eleven major companies.

Powell's national stature led to his election as president of the American Bar Association (ABA) in 1964 and as president of the American College of Trial Lawyers in 1968. Like many lawyers, he was also involved in community affairs. As president of the Richmond School Board, Powell guided the desegregation of the city's schools in the 1950s. He also served as president of the state board of education in the late 1960s. In 1971, President Richard Nixon appointed him to the Supreme Court, and, after the ABA and the Virginia chapter of the National Association for the Advancement of Colored People (NAACP) enthusiastically endorsed him, the Senate confirmed him by an 89–1 vote.

Thurgood Marshall, probably the most important American lawyer of the twentieth century, came from considerably less prosperous circumstances. The great-grandson of a slave, Marshall was born in 1908, a year later than Powell, in Baltimore, Maryland. His parents—a club steward and an elementary school teacher—stressed education. To help pay his college expenses, his mother sold her engagement ring. Marshall repaid this confidence by excelling in his studies at Lincoln University and then at Howard University Law School, where he graduated first in his class. Following graduation, Marshall enlisted in the efforts of the NAACP to combat racial discrimination through litigation. For more than twenty years as head of the NAACP Legal Defense Fund, he instituted or managed literally hundreds of cases challenging discriminatory laws dealing with voting, housing, education, and public accommodations. Several times he successfully pursued these challenges to the Supreme Court. His most important victory came with *Brown v. Board of Education* in 1954 when he persuaded the Supreme Court to invalidate racial discrimination in public education.

Marshall's formidable skills as an advocate were not limited to his service with the NAACP. Four years after his elevation to the United States Court of Appeals by President John Kennedy, President Lyndon Johnson appointed him solicitor general, the government's chief advocate before the Supreme Court. As the nation's first African American solicitor general, he won several important civil rights victories, including a Supreme Court ruling upholding the constitutionality of the 1965 Voting Rights Act. By the time President Johnson appointed him to the Supreme Court in 1967, Marshall had argued thirty-two cases before that Court, winning twenty-nine of them.

The careers of Thurgood Marshall and Lewis Powell illustrate three important points about lawyers and the legal profession.

1. Diverse legal practices.   Before their appointment to the Supreme Court, Marshall and Powell pursued altogether different legal practices. They differed in the types of clients they served, the amount of time they spent in court, the issues they addressed, and the ends they sought to achieve. Their careers demonstrate that lawyers may employ their talents in a wide variety of contexts for quite different clients and ends. They may become litigators, like Marshall, pursuing their clients' interests in the clash of courtroom conflict. Many lawyers—including prosecutors, criminal defense attorneys, and lawyers in personal injury cases—are regularly involved in trial or appellate litigation. Alternatively, like Powell, they may serve primarily as legal counselors, negotiating contracts or other legal agreements or seeking by their advice to prevent legal disputes from arising. In fact, most lawyers spend little or no time in court.

One could easily multiply examples of the sorts of career a lawyer might pursue: high-powered lawyer and lobbyist, solo practitioner serving the legal needs of average citizens, in-house counsel to a corporation, investigator for a government agency, and so on. This diversity of career choice underscores the myriad uses to which legal skills may be put and points to activities in our society that at times demand legal expertise. It also shows that lawyers tend to specialize in the sort of law they practice and clients they represent.

2. The ends of lawyering.   In his legal practice, Lewis Powell—like most lawyers—served as the "delegate" of his clients; that is, he sought to advance their aims and interests, as they defined them, within the confines of the law. In contrast, Thurgood Marshall served more as the "trustee" for his clients. He sought to advance the interests of his African American clients by promoting political goals that those clients—and other African Americans—could be assumed to share. Thus, Marshall's choice of cases and the way he framed legal issues were determined by how those choices would serve long-term political goals.[2]

Each of these relationships between lawyer and client poses dilemmas. "Delegate" attorneys may face a conflict between the interests of their clients and the demands of justice or the good of society. This conflict, though not confined to criminal law, is clearest perhaps when an attorney defends a guilty client in a criminal case. "Trustee" attorneys, however, may confront situations in which the pursuit of their political goals seems to conflict with the immediate interests of their clients. In such circumstances they must determine how to advance the interests of a particular client without compromising their own goals.

3. *The law as a public profession.*   Law is considered a "public profession" because the practice of law affects the public life of the nation. This is true not only when lawyers serve as judges, as did Marshall and Powell, but also when lawyers pursue careers in politics or in public service. But even without holding public office, lawyers affect law and public policy. They may, like Marshall, deliberately design their legal practices to advance political ends. Or, they may influence public affairs less directly, as did Powell, through their involvement in national organizations such as the American Bar Association or through their representation of large economic enterprises. Whatever the avenue, lawyers affect the public life of the nation through their expertise and the use to which they put it.

Although Americans recognize the political importance of the legal profession, they remain ambivalent about lawyers, their skills, and their power. In a 2003 Gallup Poll only 16 percent of Americans gave lawyers high marks for honesty and ethical standards.[3] A 1997 movie, *Devil's Advocate,* even portrayed Satan as a lawyer. Public ambivalence about lawyers is captured in the quotations collected in Box 4-1. Let us look more closely at the causes and consequences of American attitudes toward lawyers and the legal profession.

THE TROUBLE WITH LAWYERS

From Clarence Darrow to Thurgood Marshall, lawyers have been celebrated for seeking justice for their clients and for promoting just but unpopular causes. Yet the specialized knowledge that enables lawyers to crusade for justice may be put to other uses as well. Lawyers may use their legal expertise to advance their own interests. Critics often accuse lawyers of dishonesty or of generating business by creating disputes where none previously existed.

Perspectives on Lawyers

"Woe unto you, lawyers! for ye lade men with burdens grievous to be borne, and ye yourselves touch not the burdens with one of your fingers." (Luke 11:46)

"Underneath, most lawyers are boy scouts." (Geoffrey Hazard, Yale Law School professor)

"Lawyer: One skilled in circumvention of the law." (Ambrose Bierce, American writer and humorist)

"The zealous defense attorney is the last bastion of liberty, the final barrier between an overreaching government and its citizens." (Alan Dershowitz, defense attorney)

"Lawyers are plants that will grow in any soil that is cultivated by the hands of others; and when once they have taken root they will extinguish every other vegetable that grows around them. . . . They are here what the clergy were in past centuries. . . . A reformation equally useful is now wanted." (J. Hector St. John de Crèvecoeur, eighteenth-century writer)

"The first thing we do, let's kill all the lawyers." (William Shakespeare)

Sources: The King James Bible; Geoffrey Hazard, "Reflections on Four Studies of the Legal Profession," *Law and Society* 48 (1965), quoted in David Mellinkoff, *The Conscience of a Lawyer* (St. Paul, MN: West Publishing, 1973), p. 9; Ambrose Bierce, *The Devil's Dictionary* (Cleveland: World Publishing, 1911), p. 187; Alan Dershowitz, *The Best Defense* (New York: Random House, 1982), p. 415; J. Hector St. John de Crèvecoeur, *Letters from an American Farmer* (1782), quoted in Lawrence Friedman, *History of American Law*, 2d ed. (New York: Simon & Schuster, 1985), p. 304; and William Shakespeare, *Henry VI, Part 2*, act 4, scene 2, line 74.

Major breaches of professional ethics can presumably be handled through the disciplinary procedures of the bar or disbarment by a court. More serious is the complaint that lawyers are "hired guns" who have no compunction about shifting allegiances from one client to the next or about representing reprehensible people with immoral purposes. Illustrative of this concern was the public outcry when Abraham Sofaer, who served as legal adviser to the U.S. Department of State when the U.S. government demanded economic sanctions against Libya in 1986, agreed seven years later to represent Libya's government in litigation arising from its involvement in the destruction of Pan Am flight 103 over Lockerbie, Scotland.[4]

A further concern is the potentially distorting effect of wealth on the legal process. Legal expertise is a form of power, and the wealthy can afford more and better legal representation than can the average citizen. Some lawyers' apparent lack of concern about justice is an even more fundamental source of public distrust. Even when they believe the defendant committed the crime, criminal lawyers seek the acquittal of defendants accused of violent crimes. In personal injury suits, attorneys try to help their clients reduce or escape altogether legal liability for the injuries they caused. If the actions of clients are immoral, some argue, lawyers should not promote or defend them because doing so compounds the immorality.

It should be obvious that such criticism is at least somewhat inconsistent with the praise of fearless defense attorneys. Are only the innocent or the popular entitled to an effective legal defense? What underlies this criticism of the legal profession is a concern about how effective the American adversary system is in achieving justice. For, within this adversary system, lawyers who vigorously defend reprehensible clients are acting properly. As the American Bar Association has emphasized, "the duty of a lawyer to his client and to the legal system are the same: to represent his client zealously within the bounds of the law." Or as a practicing lawyer pungently put it: "Litigation is war. The lawyer is a gladiator and the object is to wipe out the other side."[5] (For the quite different responsibilities of a lawyer in an inquisitorial system, see Box 4-2.)

Obviously, the partisan advocacy of an attorney in an adversarial system does not by itself guarantee just outcomes. However, the attorney presenting his client's case is only one element in the process. Another lawyer will present evidence and arguments for the opposing side in the case, a judge will serve as umpire of the dispute, and a judge or jury will reach a decision by weighing the arguments and evidence presented. The assumption is that a partisan presentation by each side will ensure that all relevant facts and legal arguments are brought forward and evaluated, thereby promoting a well-informed decision. Most American lawyers believe strongly in the adversary system.

Does the adversary system guarantee justice? Obviously not; there are undoubtedly instances in which the guilty go free or the innocent are convicted, although in at least some instances, this results from the failure of attorneys to meet their responsibility of vigorous advocacy rather than from the adversary system itself. The real question is whether the adversary system works better than other legal systems. The answer to this question is unclear. Neither those nations that employ the adversarial system nor those that use the inquisitorial system seem inclined to change, as they presumably would if the alternative system were demonstrably superior. Unless the United States abandons the adversary system—and there is no real prospect that it will—lawyers will continue (quite properly) to act as advocates both for morally upright and morally dubious clients and enterprises.

Lawyers and Trials under an Inquisitorial System

To those familiar with the aggressive trial advocacy of American attorneys, a trial in an inquisitorial system will seem quite odd. In an adversarial system the opposing lawyers formulate the issues and control the development of the trial by calling their own witnesses, examining them, and vigorously cross-examining the witnesses called by the other side. The judge's role is largely to act as umpire in the battle between the opposing sides.

In contrast, in an inquisitorial system, the role of the judge is expanded and that of the lawyers reduced. The presiding judge at trial is actively involved in the search for justice. Although the lawyers for each side may nominate witnesses, the judge determines whether they will testify and whether additional witnesses, including expert witnesses, will also be questioned. The witnesses themselves are questioned by the presiding judge, not by the attorneys, although an attorney may pose additional questions after the judge has concluded his or her questioning. (In practice attorneys rarely ask further questions because too many questions might imply that the presiding judge had not done a good job, hardly a wise thing to suggest.) The lawyers cannot even prepare and rehearse their witnesses before they appear, as is regularly done in the United States. Such preparation of witnesses is viewed as inconsistent with the search for justice. In Germany, for example, the rules of legal ethics expressly forbid attorneys from coaching witnesses and even discourage them from contacting witnesses before the trial.

This is not to say that lawyers play no role in an inquisitorial system. They submit written pleadings on behalf of their clients and may, in civil

THE LEGAL PROFESSION

Becoming a Lawyer

Today in the United States, the process for becoming a lawyer is quite straight-forward. First, a student must earn an undergraduate degree. During their senior year, or in the summer immediately preceding it, prospective law students take the Law School Admission Test (LSAT), which is designed to measure their cases, prepare amended pleadings as the case progresses. They also make closing arguments at trial, although the effectiveness of rhetorical flourishes is presumably limited because the arguments are addressed to a panel of judges rather than a jury. Such flourishes are unlikely anyway because they are inconsistent with the responsibility of the lawyer under an inquisitorial system. In an adversarial system the duty of attorneys during litigation is, according to the American Bar Association, to "represent their clients zealously within the confines of the law." In an inquisitorial system, in contrast, the lawyer is—according to the German code of legal ethics—an "independent organ in the administration of justice." Thus, the American attorney's concern is for his or her client; the German attorney's, for justice.

American lawyers recognize that a wholehearted commitment to their clients is necessary to prevail at trial and that success at trial leads to greater status and (presumably) higher fees. Inquisitorial systems, however, have largely eliminated any financial inducement to vigorous advocacy. In Germany, for example, the legal fees for various types of cases are established by law. Whether one wins or loses, one receives the same fee, no matter how many hours have been devoted to case preparation. Thus, inquisitorial systems not only discourage excessive zeal in advocacy but also remove the material incentives to engage in it.

Does all this mean that an inquisitorial, judge-centered system is superior to an adversarial, lawyer-centered one? On this question there is no consensus. The inquisitorial system places considerable faith in the wisdom and fairness of the presiding judge. Americans are less willing to rely on the good faith and good judgment of a single individual. It may be that different legal systems work well for different societies.

Sources: John Langbein, "The German Advantage in Civil Procedure," *University of Chicago Law Review* 52 (1985): 823–866; David Luban, *Lawyers and Justice* (Princeton, NJ: Princeton University Press, 1988); and John Merryman, *The Civil Law Tradition* (Stanford, CA: Stanford University Press, 1969).

ability to succeed in law school. (To simplify matters, I ignore here the increasing number of applicants who enter the workforce for a period before applying to law school.) Law schools use the score on this test, along with undergraduate grades, recommendations, and other factors in deciding whom to admit. Law school itself involves three years of intensive legal studies (four or five years for students who enroll in a part-time evening program). Those who graduate typically must pass the bar examination for the state in which they wish to practice law, although a few states exempt from the exam those who attend a law school within the state. The bar exam, which lasts several days, examines the prospective lawyer's knowledge of the law of the state. Most jurisdictions also include a multistate component, which poses more general legal questions. Because so much rides on passing the bar exam, recent graduates of law school characteristically enroll in bar-preparation ("cram") courses before taking the exam. Nationally, approximately 70 percent of those who take the bar exam pass it, although success rates vary dramatically from state to state. (Some states— most notably, California and Florida—have sought to limit the number of attorneys practicing within their borders by creating very difficult bar exams.) Those who fail the bar exam are permitted to retake it, and roughly 90 percent of those who fail initially eventually pass. Those who pass the exam and survive the state bar's character check are admitted to legal practice.

Legal Education Abroad   In other countries, the path to becoming a lawyer is quite different. In France, for example, students study law as their undergraduate curriculum, then proceed to a one-year training program (half course work and half training in a law firm) that is capped by a qualifying exam. After passing the exam, they are entered on the list of trainee lawyers and receive two more years of training in a law office before admission to the rank of avocat.[6] Great Britain has a bifurcated legal profession (see Box 4-3), with the principal courtroom attorneys (barristers) historically receiving their training at the Inns of Court rather than at university law schools, although this has changed in recent years.[7] Even in the United States, the process of becoming a lawyer has changed dramatically over time.

The Transformation of Legal Education in the United States
Until the twentieth century, most American lawyers never attended law school. In 1860, there were only twenty-two law schools nationwide, and they enrolled relatively few students. Harvard Law School averaged only nine students a year from 1817 to 1829, its first twelve years of operation.[8] Thus, before 1900, most lawyers received their legal education by clerking in the office of a practicing attorney. They would read law books and assist the lawyer, often by taking on the drudge work of the practice. The quality of the preparation this apprenticeship provided varied enormously, but even poor preparation rarely prevented one from practicing law. Admission to the bar tended to be lax. In 1879, only fifteen of thirty-eight states required formal training, and bar examinations, typically conducted orally by local judges, were perfunctory at best. Gustave Koerner, who began his practice in Illinois during the 1830s, described his exam as lasting only half an hour, in which a few desultory questions were asked; then everyone adjourned for rum toddies.[9]

   The last decades of the nineteenth century witnessed the emergence of the modern law school and, with it, a movement toward formalized legal education. The central figure in these changes was Christopher Columbus

Langdell, the dean of Harvard Law School from 1870 to 1895.[10] Langdell conceived of law as a science consisting of a certain number of principles or doctrines that could be applied to "the ever-tangled skein of human affairs."[11] The way to discover these principles, he believed, was by studying appellate court opinions. Several innovations in legal education followed from these assumptions. If law is a science, then legal study belongs in an academic setting rather than in a law office; law school, not apprenticeship, is the way to produce qualified lawyers. The teachers at such schools should be selected on the basis of their knowledge of those principles rather than their experience in the law. Langdell, therefore, hired full-time law professors rather than relying on practicing lawyers who taught part-time. These instructors should introduce students to the important appellate decisions elaborating those principles, and to facilitate this process, pertinent cases were for the first time collected in casebooks. Finally, instead of merely lecturing, instructors should develop students' skill in analyzing cases and identifying legal principles. Thus, the standard mode of instruction became Socratic questioning, with the instructor calling on students to answer probing questions about the cases they had read. The contemporary flavor of these innovations testifies to the success of Langdell's efforts. Although his innovations were controversial initially, all law schools today employ faculties of full-time academics who use the case method and Socratic questioning.

The spread of Langdell's innovations coincided with enormous growth in the number of law schools and law students. Between 1889 and 1909, the number of law schools doubled, and the number of law students quadrupled.[12] The expansion occurred particularly in urban centers, where part-time schools—often with lax admissions standards—flourished by providing opportunities for recent immigrants and other working people to pursue a professional career. During the first third of the twentieth century, however, bar associations and the Association of American Law Schools campaigned to raise admissions standards for law school to upgrade the quality of the legal profession and reduce competition within it. States began to require that candidates for the bar must be graduates of an accredited law school. During the Great Depression many part-time law schools, already struggling to survive, were forced to close because they were unable to meet ABA accreditation standards. Among the casualties were three of the nation's four black law schools. Portia Law School, founded in 1908 to serve an all-female student body, abandoned its special mission and became the New England School of Law.[13]

Since World War II, legal education has expanded considerably. From 1947 to 2004, the number of ABA-approved law schools jumped from 109 to 187, and many schools also increased the size of their student bodies.[14] Nevertheless, this proliferation of law schools has not made access to the legal profession easier. Over the past thirty years, the demand for legal education has

BOX
4-3 *The Legal Profession in Great Britain*

Venture into a British courtroom and you might be surprised to discover the prosecutor and defense attorney dressed in flowing robes and wearing powdered wigs. Their attire, however, is not all that distinguishes British attorneys from their American counterparts. Upon admission to the bar, American lawyers can undertake all the functions associated with legal practice. This is not the case in Great Britain. From at least the fourteenth century, the British have had a bifurcated legal profession, with those practicing law divided into barristers and solicitors. The members of these groups receive different legal training and perform distinct functions in the British legal system.

Most legal business is taken care of by solicitors. (Currently, some 55,000 solicitors serve a population of more than 60 million.) The solicitor has traditionally been a law office practitioner, advising clients on legal, business, and personal matters. Thus, solicitors' responsibilities may run the gamut from matrimonial matters and divorce, drawing up wills, and drafting business contracts to the attempt to secure redress from debtors. Until the 1980s, solicitors also held a legal monopoly on conveying property (transferring land from one person to another), which for most solicitors was a major source of income. In addition, solicitors can appear as advocates in minor legal disputes that are resolved in limited jurisdiction courts, such as magistrates' courts or county courts.

At times, however, a client beset by more serious legal problems may require the services of a barrister as well. Note the "as well," for in all cases a client is obliged first to seek legal advice from a solicitor. If the solicitor believes that the problem will involve litigation in a general jurisdiction

outpaced the supply and allowed law schools to become increasingly selective. As late as 1960, Harvard Law School admitted half of all applicants.[15] Today, elite law schools are incredibly selective. Yale Law School admitted only 318 students in 2003, less than 7 percent of those applying. Even at less prestigious institutions, the ratio of applications to admissions has increased dramatically.[16] To assess the effects of these developments, let us consider the characteristics of the legal profession in the United States today.

court or appellate court, the solicitor then selects a barrister and "briefs" him or her on the case. The barrister then argues the case in court.

As this description suggests, barristers are an elite group specializing in trial and appellate advocacy. The elite character of the group is reinforced by its size. There are only about 6,600 practicing barristers in Great Britain. Within the ranks of barristers, there is a further division between Queen's (or King's) counsel and junior counsel. The former, also known as "silks" because of the material of their robes, comprise roughly 10 percent of all barristers. They are chosen by the Lord Chancellor, the nation's highest legal official, for their legal ability and reputation. Members of the Queen's counsel not only argue the most important cases, sometimes assisted by junior counsel, but also form the pool from which British judges are selected.

Under the British system a litigant in an important case may have three lawyers (the solicitor, the Queen's counsel arguing the case, and the junior counsel assisting in the argument). Aside from tradition, is there any reason to retain this rather cumbersome and expensive division of the legal profession? According to advocates of the current system, the fusion of the legal profession would not necessarily produce economy because in a difficult case a lawyer might still wish to bring in a specialized advocate with expert knowledge in the field. Moreover, systems with an undivided legal profession, such as in the United States, are hardly models of efficiency or economy. In addition, the selection of the barrister by the solicitor rather than the client serves to create a distance between barrister and client that enables the barrister to provide more dispassionate advice. Finally, under the "cab rank" principle that requires barristers to take any brief sent to them, the system ensures that even the most brutal or politically unpopular defendant will obtain legal representation.

Sources: Mary Ann Glendon, Michael W. Gordon, and Christopher Osakwe, *Comparative Legal Traditions*, 2d ed. (St. Paul, MN: West Publishing, 2002); Gavin Drewry, *Law, Justice and Politics* (London: Longman, 1975); and Timothy Harper, "Bye Bye Barrister: The End of Britain's Two-Tiered Bar?" *American Bar Association Journal* 76 (March 1990): 58–62.

A Portrait of the Legal Profession

Size   The United States today has more than one-quarter of the world's lawyers, with more lawyers—and more lawyers per capita—than any other country.[17] The proliferation of lawyers in the United States can be attributed in part to the nation's economic development. Economic activity tends to generate business for lawyers; thus, the nation's percentage of the world's lawyers is similar to its percentage of the world's gross national product.[18] But economic

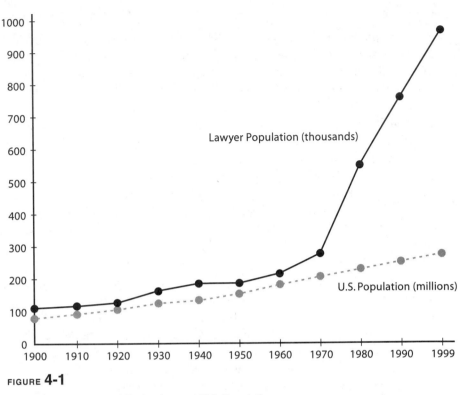

Lawyer Population (thousands)

FIGURE 4-1

The Growth of the Legal Profession and U.S. Population

Sources: Bureau of the Census, *Historical Statistics of the United States* (Washington, DC: Government Printing Office, 1975), and Bureau of the Census, *Statistical Abstract of the United States* (Washington, DC: Government Printing Office, various years).

activity alone cannot explain the size of the American legal profession. Some advanced industrial nations get along with far fewer lawyers. Japan, for example, has fewer than 18,000 attorneys—fewer than are graduated by American law schools in a single year.[19] In addition, whereas the nation's economic growth has been fairly steady, the size of the American legal profession has fluctuated, alternating between periods of rapid growth (such as the late nineteenth and late twentieth centuries) and periods of relative stability (see Figure 4-1). Nor can the increasing number of lawyers be attributed merely to the burgeoning legal demands of an increasing population; in recent years growth in the size of the legal profession has far outstripped population growth. For example, in 1970, there was one lawyer for every 790 Americans, but by 2004 the ratio had dropped to one for every 270 Americans.[20] However, this increase in the number of lawyers is not a distinctively American phenomenon: from 1960 to 1985 the number of lawyers in the United States increased 129 percent; in England the increase was 147 percent; in Canada, 253 percent.[21]

Composition   Changes have also occurred in the composition of the legal profession. One obvious effect of recent trends has been a decline in the median age of those practicing law. This generational change may affect the political perspective of the legal profession, as expressed by the American Bar Association and other legal institutions. Further, with a smaller proportion of the profession closer to retirement age, future increases in the number of attorneys are unlikely to be offset by retirements or deaths within the profession.

The recent influx of lawyers also reflects the collapse of many barriers to admission for previously excluded groups. The largest increase has been in the number of female attorneys. In 1869, Arabella Mansfield of Iowa became the first woman admitted to the practice of law, but many states did not allow women to practice law for most of the nineteenth century, and the U.S. Supreme Court ruled that the exclusion of women did not violate their constitutional rights.[22] By 1910, however, only Arkansas and Georgia persisted in excluding women, and by 1920 women constituted 1.4 percent of the legal profession. Law schools also discriminated, either by denying women admission (Harvard Law School did not admit women until 1950; Washington and Lee Law School until 1972[23]) or by capping female enrollments. The combination of overt discrimination and cultural and social barriers limited women's presence in law school (the class of 1968 at the University of Virginia Law School included only three women[24]) and, because law school had become the only avenue of entry to the legal profession, in the profession itself. As of 1970, women made up less than 5 percent of the legal profession.[25]

Since that time, as Table 4-1 documents, a revolution has occurred. Between 1960 and 2004, the enrollment of women in ABA-approved law schools increased more than 5,000 percent, so that today women make up almost half of entering law students. For the past two decades, even as overall enrollments have skyrocketed, the number of white males enrolled in law schools has remained more or less constant. Today, more than 27 percent of American lawyers are women, and this percentage will increase as current and prospective female law students enter the profession.

Dramatic gains have also been registered by members of racial and ethnic minorities. African Americans suffered systematic discrimination in the legal profession, as elsewhere, well into the twentieth century. For instance, when the American Bar Association discovered in 1914 that it had inadvertently admitted three blacks, it "persuaded" them to resign and refused thereafter to admit blacks until 1943.[26] Howard University Law School, established in 1868, ensured that African Americans were not completely excluded from legal education, but segregation remained a formidable barrier for prospective black lawyers until the 1960s. As of 1970, African Americans made up only 1.3 percent of the legal profession.

Since that time, law schools have made concerted efforts to attract qualified minority group members, and to a considerable extent they have succeeded.

TABLE 4-1 Law School Enrollments

Academic Year	Total Enrollment	Total Women Enrollment	Women Enrollment (%)	Total African American Enrollment	African American Enrollment (%)	Total Minority Enrollment*	Minority Enrollment (%)
1963–64	46,666	1,739	3.7	—	—	—	—
1968–69	59,236	3,554	6.0	—	—	—	—
1973–74	101,675	16,303	16.0	—	—	—	—
1978–79	116,150	35,775	30.8	5,350	4.6	9,952	8.6
1983–84	121,201	46,361	38.3	5,967	4.7	11,917	9.8
1988–89	120,694	50,932	42.2	6,321	5.2	14,295	11.8
1993–94	127,802	55,134	43.1	9,156	7.2	22,799	17.8
1998–99	125,627	57,952	46.1	9,271	7.4	25,266	20.1
2003–04	137,676	67,027	48.7	9,412	7.4	28,346	20.6

*Figures not available for minority enrollments until 1978–79.

Source: www.abanet.org/legaled/statistics/.

As Table 4-1 shows, enrollments of minority students in ABA-approved law schools rose from 8.6 percent in 1978 to 22 percent in 2003. However, in an era of intense competition for admissions, law schools' use of affirmative action programs to recruit minority students has provoked controversy. In 1996, voters in California approved Proposition 209, which prohibited affirmative action in admissions; but in *Grutter v. Bollinger* (2003), the U.S. Supreme Court by a 5–4 vote upheld an admissions program at the University of Michigan Law School that took race into account in order to ensure a diverse student body.[27] This ruling provides guidance for other law schools seeking to institute or continue affirmative action programs.

The Organization of the Legal Profession

The oldest and most important national legal organization is the American Bar Association (ABA). Membership in the ABA is voluntary, not compulsory, and fewer than half the nation's lawyers join. High-status lawyers and members of large law firms are disproportionately represented in its ranks. The ABA exercises no direct authority over individual lawyers or the state bar associations that regulate the legal profession. Nonetheless, the ABA conducts a wide range of activities (see www.abanet.org), and, as the recognized voice of the legal profession, it exerts considerable influence. As Chapter 3 described, until recently presidents requested that the ABA's Standing Committee on Federal Judiciary evaluate the qualifications of prospective federal judges, and nominees who received an "unqualified" rating from the committee were unlikely to be confirmed. The ABA may also take formal positions on legal or political issues and lobby on behalf of those positions. It has been particularly outspoken on issues that directly affect the legal profession, such as lawyer advertising, government-funded legal services for the poor, and the financing and conduct of judicial elections. In addition, the ABA commissions studies and issues reports that may influence political debate or the behavior of lawyers. The association's Model Code of Judicial Conduct is a prime example. Finally, the ABA supervises legal education through its power to accredit—or not accredit—law schools.

Because the states control admission to the legal profession, state bar associations are also important. Although membership in some state bar associations is voluntary, more than thirty states have an "integrated bar." This means that all persons admitted to the bar in the state must belong to the state bar association. These state bar associations generally have less political influence than the ABA. They tend to be less concerned with political lobbying than with admission to the legal profession in the state, continuing education of the state's lawyers, and disciplining attorneys guilty of illegal or unprofessional conduct.

TABLE 4-2	PRIVATE PRACTITIONERS AND THEIR PRACTICE SETTING	
Practice Setting	**Number**	**Private Practitioners (%)**
Solo practice	262,622	45
2-lawyer firm	34,152	6
3-lawyer firm	23,018	4
4–5 lawyer firm	31,418	5
6–10 lawyer firm	43,606	7
11–20 lawyer firm	41,971	7
21–50 lawyer firm	42,265	8
51–100 lawyer firm	31,353	5
Larger than 100-lawyer firm	73,883	13

Source: Barbara A. Curran and Clara N. Carson, *The Lawyer Statistical Report: The U.S. Legal Profession in the 1990s* (Chicago: American Bar Foundation, 1994), p. 25.

PRACTICING LAW

An Overview of Legal Practice

Major changes have occurred not only in the size and demographics of the legal profession but also in the types of legal practice. During the settlement of the American West, when frontier areas were sparsely populated, judges rode circuit to hold court in various locations, and lawyers often accompanied them, providing representation for those who had awaited the judge's arrival to settle their disputes. As a commentator of the era described it, "[t]he lawyer would, perhaps, scarcely alight from his horse when he would be surrounded by two or three clients requiring his services."[28] As the nation's population spread, so did the lawyers. Wherever a community grew up, a lawyer would also settle and set up his office, handling whatever legal business came his way. Thus, the typical nineteenth century lawyer was a nonspecialized solo practitioner, serving a wide diversity of clients and legal needs.[29]

By the twenty-first century, the nonspecialized solo practitioner has become the exception, not the rule.[30] Roughly one-fifth of all lawyers are employed by government or private industry. Even among private practitioners, fewer than half currently have solo practices, and one-quarter work in firms with more than twenty lawyers (see Table 4-2). Far more than in the past, then, lawyers are employees rather than autonomous professionals.

Name	Home Office	Size	Date Founded	2003 Gross Revenues ($ million)
Skadden, Arps, Slate, Meagher & Flom	New York	1,827	1948	1,310
Baker & McKenzie	Chicago	3,214	1949	1,060
Jones Day	Cleveland	2,136	1893	908
Latham & Watkins	Los Angeles	1,624	1934	906
Sidley Austin Brown & Wood	Chicago	1,559	1866	831
Mayer, Brown, Rowe & Maw	Chicago	1,376	1881	705
Shearman & Sterling	New York	1,089	1860	700
Well, Gotshal & Manges	New York	1,125	1931	688
White & Case	New York	1,681	1901	675
McDermott, Will & Emery	Chicago	1,002	1934	628

TABLE 4-3 ELITE LAW FIRMS

Sources: "The 2003 AmLaw 100," at www.legalmarketinfo.com/amlaw100.php; and www.hoovers.com.

Current Types of Legal Practice

The Elite Law Firm   Imagine defending Microsoft against an antitrust suit with billions of dollars at stake, helping the Chrysler Corporation negotiate federal guarantees for loans to avoid bankruptcy, fighting to stave off a hostile takeover of Kennecott Copper, or guiding the first stock issue of Genentech, a major genetic-engineering company, which would generate $35 million in working capital.[31] The high stakes, the powerful clients, and the intense pressures and rich rewards that accompany representing them all define the world of the elite law firm.

The large, elite firms primarily represent the nation's major economic institutions, such as corporations, banks, insurance companies, and other powerful financial enterprises.[32] Not surprisingly, then, a large number of these firms have their home offices in New York (see Table 4-3). However, most top firms today are no longer identified with a single locale; they establish branch offices in other major U.S. cities and offices overseas as well.[33] The size of successful firms has increased dramatically in recent years, in part through the acquisition of other law firms. In 1968, there were only twenty firms that employed as many as 100 lawyers, but by 2003 the United States had two firms with more than two thousand lawyers, thirteen with more than a thousand lawyers, and seventy-three with more than 500.[34]

Within these large firms, a clear hierarchy exists. Atop the hierarchy are the senior partners, who manage the firm and determine the division of profits at year's end. They are followed in descending order by junior partners, permanent associates who remain with the firm after being bypassed for partner, and associates. The most important distinction is that between partner and associate. The elite firms recruit the most promising graduates (with top grades and membership on the law review) from the nation's most prestigious law schools. These graduates start with annual salaries as high as $135,000. As associates, these young attorneys work under the direction of a partner, gradually advancing from apprenticeship to increased autonomy. The work can be demanding—70- to 80-hour weeks are not uncommon, and the pressure is enormous. Associates know that only about a quarter of them will receive partnership offers.

What these large firms claim to offer their clients is the perfection of the legal craft: a combination of legal talent and specialized expertise that ensures "no stone is left unturned, no matter how seemingly insignificant, and with virtually no regard for time or money."[35] Of course, this dedication and legal expertise is expensive. Elite firms may bill their clients more than $750 an hour for the time of a senior partner and more than $200 an hour for the work of an associate. But these figures purchase an extraordinary devotion. During the Kennecott Copper takeover fight, for instance, "the lawyers at Sullivan & Cromwell didn't have a day off from Thanksgiving 1980 to the end of January 1981, including the holidays."[36] When legal disputes involve millions of dollars, companies are quite willing to pay premium prices for top-flight legal work.

Solo Practice   At the opposite end of the spectrum from the large law firm is the solo practitioner. The solo practitioner epitomizes the idea of the independent professional and thus occupies an honored place in the mythology of the legal profession. Certainly, the prospect of being one's own boss and choosing one's own clients attracts some attorneys to solo practice. There may also be social or other barriers that prevent a lawyer from pursuing other sorts of law practice. A 1962 study found that "the individual practitioner of law in Chicago is a self-made man who came up the hard way from poor, immigrant surroundings" by attending the local law school, usually at night.[37] When neither his social background nor the quality of his legal education recommended him to major law firms, he became a solo practitioner.

The number of solo practitioners has declined sharply in recent years, particularly in urban areas, as attorneys have gravitated toward large law firms or toward employment with corporations. A contributing factor has been the tendency of corporations and other businesses to deal with their legal problems in-house or to take them to law firms with specialized expertise rather than to solo practitioners. As a result, solo practitioners are often "confined to those residual matters (and clients) that the large firms have not pre-empted."[38] Thus, solo practitioners primarily serve the legal needs of middle-class and blue-collar clients. According to a recent study of Chicago lawyers, these legal concerns generally involve personal business matters (general litigation, personal real estate, personal tax, and probate) and personal plight concerns (criminal defense, divorce, general family practice, and personal injury claims).[39]

Even in dealing with these problems, solo practitioners face increased competition today. Taking advantage of Supreme Court rulings that have removed restrictions on advertising by lawyers, legal entrepreneurs have developed "legal clinics" that seek to provide routine legal services in simple matters such as wills, uncontested divorces, and demand letters to landlords.[40] These firms have succeeded in attracting a large clientele through aggressive television advertising and branch offices in convenient locations such as shopping malls, and they have kept prices down by applying mass production techniques— standardization of services and organization of tasks—to the delivery of legal services.[41] Solo practitioners have found it difficult to compete with the clinics' high-volume, low-price approach.

Corporate Counsel   More than 16 percent of lawyers currently work in private industry, frequently in firms involved in finance, insurance, real estate, communications, or manufacturing. Major corporations are most likely to employ lawyers and maintain large legal departments. Fortune 500 firms employ approximately 30 percent of all in-house counsel (General Electric employs more than 400 attorneys, Exxon more than 200). The growth in corporate law offices represents an attempt by major companies to reduce legal costs by relying less heavily on elite law firms. By using in-house counsel, some companies have halved their legal costs. Large corporations recognize that, in the words of one board chairman, "the most active companies now require—or are best served by—the constant availability of counsel who is informed on a day to day basis of the company's activities and directions."[42] Most often the corporate counsel is engaged in preventive law, ensuring that legal problems do not arise. When large corporations do litigate, they still tend to rely on outside counsel.

From the perspective of the attorney, there are both advantages and disadvantages to working in-house. On the one hand, house counsel are not their own boss and typically earn less than a partner in a top law firm. On the other hand, corporate employment offers job security and a substantial income: forty-three companies paid their general counsel in excess of $1,000,000 in salary and bonuses in 2003.[43] Moreover, as Catherine Rein, corporate general counsel for The Continental Group, has observed, lawyers who work for a single client can see "the long-term effects of [their] legal advice, become part of a team, and can take continuing pride in [their] contribution."[44]

Government Attorney   Approximately 8 percent of American attorneys are employed by federal, state, or local governments (excluding judges, who constitute 3 percent of the legal profession). More than three-fifths of these attorneys work for state and local governments, with the largest number serving as prosecutors or public defenders (attorneys employed by the government to represent defendants who cannot afford a private attorney). Almost 40 percent of government attorneys work for the federal government. Large contingents of federal attorneys are found in the Justice Department, which handles federal civil cases and criminal prosecutions, and in the Internal Revenue Service. However, attorneys occupy positions in a wide array of departments and agencies.

The diversity of positions reflects the diverse responsibilities of government attorneys. Government attorneys dominate the practice of criminal law. Government prosecutors conduct all criminal prosecutions, and public defenders represent the vast majority of defendants. Government attorneys are also involved in civil litigation. They may initiate civil suits on behalf of federal, state, or municipal governments or their subunits. They also defend the government and its various departments against suits by private parties. In addition, the federal government supplies attorneys through the Legal Services Corporation to represent the poor in certain civil cases. Still other government attorneys work outside the courtroom. Their responsibilities may include drafting legislation or administrative regulations, administering government departments and programs, lobbying on behalf of the department before Congress, or helping governmental agencies avoid legal problems. The responsibilities of various government attorneys are considered in detail later in this chapter and in Chapters 5 and 6.

Although women and minority attorneys, perhaps concerned about discrimination in the private sector, have disproportionately chosen careers in government service,[45] government employment offers advantages for all attorneys, particularly early in their careers. Lawyers in the public sector find a degree of job security and avoid the intense competition and job pressures characteristic of large law firms. While salaries hardly match those in large firms, they are respectable, particularly for more junior attorneys. In addition, young attorneys may be given significant responsibilities in government earlier than in a large law firm. Of course, this may have its downside as well. According to one public defender, after only a day or two of orientation, he was told: "We're all attorneys and you handle the case any way you want to handle it, at your complete discretion. Just right on, brother, and good luck."[46] Nonetheless, many young attorneys gain valuable experience early in their careers through government employment, before moving into corporate work or private practice.

The migration from government to the private sector creates openings for newly minted attorneys. In addition, attorneys who have worked for a government often find their experience and expertise in demand by private employers or clients and end up representing the very groups they sought to regulate while in government service. One lawyer, when asked whether he felt any remorse about his shift in position, responded: "I have no qualms about changing sides. Will I be comfortable representing [business] in front of the [agency]? I can hardly wait! Certainly there are two sides to every story."[47]

The Divided Legal Profession

The discussion thus far has emphasized the diversity of clients that lawyers represent, the range of legal issues they address, and the varied contexts in which they practice law. Some observers would argue that contemporary legal practice is not only diverse but also fundamentally divided. According to John Heinz and Edward Laumann, the American legal profession is divided into "two hemispheres," those who represent large organizations (primarily corporations) and those who represent individuals.[48] In their study of Chicago lawyers, they found distinct differences:

> Lawyers who serve major corporations and other large organizations differ systematically from those who work for individuals and small businesses whether we look at the social origins of the lawyers, the prestige of the law schools they attended, their careers histories and mobility, their social or political values, their networks of friends and professional associations, or several other social variables. . . . [T]his fundamental difference in the nature of the client served appears to be the principal factor that structures the social differentiation of the profession.[49]

Even if, as Heinz and Laumann contend, no other profession is as divided, what difference does that make? The authors suggest that this bifurcation has at least two adverse effects. First, because the interests and perspectives of its members diverge so sharply, the legal profession cannot speak with one voice on the issues that affect it. Second, the division sends a troubling message about the orientation of the legal profession. All Americans are aware that inequalities of wealth and power exist in their society. The bifurcation of the legal profession—with the most notable members of the legal profession serving the needs of corporate America and a less prestigious group serving private persons—seems to reinforce those inequalities, raising questions about the availability of adequate legal services for the general public.

ACCESS TO LEGAL SERVICES

The Nebraska Constitution provides that "[a]ll courts shall be open, and every person, for any injury done him in his lands, goods, person, or reputation, shall have a remedy by due course of law."[50] This guarantee, repeated in similar language in several other state constitutions, reflects a commitment to the principle that all persons should have access to the courts for settling disputes and redressing injuries. Although litigants have the right to represent themselves, effective presentation of their claims usually requires the services of an attorney. So do many other commonplace activities, such as drawing up a contract, buying a house, adopting a child, and probating a will. Nevertheless, purchasing the services of an attorney to resolve even routine legal problems can be expensive, and concern about costs may deter poor or middle-class people from consulting an attorney, even when they need legal assistance.

Government, the legal profession, and private groups have attempted to ensure that all members of society obtain the legal assistance they require. Let us look at the character and success of their efforts within the criminal justice and civil-law systems.

Criminal Justice

The Sixth Amendment to the U.S. Constitution guarantees to every defendant the right "to have the Assistance of Counsel for his defense." This guarantee permits those accused of a crime to hire counsel but does not in itself oblige the government to provide an attorney to indigent defendants. However, if the government fails to provide legal assistance, the result is an unequal system of justice. It may also interfere with the operation of the adversary system. Well-to-do defendants will hire counsel, thus ensuring a rough balance of legal expertise between prosecution and defense. But indigent defendants, unable to afford an attorney, will be forced to defend themselves, despite their lack of familiarity with the law and courtroom procedures. As the discussion of *Gideon v. Wainwright* in Chapter 2 shows, such defendants are unlikely to mount a strong defense, even when they are innocent.

Because the effectiveness of the adversary system depends on a vigorous presentation of both sides, the imbalance of legal expertise between prosecution and defense in a case increases the possibility that innocent people will be convicted. Recognizing this, the U.S. Supreme Court in 1938 ruled that criminal defendants in federal courts had a constitutional right to representation by counsel, even if they could not afford to pay a lawyer.[51] Several states also recognized a right to counsel for indigent defendants as a matter of state law—Wisconsin did so as early as 1859.[52] However, the most important step toward securing equal justice for indigent defendants was *Gideon v. Wainwright* (1963), which extended the right to counsel to all felony defendants in state courts, where the bulk of criminal prosecutions take place.[53] In subsequent cases the Supreme Court extended the logic of *Gideon* to guarantee legal representation for defendants in juvenile courts and for all defendants facing the possibility of imprisonment if convicted. In addition, recognizing that such procedures as police interrogations and lineups may determine the outcome of a case, the Court extended the right to counsel to the earlier stages of the criminal justice process as well.[54]

The states had two options in responding to their obligation to provide counsel for indigent defendants. They could establish offices of government-employed defense attorneys (public defenders) or pay private attorneys to represent defendants. The second approach has not worked well because the rates that governments have paid have not been high enough to attract many good lawyers. If all attorneys in a jurisdiction are obliged to take a turn at criminal defense, defendants may well receive perfunctory representation by lawyers who have little familiarity with the criminal law. Indeed, a study of homicide cases in New York City found that, in one-third of the cases, court-appointed lawyers spent less than a week preparing the case.[55] Many jurisdictions have therefore chosen to employ public defenders to handle criminal defense. Access to legal representation has not only improved the lot of indigent defendants but also increased the fairness of the criminal justice system. Nonetheless, some critics have charged that because public defender offices are chronically underfunded and understaffed, public defenders lack the time to provide their clients with an adequate defense. Other critics have complained that public defenders have used liberal Supreme Court rulings to manipulate the criminal justice system and secure the release of guilty defendants. Whatever their validity, these allegations underscore the crucial role that public defenders play today. Public defenders provide legal representation for more than two-thirds of criminal defendants. The work of public defenders is examined more closely in Chapter 6.

Civil Law

Although the U.S. Constitution requires government to provide legal assistance for indigent defendants accused of crime, it does not guarantee legal assistance in civil cases. From time to time, however, most people do require the services of a lawyer. They may need legal representation to file suit for damages when they have been injured or divorce when a marriage fails; they may also find themselves respondents in a civil suit, or they may need legal advice for business or personal matters as well. Nevertheless, many people find it difficult to obtain legal services. They may be concerned about costs, uncertain about how to locate a lawyer, or not understand the legal implications of the problems they confront. Government, the legal profession, and private groups have pioneered various approaches to ensure the availability of legal services.

Legal Aid   Although there is no constitutional right to counsel in civil cases, government or private groups may provide an attorney for those who cannot afford one. The federal government's first involvement with legal aid for the poor grew out of the Freedman's Bureau during Reconstruction, when the bureau retained private attorneys to represent indigent African Americans in civil and criminal cases.[56] During the late nineteenth century, several private legal aid societies were formed. Illustrative of these societies were Der Deutsche Rechtsschutz Verein, established by New York City's German Society to protect recent German immigrants, and the Protective Agency for Women and Children, created by the Women's Club of Chicago to combat the "seductions and debaucheries of young girls under guise of proferred [sic] employment."[57] By 1919, legal aid societies were in operation in forty-one cities, and the number grew in succeeding decades. Despite this, the private legal aid societies lacked the resources to serve adequately the legal needs of the poor.

The federal government's more recent involvement in legal aid grew out of the "War on Poverty" launched by President Lyndon Johnson. The Legal Services Program (LSP), established in 1965, encouraged the formation of local legal aid agencies to serve the poor through grants that covered the costs of their operations. These local agencies retained considerable discretion in deciding how best to serve the needs of their clientele. Some local LSP agencies emphasized solving the legal problems of individual clients, following the approach of legal aid societies in the past, although their greater resources permitted them to serve more poor people and take more cases to court. Other local agencies placed greater emphasis on law reform, challenging laws and policies that they believed disadvantaged the poor. Such challenges, usually referred to as "impact cases," typically entailed more time and effort than the resolution of individual disputes and often involved appellate litigation. Not surprisingly, these law reform efforts were controversial. Conservative critics charged that they reduced the number of clients served, created the odd phenomenon of one part of government's suing another, and permitted left-wing lawyers to politicize the Legal Services Program by pursuing their own political agendas under the guise of helping the poor.

The political controversy over the Legal Services Program led Congress to reconstitute it as the Legal Services Corporation (LSC) in 1974, and it continues in this form to the present day. The LSC functions as a nonprofit corporation, providing funds by grant or contract to legal service programs in all fifty states, with the majority going to field offices located throughout the country. Nonetheless, like its predecessor, the LSC has often been mired in political controversy. During the 1980s, Presidents Reagan and Bush both sought to abolish the LSC, but Congress refused to go along. However, appropriations for the Legal Services Corporation were slashed, and both presidents named outspoken critics of the LSC to its board of directors. With the election of conservative Republican majorities in both houses of Congress in 1994, the attack on the LSC intensified, and limits were imposed on the LSC's funding and activities. In the Omnibus Budget Act of 1996, its budget was cut 30 percent, from $400 million in 1995 to $278 million in 1996; by 2003, however, it had increased to $338 million. Legislation specifically prohibited LSC attorneys from engaging in lobbying, initiating class action suits, representing prison inmates, or undertaking court action to block changes in federal or state welfare systems. According to the LSC's defenders, these restrictions crippled its efforts to represent the poor effectively, but to its most outspoken critics, even these restrictions did not go far enough in depoliticizing the LSC. In 2001, the U.S. Supreme Court ruled that the federal ban on LSC funding to any organization that represented clients involved in challenging existing welfare law violated the First Amendment.[58]

Whatever the deficiencies of the Legal Services Corporation, the government's involvement in legal aid has substantially increased the poor's access to legal assistance.[59] During 2001, for example, more than one million cases were closed by negotiated settlement, litigation, referral to another agency, or other means. The most common legal problems handled by legal aid lawyers involve family issues, such as divorce, child support, spousal abuse, and custody and visitation rights. Conflicts over housing matters, such as landlord–tenant disputes, and over government benefits, such as welfare and unemployment, also make up a substantial part of legal aid work.

Legal Clinics   Legal clinics are high-volume private law firms that seek to provide routine legal services for large numbers of clients at low cost. Their number increased dramatically during the 1970s: in 1974, there were only eight law clinics; by 1980 there were about 800, and their growth has continued since then.[60] The development of legal clinics was stimulated by Supreme Court rulings that opened the door to aggressive price competition within the legal profession. In *Bates v. State Bar of Arizona* (1977), the Supreme Court ruled that the First Amendment protected the right of lawyers to advertise their prices for legal services, and in *Goldfarb v. Virginia State Bar* (1975), it struck down minimum fee schedules established by bar associations as a violation of federal antitrust laws.[61] These rulings freed legal entrepreneurs to attract clients by price advertising and claims of less expensive legal services than their competitors.

In part, legal clinics can charge lower rates because of economies of scale. Although they frequently locate branch offices in neighborhoods or malls for the convenience of their clients, legal clinics are among the largest law firms in the United States. Even more important, these clinics cut personnel costs by relying on paralegals rather than lawyers for routine tasks and by employing standard forms for common legal procedures. Many clinics have prospered by focusing on such problems as divorces, wills, personal bankruptcy, and preparation of tax returns.

Legal clinics have primarily attracted middle-class and working-class clients. While they have introduced competition into the provision of legal services, it is unclear whether they have increased the availability of lawyers to those who would not otherwise use their services. It may be that legal clinics have merely displaced traditional firms, redistributing business within the legal profession.

Lifting the Lawyers' Monopoly   Like the members of other professions, lawyers have sought to establish a state-enforced monopoly over the provision of their professional services and to prevent nonlawyers from providing legal services. To a large extent their efforts have succeeded. Laws in various states mandate that only lawyers may provide legal advice, draft wills, transfer property titles, and represent persons before administrative agencies. Such laws help maintain the high cost of legal services by restricting competition to those who have law degrees.

The legal profession has justified the restrictions as necessary to protect the public, arguing that only attorneys have the expertise to provide competent legal assistance. Critics charge that the restrictions serve the interests of the legal profession rather than those of the general public. Legal clinics' intensive use of paralegals for tasks traditionally undertaken by lawyers does suggest that trained nonlawyers can perform some of the tasks currently undertaken by lawyers. The chairman of the Legal Services Corporation under President Reagan went considerably further, suggesting that the LSC could be abolished if legal restrictions on the unauthorized practice of law were lifted.

Some jurisdictions have responded to criticisms of the legal monopoly. California, for example, adopted a form for wills that is simple enough to allow most persons to draft their own. Meanwhile, groups and commercial concerns have begun to publish forms and other materials designed to enable laypersons to conduct real estate transactions, probate estates, and handle their own no-fault divorces. Although self-help materials may reduce legal costs for those who use them, they can be used only for simple and routine legal matters. Furthermore, even though reducing the monopoly position of lawyers may reduce legal costs, whether it actually increases access to legal services remain unclear.

Contingent Fees   Potential litigants may fail to consult a lawyer because they fear that the damages they are awarded may not cover the legal fees and court costs associated with their cases. To remove this disincentive to pursue legal claims, the American legal system has developed the *contingent fee*, which displaces the financial risk from the client to the lawyer. Under a contingent fee arrangement, the attorney fronts the costs of the litigation and receives an agreed-upon percentage (often one-third) of the award or settlement in the case, plus reimbursement of the costs incurred. If the lawyer's efforts net the client a large award, the lawyer shares in the good fortune. However, if the client receives nothing, neither does the attorney. Thus, a contingent fee arrangement makes sense for a lawyer only when the prospect of a substantial fee outweighs the risk of no fee at all. This occurs most often in personal injury cases where clients are suing because of injuries sustained in an accident or as the result of defects in a product they purchased. In such cases the question frequently is not whether the plaintiff will obtain damages but rather the size of the award or settlement.

Contingent fees are controversial.[62] Critics charge that they encourage frivolous suits because plaintiffs bear no financial risk. They also claim that contingent fees may create a conflict between the interests of the attorney and the client. Attorneys operating under a contingent fee arrangement may be tempted to settle cases, thereby obtaining some reward for their efforts, rather than take them to trial and risk losing both the cases and their fees. Furthermore, contingent fees allow attorneys to receive extremely high fees for relatively little work when they negotiate large settlements in straightforward personal injury cases.

Proponents counter that most criticism of contingent fees is self-interested, coming from attorneys who represent insurance companies, corporations, and other defendants in personal injury cases rather than from plaintiffs in personal injury cases. More substantively, they insist that without contingent fees average citizens would often not bring cases, even when they had suffered real injuries. They also deny that lawyers receive unduly high contingent fees. Such claims, they maintain, rely on a few atypical cases and ignore the risk that attorneys bear under contingent fee arrangements.

Although no jurisdiction has outlawed contingent fees, some have sought to regulate them. The New Jersey Supreme Court, for example, has established a graduated scale of maximum permissible contingent fees, with attorneys receiving no more than 20 percent of any award above $1,500,000.

Group Legal Services   Group legal services (GLS) plans are a form of legal insurance, under which group members pay a premium that entitles them to various legal services. GLS plans resemble medical insurance plans and, like them, vary in how they provide services. Open-panel plans are like Blue Cross/Blue Shield, in that GLS members can seek legal services from a wide range of lawyers. A closed-panel plan is more like an HMO: Members "can consult only lawyers (sometimes a single firm) who belong to the plan and have agreed to accept a schedule of fees, generally below the market rate."[63]

Such prepaid plans were developed early in the twentieth century, when the Physicians' Defense Company and automobile clubs began to offer legal services or coverage of legal fees for subscribing members. But opposition from the American Bar Association limited experimentation with group legal services until the 1970s. Promoting the renewed interest in group legal plans were a series of Supreme Court rulings during the 1960s that held that restrictions could not be placed on group efforts to ensure legal representation for their members.[64] Thus, associations could offer prepaid legal plans to their members, and unions could seek coverage for their members in collective bargaining. Whether group plans will continue to expand is unclear. Fewer workers belong to unions today than in the past, and group legal plans remain a low-priority fringe benefit for most workers.

Pro Bono Work   The ABA's Model Rules of Professional Conduct suggest that attorneys have an obligation to perform pro bono work; that is, to undertake legal work without compensation for the economically disadvantaged or for charitable causes. (The term *pro bono* comes from the Latin *pro bono publico*, "for the public good.") Much of this work is undertaken through pro bono and other private bar involvement programs. According to the American Bar Association, 17.2 percent of all lawyers participated in these organized programs in 1995, up from 10.6 percent only ten years earlier.[65] Other attorneys perform pro bono services through their law firms or as solo practitioners. Nevertheless, this professional obligation is self-enforced, and most attorneys actually engage in little or no pro bono work.

Some jurisdictions and local bar associations have begun to require attorneys to devote a minimum number of hours to pro bono work. Such pro bono requirements are controversial; some attorneys have even argued that they violate the Thirteenth Amendment ban on involuntary servitude. Even where mandatory pro bono exists, it imposes only minimal burdens (about two cases a year), and attorneys can buy out of their obligations. Thus, a knowledgeable commentator has concluded: "Although pro bono activities undoubtedly help the particular recipients and ease the consciences of lawyers, they do relatively little to fulfill the promise of equal justice."[66]

LAWYERS AND CLIENTS

In an adversary system lawyers are expected to represent the interests of their clients. Attorneys who fail to do so risk serious penalties. Those who provide inadequate or incompetent assistance can be sued for malpractice; and those who are dishonest—who, for example, make use of or steal money entrusted to them—are subject to not only criminal prosecution but also discipline by the state bar association. In serious cases a lawyer may be disbarred; that is, prohibited from practicing law again.

For attorneys who are neither incompetent nor dishonest, the perplexing issue remains: How *does* one serve the interests of one's client? The answer is inevitably tied up with the question of the proper relationship between lawyer and client. Historically, this relationship has resembled the traditional relationship between doctors and patients or between other professionals and their clients.[67] The client seeks the counsel of the professional and puts the matter in his or her hands, relying on the professional's expertise and judgment. Thus, the professional has full autonomy in deciding how best to advance the client's interests. The assumption is that the interests of both parties are best served by this arrangement.

In recent years, however, this model of professional dominance has come under attack. In medicine this is reflected in the development of the notion of informed consent: Physicians should explain the various options available to patients and proceed with a course of treatment only after receiving their consent. In law too, the idea of a more collaborative relationship between lawyer and client has gained currency. Proponents of this more cooperative approach suggest that clients should consider along with their lawyers such matters as "whether to sue at all, the ground rules of the lawyer's and client's mutual contact, the lawyer's fee, the preparation of the case, the best time to sue, whether to seek a jury trial or special trial preference, various issues of settlement strategy, and the preparation for examination before trial."[68] However, as the relationship between professional and client becomes more collaborative, defining the responsibilities of each becomes more difficult.

The appropriate relationship between lawyer and client is particularly difficult to determine in political litigation, where the aim is not merely to vindicate the interests of a single person but also to establish a legal principle of benefit to a larger group. Political litigation poses fundamental questions: Who is the lawyer's client, and whose interests should be given priority? Consider *Brown v. Board of Education,* the famous school desegregation case. Thurgood Marshall and the NAACP's Legal Defense Fund had undertaken a protracted campaign to overturn laws mandating segregation in schools and other public facilities. As part of the campaign, they actively sought out clients willing to serve as vehicles for challenging discriminatory laws. In *Brown,* which represented the culmination of this struggle, the NAACP recruited Oliver Brown, whose daughter attended a segregated school in Topeka, Kansas, to serve as plaintiff. The decision to litigate, the selection of plaintiffs, the choice of when and where to sue, and the decision as to how to frame the legal issues all remained in the hands of Thurgood Marshall and his associates.

As this account suggests, the relationship between lawyers and clients is far different in political litigation than in ordinary litigation. Lawyers in political litigation may actively seek out clients to act as parties to a suit, rather than merely provide a service to those who consult them. Moreover, the lawyers' willingness to initiate suit or file an appeal, as well as the strategy pursued in the course of the litigation, will depend upon how such action will advance the interests of the group, not those of the individual litigant. As long as the "client" understands and accepts this, as is usually the case when a group pursues a litigation strategy, no problem arises.

However, it may happen that the remedy desired by the lawyer in political litigation may diverge from that preferred by clients. In the aftermath of *Brown,* for example, a gap at times developed between the belief of civil rights lawyers in the importance of school integration and the desire of clients—parents and

children—for educational improvement, whether in a segregated or an integrated setting. Similarly, in mental health litigation, some lawyers sought to
establish a "right to treatment," whereas most residents in institutions preferred a "least restrictive alternative" suit that would release them from the
institution to a community-based mental health facility.[69] Or the choice may be
between pressing for a legal ruling that could conceivably benefit a large number of persons or accepting a settlement beneficial to one's client, as when the
government agency being sued offers a settlement that will satisfy the client's
particular concern without establishing a binding precedent. In circumstances
such as these, lawyers may well wonder how they should balance competing
interests and whose interests should be given the greatest weight.

The appropriate relationship between lawyer and client is even more
complicated when the lawyer engaged in law reform litigation is affiliated
with a legal services agency funded by the Legal Services Corporation. Critics charge that legal services lawyers in "impact cases" dominate the relationship with their clients. Instead of advancing clients' interests as they
define them, the lawyers "use their clients as mere instruments for enacting
their own political agendas."[70] Furthermore, if legal services lawyers claim to
be serving a group beyond the individual client, exactly what is that group? If
it is the poor in general, on what basis can the lawyer claim to represent their
interests, and who gave the lawyer authority to speak for them? Moreover,
because LSC lawyers work for the government, how can they justify pursuing policies in political litigation, such as increased welfare benefits or siting
public housing in middle-class neighborhoods, that diverge from the policies
endorsed by the government? In sum, critics contend that the law reform
activities of legal services lawyers go beyond even the traditional relationship
between lawyer and client because the lawyer expects clients to defer not
only to his expertise regarding how to serve their interests but also to his view
of what those interests are.

Because of these concerns, many LSC attorneys rarely engage in political
litigation, preferring to serve the day-to-day legal problems of individual clients.[71] Other LSC attorneys, however, dismiss the benefits obtained through
such legal work as "Band-Aids" and insist that real advances for the poor come
through political litigation.[72] These lawyers claim that the close ties they maintain with community groups keep them informed about the interests of their
real clients, the poor of the community. Thus, they deny that they are unilater-
ally imposing their views on their clients. Even when they seek out plaintiffs to
pursue issues or aggregate individual complaints into broad-based legal attacks
on the practices or policies of a government agency, they insist that it is the
community's interests they are seeking to advance. The concern voiced about
lawyer domination of poor clients, they argue, is insincere; those who voice the
concern are really distressed by the success of the aggressive tactics employed
by LSC attorneys.

THE TRANSFORMATION OF THE AMERICAN LEGAL PROFESSION

This chapter has shown that the American legal profession today differs from its counterparts in other countries in its training, size, and the ways in which it organizes itself and delivers legal services. The contrast with other countries, however, is no sharper than the contrast with the American past, as the transformation of American legal education illustrates. To become a lawyer in the United States today, a college graduate must survive an increasingly selective admissions process for law school and complete three years of rigorous academic training. Every element of that description represents a change from the past. The current emphasis on academic studies in a university setting marks a departure from the nation's first century, when apprenticeship was the most common form of legal training. Until well into the twentieth century, graduation from college was not a requirement for law school—indeed, some law schools accepted students who did not even have high-school diplomas— and some graduated students after as little as a single year of study. Only recently has admission to law school become fiercely competitive.

A transformation has also occurred in the composition and size of the American legal profession. Initially, the practice of law was largely confined to a relatively small group of native-born white males. But in the late nineteenth century, new groups—women, racial minorities, and immigrants—began to seek admission to the legal profession. Despite legal and social barriers, these groups had gained a tenuous foothold by the early twentieth century. Only within the last three decades, however, have women and racial minorities become a sizable presence within the American legal community. Indeed, the dramatic expansion of the American legal profession in large part reflects the opening of the profession to previously excluded or marginalized groups.

Finally, a transformation has occurred in the practice of law and the delivery of legal services in the United States. For most of the nation's history, the typical lawyer was a solo practitioner or a partner in a very small firm. But three developments during the second half of the twentieth century have altered the practice of law. First, the number of large law firms has increased dramatically, as have the size of those firms, with the largest firms employing hundreds of attorneys in branch offices throughout the nation and abroad. Second, corporations and governments at all levels now hire far more lawyers than in the past. As a result, attorneys today increasingly are employees rather than autonomous professionals. Third, governmental officials and the legal profession have recognized that segments of the American public cannot normally afford the legal services they need. This recognition has led to government programs designed to provide legal aid, such as public defender programs and the Legal Services Corporation. It has also led the legal profession to introduce innovations designed to attract new clients by making legal services more affordable. Such innovations as legal clinics, the contingent fee, and prepaid legal services have altered the way legal services are delivered and paid for. How successful these efforts to increase the accessibility of legal services have been, and to what extent they have given reality to the goal of equal justice for all, remains a matter of dispute.

NOTES

1. Background information on the two justices was obtained from Henry J. Abraham, *Justices, Presidents, and Senators: A History of the U.S. Supreme Court Appointments from Washington to Clinton,* 4th ed. (Lanham, MD: Rowman & Littlefield, 1999); Leon Friedman, ed., *The Justices of the United States Supreme Court,* vols. 4 & 5 (New York: Chelsea House, 1969, 1978); John C. Jeffries Jr., *Justice Lewis F. Powell Jr.: A Biography* (New York: Charles Scribner's Sons, 1994); and Juan Williams, *Thurgood Marshall: American Revolutionary* (New York: Times Books, 1998).

2. The distinction between attorneys as "delegates" and as "trustees" is drawn from Susan E. Lawrence, *The Poor in Court* (Princeton, NJ: Princeton University Press, 1990), chap. 1.

3. The CNN/*USA Today*/Gallup Poll, Nov. 14–16, 2003, reported at http://www.mycoolcareer.com/news/news_121203.html.

4. See Sol M. Linowitz with Martin Mayer, *The Betrayed Profession: Lawyering at the End of the Twentieth Century* (New York: Charles Scribner's Sons, 1994), p. 40.

5. American Bar Association Code, EC7-19, quoted in David Luban, *Lawyers and Justice* (Princeton, NJ: Princeton University Press, 1988), p. 51, and an unnamed lawyer, quoted in Jennifer L. Pierce, *Gender Trials: Emotional Lives in Contemporary Law Firms* (Berkeley: University of California Press, 1995), p. 59.

6. Christian Dadamo and Susan Farran, *The French Legal System,* 2d ed. (London: Sweet & Maxwell, 1996).

7. See Richard L. Abel, "England and Wales: A Comparison of the Professional Projects of Barristers and Solicitors," in *Lawyers in Society: The Common Law World,* vol. 1, ed. Richard L. Abel and Philip S. C. Lewis (Berkeley: University of California Press, 1988).

8. Robert Stevens, *Law School* (Chapel Hill: University of North Carolina Press, 1983), chap. 1.

9. Lawrence M. Friedman, *A History of American Law,* 2d ed. (New York: Simon and Schuster, 1985), p. 317.

10. The discussion of Langdell and the impact of his efforts relies on Stevens, *Law School,* chap. 3–4.

11. Quoted in ibid., p. 52.

12. Abel, *American Lawyers,* p. 41.

13. Stevens, *Law School,* chap. 11.

14. This figure was obtained from the American Bar Association's Web site: www.abanet.org.

15. Abel, *American Lawyers,* p. 59.

16. *The Official Guide to U.S. Law Schools* (New York: Law School Admissions Council, 2004), p.821.

17. Figures on the size of the American legal profession are drawn from *Statistical Abstract of the United States* at www.census.gov/prod/2004pubs/03statab/labor.pdf.

18. The connection between economic activity and the size of the legal profession is discussed in Terrence C. Halliday, "Six Score Years and Ten: Demographic Transitions in the American Legal Profession," *Law & Society Review* 20 (1986): 65–70. The relationship between GNP and number of lawyers is suggested by Marc Galanter, "News from Nowhere: The Debased Debate on Civil Justice," *Denver University Law Review* 71 (1993): 80.

19. Data on the Japanese legal profession are found in Kathryn Tolbert, "Japan Altering Legal System to Produce More Lawyers," *The Washington Post*, September 3, 2000.

20. Bureau of the Census, *Statistical Abstract of the United States* (Washington, DC: U.S. Government Printing Office, various years); American Bar Association, National Lawyer Population at http://abanet.org/marketresearch/2004nbroflawyersbystate.pdf.

21. Galanter, "News from Nowhere," p. 80.

22. *Bradwell v. Illinois*, 83 U.S. 130 (1873). For more general treatments of the barriers confronting women, see Karen Berger Morello, *The Invisible Bar: The Woman Lawyer in America 1638 to the Present* (New York: Random House, 1986), and Cynthia Fuchs Epstein, *Women in Law* (New York: Basic Books, 1981).

23. Abel, *American Lawyers*, p. 90.

24. Nancy L. Buc, "A Washington Lawyer: Using Government Experience in Private Practice," in *Women Lawyers: Perspectives on Success,* ed. Emily Couric (New York: Harcourt Brace Jovanovich, 1984), p. 50.

25. Epstein, *Women in Law*, p. 4.

26. Abel, *American Lawyers*, p. 100.

27. *Grutter v. Bollinger*, 539 U.S. 306 (2003).

28. John Dean Caton, *Early Bench and Bar of Illinois* (1893), p. 51, quoted in Friedman, *History of American Law*, p. 309.

29. See Friedman, *History of American Law*, chap. 8.

30. Data are drawn from Barbara A. Curran, "American Lawyers in the 1980s: A Profession in Transition," *Law & Society Review* 20 (1986): 27; Abel, *American Lawyers*, p. 178; Barbara A. Curran, Katherine J. Rosich, Clara N. Carson, and Mark C. Puccetti, *The Lawyer Statistical Report: A Statistical Profile of the U.S. Legal Profession in the 1980s* (Chicago: American Bar Foundation, 1985), p. 243.

31. With the exception of the Microsoft case, these examples are drawn from actual cases discussed in James B. Stewart, *The Partners* (New York: Simon and Schuster, 1983).

32. For accounts of the structure and operation of large law firms, see Marc Galanter and Thomas Palay, *Tournament of Lawyers: The Transformation of the Big Law Firm* (Chicago: University of Chicago Press, 1991), and Paul Wice, *Judges and Lawyers: The Human Side of Justice* (New York: Harper Collins, 1991), pp. 79–90.

33. Galanter and Palay, *Tournament of Lawyers*, pp. 47–48.

34. See Erwin Smigel, *The Wall Street Lawyer: Professional or Organization Man?* 2d ed. (New York: Free Press, 1969), pp. 358–359, and "The 2003 NLJ 250" at www. legalmarketinfo.com/2003_nlj250.php.

35. Stewart, *The Partners*, p. 14.

36. Ibid., p. 281.

37. Jerome E. Carlin, *Lawyers on Their Own* (New Brunswick, NJ: Rutgers University Press, 1962), p. 1.

38. Ibid., p. 17.

39. John P. Heinz and Edward O. Laumann, *Chicago Lawyers: The Social Structure of the Bar* (New York: Russell Sage Foundation and American Bar Association, 1982), p. 65, table 3-1.

40. Relevant judicial rulings include *Bates v. State Bar of Arizona*, 433 U.S. 350 (1977), and *Shapero v. Kentucky Bar Association*, 486 U.S. 466 (1988). For a discussion of the development and effects of legal clinics, see Abel, *American Lawyers*, pp. 106–107.

41. For a description of legal work in these clinics, see Jerry Van Hoy, "Selling and Processing Law: Legal Work at Franchise Law Firms," *Law & Society Review* 29 (1995): 703–729.

42. Quoted in Eve Spangler, *Lawyers for Hire* (New Haven, CT: Yale University Press, 1986), p. 71.

43. "GC Compensation Survey" at www.law.com/special/professionals/corp_counsel/2003/gc_compensation_survey.shtml.

44. Catherine A. Rein, "As Corporate General Counsel: Hierarchies with Few Women at Top," in Emily Couric, *Women Lawyers*, p. 125.

45. This discussion of the advantages of government employment for attorneys draws on Wice, *Judges and Lawyers*, p. 78.

46. Quoted in Milton Heumann, *Plea Bargaining* (Chicago: University of Chicago Press, 1977), p. 55.

47. Quoted in Spangler, *Lawyers for Hire*, p. 112.

48. John Heinz and Edward Laumann, *Chicago Lawyers*. Heinz and Laumann are currently updating their initial study; for information, see the Web site of the American Bar Foundation: www.abf-sociolegal.org.

49. Ibid., pp. 319–320. More generally, see Robert L. Nelson, David M. Trubek, and Rayman L. Solomon, eds., *Lawyers' Ideals/Lawyers' Practices: Transformations in the American Legal Profession* (Ithaca, NY: Cornell University Press, 1992).

50. Nebraska Constitution, art. 1, sec. 13.

51. *Johnson v. Zerbst*, 304 U.S. 458 (1938).

52. *Carpenter v. Dane*, 9 Wis. 249 (1859).

53. *Gideon v. Wainwright*, 372 U.S. 335 (1963).

54. Supreme Court rulings extending the right to representation at trial include *In re Gault*, 387 U.S. 1 (1967), and *Argersinger v. Hamlin*, 407 U.S. 25 (1972). Cases extending the right to representation before trial include *Escobedo v. Illinois*, 378 U.S. 478 (1964), and *Miranda v. Arizona*, 384 U.S. 436 (1966).

55. Jane Fritsch and David Rohde, "Legal Help Often Fails New York's Poor," *New York Times*, April 8, 2001, at www.nytimes.com/2001/or/08/nyregion/08LAWY.html.

56. The account of the development of legal aid for the poor, including the Legal Services Program and the Legal Services Corporation, relies primarily on Lawrence, *The Poor in Court;* Mark Kessler, *Legal Services for the Poor* (Westport, CT: Greenwood Press, 1987); and Douglas J. Besharov, ed., *Legal Services for the Poor* (Washington, DC: AEI Press, 1990).

57. Lawrence, *The Poor in Court*, p. 18.

58. For further information on the Legal Services Corporation, see Harry P. Stumpf, *American Judicial Politics*, 2d ed. (Englewood Cliffs, NJ: Prentice Hall, 1998), pp. 244–250, and the Web site of the Legal Services Corporation at www.lsc.gov/.

59. These data are drawn from Stumpf, *American Judicial Politics*, p. 248. For earlier data on the activities of LSC attorneys, which are quite similar, see Besharov, *Legal Services for the Poor*, p. 32, table 9.

60. This discussion is based on Abel, *American Lawyers*, p. 138, and Wice, *Judges and Lawyers*, pp. 75–76.

61. *Bates v. State Bar of Arizona*, 433 U.S. 350 (1977), and *Goldfarb v. Virginia State Bar*, 421 U.S. 773 (1975).

62. The critique of contingent fees is drawn from Wice, *Judges and Lawyers*, pp. 125–126.

63. Abel, *American Lawyers*, p. 136. More generally, the discussion of group legal services relies on Lillian Deitch and David Weinstein, *Prepaid Legal Services* (Lexington, MA: Lexington Books, 1976).

64. Pertinent cases include *NAACP v. Button,* 371 U.S. 415 (1963); *Brotherhood of Railroad Trainmen v. Virginia ex rel. Virginia State Bar,* 377 U.S. 1 (1964); *United Mine Workers, District 12 v. Illinois State Bar Association,* 389 U.S. 217 (1967); and *United Transportation v. State Bar of Michigan,* 401 U.S. 576 (1971).

65. American Bar Association Division for Legal Services, *The 1996 Directory of Pro Bono Programs* (Chicago: American Bar Association, 1996).

66. Abel, *American Lawyers,* p. 130.

67. See Douglas E. Rosenthal, *Lawyers and Clients: Who's in Charge?* (New York: Russell Sage, 1974), especially chap. 1 and 6.

68. Susan M. Olson, *Clients and Lawyers* (Westport, CT: Greenwood Press, 1984), pp. 28–29.

69. These examples were suggested in ibid., pp. 29–30.

70. Luban, *Lawyers and Justice,* p. 303. This is a summary of the critique, not an expression of Luban's views.

71. For a discussion of the different orientations of LSC lawyers, see Kessler, *Legal Services for the Poor.*

72. The defense of political litigation by LSC lawyers is elegantly presented by Luban, *Lawyers and Justice,* chap. 14–16.

PART two

JUDICIAL PROCESS AND JUDICIAL DECISION MAKING

TRIALS AND APPEALS   135

CRIMINAL JUSTICE AND THE COURTS   172

CIVIL JUSTICE AND THE COURTS   216

JUDICIAL DECISION MAKING   247

TRIALS AND APPEALS

During the O. J. Simpson murder trial, commentators often referred to it as "the trial of the century." But, in fact, every decade has its dramatic trial with lurid crimes and celebrities as defendants or victims. This is the story of one of those trials.

In March 1982, fifteen months after Sunny von Bulow had lapsed into an irreversible coma, twelve jurors in a Rhode Island Superior Court found her husband, Klaus von Bulow, guilty of attempted murder.[1] The sensational nine-week trial attracted reporters from all over the country, from the *New York Times* to the *National Enquirer.* And why not? The case had all the elements of a good story. The victim, who had been found lying unconscious in the marble bathroom of her Newport mansion, was an heiress, and according to her will, her aristocratic Danish husband stood to inherit an estate worth millions. But her children from a previous marriage, who also had an interest in the estate, launched the initial investigation into the case, convinced that their stepfather was guilty. In the words of the prosecutor: "This case has everything. It has money, sex, drugs; it has Newport, New York, and Europe; it has nobility; it has maids, a butler, a gardener. . . . This case is where the little man has a chance to glimpse inside and see how the rich live."[2]

The prosecution's theory of the case was simple: Although Klaus von Bulow did not love his wife, he did love her money and the lifestyle it afforded him. He also loved his mistress, soap opera star Alexandra Isles, who had threatened to leave him if he did not divorce Sunny. Rather than choose between money and mistress, Klaus decided to have them both by murdering Sunny and making it appear that she had died of natural causes. To do this, the prosecution contended, he surreptitiously injected her with insulin, thereby inducing what he expected to be a fatal coma.

The prosecution introduced physical evidence to support its theory—most important an insulin-encrusted needle allegedly found in a black bag belonging to Klaus von Bulow. It also brought forward an expert witness who stated that Sunny's coma had been induced by an insulin injection. Sunny's maid testified that Klaus owned the black bag and that she had seen needles and insulin in it in the past. Finally, Alexandra Isles admitted that she had threatened to leave Klaus unless he obtained a divorce.

The defense attorneys decided against having Klaus von Bulow take the stand in his own defense. Instead, they relied on the testimony of Joy O'Neill, a self-described confidante of Sunny's, who claimed that Sunny gave herself insulin shots. However, on cross-examination the prosecution undermined O'Neill's credibility and with it the defense case. After six days of deliberations, the jury returned a guilty verdict.

After sentencing von Bulow to thirty years in prison, the trial judge commented, "The Trial of Klaus von Bulow is over. The Trial of the Trial Judge is about to begin."[3] And so it was. Proclaiming his innocence, Klaus von Bulow appealed his conviction to the Rhode Island Supreme Court. Newly hired to represent him on appeal was Alan Dershowitz, a Harvard professor and prominent defense attorney. Although appellate courts focus on legal rather than factual questions, Dershowitz was convinced that the Rhode Island court would not overturn von Bulow's conviction unless the justices had some indication that his client was innocent. He therefore framed his argument about errors in the trial proceedings in such a way as to raise doubts about von Bulow's guilt. Whether or not this approach was necessary, it succeeded; the Rhode Island Supreme Court reversed the trial court's decision. Citing the prosecution's failure to make certain potentially relevant documents available to the defense and the police's seizure and testing of pills without a warrant, the justices awarded Klaus von Bulow a new trial.

The state of Rhode Island again prosecuted von Bulow for attempted murder, but a different defense strategy produced a different result in the second trial. The documents withheld at the first trial revealed that when questioned early in the investigation, the maid had never mentioned having seen insulin and a syringe in von Bulow's bag. Under intense defense questioning, she retracted her testimony from the first trial about the insulin. The defense also brought forward expert witnesses who countered the prosecution's claim that Sunny's coma had resulted from an insulin injection. In June 1985, the jury found Klaus von Bulow not guilty of all charges.

Although this spectacular case is hardly typical of criminal cases, or even of criminal trials, it illustrates several aspects of the roles and operations of trial and appellate courts.

*1. **Different courts, different functions.*** Dershowitz's decision to emphasize doubts about von Bulow's guilt in the appeal was a bold but risky maneuver. It is the job of trial courts, *not* appellate courts, to establish the facts and to determine whether a defendant is guilty or not guilty, liable or not liable. The job of appellate courts is to review whether trial courts have observed proper legal procedures in trying and deciding to establish the facts and to determine guilt or liability cases. If the appellate court finds, as it did in the von Bulow case, that procedural irregularities prevented a fair trial, then it can remand the case for new proceedings in which those irregularities are eliminated. This second trial will seek anew to establish the facts and to determine whether the defendant is guilty or not guilty, liable or not liable.

2. Cases and trials. Most criminal cases, unlike the von Bulow case, are resolved without a trial, usually by the defendant pleading guilty following plea negotiations between the defense attorney and the prosecutor. (Most civil cases are likewise settled before trial.) Yet trials have an importance that far exceeds their number. As the von Bulow case illustrates, the more serious the charge, the more likely a criminal case is to go to trial. Defendants charged with serious offenses may be willing to take their chances with a jury because they fear the punishment that a guilty plea would bring, and prosecutors may refuse to plea bargain because public opinion supports severe punishment for those who commit serious crimes.

In addition, both criminal and civil trials have an effect on those cases resolved without trial. Trials provide a baseline, a point of reference for resolving cases without trial. In plea bargaining, the negotiations of prosecutor and defense attorney are influenced by the punishment an offender would be likely to receive if the case were to go to trial. In civil cases the willingness of the plaintiff and the defendant to settle often depends on their perception of how they would fare if the case went to trial. Thus, even when cases are settled without trial, the negotiations take place in the shadow of the law.[4]

3. Lawyers' tactics. Under our adversarial system of justice, trial courts rely on the parties in the case to uncover relevant physical evidence (anything from documents and reports to, in the von Bulow case, a syringe and insulin) and to bring forward witnesses to testify about what happened. As the von Bulow trials reveal, this reliance allows the attorneys for each side to structure the presentation of evidence to advance their clients' interests. They can enlist expert witnesses to support their clients' version of the facts, as in the second von Bulow trial, when the defense called its own experts to counter the medical testimony of the prosecutor's experts. Attorneys can also cross-examine the witnesses called by the other side. During the first von Bulow trial, the prosecutor undermined the defense case by destroying the credibility of its main witness on cross-examination. During the second trial, sharp questioning by defense attorneys during cross-examination caused the maid to change her story. Finally, defense attorneys in criminal cases can determine whether or not they wish to call their clients to testify.

An Overview of the Chapter

This chapter analyzes trials and appeals in the United States. The examination of trials highlights how the trial is structured to ensure accurate fact-finding while safeguarding the rights of the parties at trial. It also describes the tactics that attorneys use to advance their clients' interests during the course of a trial. In doing so, it reveals the tension between the legal system's concern for impartial decision making and the quest for partisan advantage implicit in the adversary system.

This tension reappears in the discussion of the American jury. Because jurors control the fate of their clients, attorneys will use every device to persuade them, regardless of the evidence. This chapter therefore investigates the extent to which juries do consider factors other than the law and the evidence presented at trial in reaching their verdicts. It also considers whether changes in the structure and operation of the jury, such as reducing the size of the jury and partially eliminating the requirement of unanimous verdicts, have affected jury deliberations and verdicts. Finally, the discussion turns to a question raised by the reliance on juries: is justice served by tempering the rule of law with community views of substantive justice?

The last topic of this chapter is the operation of appellate courts. The operations of the U.S. Supreme Court, the most visible and most important of the nation's appellate courts, will offer an initial example of how appellate courts review trial court rulings. Consideration is then given to how the decision-making process in other appellate courts both resembles and diverges from that in the Supreme Court. This inquiry will provide insight into the various ways in which judicial systems can be organized to promote justice.

Trials

Disputes and Fact-Finding

A trial is a proceeding for resolving a dispute on the basis of law. More precisely, a trial serves to ascertain the facts about a situation, apply the law to that set of facts, and thereby determine whether a defendant is guilty or not guilty (in a criminal case) or liable or not liable (in a civil case). A trial may seek to resolve disputes about the facts in a case, the applicable law and how it applies, or questions of both fact and law.

Disputes about the Facts   In some cases, the disputing parties agree about the interpretation and application of the law but offer differing versions of the facts. A criminal assault case, for example, may turn entirely on the identity of the assailant or a robbery case on the defendant's claim that the victim actually owed him the money he took. Similarly, civil suits may focus on such questions as whether it was the defendant company's drug that produced the plaintiff's medical problems or whether an employee was refused a promotion because of her race or gender.

Disputes about the Law In some cases, both parties agree on the relevant facts but disagree on the application of the law to those facts. In a criminal case, for example, the prosecution and defense may agree that a police search uncovered evidence of wrongdoing but disagree about whether the search was legal. In civil cases too the facts may be undisputed but not the legal standards. For example, is a person legally liable for injuries he inadvertently caused? Did an administrative agency have the legal authority to issue the regulations it did?

Mixed Disputes Involving Both Facts and Law In some cases, the questions of fact and law are intertwined. For example, when a defendant claims to have shot the victim in self-defense, the outcome of the case depends on the facts surrounding the shooting and on the legal definition of self-defense. Similarly, when a plaintiff sues for sexual harassment, the judge or jury must decide what the defendant did and whether those actions meet the legal definition of sexual harassment.

Although trial courts decide questions of both fact and law, their primary task is gathering the evidence necessary to resolve disputes. Indeed, their success in fact-finding is crucial to the administration of justice. If a trial court misinterprets or misapplies the law, its error can be corrected on appeal. But if a trial court does not uncover all the relevant facts, there is no mechanism for introducing new testimony on appeal. Moreover, because they did not hear the witnesses, appellate courts are extremely reluctant to reverse a trial court ruling even if they suspect the trial judge may have misinterpreted the facts of the case.

Thus, if justice is to prevail, trial courts must uncover all evidence pertinent to the cases they are deciding and correctly evaluate that evidence. To ensure that all pertinent evidence is introduced at trial, the American legal system relies on the adversary system, which assumes that each side will bring forward all the evidence and legal arguments that support its position. The adversary system also serves to ensure the reliability of the evidence that is introduced by permitting each side to challenge the testimony of opposing witnesses during cross-examination. Further safeguarding the reliability of testimony and physical evidence at trial is the law of evidence, which prescribes what evidence can be admitted, who can present this evidence, and how it should be introduced.

The Diversity of Trials

Most people form their picture of trials from highly publicized cases, such as the O. J. Simpson murder trial, or from courtroom dramas depicted on television or in books. Such trials, however, are exceptional. Most trials do not involve months of testimony, as the Simpson trial did, nor do they feature dramatic revelations from the witness stand or a barrage of motions and objections by the attorneys. Rather, they are brief and at times perfunctory affairs.

A study of criminal trials in the late nineteenth century found that most defendants were tried "in slapdash and routine ways, in trials that lasted a few hours or a few minutes at best."[5] Because criminal defendants today are guaranteed legal representation at trial, they are better able to mount a defense than were their counterparts a century ago. Still, unless the charges against a defendant are very serious or the defendant demands a jury trial, most contemporary criminal trials do not last long either. In Philadelphia, for example, felony trials conducted without a jury averaged less than an hour.[6] Most trials in civil cases are also short, particularly when the amount at stake is small. In the Los Angeles Small Claims Court, for example, the average trial in contested cases lasted only 8.9 minutes, with the shortest trial taking only 1 minute.[7]

Not all trials, however, are abbreviated affairs in which procedural safeguards, such as trial by jury, are waived and various stages of the process compressed or eliminated. Let us look more closely at the legal safeguards available to defendants and at the various stages of a "full-dress" trial.

Rights at Trial

The Fifth and Fourteenth Amendments to the U.S. Constitution guarantee that neither the federal government nor the state governments may deprive any person of life, liberty, or property without due process of law. Nevertheless, exactly what process is "due" at trial and what procedures are constitutional is difficult to determine. Justice Felix Frankfurter described the problem:

> "Due Process," unlike some legal rules, is not a technical conception with a fixed content unrelated to time, place, and circumstances. Expressing as it does in its ultimate analysis respect enforced by law for the feeling of just treatment . . . [and] representing a profound attitude of fairness between man and man, and more particularly between the individual and government, due process is compounded of history, reason, the past course of decisions, and stout confidence in the strength of the democratic faith that we profess.[8]

To give substance to this general guarantee of procedural fairness, judges have looked to the rights established by the federal and state constitutions, statutes, judicial precedents, and the common law. Among these rights are:

1. Trial by jury.   Trial by jury allows ordinary citizens to participate in the administration of justice and thus acts as a barrier against governmental tyranny. In *Duncan v. Louisiana,* Justice Byron White wrote: "Providing an accused with the right to be tried by a jury of his peers gave him an inestimable safeguard against the corrupt or overzealous prosecutor and against the compliant, biased, or eccentric judge."[9] The Sixth Amendment to the U.S. Constitution secures the right to trial by jury in federal criminal cases and the Seventh Amendment in civil cases in which more than twenty dollars is at stake. In 1968, the Supreme Court ruled that defendants in state courts also have a federal constitutional right to a jury trial in most *criminal* cases.[10] Various state constitutions and state statutes also guarantee a right to trial by jury.

2. *Speedy and public trial.* The Sixth Amendment to the U.S. Constitution, along with analogous state provisions, secures to defendants in criminal cases the right to a speedy and public trial. The Constitution prohibits secret trials on the assumption that public scrutiny of the administration of justice protects against governmental abuse of its prosecutorial power and promotes judicial impartiality. State and federal guarantees of a speedy trial ensure that the government cannot charge people with crimes and then, by delaying their trials, keep them in jail or prevent them from proving their innocence. The Speedy Trial Act of 1974 requires that defendants in federal court must be brought to trial no more than 100 days after they are charged with a crime.

3. *Right to counsel.* Protected by the Sixth Amendment, the right to counsel was originally understood to ensure only that those accused of crime could employ and bring to trial an attorney of their own choosing. But over time it became clear that, in the words of Justice Hugo Black, "any person hauled into court, who is too poor to hire a lawyer, cannot be assured a fair trial unless counsel is provided for him."[11] Thus, beginning in the nineteenth century, several states undertook to furnish counsel to indigent defendants. In *Johnson v. Zerbst* (1938), the U.S. Supreme Court followed their lead, ruling that the right to counsel included appointment of counsel for indigent defendants in all criminal proceedings in federal courts. In *Gideon v. Wainwright* (1963), the Court further extended this protection to indigent defendants in state courts.[12] But the federal Constitution does not oblige federal or state governments to provide attorneys to indigent plaintiffs in civil cases.[13]

4. *Securing and confronting witnesses.* The adversary system of justice works on the principle that truth will emerge from the clash of partisan presentations by the parties in a case. Each party is expected to bring forth all the evidence and arguments that support its position. The prosecution can secure the evidence it needs through its power to subpoena witnesses—that is, to require them to appear under threat of legal punishment. To equalize matters, the Sixth Amendment gives defendants in criminal cases this same power to compel witnesses to appear. The adversary system also assumes that each party will seek to discredit the evidence and arguments of the opposing party, and so the Sixth Amendment guarantees defendants the right to confront and question witnesses against them. However, the Supreme Court has narrowed the right to confront witnesses, permitting, under some circumstances, children to testify about sexual abuse they suffered without having the defendant present before them.[14]

5. *The burden of proof.* In both criminal and civil cases the burden of proof rests on the party who initiates the proceeding. However, the standard of proof depends on the type of case. For a conviction in a criminal case, the prosecution must prove guilt "beyond a reasonable doubt."[15] Thus, defendants in criminal cases need not prove their innocence; they need merely raise doubts about their guilt. This high threshold of persuasion reflects the belief that it is better to risk letting the guilty go free than to risk convicting the innocent. In civil cases a lower standard of proof—proof by a preponderance of the evidence—suffices. This standard is satisfied when the balance of probabilities favors the plaintiff or the defendant in the case.

In a criminal trial the prosecution must meet its burden of proof at trial without relying on the assistance of the defendant. Thus, the Fifth Amendment, along with analogous state guarantees, forbids compelling witnesses to testify against themselves. Indeed, the prosecution cannot even comment on the defendant's failure to testify, and jurors are cautioned not to draw any inferences from the defendant's not taking the stand.[16]

The Trial Process

Although procedures vary somewhat from state to state, a full-scale trial tends to follow certain set steps (see Box 5-1). These steps are basically the same in both civil and criminal litigation, although in civil cases the term "plaintiff" is used instead of "prosecutor."

Bench or Jury Trial? The initial step is the decision whether to choose a jury trial, in which a group of ordinary citizens renders the verdict, or a bench trial, in which a judge conducts the trial without a jury and then renders the verdict. In criminal cases in which jury trial is an option, the choice is left to the defendant. In civil cases for which jury trial is available, the plaintiff and the defendant usually must agree to waive a jury trial.

More jury trials are conducted in the United States than in any other country, although the number of jury trials has declined in recent years. Still, not all defendants are entitled to a trial by jury. For example, there is no federal constitutional right to a jury trial in criminal cases involving petty offenses, although state law may provide for one.[17] Thus, drunk drivers in five states— Louisiana, Mississippi, Nevada, New Jersey, and New Mexico—are not entitled

> **BOX 5-1** *The Stages of a Trial*
>
> 1. Choice of a jury trial or a bench trial
> 2. Jury selection*
> 3. Opening statement of the prosecutor**
> 4. Opening statement of the defendant's attorney
> 5. Presentation of the prosecution's case**
> 6. Presentation of the defendant's case
> 7. Rebuttal witnesses
> 8. Closing argument for the prosecution**
> 9. Closing argument for the defendant
> 10. Closing argument in response for the prosecution**
> 11. Judge's instructions to the jury*
> 12. Deliberations by the judge (bench trial) or the jury
> 13. Announcement of the verdict
>
> *Occurs only in jury trials
> **Involves the prosecutor in a criminal trial; the plaintiff's attorney in a civil trial

to a jury trial unless they face jail terms of more than six months.[18] Nor are jury trials available in all civil cases. Most states, for example, mandate bench trials for family matters such as divorce or child custody disputes.

Litigants choose between a jury trial and a bench trial on the assumption that who decides the case will affect its outcome. Thus, those who are accused of particularly heinous crimes may waive their right to a jury trial, because they assume a judge would be less influenced by emotional factors than would a jury. Conversely, if defendants believe the community would be reluctant to apply the law to them, as in the case of a "mercy killing," then they may well opt for a jury trial. Finally, individuals suing corporations or other large organizations may insist on a jury trial because they expect that jurors will identify with them and sympathize with their plight.

Jury Selection   If a jury trial is chosen, the next step is jury selection. Long before the trial, the jurisdiction will have compiled a master jury list (also called a "wheel") that is designed to include all potential jurors within its borders. Many jurisdictions create their master jury list from voter rolls, sometimes supplemented by the local census, lists of taxpayers, or driver's license records.

From the master jury list, the jury commissioners or court clerks randomly select enough names to make up a "venire" (jury pool). Those who are selected receive questionnaires designed to determine their eligibility for jury service. Some are disqualified by statute from serving on juries because they are aliens, do not meet local residency requirements, cannot read or speak English, or because they have previously been convicted of a felony. Others enjoy statutory exemptions for various reasons: their occupations are considered vital (elected officials, physicians, and members of the military); they might exert too much influence on jury deliberations (lawyers and police officers); they might have an occupational prejudice on the question of guilt or innocence (police officers and clergy). Finally, some potential jurors are excused because jury service would impose an undue hardship on them. Most states excuse all persons who request to be excused, because their reluctance to serve would probably make them poor jurors. Citizens who are not excused receive a summons ordering them to appear at the courthouse on a specified day. The court clerk's office then randomly selects groups of prospective jurors from the venire and directs them to courtrooms where they might be needed.

Jurors and alternates are selected for trial through a process called the "voir dire" (a French term usually translated as "to speak the truth"). During voir dire, prospective jurors are questioned to determine whether they can decide the case fairly and impartially. Based on their answers, the prosecution or the defense can challenge prospective jurors "for cause," claiming that they are biased about the defendant, the prosecution, or the case. Among the factors that might justify a challenge for cause are personal relationships between the juror and a litigant, preconceptions about the case or the parties to it, or, if applicable to the case, prejudice against a particular racial, ethnic, or religious group. If the judge rules that cause has been shown, then a challenged juror is excused. There is no limit on the number of jurors who can be challenged for cause, and in highly publicized cases the process of jury selection can be quite drawn out. In the "Hillside Strangler" murder trial in Los Angeles, for example, voir dire and jury selection took forty-nine court days.[19]

Attorneys may also remove a limited number of prospective jurors through peremptory challenges. In exercising peremptory challenges, attorneys need not specify their reasons nor gain the judge's approval for removing a juror. Thus, peremptory challenges enable each side to eliminate prospective jurors whom they suspect of being predisposed against their client, even if the jurors have not displayed any overt prejudice that would justify a challenge for cause. Even more important, lawyers also attempt to use peremptory challenges to eliminate prospective jurors whom they believe will be unsympathetic and to empanel a jury favorable to their client (see Box 5-2). There are, however, legal limitations on the use of peremptory challenges. The U.S. Supreme Court has ruled that the Constitution prohibits their use to exclude prospective jurors exclusively on the basis of race or gender.[20] The number of peremptory challenges exercised is

BOX
5-2 *Jury Selection in the Simpson Murder Trial*

From the outset the prosecution and defense in O. J. Simpson's murder trial knew that jury selection would be crucial to the outcome. The defense team retained Jo-Ellen Dimitrius, a crack jury consultant with a record of success with Los Angeles juries. Donald Vinson, president of Decision Quest, one of the nation's top jury consultants, offered his services for free to the prosecution.

Dimitrius and Vinson both polled residents of Los Angeles to determine their attitudes on the Simpson case, as well as on various issues that might arise at trial. In addition to polling, the defense conducted focus groups, whose discussions helped the attorneys devise the questionnaire to be submitted to prospective jurors during voir dire. The prosecution, meanwhile, staged "mock trials"—presentations of opening arguments before demographically diverse groups—and observed the groups' subsequent deliberations through one-way glass.

With this information Dimitrius and Vinson each constructed profiles of the ideal defense juror. Their profiles largely coincided: a blue-collar, middle-aged, African American woman who had some personal or familial experience with law enforcement. Simpson's attorneys heeded Dimitrius's advice and sought to select jurors who fit this profile. However, prosecutor Marcia Clark rejected Vinson's advice, confident that the spousal-abuse issue in the case and her experience in establishing rapport with African American women jurors would be decisive. The prosecution thus failed to use its full allotment of twenty peremptory challenges, and the jury that finally acquitted Simpson included eight African American women, one African American man, two white women, and one Hispanic man.

Sources: Jeffrey Toobin, *The Run of His Life: The People vs. O. J. Simpson* (New York: Random House, 1996); Johnnie L. Cochran, *Journey to Justice* (New York: Ballantine Books, 1996); and Marcia Clark, *Without a Doubt* (New York: Penguin, 1997).

established by statute and varies by jurisdiction and the seriousness of the charges. Arkansas, for example, permits the prosecution ten peremptory challenges and the defense twelve in capital cases, but only six and eight in other felony cases, and three apiece in misdemeanor cases.[21]

The mechanics of the voir dire also vary by jurisdiction. In some states, the judge alone questions prospective jurors, in others attorneys may pose supplemental questions, and in still others the attorneys conduct all questioning of prospective jurors.[22] In major cases, the scope of questioning during voir dire can be quite extraordinary. In the O. J. Simpson murder trial, for example, prospective jurors were asked to complete an 80-page questionnaire that included 294 questions, ranging from "Have you ever dated a person of a different race?" to "Have you ever asked a celebrity for an autograph?"[23] Because the jury's composition may be crucial to their success at trial, most trial lawyers want to conduct voir dire questioning.[24] Doing so enables them to probe for the information they need to exercise their challenges wisely. Equally important, conducting voir dire gives them an opportunity to influence the jury and lay the foundation for the case they plan to present.

How do attorneys choose jurors? In most cases, given the unavailability of information on juror attitudes, attorneys rely on broad generalizations and gut feelings. Thus, fabled defense attorney Clarence Darrow acknowledged that he based his choices largely on stereotypes, choosing as candidates for peremptory challenges the "cold as the grave" Presbyterians, the "almost sure to convict" Scandinavians, and, above all, the very rich, for whom "next to the Board of Trade, the Penitentiary is the most important of all public buildings."[25] For modern defense attorneys, the stereotypes may have changed, but not the approach. Famous defense attorney Gerry Spence says he prefers men rather than women because he believes men have done more hell-raising and are more forgiving of it, and fat people rather than thin people because fat people lack self-control and therefore would not demand as much from others.[26]

Over the last thirty years, attorneys in some major cases have sought to replace such guesswork with science and have enlisted social scientists to assist in jury selection. The first use of scientific jury selection, during the 1972 conspiracy trial of Daniel Berrigan and other anti-Vietnam War activists, exemplifies the basic approach.[27] Researchers sympathetic to the defendants conducted a telephone survey of the area in which the trial was to take place, asking questions about the issues in the coming trial and obtaining demographic information from respondents. From this they developed demographic profiles of the kinds of persons likely to be hostile or sympathetic to the defendants. Defense attorneys carefully questioned prospective jurors with unfavorable demographic profiles and used their peremptory challenges to eliminate those who had not been excused for cause. Whatever the success of this selection process, Berrigan and his fellow defendants were acquitted of all charges.

Nowadays, attorneys in major trials often use social science to advance their clients' interests. Attorneys may hire jury consultants to assist in jury selection, try out arguments in front of "mock juries" before trial, or employ "shadow juries" (people similar to those serving on the jury, who are hired to provide daily feedback on how the arguments presented in court might have been received by the jury). To the extent that these approaches can predict juror behavior—a claim disputed by some commentators, who dismiss the jury consultants' claims of success as highly inflated[28]—they raise serious questions: Does scientific jury selection increase the likelihood that trial outcomes will be determined by the predispositions of jurors rather than by evidence? Should jury selection techniques be permitted if they give an advantage only to those who can afford to use them?

Opening Statements   Before any evidence is presented, the attorney for the party that initiated the litigation (the prosecution in criminal cases or the plaintiff in civil cases) presents an opening statement to the jury—or, in bench trials, to the judge. This opening statement provides a preview of the prosecution's case, identifying the issues and describing the evidence that the prosecutor intends to offer. It thus serves as a road map for jurors throughout the trial. The defense usually follows with its opening statement, raising questions about the prosecution's evidence and promising contradictory evidence. On occasion a defense attorney may postpone giving an opening statement until after the presentation of the prosecution's case.

By law, opening statements are supposed to be bare outlines of the substance of the evidence, free of argument or appeals to emotion. Many trial lawyers, however, believe that opening statements can make or break a case. These statements, they note, provide attorneys their first opportunity to establish a rapport with the jury, and the impression attorneys make with their opening statements may predispose jurors toward the prosecution's or the defense's position, even before testimony is presented.[29] Thus, attorneys must view the opening statement as an opportunity to persuade. The challenge, given the strictures on persuasive appeals, is to "prepar[e] a persuasive opening statement that appears to be devoid of persuasive appeal."[30]

Presentation of the Prosecution's (Plaintiff's) Case   Each party in a trial offers its evidence in turn, with the party who initiated the litigation—and who therefore must prove its case—presenting witnesses and physical evidence first. The questioning of each witness typically occurs in three stages: direct examination, cross-examination, and redirect examination. During direct examination, the prosecutor elicits testimony about the facts needed to prove the prosecution's case. The defense attorney may then cross-examine prosecution witnesses, attempting to discredit their testimony or undermine their credibility. Finally, the prosecutor may ask additional questions of its witnesses during redirect examination. These questions may undo damage resulting from an effective cross-examination.

Considerable planning goes into the presentation of the prosecution's case. First, prosecutors must identify the facts that they need to prove to win the case, and, by interviewing prospective witnesses, they must determine who will testify to those facts. Prosecutors usually seek more than one witness for each important fact, because multiple witnesses can corroborate each other's testimony. Next, prosecutors prepare their witnesses to testify by going over what the witness will say. Although they cannot dictate the substance of witnesses' testimony, experienced prosecutors never ask a question on direct examination without knowing beforehand the answer they should receive. They may also coach the witnesses on how to present their stories effectively and on what questions to expect during cross-examination. Finally, prosecutors must determine in what order to present their witnesses to ensure a clear and persuasive case. One manual for trial lawyers describes a jury trial "as a drama, with the jury the audience, the judge the critic (who delivers his reviews during, not after, each scene), and the witnesses the actors. The trial lawyer is the director, producer, and narrator. To reach your audience, you must view each element of the trial for its potential impact on the jury."[31]

The prosecution, like the defense, is governed by rules of evidence that pre-scribe what evidence can be presented and how it can be presented. These rules serve to promote reliable fact-finding by only admitting evidence that is trust-worthy and relevant. For example, the rules of evidence generally exclude hearsay—that is, testimony a witness provides based not on personal knowledge but on what another person has said—because there is no way to test its trust-worthiness through cross-examination. Many rules of evidence are not so clear, however, and the prosecution and defense may differ on whether some testi-mony or physical evidence is admissible. For example, courts usually exclude tes-timony about a victim's sexual history in rape trials because it has no bearing on whether the crime was committed and may prejudice jurors' consideration of the case. But in the period prior to the scheduled opening of the sexual assault trial of Kobe Bryant, defense attorneys and prosecutors sparred over whether the defense could introduce evidence of other sexual encounters by Bryant's accuser. When either side objects to the admission of a piece of evidence, the judge must apply the law of evidence in ruling on the objection. If the defense unsuccessfully objects to the admission of evidence that is then used to secure a conviction, it may appeal the judge's interpretation of the law of evidence. Similarly, the pros-ecution may appeal the exclusion of evidence it deems vital to its case.

Presentation of the Defendant's Case   Once the prosecution has com-pleted the presentation of its case, the defense may introduce its own evidence. In a criminal case, in which the prosecution must prove guilt beyond a reason-able doubt, the defense need not prove its own version of the facts; it need merely create reasonable doubt about the prosecution's version. Skillful defense attorneys will already have begun to sow such doubts during their cross-examination of the prosecution's witnesses and will continue to do so by offering physical evidence, testimony of defense witnesses, or both.

The most difficult question defense attorneys face is whether the defendant should testify. On the one hand, jurors are naturally curious about the defendant's version of events, and a convincing assertion of innocence by the defendant may lead to acquittal. Moreover, despite warnings by the judge that no inferences should be drawn from a defendant's failure to testify, jurors may well expect a defendant to take the stand if he or she is innocent, so the failure to testify could hurt the defendant's chances. On the other hand, a defendant who testifies is subject to cross-examination by the prosecutor, who may expose difficulties with the defendant's story. In addition, the prosecutor can impeach the defendant's credibility by introducing, with certain limitations, evidence of his past criminal record. Thus, the defense attorney must judge, and advise the client on, whether jurors will view the defendant as a truthful witness with a believable story.[32]

In civil cases the plaintiff need merely prove its case by a preponderance of the evidence, so the defense must offer a version of the facts at least as convincing as the plaintiff's account. Therefore, although the process of offering testimony and other evidence is the same in civil cases as in criminal cases, the greater burden on the defense usually requires presentation of a more elaborate case for the defense.

After the defense presents its case, the prosecution may call rebuttal witnesses to attempt to discredit the testimony of defense witnesses or impeach their credibility. The testimony of rebuttal witnesses concludes the presentation of evidence at trial.

Closing Arguments   As the name implies, closing arguments provide attorneys their last chance to sway the jury. An effective closing argument "pulls together the disparate threads of evidence and weaves them into a coherent and compelling whole" that leads to a favorable verdict.[33] Even though rhetorical flourishes and emotional appeals alone are unlikely to win a case, closing arguments offer a unique opportunity for eloquent advocacy, and the most effective attorneys can turn a closing argument into a rhetorical tour de force. But there are limits here as well, and the use of prejudicial material can result in the verdict being overturned on appeal.

In its closing argument the prosecution explains the issues in the case, summarizes the facts as it understands them, and explains why the testimony it presented is more reliable than the conflicting testimony offered by the defense. If the jurors are persuaded by this interpretation of what transpired at the trial, then conviction becomes the obvious and inevitable verdict. In its closing argument, of course, the defense portrays the evidence quite differently, arguing either that the prosecution failed to meet its burden of proof or that the defense's version of events is more persuasive. The party bearing the burden of proof, the prosecution in criminal cases or the plaintiff in civil cases, is allowed to make the final argument to the jury.

Jury Instructions   In a bench trial, the judge decides both questions of fact and questions of law. A jury trial, however, involves a division of labor, with the jury responsible for deciding questions of fact and the judge responsible for determining the law to be applied. Thus, after closing arguments, the judge instructs the jury about the law in the case to guide it in its deliberations. The judge's instructions are written explanations of the law, which the judge reads to the jury in open court. Often the instructions are technical and detailed, and some judges therefore allow the jurors to take a copy of the instructions with them to the jury room.

Instructions to the jury include explanations of general matters, such as the responsibilities of the jury, the evidence it may consider, and the burden of proof to be met in the case. In criminal cases the instructions also include detailed explanations of the specific legal offenses a defendant is charged with and the legal defenses the defendant may have advanced as they apply to the facts of the case. Thus, in a homicide case the instructions might clarify such matters as the distinction between first-degree and second-degree murder, the concept of premeditation, and the legal meaning of self-defense. Finally, the judge instructs the jury about the possible verdicts it might render.

Judges do not draw up these instructions all by themselves. Rather, they rely on attorneys for the parties to draw up the instructions that they wish the jury to receive. The attorneys themselves tend to rely on volumes containing "model jury instructions," which they then tailor to the facts of the case. From the alternative versions of instructions the attorneys submit on each legal issue in the case, the judge selects the instructions that seem most appropriate, modifying them if necessary. An attorney whose version is rejected may base an appeal on that rejection, arguing that the jury was misinformed about the law in the case.

After it hears the judge's instructions, the jury retires to discuss the case. Once it completes its deliberations, the jury communicates its decision to the judge, who announces the verdict. Because the jury is such an important part of the American legal system, it deserves detailed consideration.

THE JURY IN THE UNITED STATES

The Changing Jury

Although the American jury has its roots in the English jury, which originated before the Norman conquest in 1066, it differs from its early counterpart in several respects. Juries in England were initially composed of local residents who had personal knowledge of the dispute at trial. Only gradually did the modern notion develop that the jurors should be disinterested citizens who decide cases solely on the basis of evidence presented at trial. It was also not uncommon in England for judges or political authorities to pressure a jury to reach the verdict they desired. A particularly egregious example occurred in the trial of William Penn in 1670 for unlawful assembly and breach of the peace. When the jurors found Penn not guilty of the charges, the judge refused to accept their verdict and sent them back to deliberate some more. After two-and-a-half days of deliberation without food, water, or chamber pot, the jury still would not convict Penn; so the angry judge fined each of the jurors and kept them in jail until they could pay their fines. This outrageous conduct produced a backlash and effectively ended the practice of coercing juries to reach "correct" verdicts.[34]

A more recent change involves the scope of the jury's responsibilities. Currently in jury trials the judge determines the law and instructs the jury about it, while the jury determines the facts and applies the law to those facts. This division of labor did not develop in the United States until the nineteenth century. Before that, the jury determined both the facts and the law. Although the judge instructed jurors about the law, they remained free to ignore the judge's instructions and render verdicts based on their consciences or their own independent interpretation of the law.[35] Such "jury nullification" undercut unpopular laws by allowing groups of ordinary citizens to decide which laws would be enforced. In the decade preceding independence, for example, juries in the American colonies effectively nullified seditious libel laws (outlawing criticism of the English government) by consistently refusing to convict those charged with violating these laws.

Although the province of the jury diminished when judges were assigned the responsibility to determine the applicable law, the change has not altogether eliminated jury nullification. Community sentiment still may play a part in jury verdicts. During the 1920s, juries often refused to convict ordinary citizens who had run afoul of the Prohibition laws. And throughout the first half of the twentieth century, segregated juries in the South frequently acquitted whites accused of violence against blacks. Yet in refusing to convict those guilty of violating criminal law, contemporary jurors exceed their legal authority, and the recognition of their legal obligation to apply the law may lead jurors to do so even when they disagree with the law.

I have already discussed the greatest change in the American jury during the twentieth century, the creation of more representative juries through the inclusion of previously excluded groups, such as African Americans, Hispanic Americans, and women. Important changes have also occurred in the size and decision rules of juries, and it is to these I now turn.

Jury Size and Jury Decision Making

Quite early in the history of the Anglo-American jury, it was established that juries would include twelve members and would reach their verdicts by unanimous vote. If, after deliberation, the jurors could not agree on a verdict, the judge would rule that the jury was "hung" and dismiss it. If the jury "hung" in a criminal trial, the accused, having been neither convicted nor acquitted, could be tried again for the same offense. Often, however, the prosecution would decline to reinstitute charges after having failed to win a conviction in the first trial.

During the twentieth century, several states sought to reduce the costs of trials and promote efficiency by reducing the size of juries and experimenting with nonunanimous verdicts. When disappointed litigants challenged these experiments as unconstitutional, the Supreme Court for the most part backed the states. In *Williams v. Florida* (1970), the Court ruled that a jury of twelve was not required in state criminal or civil trials, although in 1978 it established a minimum size of six members in state criminal trials.[36] In two cases decided in 1972, *Johnson v. Louisiana* and *Apodaca v. Oregon,* the Court also upheld the use of nonunanimous (9–3) verdicts in criminal cases, although, seven years later, it held that a six-member jury could convict a defendant only by unanimous vote.[37] These rulings have encouraged previously reluctant states to modify their jury systems. Currently, twenty-two states use juries of less than twelve to try civil cases, twenty-four states use them to try misdemeanors, while forty-three states continue to employ twelve-member juries in felony cases.[38]

Critics of the changes in jury size and decision rules have argued that the changes affect jury deliberations and the outcome of cases. A six-member jury is likely to be less diverse and, therefore, less representative of the community than a twelve-member jury. Furthermore, decreasing the size of the jury reduces the likelihood of hung juries because a single juror is unlikely to hold out against group sentiment or to find allies on a six-member jury. Also, when nonunanimous verdicts are permitted, the majority on a jury need not persuade holdouts that the verdict is correct. This not only means that nonunanimous juries are less likely to hang but also that they are less likely to listen carefully to the holdouts' perspectives on the case. Finally, critics argue that nonunanimous juries convict defendants who are not guilty "beyond a reasonable doubt," citing the reluctance of some jurors to convict as conclusive evidence that a reasonable doubt exists.

Empirical studies have largely confirmed these criticisms. They have shown that permitting nonunanimous verdicts reduces the frequency of hung juries in criminal, but not in civil, cases. Studies have also found that twelve-member juries and those deciding unanimously tend to deliberate longer before reaching their verdicts, which may suggest a more thorough consideration of the evidence. Finally, studies have discovered that the variety of viewpoints tends to increase on twelve-member juries; further, on unanimous juries, jurors holding minority viewpoints are more likely to participate actively in discussions and to be listened to than on majority-rule juries.[39]

Evaluating the Jury

As Box 5-3 indicates, there is considerable controversy about whether the jury serves the cause of justice. In England, the birthplace of the modern jury, jury trials have declined in criminal cases and have virtually disappeared in civil cases. In the United States, jury trials have likewise declined, particularly in civil cases, where fewer than one-third of trials are jury trials. Indeed, an appellate court ruled in one civil case that the issues were so complex that a trial by jury would constitute a denial of due process.[40] Underlying this ruling is the belief that ordinary citizens lack the capacity to comprehend highly technical evidence and apply complicated legal standards so as to render decisions in accordance with law. As Box 5-3 indicates, many opponents of the jury system believe that this criticism is equally applicable to jury decision making in ordinary cases. According to these critics, bench trials are preferable to jury trials because judges are better able to understand and evaluate evidence, more knowledgeable about the law, less affected by prejudice and emotion, and therefore, more likely to render law-based decisions.

Do juries, in fact, misunderstand or ignore the law and reach legally indefensible decisions based on prejudice or emotion? The most thorough investigation of this question is *The American Jury,* which compared jury verdicts in more than 3,500 criminal trials and in more than 4,000 civil trials with the verdicts that trial judges would have rendered in bench decisions.[41] This study found that jury decision making was not arbitrary. In more than three-fourths of the criminal and civil trials, the jury and judge agreed on the verdict, suggesting that the jury reached the legally required result. Moreover, in most cases in which trial judges disagreed with jury verdicts, they viewed those disagreements as arising not from jury caprice or incompetence but primarily from different evaluations of the evidence or the defendant. In only 9 percent of the cases did trial judges maintain that the jury's verdict was without legal merit. Subsequent studies have corroborated the conclusion of *The American Jury* that jurors generally follow the law and evidence presented to them in reaching their verdicts.[42]

But if the decisions of judges and juries generally coincide, doesn't it make sense to dispense with jury trials, which may be costly and time-consuming, and allow judges to decide all cases? According to advocates of jury trials, the costs of eliminating trial by jury far outweigh the benefits (see Box 5-3). The jury is valuable, they insist, because it provides one of the few opportunities Americans have to participate directly in government. In addition, analysis of those instances in which the judge and jury disagree suggests that the jury brings a distinctive perspective to the administration of justice. In civil cases, according to *The American Jury,* juries do not consistently favor either the plaintiff or the defendant. However, in criminal cases, juries are more likely to rule in favor of defendants, acquitting them or hanging when the judge would have convicted, or convicting the defendant of a lesser charge. This greater lenience in some instances reflects a willingness to give the benefit of the doubt to defendants without a criminal record and in some instances a rigorous interpretation of the "beyond a reasonable doubt" standard. Jury nullification also plays a role. Jurors sometimes refuse to convict when they disagree with the law

---

Evaluating the Jury

"We have a criminal jury system which is superior to any in the world; and its efficiency is only marred by the difficulty of finding twelve men every day who don't know anything and can't read." (Mark Twain)

"[T]rial by jury is more than an instrument of justice and more than one wheel of the constitution: it is the lamp that shows that freedom lives." (Lord Justice Devlin, English judge)

"[W]hile the jury can contribute nothing of value so far as the law is concerned, it has infinite capacity for mischief, for twelve men can easily misunderstand more law in a minute than the judge can explain in an hour." (Jerome Frank, legal scholar and judge)

"Although jurors are extraordinarily right in their conclusion, it is usually based upon common sense 'instincts' about right and wrong, and not on sophisticated evaluations of complicated testimony. . . . Because judges, sometimes, consciously reject this laymen's approach of who is right or wrong and restrict themselves to the precise legal weights, they come out wrong more often than the juries." (Louis Nizer, defense attorney)

---

or when they believe that defendants have already suffered enough for their wrongdoing.[43]

According to advocates of jury trials, these findings demonstrate the value of the jury as a mechanism for bringing community sentiment to bear and correcting the harshness of the law when it would lead to unjust results. Put differently, the value of the jury lies in its political role. To its critics, however, these findings confirm that the jury system is at odds with the rule of law and substitutes community prejudices for the even-handed administration of justice. One's verdict on the jury thus largely depends on whether one views the infusion of community values into the administration of justice as a positive or a negative phenomenon.

"I submit that the jury is the worst possible enemy of [the] ideal of the 'supremacy of law.' For 'jury-made law' is, par excellence, capricious and arbitrary, yielding the maximum in the way of lack of uniformity and unknowability." (Jerome Frank)

"The jury . . . represents an impressive way of building discretion, equity, and flexibility into a legal system. Not the least of its advantages is that the jury, relieved of the burdens of creating precedent, can bend the law without breaking it." (Harry Kalven and Hans Zeisel, legal scholars)

"Jurymen seldom convict a person they like, or acquit one that they dislike. The main work of a trial lawyer is to make a jury like his client, or, at least to feel sympathy for him; facts regarding the crime are relatively unimportant." (Clarence Darrow, defense attorney)

"The jury contributes most powerfully to form the judgment, and to increase the natural intelligence of a people; and this is, in my opinion, its greatest advantage. It may be regarded as a gratuitous public school ever open, in which every juror learns to exercise his rights. . . . I think that the practical intelligence and political good sense of the Americans are mainly attributable to the long use which they have made of the jury in civil causes." (Alexis de Tocqueville, French commentator on America)

Sources: Mark Twain, quoted in Randolph N. Jonakait, *The American Jury System* (New Haven, CT: Yale University Press, 2003), p. xx; Patrick Devlin, *Trial by Jury* (London: Stevens, 1956) p. 164; *Skidmore v. Baltimore & Ohio Railroad*, 167 F.2d 54 (2d Cir. 1948); Louis Nizer, *My Life in Court* (New York: Jove, 1978), p. 359; Jerome Frank, *Courts on Trial: Myth and Reality in American Justice* (Princeton, NJ: Princeton University Press, 1949), p. 132; Harry Kalven, Jr. and Hans Zeisel, *The American Jury* (Boston: Little Brown, 1966), p. 498; Clarence Darrow, quoted in Valerie P. Hans and Neil Vidmar, *Judging the Jury* (New York: Plenum Press, 1986), p. 131; Alexis de Tocqueville, *Democracy in America*, ed. Richard D. Heffner (New York: New American Library, 1956), p. 128.

APPEALS

The Appellate Process

In the United States, after trial courts render their decisions, dissatisfied litigants are entitled to one appeal. Fewer than 10 percent of state trial court decisions and roughly 13 percent of federal district court rulings are appealed.[44] The appellate court's main job is error correction—that is, ensuring that the law was correctly interpreted and applied at trial. After a first-level appellate court (such as a federal court of appeals or a state intermediate court of appeals) rules on their cases, litigants may appeal those decisions as well. However, the second-level appellate court typically has some discretion over whether it will hear the case. For cases that fall within the jurisdiction of the federal courts, the final resort for litigants is the U.S. Supreme Court. For cases that do not, the final appeal is to the state's supreme court.

Appellate courts differ among themselves in terms of:

1. Agenda setting. To what extent do legal guidelines determine what cases a court must decide, and to what extent does the court exercise discretion in deciding what cases to hear?
2. Information gathering. How does the court secure the information it needs about the facts of the case, the applicable law, and the likely consequences of its decisions?
3. Decision making. What is the process by which the members of the court resolve their differences and reach decisions?
4. Promulgating decisions. How does the court convey its decisions to litigants and the general public?

Rather than considering in detail how all appellate courts deal with these matters, I will focus on the operations of the U.S. Supreme Court and then compare that court with other appellate courts in the United States.

The U.S. Supreme Court

Agenda Setting

The Cases   Each year the Supreme Court receives more than 7,000 petitions for review, the vast majority of them appealing rulings of federal courts of appeals or state supreme courts. Litigants who cannot afford the costs of an appeal (like Clarence Gideon, whose case is discussed in Chapter 2) can file their petitions "in forma pauperis" (literally, "in the manner of a pauper"), and the Court will waive fees and other costs. In recent years, the Court has accepted fewer than 100 cases annually—less than 3 percent of the cases it receives on appeal—for oral argument and decision. Over the course of the twentieth century, Congress has gradually expanded the justices' control over their agenda. Today, the justices exercise virtually total discretion in deciding which appeals to hear and which to reject.

Of course, like other courts, the Supreme Court operates within legal constraints. It can only rule on cases that fall within its jurisdiction. In addition, the justices cannot address an issue unless a litigant brings it before them. Thus, the pool of cases from which the justices select is outside their direct control. Despite these constraints, the Court does have the opportunity, as a matter of course, to address most of the important political issues of the day. As Alexis de Tocqueville observed 170 years ago, "there is hardly a political question in the United States which does not sooner or later turn into a judicial one."[45]

Ultimately, the cases appealed to the Court tend to reflect the political concerns of the era. Over the last decade, for example, the Court confronted such contentious political issues as the rights of accused terrorists, abortion, affirmative action, and the use of racial factors in electoral districting. Indeed, groups may seek to shape the political agenda of their era by bringing their concerns before the Court. Examples include the NAACP's campaign against racial segregation from the 1930s to the 1950s, efforts of Legal Services lawyers to establish new rights for the poor in the late 1960s and the 1970s, and attempts of right-to-life groups to overturn the Court's abortion rulings during the 1980s and 1990s.

By their decisions, the justices may also influence the pool of cases brought before them. An extreme example occurred in the Supreme Court's flag-salute cases. In 1940, the Court had ruled that states could require public school students to salute the American flag, notwithstanding their religious objections to the practice. Two years later, however, three members of the Court majority used the occasion of an unrelated case to admit that they had erred and to repudiate their votes. This admission, along with personnel changes on the Court, invited new litigation, and the Court overruled its earlier flag-salute decision only three years after it was rendered.[46]

Generally, the Court's influence on the types of cases appealed to it is less direct. If the justices reveal a willingness to entertain a type of claim, then litigants are encouraged to bring cases to the Court that raise such claims. During the 1960s, the Court's receptivity to the rights claims of criminal defendants prompted a proliferation of claims by those who sought to overturn their convictions. More recently, after the Court indicated in 1989 that it would reconsider its position on abortion, several cases were initiated to provide a vehicle for the Court to overrule *Roe v. Wade*.[47] Conversely, if the Court consistently rejects certain types of legal claims, litigants will be reluctant to bring such claims before the Court. Thus, the Court's tendency to read defendants' rights narrowly during the 1980s and 1990s has discouraged some defendants from appealing their cases to the Court.

Finally, at times the Court purposely announces rulings that leave important questions unresolved. In such circumstances, the justices can expect litigants to raise those questions in the lower courts and to appeal adverse rulings to the Supreme Court. This allows the Court to address those unresolved questions at a later date, with their judgment illuminated by the opinions of the lower court judges who have already confronted those questions. A prime example involves police interrogations. In *Escobedo v. Illinois* (1964), the Court ruled that police could not deny an accused person access to his attorney during a police interrogation.[48] But the ruling in *Escobedo* did not indicate whether the accused had to request an attorney, whether the police could delay granting access to one, or whether they had to provide one for indigent persons. Over a period of 18 months, 150 cases raising *Escobedo*-type issues were appealed to the Court.[49] In 1966, the Court resolved most of those issues with its decision

---

BOX

5-4   *Law Clerks*

Imagine being a recent law-school graduate and yet drafting judicial opinions for the U.S. Supreme Court. Farfetched as this may sound, drafting
opinions would likely be one of your responsibilities if you were one of the
elite group of young lawyers chosen annually to clerk for the justices of the
Supreme Court. This does not mean, of course, that the clerks determine
how the Court decides. As Chief Justice William Rehnquist has noted,
they are not "legal Rasputins," manipulating the justices to advance their
own legal or policy goals. Nevertheless, working under the close supervision of the justice who selected them, law clerks do play a crucial role in
the operations of the Supreme Court.

The first Supreme Court justice to hire a law clerk was Justice
Horace Gray, who initiated the practice while a member of the Supreme
Judicial Court of Massachusetts and brought his clerk with him when
appointed to the Supreme Court in 1882. Gray's successor on the Court,
Oliver Wendell Holmes, continued the practice, and gradually other justices followed their lead. Today, each justice chooses four clerks each year
to assist with his or her work. The clerks are truly a select group. Typically, they include the top graduates of major law schools. For a long time,
Harvard and Yale dominated, but in recent years other law schools have
contributed their share. The clerks usually come to the Court with the
experience of a year's clerkship for another judge, most often on a court
of appeals. The justices are free, however, to employ their own criteria in
selecting their clerks, and some have been partial to clerks from their
own region or law school. For example, Justice William O. Douglas, a
native of Washington, characteristically chose Westerners as his clerks.

Because the clerks are to assist the justices, each justice determines
the tasks his clerks will perform. Justice Gray, for example, asked his
clerk's advice in picking out a ring when he became engaged at age 60,
and Justice Hugo Black required his clerks to play tennis with him.

---

in *Miranda v. Arizona,* which outlined the warnings that had to be given before
police interrogations.[50]

The Process of Case Selection   The process by which the justices select cases
for review begins with the party appealing the lower court's decision petitioning the Court for a writ of *certiorari* (from the Latin, "made more certain"),

However, almost all clerks share certain common tasks. The clerks assist their justice first of all in reviewing the petitions for certiorari, drafting memos that detail the issues and legal arguments in each case, and recommending whether certiorari should be granted. Or, if their justice belongs to the "cert pool," the clerks prepare memos on their assigned cases that are then circulated to all the justices participating in the pool. The limited data available suggest that the justices usually go along with their clerks' recommendations, perhaps because the recommendations take into account the perspectives of the justice to whom they are addressed. Justice John Paul Stevens has underscored the importance of the clerks' work in screening petitions for review, noting, "I don't even look at the papers in over 80 percent of the cases that are filed."

Clerks also participate in preparing opinions. Although the justices differ in the responsibilities they assign their clerks, all clerks conduct legal research for their justices. Some do little actual writing (one of Justice Felix Frankfurter's clerks said that the justice wrote the opinion, and he wrote the footnotes). Most justices, however, allow their clerks to prepare rough drafts along lines dictated by the justice. The justice will then revise the draft before circulating it to other members of the Court, whose comments will lead to further revisions. The opinion that is eventually published may bear little resemblance to the draft the clerk prepared. Finally, some clerks serve as "sounding boards" for their justices, providing them with opportunities to discuss the issues in the cases they are deciding. Justice Lewis Powell, for example, reputedly chose clerks whose views were more liberal than his own to ensure that he confronted the arguments against his own conservative proclivities. Although justices could conceivably be swayed by the arguments of their clerks, this probably does not happen often. The justices have enough political experience to have become used to working with a staff without being dominated by it. In addition, the clerks themselves are transients; with rare exceptions, they serve for only a single year.

Sources: David O'Brien, *Storm Center*, 5th ed. (New York: Norton, 1999); William H. Rehnquist, *The Supreme Court*, 2d ed. (New York: Knopf, 2001); Joan Biskupic and Elder Witt, *Guide to the U.S. Supreme Court*, 3d ed. (Washington, DC: Congressional Quarterly Press, 1997); and David Crump, "Law Clerks: Their Roles and Relationships with Their Judges," *Judicature* 69 (December–January 1986): 236–240.

asking that the Court hear the case. The various justices, in conjunction with their law clerks (see Box 5-4), review the petitions and individually determine which cases they believe merit consideration. The chief justice prepares and circulates a "discuss list," which includes the cases he believes warrant collective consideration, and other justices may add cases to the list. Unless a justice requests that a petition be discussed in conference, the petition is automatically denied. More than 70 percent of all petitions for certiorari are thereby disposed of before conference.

Collective consideration of the petitions on the discussion list begins at the three- to four-day conference held before the beginning of the Court's term in October. During this conference, which like all the Court's conferences is attended only by the justices themselves, the justices screen the large number of petitions for certiorari that have accumulated over the preceding summer. At weekly Friday conferences held throughout the Court's term, justices continue their screening. If four justices vote to hear a case (the so-called Rule of Four), it is accepted for review and scheduled for oral argument. If fewer than four justices favor review, the petition for certiorari is denied, and the decision of the lower court stands.

Criteria for Case Selection   It is difficult to determine the factors that influence the justices' decisions to grant or deny review, because the justices neither publish nor explain their votes. The Court's own Rule 10, "Considerations Governing Review on Certiorari," offers some guidance (see Box 5-5), but the justices can grant review when the listed factors are absent or deny review even when they are present. To some extent the criteria used in voting on certiorari petitions may be idiosyncratic, varying from justice to justice and even from case to case. Thus, Chief Justice Earl Warren asserted that the standards governing the justices' determinations "cannot be captured in any rule or guideline that would be meaningful."[51] Nonetheless, some general observations are possible.

First, the Court accepts cases that involve political disputes of national import. Thus, during the Korean War it ruled on the constitutionality of President Truman's seizure and operation of the nation's steel mills; and during the Watergate scandal of the early 1970s, it reviewed a challenge to President Nixon's claim that he could withhold incriminating tape recordings from a special prosecutor.[52] More recently, the Court resolved a dispute over election returns in Florida that in effect determined the outcome of the 2000 presidential election.[53] Nevertheless, the Court tends to avoid becoming embroiled in political disputes that it feels it cannot resolve. For example, it refused to hear several challenges to the constitutionality of the Vietnam War.[54] Moreover, it may postpone consideration of sensitive issues to avoid losing public support. Thus, after the Court had angered many white Southerners by invalidating state laws mandating racial segregation in public schools, it refused for more than a decade to consider challenges to state laws banning racial intermarriage.[55]

Some political scientists have suggested that the Court's decisions on whether to grant certiorari can be predicted on the basis of certain "cues" that trigger review.[56] Underlying this theory is the assumption that, faced with a

> **BOX**
> **5-5**   *Rule 10: Considerations Governing*
>   *Review on Certiorari*
>
> 1. A review on writ of certiorari is not a matter of right, but of judicial discretion, and will be granted only when there are special and important reasons therefor. The following, while neither controlling nor fully measuring the Court's discretion, indicate the character of reasons that will be considered:
>
>   (a) When a federal court of appeals has rendered a decision in conflict with the decision of another federal court of appeals on the same matter. . . .
>
>   (b) When a state court of last resort has decided a federal question in a way in conflict with the decision of another state court of last resort or of a federal court of appeals.
>
>   (c) When a state court of last resort or a federal court of appeals has decided an important question of federal law which has not, but should be, settled by this Court, or has decided a federal question in a way in conflict with applicable decisions of this Court.
>
> 2. The same general considerations outlined above will control in respect of petitions for writs of certiorari to review judgments of the Court of Claims, of the Court of Customs and Patent Appeals, and of any other court whose judgments are reviewable by law on writ of certiorari.

deluge of petitions for review, the justices and their clerks develop shortcuts to identify meritorious cases. In recent years, the most important cue seems to be whether the party seeking review is the federal government. Other relevant cues include conflict between a lower court decision and a Supreme Court precedent, conflict between circuits on a matter of federal law, and the presence of a civil liberties issue. When several of these cues are present in a single case, the likelihood of Supreme Court review increases. Although the research may account for patterns in the Court's agenda setting, it cannot explain the Court's decision to hear or not hear a particular case. Moreover, the theory must be continually updated because the cues that are important change in response to changes in the membership and orientation of the Court.

Other scholars have concluded that the justices' votes on certiorari reflect strategic considerations. Their votes to hear cases or to deny certiorari are designed to advance their views on constitutional policy.[57] Two considerations are involved: the justices' perception of whether the lower court decided the case correctly, and their perception of how the Supreme Court is likely to rule on the case. Thus, justices may vote for review when they disagree with a lower court's ruling in order to "correct" the perceived error and establish precedent that reorients lower court decisions. But justices may vote against granting certiorari despite disagreeing with a lower court's ruling if they believe that the Court will affirm the lower court. As one justice explained, the concern in such circumstances is damage control: "I might think the Nebraska Supreme Court made a horrible decision, but I wouldn't want to take the case, for if we take the case and affirm it, then it would become a precedent."[58] Interviews with the justices suggest, however, that legal considerations—conflicts among the circuits, the *legal* importance of the issue—also figure heavily in the justices' votes on certiorari.[59] In sum, it appears that the legal or political importance of the issue, the lower courts' rulings on the issue, the parties to the case, and the justices' own policy views all figure into the decision to grant or deny certiorari.

Information Gathering   To decide a case, the Supreme Court needs information about the facts, the applicable law, and the likely consequences of its decision. Under our adversary system the justices look to the litigants in the case for much of this information. The attorneys for each party file legal briefs and then argue the case orally before the justices. Other groups interested in the outcome of the case may, with the Court's permission, also submit legal briefs—called *amicus curiae* (literally, "friend of the court") briefs. Finally, the justices can rely on the record of proceedings and the opinions of the lower courts.

Legal Briefs   Legal briefs are first and foremost partisan documents, designed to persuade the Court to rule in favor of one's client or position. This persuasion takes the form of marshaling and interpreting pertinent legal materials (precedents, statutes, constitutional provisions) and factual information in a manner that favors one's client and supports one's position.

For amicus curiae briefs as well as for briefs submitted by the litigants, the goal is to gain a favorable ruling. Typically, those who file amicus briefs are more interested in the constitutional issue raised by the case than in the fate of particular litigants. Some organizations file amicus briefs out of concern for the effects the Court's decision might have on them or their members. Twenty-seven states, for example, submitted a brief in *Miranda v. Arizona* urging the Court not to get involved in setting standards for police interrogations. For other groups the concern is primarily ideological. Thus, the American Civil Liberties Union, a group committed to a broad interpretation of constitutional rights, also filed a brief in *Miranda* urging the Court to extend the rights of the accused. Some groups file amicus briefs to signal the Court that their members care about the issue. Finally, on occasion groups file amicus briefs because they lack confidence in the lawyer arguing the case and hope to win the case through the arguments advanced in their briefs.[60]

Oral Argument   During oral argument, the attorneys for each party have their final opportunity to influence the Court's ruling. Early in the nation's history, when the Court's docket was less crowded, the oral argument in a case could extend over several days, and the flowery oratory of the attorneys attracted large audiences. Daniel Webster is actually reputed to have moved those in the Court to tears as he concluded his argument in *Dartmouth College v. Woodward*.[61] As the demands on the Court's time have increased, it has gradually cut back on the time available to each party for oral argument. Since 1970, the Court has limited arguments to thirty minutes for each side except in those rare circumstances in which the importance and complexity of a case justified additional time.

Lawyers soon discover that oral argument is not an opportunity to make a set speech. The justices pepper the attorneys with questions, testing the soundness of the legal positions they are advancing. These questions frequently force attorneys to confront weaknesses in their arguments or to clarify the implications of the positions they are urging on the Court. For an ill-prepared attorney, the half-hour may seem a lifetime. Although oral argument can be a harrowing experience, it also provides a unique opportunity. As Chief Justice William Rehnquist has observed, "it is the only time before conference discussion of the case later in the week when all of the judges are expected to sit on the bench and concentrate on one particular case."[62]

Does oral argument make a difference? Most justices insist that it does. According to Justice Antonin Scalia, "things can be put in perspective during oral argument in a way that they can't in a written brief."[63] In response to the justices' questions attorneys can correct misunderstandings, demonstrate unappreciated strengths in their positions, and remove obstacles to the justices voting for their clients. Indeed, Justice John Marshall Harlan concluded that oral argument "may in many cases make the difference between winning and losing, no matter how good the briefs are."[64]

Decision Making   During the Court's term, the justices meet in conference twice a week to consider the cases that have been argued. Only the justices are present at these conferences. On Wednesday afternoons, they discuss and vote on the four cases argued the previous Monday, and on Fridays the justices consider the cases argued on Tuesday and Wednesday. The chief justice begins the discussion of each case by summarizing the facts and legal arguments and offering his own views on how it should be decided. The senior associate justice then explains his views, and the remaining justices follow in order of seniority. By the time their turns arrive, the most junior justices may have little new to offer other than their votes. When all the justices have spoken, the chief justice tabulates the justices' votes and announces the Court's tentative decision.

These deliberations have little of the sharp give-and-take characteristic of legislative debate. In fact, according to Chief Justice Rehnquist, there is surprisingly little interplay among the justices at conference, and Justice William Douglas observed that conference discussions rarely changed a justice's view of the case.[65] This may reflect the format for discussion: Allowing each justice to express his or her views without interruption is hardly conducive to lively debate.

In contrast with legislators, the justices have only limited means to influence the votes of fellow justices. Judicial ethics prevent them from offering to trade votes to gain support on issues of importance to them. And, given judicial independence, justices cannot bring outside pressures to bear on their colleagues. Thus, their main source of influence is the quality of the arguments that they can marshal. If the chief justice is also the intellectual leader of the Court, then his power to frame the issues—and thereby direct the course of debate—can give him some advantage. Thus, according to Justice Felix Frankfurter, Chief Justice Charles Evans Hughes "radiated authority," and the other justices did not venture an opinion after the chief justice had spoken unless they were sure they knew what they were talking about.[66] An associate justice also may exhibit the intellectual acuity and force of personality necessary to assume a leadership role on the Court, as Justice William Brennan did during the 1960s and 1970s. Still, it is difficult to present a fully developed argument on complex legal issues orally, and it is certainly difficult to follow such an argument. Thus, intellectual leadership on the Court is likely to manifest itself more in written opinions than in debate during conference.

Once the Court has reached its tentative decision on a case (the vote in conference is tentative because justices can change their minds up to the time that the decision is announced), a justice is assigned to write the opinion of the Court. If the chief justice has voted with the majority, then he assigns the opinion of the Court to himself or to another member of the majority coalition. When the case is a momentous one, the chief justice typically assigns himself the opinion, as Chief Justice Warren did in *Brown v. Board of Education* and as Chief Justice Burger did in *United States v. Nixon.* If the chief justice is in dissent, then the senior associate justice aligned with the majority assigns the opinion of the Court. Other justices, of course, remain free to write concurring or dissenting opinions.

Writing opinions is a long and difficult process. Most justices permit their clerks to draft the initial version of opinions, along lines specified by the justice. Once the justice has made whatever changes seem appropriate, the draft opinion is circulated among the justices. Other justices may also circulate concurring and dissenting opinions at this time, seeking support for their views. The justices carefully scrutinize the opinions that are circulated and often return them with requests for changes, sometimes making such changes a condition for joining the opinion. Particularly crucial are the negotiations over the opinion of the Court, because the justice assigned the opinion must craft an opinion that can gain the support of five justices. Often an opinion goes through several drafts before it is accepted. Justice William Brennan once circulated ten versions of an opinion before it became the opinion of the Court.[67] Sometimes deep-seated divisions prevent a majority of justices from coalescing behind a single opinion. In *Webster v. Reproductive Health Services,* for example, a majority of five justices upheld various state restrictions on abortions, but Justices Antonin Scalia and Sandra Day O'Connor refused to join Chief Justice Rehnquist's opinion and filed separate concurring opinions. When no opinion commands a majority of the Court, it complicates the efforts of lower court judges to determine the exact meaning of the Court's ruling.

The opinion writing phase provides an opportunity for further consideration of cases, and justices may change their votes after reading the draft opinions. Indeed, on several occasions justices assigned to write the opinion of the Court have reported back that additional research had led them to change their votes. In a closely divided court, defection by a single justice can produce a new majority and, with it, a different decision. According to one study of a ten-year period, the justices' final votes differed from those in conference 9 percent of the time. In most instances, however, the changes served to increase the size of the Court majority rather than to create a new majority, because justices merely refrained from dissenting.[68]

Even if no votes change, the opinion writing phase is crucial. The Court's decisions have a dual aspect, resolving particular disputes and announcing legal standards to be applied in future cases. Often the grounds on which the Court decides, or the breadth of the legal principles it announces, is as important as the vote itself. In *Miranda v. Arizona,* for example, the Court not only overturned Miranda's conviction but also used the case to establish standards governing all future police interrogations. By framing the opinion this way, the Court ensured that its decision would have a broad effect. In contrast, in *Webster v. Reproductive Health Services* the justices upheld state restrictions on abortion but decided on narrow grounds so as to avoid directly overruling *Roe v. Wade,* which established a constitutional right to abortion. By leaving open the question of whether *Roe* remained a viable precedent, the Court encouraged further litigation on the issue.

Promulgating Decisions   A term of the Supreme Court follows a predictable pattern. Oral argument commences immediately on the first Monday in October, but because preparing opinions is time-consuming, the Court does not begin announcing decisions immediately. Early in the term, it follows the traditional practice of announcing its decisions on Mondays ("decision Mondays"). As the term rushes toward its conclusion, the increasing number of decided cases leads the Court to announce its decisions on other days as well. By the conclusion of the Court's term in late June or early July, it will have decided and written opinions in nearly 100 cases.

The Court jealously guards the secrecy of its decisions. Once the opinions in a case are written, they go to the print shop in the basement of the Court, which prepares copies for transmission to reporters and the general public. In the print shop each copy of an opinion is numbered to prevent any from being removed from the premises. "Leaks" are rare; reporters at the Court are not even informed ahead of time which decisions the justices will announce that day.

The Court announces its decisions in open court. Usually, the justice who wrote the opinion of the Court announces the decision, and justices who filed concurring or dissenting opinions may also state their views. When several decisions are handed down on the same day, the justices delivering the opinions of the Court do so in reverse order of seniority. In the past, justices used to read their full opinions from the bench, but time pressures have eliminated that practice. Still, justices may occasionally read portions of their opinions or offer extemporaneous remarks about a case. Dissenting in one contentious case, Justice James McReynolds hit the bench with his fist, exclaiming, "The Constitution is gone!"[69]

While the justices are announcing the Court's decisions, the Court's press office releases copies of the opinions to reporters. Although most members of the general public will get their notions of the Court's rulings from the news stories the reporters file, the Court's opinions are available from a variety of other sources. The official source for the Court's rulings is *United States Reports,* a set of bound volumes containing all the Court's opinions and other actions. Cornell Law School offers a free e-mail subscription service that sends summaries of Court rulings on the day that they are announced, and various organizations maintain Web sites that provide the full opinions on current cases (see "For Further Reading" for a listing of pertinent sites).

Other Appellate Courts

Agenda Setting   The U.S. Supreme Court's power to decide which cases it will hear distinguishes it from most other appellate courts. First-level appellate courts, such as federal courts of appeals and state intermediate appellate courts, have no control over their dockets. Because all litigants are entitled to one appeal, these first-level appellate courts must hear whatever cases are brought before them. Most second-level appellate courts, such as state supreme courts, also have only limited control over their dockets. Statutes or constitutional provisions in most states mandate that their supreme courts hear certain types of appeals. States with the death penalty, for instance, generally require their supreme court review convictions in all cases in which the defendant has been sentenced to death. Beyond that, the states vary in the mandatory jurisdiction they assign to their supreme courts, although only about 15 percent of all appeals are mandatory. These constitutional or statutory mandates increase the caseloads of state supreme courts—most hear many more cases per year than the U.S. Supreme Court—and may burden them with cases of little legal importance.

Information Gathering   As previously discussed, the U.S. Supreme Court obtains information for its decision making from the briefs of the parties in the case, amicus curiae briefs, and oral argument. But amicus curiae briefs are less often filed in cases before other appellate courts because the appeals raise issues of interest solely to the parties, without the broad legal significance that attracts groups to a case. Other appellate courts also rely less heavily on oral argument. Indeed, some dispense with it altogether or reserve it for complex or important cases. As a result, the lower-level appellate courts decide most appeals on the basis of the briefs of the parties and the lower court record.

Decision Making   Because all appellate courts are multimember courts, appellate decision making necessarily has a group dimension. The process of decision making on many appellate courts resembles that on the U.S. Supreme Court; that is, the judges meet in conference, and the writing of the opinion of the court is assigned to a member of the majority coalition following the vote in conference. A few state appellate courts rotate opinion assignments, so that a judge is assigned the opinion in a case even before it is argued. Under this system, the judge assigned the opinion tends to be far more knowledgeable about the case than his or her colleagues, and they therefore tend to defer to the assigned judge's view of how it should be decided.

When cases merely resolve disputes between the contending parties and have no broader legal significance, some appellate courts do not issue opinions but merely announce their decisions. When they are published, most appellate court opinions are shorter than those authored by Supreme Court justices. Judges on other appellate courts also tend to file fewer concurring or dissenting opinions. Federal courts of appeals decide most cases in three-judge panels, and dissents occur in less than 10 percent of the decisions. Most state supreme courts report dissents in less than a quarter of the cases they decide, but dissent levels vary considerably from court to court. On some courts dissent is rare, perhaps because of a tradition of unanimity, a homogeneous group of judges, or the routine character of the cases they decide. Thus, the Alabama Supreme Court until recently had dissents filed in fewer than 5 percent of its cases. On other courts—for example, the Ohio Supreme Court—dissent is an established tradition, occurring in roughly half the cases.[70]

Promulgating Decisions   Few decisions of state appellate courts and lower federal courts attract the sort of public attention that is given to Supreme Court rulings. Indeed, some are of such minimal interest even to the legal profession that the court merely announces its decision without writing an opinion in the case.

Written opinions for decisions in federal court of appeals cases can be found in the *Federal Reporter* series. Many states publish important state appellate rulings in their own state reporter series. Other states rely on the privately published *National Reporter* series, which groups the decisions of state appellate courts in regional reporters. The *Southeastern Reporter*, for example, includes state appellate rulings from West Virginia, Virginia, North Carolina, South Carolina, and Georgia.

BEYOND TRIALS AND APPEALS

This chapter examined the conduct of trials and the review of trial court rulings by appellate courts. Important as these processes are, they comprise only a small portion of the activities of U.S. courts. Appellate courts can review lower court rulings only if litigants appeal those rulings, and most litigants do not appeal. Trial courts can conduct trials only when there is an ongoing dispute between two parties. In criminal cases, however, most defendants plead guilty before trial, and, in the vast majority of civil cases, parties settle rather than go to trial. Thus, a complete understanding of court operations requires looking beyond the formal processes of trial and appeal. This is the project of the next two chapters.

NOTES

1. This account of the von Bulow case relies on Alan M. Dershowitz, *Reversal of Fortune* (New York: Random House, 1986), and William Wright, *The von Bulow Affair* (New York: Delacorte, 1983). A film about the case, *Reversal of Fortune*, was based on the Dershowitz book.

2. Quoted in Dershowitz, *Reversal of Fortune*, p. xvii.

3. Quoted in Wright, *The von Bulow Affair*, p. 354.

4. Robert Mnookin and Lewis Kornhauser, "Bargaining in the Shadow of the Law: The Case of Divorce," *Yale Law Journal* 88 (1979): 950–997.

5. Lawrence M. Friedman, *A History of American Law*, 2d ed. (New York: Simon & Schuster, 1985), p. 576.

6. Stephen J. Schulhofer, "Is Plea Bargaining Inevitable?" *Harvard Law Review* 97 (March 1984): 1096.

7. Barbara Yngvesson and Patricia Hennessey, "Small Claims, Complex Disputes: A Review of the Small Claims Literature," *Law and Society Review* 9 (winter 1975): 219–274.

8. *Joint Anti-Fascist Refugee Committee v. McGrath,* 341 U.S. 123, 162 (1951).

9. *Duncan v. Louisiana,* 391 U.S. 145, 156 (1968).

10. *Duncan v. Louisiana,* 391 U.S. 145 (1968); *Baldwin v. New York,* 399 U.S. 66 (1970).

11. *Gideon v. Wainwright,* 372 U.S. 335, 348 (1963).

12. Supreme Court rulings extending the right to counsel in criminal cases are *Johnson .v. Zerbst,* 304 U.S. 458 (1938); *Gideon v. Wainwright,* 372 U.S. 335 (1963); and *Argersinger v. Hamlin,* 407 U.S. 25 (1972). The details of the *Gideon* case are presented in Chapter 2. Among state rulings that extended the right to counsel under state law are *Carpenter v. Dane,* 9 Wis. 249 (1859), and *Cogdill v. State,* 246 S.W.2d 5 (Tenn. 1951).

13. *Lassiter v. Department of Social Services of Durham, N.C.,* 452 U.S. 18 (1981).

14. *Maryland v. Craig,* 497 U.S. 836 (1990).

15. *In re Winship,* 397 U.S. 358 (1970).

16. *Griffin v. California,* 380 U.S. 609 (1965).

17. *Baldwin v. New York,* 399 U.S. 66 (1970).

18. *Blanton v. City of North Las Vegas,* 489 U.S. 538 (1989).

19. Jon M. Van Dyke, *Jury Selection Procedures* (Cambridge, MA: Ballinger, 1977), p. 180.

20. Pertinent cases include *Batson v. Kentucky,* 476 U.S. 79 (1986); *Powers v. Ohio,* 499 U.S. 400 (1991); *Edmonson v. Leesville Concrete Co.,* 500 U.S. 614 (1991); *Georgia v. McCollum,* 505 U.S. 42 (1992); and *J.E.B. v. Alabama ex rel. T.B.,* 511 U.S. 127 (1994).

21. Van Dyke, *Jury Selection Procedures,* appendix D, p. 282.

22. Ibid., pp. 282–284.

23. Jeffrey Toobin, *The Run of His Life: The People vs. O. J. Simpson* (New York: Random House, 1996), pp. 196–197.

24. This analysis derives from Gordon Bermant and John Shapard, "The Voir Dire Examination, Juror Challenges, and Adversary Advocacy," in *The Trial Process,* ed. Bruce D. Sales (New York: Plenum Press, 1981), and Valerie P. Hans and Neil Vidmar, *Judging the Jury* (New York: Plenum Press, 1986), chap. 5.

25. Darrow's remarks are recounted in Stephen J. Adler, *The Jury: Trial and Error in the American Courtroom* (New York: Random House, 1994), pp. 53–54.

26. Spence's views are summarized in Adler, *The Jury,* p. 55.

27. See Hans and Vidmar, *Judging the Jury,* chap. 6.

28. See Jeffrey Abramson, *We, the Jury: The Jury System and the Ideal of Democracy* (New York: Basic Books, 1994), chap. 4; and Randolph N. Jonakait, *The American Jury System* (New Haven, CT: Yale University Press, 2003), pp. 157–164.

29. Maxwell M. Blecher and Robert M. Lindquist, "Opening Statements," in *Civil Trial Practice: Strategies and Techniques,* ed. William A. Masterson (New York: Practicing Law Institute, 1986), p. 115. See also E. Allen Lind and Gina Y. Ke, "Opening and Closing Statements," in *The Psychology of Evidence and Trial Procedure,* ed. Saul M. Kassin and Lawrence S. Wrightsman (Beverly Hills, CA: Sage Publications, 1985), pp. 232–233.

30. Lind and Ke, "Opening and Closing Statements," p. 234.

31. Jerold S. Solovy and Robert L. Byman, "Direct Examination," in Masterson, *Civil Trial Practice,* p. 134.

32. David W. Neubauer, *Judicial Process: Law, Courts, and Politics in the United States* (Pacific Grove, CA: Brooks/Cole, 1991), pp. 318–320.

33. Paul A. Renne, "Final Argument," in Masterson, *Civil Trial Practice,* p. 293.

34. Valerie P. Hans and Neil Vidmar, *Judging the Jury* (New York: Plenum Press, 1986), pp. 21–22, and Paula DiPerna, *Juries on Trial* (New York: Dembner Books, 1984), p. 28.

35. Gary J. Jacobsohn, "Citizen Participation in Policy-Making: The Role of the Jury," *Journal of Politics* 39 (February 1977): 73–96, and Hans and Vidmar, *Judging the Jury,* pp. 31–37.

36. *Williams v. Florida,* 390 U.S. 78 (1970); *Ballew v. Georgia,* 435 U.S. 223 (1978). In federal courts twelve-member juries are required in criminal cases, and no less than six-member juries in civil cases. See *Thompson v. Utah,* 170 U.S. 343 (1898), and *Colegrove v. Battin,* 413 U.S. 149 (1973).

37. *Johnson v. Louisiana,* 406 U.S. 356 (1972); *Apodaca v. Oregon,* 406 U.S. 404 (1972); *Burch v. Louisiana,* 441 U.S. 130 (1979). Under rules for federal courts established by the Supreme Court, all verdicts in federal cases must be unanimous.

38. DiPerna, *Juries on Trial,* pp. 70–71.

39. Major social science studies of the effects of jury size and decision rules, many of them quite critical of the Supreme Court's rulings, include Jonakait, *The American Jury System*; Reid Hastie, Steven D. Penrod, and Nancy Pennington, *Inside the Jury* (Cambridge, MA: Harvard University Press, 1983); Hans Zeisel, ". . . And Then There Were None: The Diminution of the Federal Jury," *University of Chicago Law Review* 38 (1971): 710–724; Hans Zeisel and Shari Diamond, "Convincing Empirical Evidence on the Six Member Jury," *University of Chicago Law Review* 41 (1974): 281–295; Robert Roper, "Jury Size: Impact on Verdict's Correctness," *American Politics Quarterly* 7 (1979): 438–452; and C. Nemeth, "Interactions between Jurors as a Function of Majority vs. Unanimity Decision Rules," *Journal of Applied Social Psychology* 7 (1977): 38–56.

40. *In re Japanese Products Antitrust Litigation,* 631 F.2d 1069, 1084 (3d Cir. 1980). For analyses of jury performance in complex litigation, see Arthur D. Austin, *Complex Litigation Confronts the Jury System: A Case Study* (Frederick, MD: University Publications of America, 1984); Molly Selvin and Larry Picus, *The Debate over Jury Performance: Observations from a Recent Asbestos Case* (Santa Monica, CA: Rand Corporation, 1987); and Peter Sperlich, "The Case for Preserving Trial by Jury in Complex Litigation," *Judicature* 65 (March–April 1982): 395–419.

41. Harry Kalven Jr. and Hans Zeisel, *The American Jury* (Boston: Little Brown, 1966).

42. This research is discussed in Hans and Vidmar, *Judging the Jury,* chap. 8–10.

43. Kalven and Zeisel, *The American Jury,* chap. 5–6 and 18–22.

44. The percentage of rulings by federal district courts that are appealed to federal courts of appeals is computed from *Annual Report of the Director of the Administrative Office of the United States Courts 2002,* available online at www.uscourts.gov. The percentage of state trial court rulings that are appealed is drawn from *State Court Caseload Statistics, 2003,* available online at www.ncsconline.org.

45. Alexis de Tocqueville, *Democracy in America,* edited by J. P. Mayer (Garden City, NY: Doubleday, 1969), p. 270.

46. The compulsory flag salute was upheld in *Minersville School District v. Gobitis,* 310 U.S. 586 (1940). Justices Black, Douglas, and Murphy repudiated their *Gobitis* votes in *Jones v. Opelika,* 316 U.S. 584 (1942). The Court overruled *Gobitis* in *West Virginia State Board of Education v. Barnette,* 319 U.S. 624 (1943).

47. The Supreme Court recognized that the right to privacy encompassed the right to terminate a pregnancy in *Roe v. Wade,* 410 U.S. 113 (1973). However, the Court narrowed *Roe* and raised questions about its continued viability in *Webster v. Reproductive Health Services,* 492 U.S. 490 (1989), and *Planned Parenthood of Southeastern Pennsylvania v. Casey,* 502 U.S. 1056 (1992).

48. *Escobedo v. Illinois,* 378 U.S. 478 (1964).

49. Liva Baker, *Miranda: Crime, Law and Politics* (New York: Atheneum, 1983), p. 98.

50. *Miranda v. Arizona,* 384 U.S. 436 (1966).

51. "Retired Chief Justice Warren Attacks . . . Freund Study Group's Composition and Proposal," *American Bar Association Journal* 59 (July 1973): 728.

52. *Youngstown Sheet & Tube Company v. Sawyer,* 343 U.S. 579 (1952); *United States v. Nixon,* 418 U.S. 683 (1974).

53. *Bush v. Gore,* 531 U.S. 525 (2000).

54. See, e.g., *Katz v. Tyler,* 386 U.S. 942 (1967), and *Sarnoff v. Schultz,* 409 U.S. 929 (1971).

55. The Court finally struck down state laws forbidding racial intermarriage in 1967, thirteen years after its decision in *Brown v. Board of Education,* 347 U.S. 483 (1954). The case striking down such laws was the aptly named *Loving v. Virginia,* 388 U.S. 1 (1967).

56. The original attempt to apply the cue theory to the Court's certiorari decisions was Joseph Tanenhaus, Marvin Schick, M. Muraskin, and D. Rosen, "The Supreme Court's Certiorari Jurisdiction: Cue Theory," in *Courts, Law, and Judicial Processes,* ed. S. Sidney Ulmer (New York: Free Press, 1981). Refinements of the theory were proposed in S. Sidney Ulmer, "The Supreme Court's Certiorari Decisions: Conflict as a Predictive Variable," *American Political Science Review* 78 (December 1984): 901–911; and Stewart Teger and Donald Kosinski, "The Cue Theory of Supreme Court Certiorari Jurisdiction: A Reconsideration," *Journal of Politics* 42 (August 1980): 834–846.

57. For discussions of strategic voting on certiorari, see Lee Epstein and Jack Knight, *The Choices Justices Make* (Washington, DC: CQ Press, 1998), and Walter Murphy, *Elements of Judicial Strategy* (Chicago: University of Chicago Press, 1964).

58. Quoted in H. W. Perry Jr., *Deciding to Decide: Agenda Setting in the United States Supreme Court* (Cambridge, MA: Harvard University Press, 1991), p. 200.

59. Ibid., chap. 6–8.

60. On amicus briefs in *Miranda,* see Baker, *Miranda: Crime, Law and Politics,* pp. 108–109. More generally, see Joseph D. Kearney and Thomas W. Merrill, "The Influence of Amicus Curiae Briefs on the Supreme Court," *University of Pennsylvania Law Review* 148 (January 2000): 743–855.

61. David M. O'Brien, *Storm Center: The Supreme Court in American Politics,* 5th ed. (New York: Norton, 1999), pp. 286–287, discussing *Dartmouth College v. Woodward,* 4 Wheat. 518 (1819).

62. William H. Rehnquist, *The Supreme Court,* 2d ed. (New York: Knopf, 2001), p. 244.

63. Quoted in O'Brien, *Storm Center,* p. 260.

64. Quoted in Anthony Lewis, *Gideon's Trumpet* (New York: Random House, 1964), p. 162, n. 23. For an effort to document the effect of oral argument, see Timothy R. Johnson, "Information, Oral Arguments, and Supreme Court Decision Making," *American Politics Review* 29 (July 2001): 331–351.

65. Rehnquist, *The Supreme Court,* p. 254–255, and William O. Douglas, *The Court Years, 1939–1975* (New York: Random House, 1980), p. 34.

66. Rehnquist, *The Supreme Court,* p. 256.

67. O'Brien, *Storm Center,* p. 284.

68. Saul Brenner, "Fluidity on the United States Supreme Court: A Reexamination," *American Journal of Political Science* 24 (August 1980): 526–535.

69. Quoted in O'Brien, *Storm Center,* p. 323.

70. For discussion of dissent rates on federal courts of appeals, see Ashlyn Kuersten and Donald Songer, *Decisions of the U.S. Courts of Appeals* (New York: Garland, 2000). For dissent rates on the Alabama and Ohio supreme courts, see G. Alan Tarr and Mary Cornelia Aldis Porter, *State Supreme Courts in State and Nation* (New Haven, CT: Yale University Press, 1988), p. 106, n. 111, and p. 139, n. 23. For an overview of dissent on state supreme courts, see Henry R. Glick and Robert W. Pruet Jr., "Dissent in State Supreme Courts: Patterns and Correlates of Conflict," in *Judicial Conflict and Consensus: Behavioral Studies of American Appellate Courts,* ed. Sheldon Goldman and Charles M. Lamb (Lexington: University of Kentucky Press, 1986).

CRIMINAL JUSTICE AND THE COURTS

The scene, a hall outside a Detroit courtroom; a defendant and his attorney deep in conversation; the subject, whether to plead guilty or go to trial.

> DEF[ENSE] COUNSEL: *We've got a problem. It looks like the prosecutor has a pretty good case—there are the people in the store and the customer's paycheck found in your wallet. Judge Singleton will probably find you guilty if we go without a jury. Of course, nobody ever knows what a jury will do, but my feeling is they'll probably convict you in a case like this.*
>
> DEFENDANT: *One of those dudes can't say for sure it was me robbed the place.*
>
> DEF. COUNSEL: *I know, I know. Look, the other two can. And you were in the neighborhood and had that paycheck. What do you think a jury will do?*
>
> DEFENDANT: *Well, what can I do?*
>
> DEF. COUNSEL: *I'll give it to you straight. If we go to trial, it will be on the armed robbery. You'll probably be convicted, and the law says the judge has got to give you some time. Knowing Singleton, if the jury convicts you, he won't hesitate to give you time either. You can plead guilty to the other charge—assault with intent to rob while being armed.*
>
> DEFENDANT: *What would I get then?*
>
> DEF. COUNSEL: *Well, if you plead, it will be a conviction. You could get probation, but you might still get some time. I really don't know what he'll give you.*
>
> DEFENDANT: *Damn! What should I do, man?*
>
> DEF. COUNSEL: *Look, I'm just your attorney. You have to decide. I guess if I were in your shoes, I'd take the plea.*
>
> DEFENDANT: *Yeah. Yeah. OK.*[1]

Source: "From Felony Justice," p. 131. Reprinted by permission of James Eisenstein.

After pleading guilty, the defendant was sentenced to three to five years in prison.

This conversation between defendant and counsel illustrates a basic aspect of criminal justice in the United States. Most of those who are accused of a crime plead guilty rather than go to trial. Although the frequency of guilty pleas varies from jurisdiction to jurisdiction, defendants plead guilty in more than 80 percent of felony cases (those involving serious crimes) and in an even larger percentage of misdemeanor cases.

Therefore, this chapter focuses primarily on criminal cases that do not go to trial. It first identifies the major actors in the criminal justice process and follows them from arrest to guilty plea, looking in detail at key aspects of the process. It then discusses plea negotiations (or plea bargaining), which frequently precede guilty pleas. Finally, the chapter examines the policy debates over the exclusionary rule, the insanity defense, the sentencing of criminals, and drug courts.

PROSECUTORS AND DEFENSE ATTORNEYS

Prosecutors

Known in different jurisdictions as the district attorney, the state's attorney, or the U.S. attorney, the prosecutor is the community's chief law enforcement official. Typically, prosecutors in the states are elected locally and have a political base that enables them to operate independently of the state's attorney general. (Federal prosecutors are appointed by the president with the advice and consent of the Senate.) In some rural jurisdictions, prosecutors serve part-time while maintaining a private practice. But in urban areas, the prosecutor occupies a full-time position and usually has a staff of assistant prosecutors to help deal with the heavy workload of criminal cases. Many of these assistant prosecutors are recent law school graduates seeking litigation experience before moving on to other positions, so turnover in the prosecutor's office is continuous.

Prosecutors are the most powerful officials in the criminal courts because of the broad discretion they exercise.[2] In most jurisdictions, they screen felony arrests to determine whether charges should be filed and, if so, which charges. If they decide not to file charges, the suspects are released. At later stages of the criminal process, they may decide whether to seek a grand jury indictment, oppose bail for a suspect, drop or reduce the charges they initially filed, and plea-bargain—or refuse to plea-bargain—with defendants.

In exercising this discretion, the assistant prosecutors are guided by the policies and expectations of the prosecutor who heads the office. But they usually are accorded considerable leeway in conducting cases, as long as they safeguard the prosecutor's reputation by maintaining a high conviction rate. This emphasis on convictions affects how assistant prosecutors view cases. Often "they prefer dismissing charges to subjecting themselves to possible criticism for 'losing.'"[3]

Defense Attorneys

The Sixth Amendment and analogous state constitutional provisions guarantee defendants the right to counsel. As a result of the Supreme Court's decision in *Gideon v. Wainwright* (see Chapter 2), states are required to furnish counsel to indigent defendants in felony cases.[4] A subsequent Supreme Court ruling, *Argersinger v. Hamlin* (1972), extended this right to counsel to all cases in which the defendant could be sentenced to jail or prison. Some states have gone even further, providing counsel to all indigents charged with misdemeanors.[5] Before these initiatives, many indigent defendants were not represented by counsel, which placed them at a severe disadvantage. The requirement that counsel must be provided to indigent defendants revolutionized criminal justice in the United States.

Because most defendants are indigent, they cannot afford a private attorney, thus, relatively few lawyers specialize in criminal law. States and localities have devised three systems to provide representation for indigent defendants.[6]

1. Public defender programs.   Fifteen states and many localities, particularly in urban areas, operate public defender programs, employing attorneys whose sole responsibility is to represent indigent defendants. Many of these attorneys, like their counterparts in the prosecutor's office, are recent law school graduates who do not remain in the public defender's office for their entire careers. Their skills as advocates have sometimes been questioned. One inmate, when asked if he had a lawyer at his trial, replied: "No, I had a public defender." There is little evidence, however, that public defenders provide less effective representation than other defense attorneys do.[7]

2. Assigned counsel systems.   Assigned counsel systems operate in almost two-thirds of all counties but are particularly prevalent in counties with fewer than 50,000 residents. Under an assigned counsel system, the judge appoints private attorneys from a list of available lawyers to represent indigent defendants. In some jurisdictions, this service is considered a professional obligation, and the attorney is not paid. In others, the lawyer receives a reduced fee. Although this system disperses the responsibility of defending the poor among all practicing attorneys, the defendant runs the risk of being represented by a lawyer who has neither expertise nor experience in criminal law.[8]

3. Contract systems.   Some communities have experimented with contract systems as an alternative to other systems or as a supplement to public defender offices. Under a contract system, the government awards defender services contracts to individual attorneys or private law firms, which agree to provide representation for a specified dollar amount.

THE PROCESS OF CRIMINAL JUSTICE

Figure 6-1 illustrates the sequence of events in the criminal justice system from the commission of a felony to the final disposition of a case. Until the initial appearance in court, the process is similar for misdemeanors. However, unlike those who are accused of felonies, most defendants in misdemeanor cases plead guilty at their initial appearance in court. Most do so because they are guilty of the offenses with which they are charged, but another factor may also be involved. The costs of making bail and paying an attorney, as well as the prospect of docked wages and possible loss of a job because of days spent in court or in jail awaiting trial, may deter defendants from contesting their innocence, especially when the penalties for conviction (usually a fine, probation, or both) are not severe. As Malcolm Feeley has observed: "The time, effort, money, and opportunities lost as a direct result of being caught up in the system can quickly come to outweigh the penalty that issues from adjudication and sentence." Or more succinctly, "the process is the punishment."[9]

For those who are accused of felonies, however, the potential penalty upon conviction may be severe (see Box 6-1). Thus, defendants may be less willing to admit their guilt: the more serious the charges, the more likely a trial. Or defendants may be willing to admit guilt only in exchange for some concession from the prosecution. As a result, processing felony cases is more drawn out and complex.

The following analysis will focus on four key aspects of the process: (1) the commission of the crime and the arrest, (2) the prosecutor's charging decision, (3) the setting (or denial) of bail, and (4) the official accusation of the accused in felony cases through indictment by a grand jury or other procedures.

Crime and Arrest

Most crimes are never solved, and their perpetrators are never arrested or punished. What accounts for this striking fact? For one thing, most crimes are not reported to the police. Survey data suggest that the level of crime is three times as high as reported by the Federal Bureau of Investigation's (FBI's) Uniform Crime Reports (UCR), which are based on crime statistics submitted by police departments nationwide. Some victims of crime simply are not in a position to report offenses to the police—for example, a drug purchaser can hardly complain of being cheated by a dealer. Other victims may not report crimes because they either distrust the police or, as in the case of some rape victims, wish to avoid the unpleasantness of a police investigation and testimony at trial. Also, some victims of crime are in a continuing relationship with an offender— for example, in incidents of domestic violence—and they may either be too intimidated to report offenses or wish to deal with the problem privately. Some

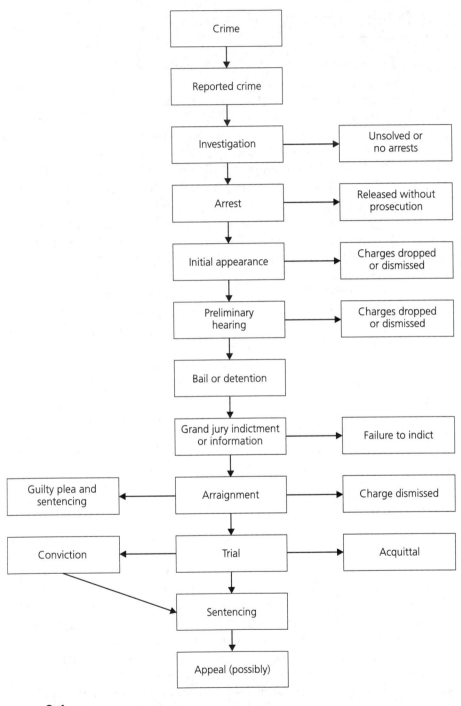

FIGURE **6-1**

Serious Crimes and Criminal Justice

Source: Adapted from *The Challenge of Crime in a Free Society* (Washington, DC: President's Commission on Law Enforcement and Administration of Justice, 1967).

BOX
6-1 *Crime in the United States*

Level and Type of Crime

- From 1981 to 1990, the crime rate in the United States—as measured by the FBI's *Uniform Crime Reports*—increased by 78 percent. From 1993 to 2002, however, the crime rate decreased almost 25 percent.
- Property crimes outnumber violent crimes approximately 8 to 1.
- Crime surveys suggest that only one-third or so of all crimes are reported to the police.

Victims of Crime

- Younger people are more likely than the elderly to be victims of crime. Young males are most likely to be victims of violent crime, and elderly women the least likely. One-third of the victims of violent crime in 2002 was between twelve to nineteen years old.
- African Americans are more likely than members of other racial groups to be victims of crime in general and violent crime in particular.
- FBI reports indicate that almost half the persons victimized by nonfatal violence (e.g., rape and assault) knew their assailant.

Offenders and the Criminal Law

- Police "clear" by arrest only about one-fifth of all reported crimes.
- Most cases that are prosecuted result in a conviction either by a guilty plea or following a trial (80 percent of trials result in a guilty verdict).
- Of those convicted of felonies, more than 70 percent are sentenced to serve time in prison or jail.
- From 1980 to 2003, the incarceration rate more than tripled. An increase in prisoners convicted of violent offenses accounts for more than half of this increase in prison population. In 2003, state and federal prisons held 1,460,920 prisoners.

Sources: Bureau of Justice Statistics Web site, http://www.ojp.usdoj.gov/bjs, and the Federal Bureau of Investigation Web site, www.fbi.gov.

crimes, such as minor thefts, are viewed by victims as "not important enough to report." Finally, some crimes, such as illegal gambling or underage drinking, do not have an identifiable victim and so often go unreported.[10]

Even when crimes are reported to police, in most instances the perpetrators are never arrested. According to the Bureau of Justice Statistics, police "cleared" by arrest only 20 percent of all *UCR* felonies.[11] However, clearance rates differ dramatically from offense to offense. The highest clearance rates for reported crimes are for victimless crimes—typically the discovery (report) of the crime and the arrest are made simultaneously by a police officer.[12] Arrest rates tend to be higher for violent crimes such as aggravated assault and rape, in which the victim may be able to identify the assailant, than for crimes against property, such as larceny, auto theft, and burglary, which may occur without the presence of the victim.[13] Most arrests depend not on investigative work by the police but on immediate or almost immediate apprehension of a suspect. According to one study, 56 percent of felony arrests took place either at the scene of the crime or nearby, with another 24 percent occurring because the victim was able to identify the offender.[14]

Charges and Dismissals

As political scientist James Q. Wilson has observed, "In the real world, an arrest rarely ends anything."[15] Figure 6-2, which depicts what happens after arrest, confirms this. In none of the four cities in the figure were as many as one-third of those arrested in felony cases convicted of felonies. Prosecutors dismissed many cases or downgraded them to misdemeanors and sent them to a trial court of limited jurisdiction. Often the cases sent to the lower court were dismissed there. Thus, although most cases that were prosecuted resulted in convictions, large numbers of cases were not prosecuted. What accounts for this attrition?

The most important factor leading prosecutors to dismiss cases is the absence of evidence sufficient to prove guilt beyond a reasonable doubt.[16] Potential witnesses may be reluctant to testify or may lack credibility because they have, for example, criminal records or a drug or alcohol dependency. Complainants may also withdraw their complaints, especially if they had a prior relationship with the accused and have reconciled their differences. This occurs most often in intra-family disputes. Even if there is sufficient evidence to convict, prosecutors may dismiss potentially convictable cases when they believe that prosecution will not serve the cause of justice. For example, a prosecutor may not file charges against a person arrested for a minor felony to avoid giving a criminal record to a first offender.[17] Such an exercise of prosecutorial discretion has the same effect as an acquittal.

If the prosecutor files charges, the defendant is brought to court for his or her *initial appearance,* usually before a judge in a court of limited jurisdiction. At this stage, most defendants accused of ordinance violations and minor

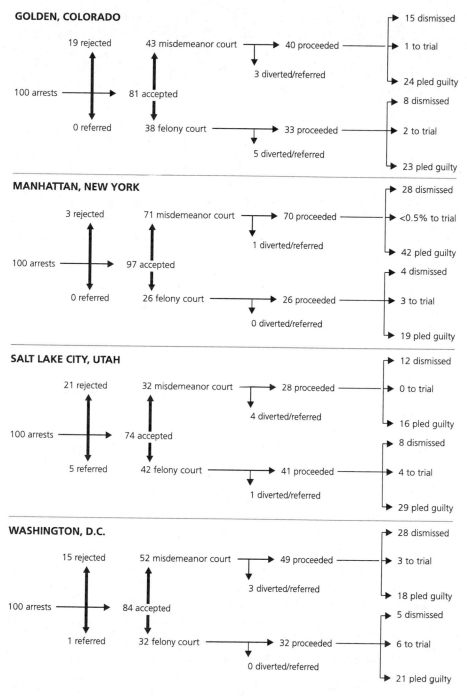

GOLDEN, COLORADO

MANHATTAN, NEW YORK

SALT LAKE CITY, UTAH

WASHINGTON, D.C.

FIGURE **6-2**

How Criminal Cases Are Processed

Source: *Report to the Nation on Crime and Justice*, 2d ed. (Washington, DC: U.S. Department of Justice, Bureau of Justice Statistics, 1988), p. 71.

misdemeanors plead guilty. The judge informs those accused of more serious crimes of the charges against them, advises them of their constitutional rights, and appoints an attorney for defendants who are indigent. The judge also determines whether the defendants will be released from custody pending trial and schedules their next appearance in court.

Bail and Pretrial Release

As befits a system in which the accused is presumed innocent until proven guilty, most defendants are eligible for release before trial. Typically, the accused must post bail as a guarantee that he or she will return for trial and other court proceedings. In medieval times, the accused was bailed to a third party, who was tried in place of the accused if he or she failed to appear for trial. Today, bail involves posting a monetary bond with the court that is forfeited if the accused fails to appear.

Usually, the bail required depends on the seriousness of the charges against defendants and on their prior criminal record—the more serious the charges and the more extensive the record, the higher the bail. As long as they do not violate the Eighth Amendment's ban on "excessive bail," however, judges have considerable discretion in setting bail. Some states have sought to eliminate undue leniency or harshness in setting bail by establishing a fixed schedule that specifies the bail for various offenses. Critics have claimed, however, that this substitution of a "going rate" prevents judges from responding to the circumstances in individual cases.

In some jurisdictions, defendants are required to post the full amount of bail with the court. In others, defendants rely on bail bondsmen, who sign a promissory note to the court for the bail and charge defendants a nonrefundable fee for their service (usually 10 percent of the bail). Both of these systems—the only ones in operation until bail reforms began in the 1960s—place a particular burden on indigent defendants, who may be unable to raise the money or afford the bondsman's fee. A study of twenty cities during the early 1960s found that more than half of all defendants remained in jail, often for months, awaiting trial.[18]

Reformers attacked this incarceration as "punishment before trial." They claimed that it cost indigent defendants their jobs, undermined family relationships, and made it more difficult for defendants to mount an effective defense.[19] They sought to sever the connection between indigency and pretrial confinement by limiting the role of bail bondsmen and by developing alternatives to monetary bail. Their reforms included:[20]

1. Deposit bail. Defendants secure their release by depositing a percentage of the full bail with the court rather than with a bondsman, and recover the full amount deposited when they appear for trial.
2. Unsecured bail. When bail is set, defendants are released without paying any money to the court but they are liable for the full amount if they fail to appear for trial.

3. Release on recognizance. Defendants with strong ties to the community, who are therefore unlikely to flee prosecution, are released on their promise to appear in court.
4. Conditional release. Defendants are released on certain nonmonetary conditions, such as that they will seek treatment or check in with court officials periodically.

The widespread adoption of these alternative release options during the 1960s and 1970s had dramatic effects. A study of 20 cities found that the release rate rose from 48 percent of all defendants in 1962 to 67 percent in 1971, and a more recent study of eight communities found a release rate of 85 percent.[21] Despite the liberalization of pretrial release, few defendants—less than 4 percent, according to one study—try to flee or otherwise fail to appear in order to avoid conviction.[22]

But as the number of defendants released before trial rose, so did concern that the release of some defendants posed a threat to the community. Research offers some support for this concern. The eight-community study mentioned in the preceding paragraph found that 16 percent of all released defendants were rearrested before trial and that 30 percent of those rearrested were rearrested more than once.[23] Most states have responded to this concern by requiring judges to consider community safety as well as the likelihood of appearance at trial in deciding on pretrial release.[24] Critics have charged that there is no reliable basis for predicting criminal behavior and that therefore some offenders will be unnecessarily confined awaiting trial while dangerous ones will be released.[25] The haphazard implementation of these "preventive detention" enactments has made it difficult to determine their effectiveness.[26]

Preliminary Hearings and Grand Juries

To protect against governmental abuse of its prosecutorial power, defendants in the United States cannot be tried for a felony until the case against them has been reviewed by someone other than a law enforcement official. During this process of formal accusation, the prosecutor must demonstrate that there is probable cause to believe that a crime has been committed and that the accused has committed the crime. In most states, this process of formal accusation occurs during a preliminary hearing before a lower court judge.

In federal courts and in some state courts, however, the process of formal accusation takes a different form. The Fifth Amendment to the U.S. Constitution requires that felony prosecutions in federal court be initiated by a grand jury indictment; that is, by a determination by an independent body of citizens that there is sufficient evidence to go to trial. Eighteen states likewise mandate that indictment by a grand jury precede all felony prosecutions, and six more states require indictments in capital cases.[27] In these twenty-four states, the defendant at the preliminary hearing is bound over to a grand jury for indictment.

The Grand Jury   The grand jury differs from the trial (petit) jury in four respects.[28]

1. Membership and length of service.   Although the grand jury, like the trial jury, is composed of ordinary citizens, its size varies from as few as six members (in Indiana) to as many as twenty-three (for federal grand juries). Also, whereas trial jurors sit on a single case, grand jurors are empaneled for a set term (frequently three months) and during that period the prosecutor brings a large number of cases before them for review.

2. Function.   Grand juries, unlike petit juries, do not determine the guilt or innocence of defendants. Instead, they serve investigative and accusatory functions. In some states, grand juries investigate issues of official corruption and organized crime, but in most states, their primary responsibility is to determine whether there is sufficient evidence to indict defendants.

3. Standard for decision.   In most states, trial juries in serious criminal cases can convict defendants only by a unanimous vote. Grand juries, however, indict defendants by a plurality vote—from a simple majority to a two-thirds vote, depending on state law. Moreover, the standard that grand juries use in deciding whether to indict is "probable cause" rather than the more stringent standard of "beyond a reasonable doubt."

4. Mode of operation.   Unlike trials, grand jury hearings are conducted in secret, partly to protect the reputations of those against whom there is insufficient evidence for an indictment. Most states relax the rules of evidence that operate at trial. For example, prosecutors in a grand jury hearing may introduce hearsay or illegally seized evidence that would be inadmissible at trial. Also, in most states witnesses do not have a right to have counsel with them during grand jury proceedings.

If a grand jury concludes that there is sufficient evidence to proceed to trial, it votes an indictment, or "true bill." If not, it votes "no true bill" and the case is dismissed. This requirement of grand jury indictment before prosecution serves, according to the U.S. Supreme Court, as "a primary security for the innocent against hasty, malicious, and oppressive prosecution."[29] Prosecutors seldom find it difficult to secure a grand jury indictment, however. One study found that over the course of a year federal grand juries voted for more than 17,000 indictments but voted no true bill in fewer than 70 cases.[30] Even when a grand jury does refuse to indict, it may be following the direction of a prosecutor who was obliged to bring a politically sensitive case before the grand jury but did not want to prosecute. Small wonder, then, that one judge concluded that most grand juries would "indict a ham sandwich" if the prosecutor asked them to.[31]

The Preliminary Hearing   As an alternative to grand jury indictment, some states permit the prosecutor to present evidence at the preliminary hearing that the defendant has committed the crimes with which he is charged. The decision of whether to proceed to trial then rests with the judge presiding over the hearing. If the prosecutor fails to establish probable cause, the judge dismisses the charges and the defendant is released. If probable cause is established, the defendant is held for trial.

Researchers have discovered wide variation in how jurisdictions conduct their preliminary hearings.[32] In some jurisdictions—for example, in Los Angeles— preliminary hearings resemble miniature trials, with both prosecutor and defense attorney calling and cross-examining witnesses. But in most jurisdictions, preliminary hearings are perfunctory proceedings lasting only a few minutes, with the main evidence presented by a police officer testifying from a police report. In a few jurisdictions—Chicago is one—the preliminary hearing is used to screen cases, with judges either dismissing cases or reducing charges in many instances. More typical is David Neubauer's finding that less than 2 percent of defendants had their cases terminated at preliminary hearings.[33] In jurisdictions in which judges routinely find that probable cause exists, defendants may waive their right to a preliminary hearing.

PLEA BARGAINING

As we have seen, the American criminal justice system is designed to screen out weak cases early in the process. The cases that are not screened out are those in which the prosecutor believes there is strong evidence of guilt. Not surprisingly then, the overwhelming majority of cases that are prosecuted result in convictions. More than two-thirds of defendants who go to trial are found guilty.[34] Most criminal cases, however, are resolved through a defendant's admission of guilt before trial (see Box 6-2). In many instances defendants plead guilty with the expectation that they will receive some consideration in exchange for their plea, such as a reduction in the number or severity of the charges against them, a more lenient sentence, or both. Often this expectation is based on a specific agreement negotiated between the prosecutor and the defense attorney and ratified by the judge. The process by which such agreements are negotiated is known as plea bargaining.

The Process of Plea Bargaining

Although "there probably is no such thing as a typical criminal court," certain aspects of plea bargaining are relatively uniform from court to court.[35] Plea negotiations are generally initiated by the defense attorney, whether public defender or private counsel, rather than by the prosecutor. When a defense

| BOX 6-2 | *Plea Bargaining in Comparative Perspective* |

Although other countries share the United States's need to process large numbers of relatively routine criminal cases, they have developed their own mechanisms for doing so. Some countries have plea negotiations similar to those in U.S. criminal courts. In Great Britain, for example, plea bargaining flourishes despite official policies and appellate rulings discouraging the practice. One study found that roughly 85 percent of defendants pled guilty, often changing their plea from "not guilty" shortly before their trial was scheduled to begin. In most cases, defendants were induced to plead guilty by concessions on the sentence they would receive, and by pressure from the judge, who promised defendants a more severe sentence if they went to trial.

In Germany—and also, apparently, in other civil-law countries— plea bargaining is unknown. Still, most routine cases involving less serious crimes are resolved without trial. The mechanism developed in Germany for disposing of these cases is called the penal order. Prepared by the prosecutor and signed by the judge, this order describes the wrongdoing of the defendant, the evidence gathered by the state, and the penalty to be imposed on the defendant. The penalty cannot involve imprisonment (the most common penalties are fines or the loss of one's driver's license). If the defendant accepts the penal order (about 75 percent

attorney believes that a client is likely to be convicted at trial, the attorney may approach the prosecutor offering a plea of guilty. In exchange, the defense attorney seeks concessions relating to either the charges against the defendant or the sentence to be imposed.

That defense attorneys typically initiate plea negotiations suggests that most defendants whose cases progress to this stage are either guilty of criminal violations or at least are likely to be convicted at trial. This is hardly surprising given the screening of cases that occurs early in the criminal justice process. Experienced defense attorneys readily admit that most of their clients are guilty. As one put it:

> We make an initial determination whether we've got a defense, and many times we don't. When somebody's apprehended in the midst of a break-in, caught in a store or a house, you have to go some to explain what you're doing there at two or three o'clock in the morning. We get a fair number of these. If you are apprehended

of defendants do), then the order becomes effective and has the same effect as a conviction after trial. If the defendant objects, then the order is nullified, and the case is scheduled for trial.

The German use of penal orders differs from plea bargaining in several respects. First, the defendant need never appear in court. If in misdemeanor cases the process is the punishment, as Malcolm Feeley has argued, the penal order eliminates that punishment. The closest analogy to the penal order in American law is the traffic ticket, which allows defendants to mail in the fine or go to court and contest their innocence. Second, penal orders involve no negotiations, no offer and counteroffer. If the accused rejects a penal order, the prosecutor cannot make a second offer; the matter must go to trial. However, the defendant's rejection of a penal order is not final; the defendant can accept the penal order (and the punishment it specifies) during the course of the trial or anytime up to the court's announcement of its decision. Finally, the defendant does not risk a harsher punishment by going to trial. The defendant can accept the penal order after the trial has commenced, so the penalty it specifies is not an inducement to forego trial. In addition, studies have shown that German judges do not impose a more severe punishment on those who reject penal orders and demand a trial. Put differently, defendants in Germany are not penalized for asserting their rights.

Sources: The analysis is based on John Baldwin and Michael McConville, "Plea Bargaining and Plea Negotiation in England," *Law & Society Review* 13 (winter 1979): 287–307; William L. F. Felstiner, "Plea Contracts in West Germany," *Law & Society Review* 13 (winter 1979): 309–325; and Malcolm M. Feeley, *The Process Is the Punishment: Handling Cases in a Lower Criminal Court* (New York: Russell Sage Foundation, 1979).

fleeing the scene of a crime, you are going to be hard pressed to explain why [you're] running away from the scene.[36]

Yet the virtual certainty of conviction at trial does not prevent plea bargaining. Prosecutors are willing to offer concessions even in cases in which the evidence of guilt is conclusive. Thus, sometimes defense attorneys best represent their clients' interests by encouraging them to plead guilty rather than by taking their cases to trial.

Plea bargaining may make sense for the defendant because the prosecutor can offer important concessions in exchange for a guilty plea. A defendant may face multiple charges arising from a series of crimes or even from a single incident. For example, a person who gets drunk and takes a car for a joyride might be charged with grand larceny, possession of a stolen automobile, use of an automobile without authorization from the owner, drunk driving, and reckless driving.[37] The prosecutor may then offer to drop some charges or reduce others—for instance, from grand larceny to petit larceny—in exchange for a guilty plea. In so doing, of course, the sentence that a defendant might receive on conviction is also reduced. If the "discount" is substantial, then the defendant may have a strong incentive to plead guilty. The prosecutor may also agree to recommend a relatively lenient sentence or to refrain from demanding a harsh one in exchange for a guilty plea. Faced with the choice between an assured sentence and the possibility of a more severe one if convicted at trial, the defendant may avoid the risk by pleading guilty.

Plea negotiations characteristically reflect established patterns of interaction between prosecutors and defense attorneys.[38] In many jurisdictions a single prosecutor handles all cases that arise in a particular judge's courtroom. Public defenders' offices, which represent the majority of defendants, often operate on the same basis, assigning their defenders to specific courtrooms. Even when defendants can afford private counsel, they typically select someone from the local criminal bar who has represented numerous defendants in that court. As a result, when a prosecutor and defense attorney (and possibly the judge) enter into plea negotiations, they usually have experience dealing with each other, sometimes in cases similar to the one under discussion.

This personal and professional familiarity helps plea negotiations by promoting easy interaction between the attorneys. Even more important, the outcomes of negotiations in previous cases furnish a basis for resolving the prime question in any plea bargain, namely, what is an appropriate punishment for the defendant? If the defense attorney is attempting to convince the prosecutor that his client should be given probation, then he may bring up past instances in which the prosecutor agreed to probation for defendants facing similar charges. If previous defendants received jail time for the same offense, he may emphasize factors that distinguish his client from them (such as a stable family life or no prior criminal record) to justify a more favorable outcome. But the prosecutor independently considers how this case resembles past cases and whether any factors aggravate the situation and warrant unusual severity. Once the prosecutor and defense attorney have resolved the facts of the case—that is, the nature of the crime and the character of the defendant—their settlement of similar past cases guides them in determining what the case is worth. In other words, because both prosecutor and defense attorney share the assumption that like cases should be treated alike, plea bargains occur in a rough system of precedent in which the outcomes of past negotiations provide standards for the resolution of current ones.

If the defendant accepts the settlement the attorneys have negotiated, they then recommend that the judge resolve the case in line with their agreement. Some judges are actively involved in plea negotiations from the outset, partly to expedite the flow of cases and partly to influence sentencing, which they consider a judicial prerogative. Because they participated in the negotiations, they will, of course, ratify the plea agreement. Most judges do not participate in plea negotiations, however, and are first involved with a case when they decide whether to accept the proposed plea bargain.

Although in theory judges can reject the agreements negotiated by the attorneys, they typically are reluctant to do so. Because both the prosecutor and defense attorney agreed to the plea bargain, the judge may well conclude that their agreement adequately protects the interests of both the community and the defendant. The prosecutor and defense attorney also can supply the judge with information supporting their recommendation, and the judge usually has little basis for a contrary assessment of the case. Furthermore, if the judge rejects a plea bargain, the defendant may elect to go to trial, something the judge usually wants to avoid. Finally, the judge's desire to maintain a harmonious working relationship with attorneys who regularly practice before her promotes an inclination to accept their recommendations. As James Eisenstein and Herbert Jacob have put it, "The higher the proportion of dispositions accounted for by the same set of participants, the more interdependent they become."[39]

Nevertheless, the interdependence of judge, prosecutor, and defense attorney enhances the judge's indirect influence over plea bargains. The prosecutor and defense attorney, mindful that the judge can reject their recommendations, must factor the judge's views into their discussions. This anticipation and consideration of the judge's perspective means that all participants influence the outcomes of plea negotiations.

Why Plea Bargaining Occurs

Plea bargaining is most commonly viewed as a response to the case pressures that afflict all those who are involved in the criminal courts.[40] According to this view, which is endorsed by many judges and practicing attorneys, escalating crime rates increased the number of cases coming to the courts, often without a corresponding increase in the resources available for dealing with them. Courts thus turned to plea bargaining as a way to resolve cases more quickly. Underlying this view are several key assumptions: that plea bargaining, like the burgeoning caseloads that caused it, is a relatively recent phenomenon; that plea bargaining is a necessary evil rather than a conscious policy choice, a second-best means of dealing with defendants; and that with sufficient resources courts would decide criminal cases with trials rather than by plea bargaining.

Recent research does not altogether support this account of plea bargaining. Although U.S. courts actively discouraged guilty pleas during the early nineteenth century, by the early 1900s, plea bargaining had become the primary means of processing cases in many criminal courts.[41] This can be seen not only in the frequency of guilty pleas—in 1926, more than 90 percent of all felony convictions in Manhattan and Brooklyn resulted from such pleas—but also in prosecutors' willingness to reduce charges against defendants. In New York in 1926, for instance, 85 percent of all guilty pleas in felony cases were to offenses less serious than the original charges, and in Chicago the figure was 78 percent.[42] Because these figures suggest that plea bargaining was as frequent in the 1920s as it is today, recent increases in crime cannot explain the prevalence of plea bargaining. Furthermore, if plea bargaining is a result of heavy caseloads, then those courts with particularly heavy caseloads should rely on plea bargaining more than should courts with lighter caseloads. This is not the case. Some low-volume courts rely heavily on plea bargaining while some high-volume courts do not.[43] Indeed, some high-volume courts—those in Baltimore and Los Angeles, for example—conduct large numbers of trials.[44] So caseload pressures alone do not account for plea bargaining.

Another common view is that prosecutors plea-bargain when they lack sufficient evidence to get a conviction at trial.[45] According to this view, a prosecutor's willingness to plea-bargain is a sign of weakness, an indication that the aim of securing the full punishment the law allows must be sacrificed so that the accused receives some punishment. Although the strength of the evidence affects plea bargaining in some instances, the frequency of plea negotiations suggest that this explanation is inadequate. If the evidence were weak in the majority of cases, defense attorneys would plea-bargain less and take more cases to trial. And if the evidence was strong in most cases, as might be expected after weak cases were screened out, then prosecutors would plea-bargain less frequently. This explanation cannot account for the behavior of either defense attorneys or prosecutors because it inaccurately assumes that prosecutors seek the harshest possible punishment for defendants.

But if neither caseload pressures nor evidentiary problems account for plea bargaining, then what does? One view is that attorneys and judges engage in plea bargaining to enhance their discretion, so that they can seek *what they perceive* as substantive justice in each case.[46] According to this view, the participants in plea bargaining all agree that strict application of criminal law does not produce justice. Because the law necessarily defines offenses in general terms (for example, robbery and assault) and prescribes penalties (or a limited range of penalties) for them, it cannot take into account the specifics of each case. Thus, an insistence on strict application of the law means treating dissimilar cases as similar. Furthermore, when legislators enact criminal laws, the penalties they prescribe may reflect their strong disapproval of the actions they are outlawing instead of a thoughtful consideration of what punishment is appropriate. According to this view, plea bargaining permits those who administer justice to escape the rigidity and excessive harshness of criminal law and to focus on the character of the defendant and the nature of his offense in determining punishment.

This does not mean, of course, that eavesdroppers on plea negotiations are treated to extended discussions about the nature of justice. Because the participants in a plea bargain have dealt with each other on numerous occasions, previous understandings usually permit a quick determination of the "worth" of a case and the appropriate punishment. According to this explanation, then, plea bargaining is not a kind of assembly line justice necessitated by heavy caseloads but is instead an attempt to individualize criminal justice.

Other studies have attributed the prevalence of plea bargaining less to a shared concern for substantive justice than to the shared interest of attorneys and judges in processing cases quickly.[47] This interest in the speedy disposition of cases exists in both low-volume and high-volume courts and so does not depend on caseload pressures. For private attorneys, the desire for speedy disposition comes largely from monetary considerations: Few defendants can afford the costs, such as investigative work, trial preparation, and court time, associated with an extended trial, so private attorneys usually lose money when cases go to trial. But plea bargaining enables them both to benefit their clients (with reduced sentences) and to take on more cases, thus increasing their income. For judges and for attorneys (prosecutors and public defenders) employed by the state, compensation does not depend on the number of cases processed. Other incentives, however, promote a common concern for expeditious case processing. Chief among these is the natural desire to reduce one's workload. As Peter Nardulli has observed, "When the cases on their respective calls are completed in a given day, normally the formal work requirements of the judge, public defender, and prosecutor are fulfilled. Thus, it is in their mutual self-interest to process expeditiously the cases on the call for a given day, regardless of how many cases are scheduled."[48] Plea bargaining not only allows cases to be disposed of more quickly but also lightens the workloads of judges and attorneys, who can dispense with time-consuming preparation for trial. Also, participants in plea bargaining can justify the practice by insisting that trial is rarely warranted because weak cases are screened out early in the process. The only question in the remaining cases is the appropriate punishment for the defendant. Furthermore, each participant in plea bargaining recognizes that expeditious case processing requires a willingness to cooperate, that the refusal to do so imposes burdens on other participants and thus, may reduce their willingness to cooperate on future cases. In sum, the mutual interdependence of judge, prosecutor, and defense attorney, the prospect of continuing interaction among them, and the common goal of quick case processing all serve to reduce adversariness and promote the cooperative resolution of cases through plea bargaining.

Attacks on Plea Bargaining

Despite the prevalence of plea bargaining, or perhaps because of it, many critics argue that plea bargaining is an inappropriate and undesirable method of establishing sentencing policy.[49] According to these critics, plea bargaining diminishes the role of the judge by investing prosecutors with excessive control over sentencing decisions. Also, the discretion in sentencing that plea bargaining affords undermines the decisions on punishment established by the state legislature, in effect transferring power from a popularly elected, accountable body to officials whose actions are not subject to public scrutiny.

Critics have also attacked the sentencing policies that plea bargaining promotes. Some charge that plea bargaining coerces defendants into waiving their constitutional right to assert their innocence by penalizing them for going to trial.[50] If pleading guilty guarantees more lenient sentences, then the pressure on defendants to plea-bargain may be considerable, especially for those who cannot raise bail and must remain in jail until trial. Other critics complain that plea bargaining results in excessively lenient sentences because prosecutors must offer substantial concessions to obtain guilty pleas.[51] As a result, dangerous offenders escape the harsh punishment they deserve and soon threaten the community again. This undermines both respect for the law and its ability to deter crime. Still other critics, noting the interdependence that develops among the participants in plea bargaining, worry that defense attorneys end up sacrificing their clients' interests to maintain good relations with prosecutors.[52] Finally, some critics insist that because plea bargaining permits the exercise of broad discretion free from regulation and publicity, it fosters favoritism, corruption, and discrimination.[53] At the very least, it aggravates the problem of securing equal treatment for offenders because similar offenses may be dealt with dissimilarly in different parts of the state or even from courtroom to courtroom in the same community.

Responding to these criticisms, several jurisdictions tried during the 1970s and 1980s to restrict or abolish plea bargaining. The most successful effort was in Alaska. In 1975, the state's attorney general, Avrum Gross, prohibited prosecutors from offering concessions as a means of obtaining guilty pleas in felony and misdemeanor cases. Gross's ban, which effectively abolished plea bargaining in the state, produced some surprising results:

- contrary to expectations, guilty pleas in criminal cases declined only marginally (from 94 percent to 92 percent of all cases), so the number of trials increased only slightly;
- when trials were held, prosecutorial success increased, so there was no decline in the percentage of defendants convicted;
- because the number of trials did not increase substantially after the ban on plea bargaining, the courts did not experience case backlogs; the time required to process a case actually decreased;
- the conviction rates and sentences for those charged with serious violent crimes did not change as a result of the ban, suggesting that serious offenders were not escaping punishment as a result of plea bargaining;
- those charged with less serious property offenses—such as burglary, receiving stolen property, and malicious destruction of property— tended to receive more severe sentences than before the ban. This was particularly true for first offenders.[54]

Evaluating Plea Bargaining

What conclusions can be drawn from this description of plea bargaining and of the criticisms directed against it? As critics claim, plea bargaining does transfer control over sentencing from state legislatures and judges operating within statutory guidelines to judges, prosecutors, and defense attorneys collectively exercising broad discretion. Yet the critics' charge that this insulates sentencing from popular control is only partly valid. As the abolition of plea bargaining in Alaska and elsewhere shows, popular efforts to reassert control can succeed. More important, studies of criminal courts in various communities confirm that public opinion, as embodied in the broader political and legal culture of the community, does constrain participants in plea bargaining.[55] Of course, that public opinion affects plea bargaining does not by itself legitimate the practice. The fundamental question is whether plea bargaining promotes justice in sentencing.

Other criticisms of plea bargaining seem on inspection to be complaints about the American criminal justice system in general rather than specifically about plea bargaining. Take, for example, the charge that plea bargaining creates opportunities for favoritism, discrimination, and corruption. Clearly it does, and presumably one could find instances of such abuses.[56] The real question, however, is not the potential for abuse but the frequency of abuse. Even more, the question is whether such abuse is more prevalent in cases that are plea-bargained than in cases that go to trial. There is no evidence that plea bargaining is more infected by corruption and discrimination than are other ways of disposing of cases.

The charge that plea bargaining promotes excessive leniency in sentencing, endangering people by putting violent criminals back on the street, likewise might be better addressed to the American criminal justice system as a whole. Although sentencing in American courts may be too lenient, there is little evidence that plea bargaining alone promotes lenient sentences. Contrary to the views of many attorneys and judges, the most sophisticated studies of plea bargaining have discovered no evidence that defendants receive more lenient sentences through this method.[57] Also, the more serious the crime, the less likely plea bargaining is to occur. Defendants charged with serious offenses, who face the prospect of serving time in prison, are more likely to take their chances at trial and less likely to plea-bargain. And prosecutors, aware of community sentiment, are less willing to cut "sweet" deals with such offenders. When plea bargaining does occur in serious cases, offenders still receive lengthy sentences. The studies of sentencing in Alaska confirm the point. The sentences serious offenders received when plea bargaining was legal were just as severe as those they received after it was abolished.

More troubling is the charge that in plea bargaining defendants are coerced into pleading guilty and waiving their constitutional right to trial. Advocates of plea bargaining observe that most defendants are eager to plead guilty. They even plead guilty when, as in Alaska after the abolition of plea bargaining, they can expect no concessions for their admission of guilt. Critics insist, however, that defendants' willingness to plead guilty and plea-bargain often depends on their fear that they will be penalized if they go to trial. This fear may be groundless. Judges have insisted that they penalize defendants who demand a trial only when their demand is "frivolous"—that is, when they have no basis for contesting the charges against them.[58] And as we have seen, the best empirical evidence suggests that defendants who go to trial do not automatically receive harsher sentences. Yet ultimately this evidence is not decisive. Many judges and attorneys who participate in plea bargaining believe that defendants who go to trial do receive harsher sentences.[59] If defendants take their cues from what their attorneys say, they are likely to share the belief that conviction at trial will lead to a harsher sentence. Whether this perception deters defendants from contesting their innocence is unclear.

Also troubling is the charge that the established working relationships among participants in plea bargaining deter defense attorneys from vigorously pursuing their clients' interests. Advocates of plea bargaining deny that the strong pressure to cooperate undermines the vigorous representation of defendants. Prosecutors, they insist, expect defense counsel to pursue legitimate avenues for acquittal and do not penalize such efforts by refusing to plea-bargain.[60] Somewhat inconsistently, advocates also contend that a less adversarial stance usually works for the benefit of defendants, who are usually guilty of the charges against them and eager to negotiate a plea. Still, many defense attorneys are ambivalent about their close relationship with prosecutors, concerned that the need to maintain harmonious relations leads them to become "part of the system."[61] Whether plea bargaining is a legitimate and desirable element of the American criminal justice system thus remains a perplexing and hotly contested issue.

POLICY ISSUES IN CRIMINAL JUSTICE

Beginning in the 1960s, crime rates in the United States soared and conservative critics claimed that the courts were responsible for much of the rise in crime.[62] By freeing criminals on "legal technicalities" and giving lenient sentences to those convicted, they contended, the courts allowed dangerous criminals to return to the streets and undermined the deterrent effect of criminal law. To remedy the situation, these critics proposed several policy changes that would affect the operation of the courts. Among the changes were the reform or elimination of the exclusionary rule, which prevents the use of illegally obtained evidence to secure convictions; the reform or elimination of the insanity defense in criminal trials; and the establishment of minimum sentences for offenders, with sharply escalating sentences for repeat offenders. Many of these changes were enacted into law.

Liberal critics have also challenged the sentencing practices of the courts but from a different perspective.[63] They contend that those guilty of the same crime often receive different sentences, with particularly harsh sentences meted out to minorities and to the poor. Reforms must be instituted, they argue, to ensure more equitable sentencing. Other liberal critics have decried the incarceration of so many offenders and sought alternatives designed to rehabilitate instead of punish offenders.

Both conservative and liberal critiques have drawn fire. Proponents of the exclusionary rule believe that it deters police from violating constitutional rights and maintains the integrity of the judicial process.[64] Supporters of the insanity defense contend that it reaffirms the moral underpinnings of criminal justice by distinguishing those who are responsible for their actions from those who are not.[65] And some researchers have challenged claims that courts are unduly lenient or that they discriminate in sentencing offenders, while others lament the loss of judicial discretion to tailor sentences to the specifics of the offense and the offender.[66]

In the next sections, policy debates over the exclusionary rule, the insanity defense, the sentencing of criminals, and drug courts are examined. Each section analyzes both the justifications offered for and the objections to traditional policies and practices. It also considers the empirical evidence bearing on competing claims and assesses the consequences of the reforms that have been adopted.

The Exclusionary Rule

The exclusionary rule forbids the use in a criminal prosecution of any evidence that is illegally obtained by law enforcement officials. This evidence is usually either physical evidence, such as drugs or weapons, uncovered through illegal searches in violation of the Fourth Amendment, or confessions extracted from defendants in violation of their rights under the Fifth or Sixth Amendments. When a trial judge rules that a police officer violated the defendant's rights in securing evidence, the prosecution cannot use that evidence to obtain a conviction. Nor can it use any additional evidence obtained by following leads generated by the initial illegality—what courts have referred to as "the fruit of the poisonous tree."[67] The exclusionary rule may have an effect even before trial. If the only evidence of guilt is inadmissible, the prosecutor has no case and thus is unlikely to charge a suspect.

Yet the exclusionary rule does not immunize lawbreakers from prosecution. Prosecutors can still pursue convictions with any evidence that the police have obtained legally. Put differently, the exclusionary rule merely places the government in the same position it would have been in had the illegal search or interrogation not taken place. If a conviction is overturned on appeal because illegally obtained evidence was used to secure it, the defendant can be retried with that evidence excluded from consideration.

The Development of the Exclusionary Rule   The United States is unique in its reliance on the exclusionary rule as a means of dealing with police misconduct. Great Britain, Canada, and other common-law countries admit all reliable evidence at trial but permit suits for damages against police officers alleged to have committed illegal acts. No civil-law country disciplines its police by excluding illegally seized evidence. Indeed, for most of the nation's history, U.S. courts also followed the common-law rule and permitted the introduction of all probative evidence at trial.

The adoption of the exclusionary rule began early in the twentieth century when a few states banned the admission of illegally seized evidence as a matter of state law.[68] In *Weeks v. United States* (1914), the U.S. Supreme Court adopted the exclusionary rule for federal prosecutions, maintaining that the exclusion of illegally seized evidence was necessary to protect defendants' Fourth Amendment rights.[69] But *Weeks* had no direct effect on the states, which conduct more than 99 percent of criminal prosecutions. Even after the Court applied the Fourth Amendment's search-and-seizure requirements to the states in *Wolf v. Colorado* (1949), most states did not adopt the exclusionary rule. As late as 1960, only half the states required the suppression of illegally seized evidence.[70] This changed dramatically after the Court's decision in *Mapp v. Ohio* (1961).[71] In *Mapp,* the Supreme Court extended the exclusionary rule to the states, inaugurating (in the view of its critics) a constitutional revolution. Although since the 1980s the Court has somewhat limited the reach of the exclusionary rule, the rule continues to affect the kind of evidence admissible at trial.[72]

Underlying the Supreme Court's decisions establishing the exclusionary rule are three complementary arguments. One is that the exclusionary rule is necessary to vindicate the protections of the Fourth and Fifth Amendments. Indeed, advocates of the exclusionary rule have turned the critics' rhetoric back on them. If *Mapp* truly inaugurated a constitutional revolution, the obvious question is why? After all, the ruling did not institute any new requirements regarding searches and seizures. The answer, according to proponents of the exclusionary rule, is that before *Mapp* the Fourth Amendment's requirements were routinely ignored. If that is true, it demonstrates that other remedies did not adequately safeguard Fourth Amendment rights.

Advocates claim that the exclusionary rule can safeguard those rights because it deters police misconduct. By preventing convictions on the basis of illegally seized evidence, the rule removes the incentive for police to gather evidence illegally. As a result, far fewer unconstitutional searches or interrogations will occur. Thus, the exclusionary rule not only vindicates the rights of a defendant subjected to an illegal search or interrogation but also deters future police misconduct, thereby protecting all citizens.

Proponents also maintain that the exclusionary rule protects the integrity of the judicial process by preventing the government from benefiting from the misconduct of its agents. To permit the use of illegally obtained evidence in court would signal an implicit approval of the officers' methods in obtaining the evidence. This would send the message that it is okay to violate constitutional rights for a good cause. But the exclusion of such evidence sends a different message: The government must respect rights even as it pursues legitimate ends.

The Case Against the Exclusionary Rule   Not surprisingly, critics of the exclusionary rule dispute these arguments. They charge that the rule requires the release of dangerous criminals. Under the exclusionary rule, the reliability of the illegally obtained evidence has no effect on its admissibility. If a suspect under extreme duress confesses to a crime, then there may be reason to doubt the truth of his statements. If a police officer discovers a stolen wallet during an illegal search of a suspect, however, the wallet provides clear evidence of guilt. Yet in neither case is the evidence admissible. This holds true no matter how serious the charges against a defendant. Even if the illegally seized evidence conclusively proves that the defendant is guilty of murder, it cannot be used to convict him. If there is no other evidence adequate to obtain a conviction, the defendant is released. Opponents of the exclusionary rule claim that this is too high a cost to pay. They insist that all pertinent and reliable evidence should be admitted at trial so that guilty persons receive their just punishment.

Critics also charge that the exclusionary rule is too inflexible. In determining the admissibility of evidence, the rule does not consider how seriously the defendant's rights were infringed upon in obtaining that evidence. The same penalty of exclusion operates whether the police officer's violation of the defendant's rights was slight and inadvertent or blatant and intentional. In the words of Justice Benjamin Cardozo, this may mean that "the criminal is to go free because the constable blundered."[73] Some critics of the exclusionary rule have proposed a "good faith" exception to the rule, permitting the introduction of evidence resulting from illegal searches or interrogations that officers believed were lawful. This would preserve the rule only for intentional, and therefore serious, violations of constitutional rights.

Critics contend that the exclusionary rule is ineffective in protecting rights. It can deter police misconduct only if police engage in illegal searches to develop evidence for trial. It has no effect on illegal searches undertaken for other reasons—to harass individuals or to confiscate contraband, for example. Even when police search to gather evidence, the exclusionary rule can deter misconduct only if the offending officers realize that they are violating Fourth Amendment rights. An officer who mistakenly believes a search is permissible under the Fourth Amendment will not be deterred by the exclusionary rule.

Finally, critics claim that the exclusionary rule protects only criminals, not law-abiding citizens. If police officers illegally ransack a person's house and find evidence of criminality, that evidence is excluded at trial. But if police discover no evidence of crime, there is no evidence to exclude and no trial at which to exclude it, so the exclusionary rule does not help the victim of the illegal search. Opponents propose replacing the exclusionary rule with other mechanisms, such as civil suits against police by victims of illegal searches or interrogations.

Evidence on the Exclusionary Rule   The debate over the exclusionary rule revolves largely around competing claims about the rule's effect on criminal justice. Numerous studies have been conducted to assess those claims. This section considers the findings of these studies.

Does the Exclusionary Rule Deter Police Misconduct?   If the exclusionary rule has a deterrent effect, then one would expect illegal police searches to decline after *Mapp.* In a few jurisdictions, researchers did find a decrease in the number of defense motions to suppress illegally seized evidence, which might signal a decline in illegal searches.[74] In several jurisdictions after *Mapp,* however, there was an increase in the number of motions to suppress illegally seized evidence.[75] One might attribute this increase to the failure of the exclusionary rule to deter police misconduct. But the increase might indicate a greater willingness on the part of defense attorneys to challenge police searches so that illegally seized evidence would be excluded at trial. Thus, the available evidence does not conclusively resolve the deterrence issue.

What Effect Does the Exclusionary Rule Have on Convictions?   Critics contend that large numbers of guilty persons go free because of the exclusionary rule. Empirical studies of the effects of the exclusionary rule do not bear out this claim, however. A National Institute of Justice study of prosecutions in California found that prosecutors decided not to press charges because of illegal search problems in 2.4 percent of drug cases and in less than 1 percent of their cases overall.[76] A nine-county study of criminal courts found that defense attorneys filed motions to suppress evidence in more than 7 percent of all cases but that only 5 percent of those motions succeeded (with a slightly higher success rate in drugs and weapons cases).[77] The study also found that defendants were convicted in one-third of those cases in which evidence was suppressed.[78] Thus, few defendants escape conviction because of the exclusionary rule.

Does the Exclusionary Rule Let Dangerous Criminals Go Free?   Even if few defendants avoid conviction as a result of the exclusionary rule, those defendants who do may pose a serious threat to public safety. In general, however, studies of the exclusionary rule do not support that notion. For example, the nine-county study found that almost 60 percent of the cases "lost" as a result of the exclusionary rule involved so-called victimless crimes (drug possession or possession of a weapon), while fewer than 20 percent involved serious offenses such as armed robbery, burglary, and arson. Also, if the defendants in the "lost" cases had been convicted and received sentences comparable to those given to defendants convicted of the same offenses, almost two-thirds would have received jail sentences of less than six months.[79] These findings suggest that few dangerous criminals are freed by the exclusionary rule. Of course, they do not determine whether the release of even a few such criminals is too heavy a price to pay for the exclusionary rule.

Are There Alternatives to the Exclusionary Rule?   Critics concede that if the exclusionary rule is eliminated because it is ineffective or results in too many "lost convictions," then some other means must be devised to vindicate constitutional rights and prevent police misconduct. The two most frequently proposed alternatives are the "good faith" exception to the exclusionary rule and a reliance on civil suits against those who violate constitutional rights.

The idea of a good faith exception has received considerable support. It was recommended by the Attorney General's Task Force on Violent Crime in 1981 and has been partly endorsed in Supreme Court decisions.[80] Under this proposal, illegally obtained evidence can be used at trial only if the officers who obtained it acted in good faith; that is, with a reasonable belief that they were complying with constitutional requirements. Proponents note that the good faith exception retains the exclusionary rule when it might serve as a deterrent. But barring evidence obtained in good faith does not deter police misconduct because the problem is a lack of knowledge about constitutional requirements, not an unwillingness to observe them. Unfortunately, there are no data on how frequently constitutional violations by the police result from good faith mistakes rather than intentional disregard of constitutional mandates.

Many critics who favor abolishing the exclusionary rule have proposed that the United States emulate Great Britain in permitting civil suits against police officers by those whose constitutional rights have been violated.[81] This would not only ensure the availability of all reliable evidence in criminal cases but also offer recourse for innocent victims of illegal searches. But proponents of the exclusionary rule caution that juries would sympathize with police officers and be reluctant to decide in favor of "disreputable" plaintiffs, especially those who had committed criminal offenses. The lack of success of civil suits against police officers offers at least some support for this contention.[82] The exclusionary rule will probably not be eliminated soon.

The Insanity Defense

In 1981, John Hinckley, Jr. fired six shots at President Ronald Reagan. One hit the president in the chest, two wounded members of the president's security detail, and a fourth penetrated the brain of Press Secretary James Brady, permanently disabling him. A year later, a jury found Hinckley not guilty by reason of insanity, concluding that the government had failed to prove beyond a reasonable doubt that Hinckley was sane at the time of the shooting. The public was outraged. Some people, thinking that Hinckley had hoodwinked the jury, proposed tightening the legal definition of insanity, while others—including Attorney General William French Smith—demanded the abolition of the insanity defense.

The reaction to the Hinckley verdict was reminiscent of an earlier controversy over the insanity defense. Queen Victoria herself criticized the acquittal by reason of insanity of Daniel M'Naghten, who—under the delusion that he was being persecuted by the Pope, the Jesuits, and Prime Minister Robert Peel—mistakenly shot Peel's secretary. The importance of the M'Naghten case derived less from the unpopularity of its verdict than from the standard it established, the so-called M'Naghten test, for determining whether defendants were responsible for their criminal actions.

Tests of Insanity   The criminal law justifies holding individuals responsible for their actions on the assumption that they have the ability to choose between acceptable and unacceptable behavior. This assumption supplies the rationale for the insanity defense: Criminal law should not punish those who are unable to choose between acceptable and unacceptable behavior. But how does one define the inability to choose that exempts a person from the operation of criminal law? Under the M'Naghten test, a defendant is responsible for criminal actions unless "the party accused was labouring under such a defect of reason, from disease of the mind, as not to know the nature and quality of the act he was doing; or, if he did know it, he did not know he was doing what was wrong."[83] Under this test, as under other insanity standards, the incapacity must come from mental disease. An incapacity due to drunkenness or drug addiction does not excuse criminal conduct. What is distinctive about the M'Naghten test is its emphasis on the cognitive capacity of defendants—that is, their ability to distinguish right from wrong. Lack of understanding, not an inability to control one's behavior, is decisive.

For most of the twentieth century, efforts to reform the insanity defense have focused on introducing a volitional element into the legal definition of insanity (see Table 6-1). Defendants would be judged insane not only if they lacked the ability to distinguish right from wrong, but also if mental illness prevented them from choosing socially acceptable behavior. This is reflected in the "irresistible impulse" test, which was adopted in some states as a supplement to the M'Naghten test. The irresistible impulse test permits the acquittal of defendants who could not control their behavior, even though they knew it was wrong. It is also reflected in the American Law Institute's (ALI) Model Penal Code, which has served as the basis for reform in several states. According to the ALI's code, "A person is not responsible for criminal conduct if at the time of such conduct as a result of mental disease or defect he lacks substantial capacity either to appreciate the criminality of his conduct or to conform his conduct to the requirements of the law."[84] Although the ALI standard

TABLE 6-1	INSANITY DEFENSE STANDARDS		
American Law Institute	**M'Naghten Rule**	**M'Naghten Rule and Irresistible Impulse**	**Guilty but Mentally Ill***
Alabama	Arizona	Colorado	Alaska
Alaska	Delaware	Florida[a]	Delaware
Arkansas	Iowa	New Mexico	Georgia
California	Kansas	New York[a]	
Georgia	Louisiana	Virginia	
Hawaii	Mississippi	Illinois	
Illinois	Nebraska*	Indiana	
Indiana	Nevada	Kentucky	
Kentucky	New Jersey	Michigan	
Maine	North Carolina	New Mexico	
Maryland	North Dakota[a]	Pennsylvania	
Massachusetts	Oklahoma	South Dakota	
Michigan	Pennsylvania	Utah	
Missouri	South Carolina		
Ohio[a]	South Dakota[a]		
Oregon	Washington		
Rhode Island[a]			
Tennessee			
Texas[a]			
Vermont			
West Virginia			
Wisconsin			

*States that have instituted the "guilty but mentally ill" verdict appear in other columns listing insanity standards because they employ those standards in determining whether a defendant is mentally ill. Utah has abolished the insanity defense but, somewhat inconsistently, retained the verdict of guilty but mentally ill.

[a]With some modification.

Source: Rita J. Simon and David E. Aaronson, *The Insanity Defense: A Critical Assessment of Law and Policy in the Post-Hinckley Era* (New York: Praeger, 1988), Appendix, pp. 251–263.

resembles the M'Naghten test, it includes both cognitive and volitional elements and seems, in using "appreciate" rather than "know," to allow consideration of whether the defendant was emotionally as well as intellectually aware of the significance of his behavior.[85]

Following the verdict in the Hinckley case, however, reform efforts took a decidedly different direction, as the federal government and more than thirty states reconsidered the insanity defense. In the Comprehensive Crime Control Act of 1984, the federal government shifted the burden of proof on the issue of insanity. The defense would have to prove that the accused was insane at the time of the crime instead of the government having to prove he was not. The Act also narrowed somewhat the legal definition of insanity by, in effect, resurrecting the M'Naghten standard for federal prosecutions. Several states also tightened their requirements for insanity acquittals and for the release of offenders acquitted by reason of insanity. Finally, eleven states followed the example of Michigan, which in 1975 attempted to reduce the use of the insanity defense by establishing the verdict of "guilty but mentally ill."[86]

The Effects of the Insanity Defense   Although there are no nationwide data, various studies indicate that few defendants plead not guilty by reason of insanity (NGRI) and even fewer are acquitted on that basis. A study in New Jersey found that successful NGRI pleas amounted to only 1/20 of 1 percent of all criminal cases handled by the Office of Public Defender.[87] But researchers did find that the test for determining insanity affects both the frequency of insanity pleas and their success. Apparently jurors do attempt to apply the standard outlined by judges in their instructions to the jury.[88] Perhaps surprisingly, the establishment of the "guilty but mentally ill" verdict has not decreased NGRI pleas or acquittals, as it appears that those defendants in Michigan who pled guilty but mentally ill would have pled guilty in the absence of that additional verdict.[89]

Just who are the defendants pleading NGRI, and with what crimes are they charged? Highly publicized cases such as that of Hinckley suggest that defendants plead insanity when they face severe punishment for violent crimes. But research on this point is inconclusive. A study of insanity acquittees in Hawaii found that only 22 percent were charged with murder and that although slightly more than half the acquittals were in cases involving crimes against persons (e.g., homicide, rape, assault), a sizable number involved crimes against property (e.g., burglary) or crimes against public order (e.g., indecent exposure).[90] A New York study found that as many as 70 percent of NGRI acquittals involved violent crimes but research on NGRI acquittees in Colorado found only 19 percent were charged with murder.[91]

Finally, many states commit all defendants found not guilty by reason of insanity to a fifty-day observation period before determining whether they are fit to be released. Few are released at the conclusion of that observation period. Several studies have found that in comparison with those convicted and sentenced, insanity acquittees tend to spend an equivalent time in confinement for violent crimes such as murder or attempted murder and more time in confinement for less serious crimes.[92] Thus, recent research suggests that defendants seldom "beat the rap" if found not guilty by reason of insanity.

Crime and Punishment: Sentencing

From the late 1940s to the early 1970s, the idea of rehabilitation dominated the sentencing of criminals in the United States. It was assumed that the aim of imprisonment was to change the characters, attitudes, and behavior of offenders, both to benefit them and to make them less threatening to society.[93] Punishment was to be tailored to the offender, with the length of confinement depending less on the character of the offense and more on how long it took to rehabilitate the offender. To fit the punishment to the offender, sentencing policy emphasized the use of indeterminate sentences as well as broad discretion for judges in sentencing. Prisoners were sentenced for a range of years and the prison parole board released offenders when they demonstrated sufficient signs of rehabilitation. California, perhaps the state most committed to the rehabilitative model, sentenced most serious offenders to an indeterminate term of between one year and life in prison, with the duration served determined by parole authorities.

In the early 1970s, rehabilitation as the aim of punishment came under attack from many directions. Conservatives charged that the emphasis on rehabilitation promoted excessive leniency in sentencing and that punishment should serve the purposes of retribution and incapacitation. Liberals attacked the potential for unfairness and discrimination in a system under which offenders committing the same crime could serve widely disparate sentences, especially when those deciding sentences (judges and parole boards) did not need to explain or justify their choices. Social science research also undermined the case for rehabilitation, demonstrating that imprisonment rarely promoted rehabilitation and that, even when it did, officials could not reliably determine which offenders had been rehabilitated.[94]

Reforming Sentencing   These criticisms led to reforms designed to curb excessive leniency in sentencing and to eliminate disparities in sentencing for the same offense. One such reform was the establishment of "mandatory minimum" sentences for certain offenses.[95] Massachusetts, for example, established a one-year minimum sentence for anyone convicted of carrying a firearm in violation of the state's firearm laws. Michigan prescribed a two-year prison sentence, in addition to the primary sentence, for possession of a firearm during the commission of a felony (as publicized on billboards, "One with a Gun Gets You Two"). More recently, some states extended the mandatory sentencing concept to target repeat offenders, using "three strikes and you're out" laws that call for life imprisonment for third-time felons.[96]

Another reform has been to limit judicial discretion by establishing guidelines for judges to use in sentencing offenders. Some states—Florida and Maryland, for example—adopted guidelines that judges might voluntarily adhere to in sentencing. Others such as California enacted specific sentences

---

BOX

6-3   *Federal Sentencing Guidelines: How They Work*

This begins with section 2B3.1 of the Federal Sentencing Guidelines, on robbery, which has a base offense level of 18, and the following special offense characteristics:

(1) If the value of the property taken or destroyed exceeded $2,500, increase the offense level as follows:

Loss	*Increase in Level*
(A) $2,500 or less	no increase
(B) $2,501–$10,000	add 1
(C) $10,001–$50,000	add 2
(D) $50,001–$250,000	add 3
(E) $250,001–$1,000,000	add 4
(F) $1,000,001–$5,000,000	add 5
(G) more than $5,000,000	add 6

Treat the loss for a financial institution or post office as at least $5,000.

(2) (A) If a firearm was discharged increase by 5 levels; (B) if a firearm or a dangerous weapon was otherwise used, increase by 4 levels; (C) if a firearm or other dangerous weapon was brandished, displayed, or possessed, increase by 3 levels.

(3) If any victim sustained bodily injury, increase the offense level according to the seriousness of the injury:

---

for various offenses, allowing judges to increase or decrease the prescribed sentence only slightly based on mitigating or aggravating factors. In the Sentencing Reform Act of 1984, Congress adopted a third approach, delegating to a commission the responsibility for devising detailed sentencing criteria. The commission produced an over 900-page manual to regulate sentencing in federal courts. Under the guidelines, offenders are assigned a score based on the seriousness of the offense and personal characteristics such as age, mental condition, and prior record. For each combination of offense and offender scores, a presumptive sentence was established. Federal judges are obliged to justify any sentences outside the guidelines and both the defendant and prosecutor can appeal the justification offered by the judge. (See Box 6-3)

Degree of Bodily Injury	Increase in Level
(A) Bodily Injury	add 2
(B) Serious Bodily Injury	add 4
(C) Permanent or Life-Threatening Bodily Injury	add 6

Provided, however, that the cumulative adjustments from (2) and (3) shall not exceed 9 levels.

(4) (A) If any person was abducted to facilitate commission of the offense or to facilitate escape, increase by 4 levels; or (B) if any person was physically restrained to facilitate commission of the offense or to facilitate escape, increase by 2 levels.

(5) If obtaining a firearm, destructive device, or controlled substance was the object of the offense, increase by 1 level.

How do the Guidelines operate in practice? Imagine a bank robber, with one prior serious conviction, who robs a bank of $40,000 by pointing a gun at the teller. Then, according to Guideline Sec.2B3.1, the offender would receive an offense score of 23 (18 for the offense, plus 2 for the amount of the robbery and 3 for brandishing the gun), with an additional 3 points for the prior conviction. Looking up the Guideline sentence for the score, one would find a sentencing range of from 51 to 63 months in prison. If the judge sentences the defendant to a sentence outside the range indicated by the Guidelines, he or she must give reasons for departing from the Guidelines, and an appeals court may then review the reasonableness of the departure.

Source: Stephen Breyer, "The Federal Sentencing Guidelines and the Key Compromises upon Which They Rest," *Hofstra Law Review* 17 (fall 1988): 1–50.

In *Blakely v. Washington* (2004), the U.S. Supreme Court cast a shadow on the federal sentencing guidelines and on similar guidelines in other states. Citing defendants' Sixth Amendment right to trial by jury, the Court ruled that any aggravating factors used to increase a criminal sentence must be proven to a jury, not decided by a judge. Although the Court did not directly address the federal guidelines, those guidelines authorized the trial judge to determine whether aggravating factors existed and to adjust the defendant's sentence accordingly. In a speech after the Court's ruling, Justice Sandra Day O'Connor told a group of federal judges: "It looks like a No. 10 earthquake to me. I think that the consequences are severe and it's going to take a little time to figure out what to do." In *United States v. Booker* (2005), she joined four other justices in holding that the congressional statute making the federal sentencing guidelines mandatory was unconstitutional. Thus, *Booker* made the guidelines essentially advisory, but federal judges were obliged to consider them in arriving at their sentencing decisions. How this will operate, and whether Congress will seek an alternative approach to curtailing the sentencing discretion of federal judges remains uncertain.[97]

The Effects of Sentencing Reforms   Studies of the gun laws in Massachusetts and Michigan suggest that the establishment of mandatory sentences does not guarantee greater severity for offenders or eliminate disparities in sentencing.[98] Prosecutors have circumvented the laws when they believed them unduly harsh, often with the approval of judges and police, usually by refusing to charge arrestees with offenses that carry a mandatory sentence. After the adoption of Michigan's gun law, parole officers routinely began parole hearings with the comment, "I see you were convicted of unarmed robbery in Detroit. What caliber of gun did you use?"[99] Also, defendants charged with crimes carrying a mandatory sentence have more frequently gone to trial, thus slowing the processing of cases. Those convicted under mandatory-sentence statutes have received more severe sentences. Mandatory-sentence laws have increased sentencing disparities, however, among offenders committing the same crime. This increase occurred because the sentence such offenders receive depends on whether the prosecutor charges them with violating the mandatory-sentence law.

Sentencing guidelines seem a more promising approach to sentencing reform.[100] In Minnesota and some other states, these guidelines have succeeded in reducing unjust (e.g., racially discriminatory) sentencing disparities by eliminating the unchecked discretion of judges and parole boards to determine the length of imprisonment. The federal sentencing guidelines have been subject to intense criticism, however, especially from judges. Although one aim of the guidelines was to increase the severity of sentences, some critics insist that the guidelines treat offenders too harshly. Far fewer offenders receive probation under the guidelines and the average prison time for offenses has increased dramatically. For example, the term served for drug offenses rose from twenty-two months before the guidelines to sixty-five months after, and the time for robbery increased from fifty-two to ninety-one months.[101] Critics also charge that the guidelines have made sentencing too rigid and mechanical, preventing judges from considering the personal characteristics of individual defendants, which leads to arbitrary and unjust results. Indeed, one federal judge claimed his role had been reduced to that of a notary public; another compared his role to that of an accountant.[102] Finally, critics contend that one unanticipated result of the sentencing guidelines was to increase the power of prosecutors. Kate Stith and Jose Cabranes observed that "[b]ecause the sentencing rules are known in advance, prosecutors may greatly influence the ultimate sentence through their decisions on charges, plea agreements, and motions to depart [from the prescribed sentence] for substantial assistance to law enforcement authorities."[103] In sum, critics of sentencing guidelines deny that the elimination of judicial discretion promotes justice in sentencing.

Some federal district judges have responded to the rigidity and severity of the sentencing guidelines by invoking with some frequency their discretion to depart downward from sentences prescribed by the guidelines. In 2003, Congress enacted new legislation designed to limit judges' downward departures from the sentencing guidelines. This underscores the continuing controversy over the appropriate discretion for judges in sentencing.

Crime and Punishment: Drug Courts

The rapidly increasing use of cocaine and "crack" cocaine during the 1980s sparked concern about the drug problem in the United States.[104] The federal government responded by launching a "war on drugs," devoting substantial resources to drug interdiction and to the arrest of drug users and drug traffickers. Congress enacted a series of laws that increased penalties for drug trafficking and drug use, and state legislatures followed suit, prescribing mandatory minimum sentences for drug offenders. The war on drugs produced a dramatic rise in drug arrests (up 134 percent nationally from 1980 to 1989). Prosecution of these offenders imposed serious caseload pressures on state and federal courts. By 2002, convictions for drug trafficking and drug possession constituted almost one-third of felony convictions in state courts. This in turn led to increased demands on state and federal prisons. By 2002, over half of federal prisoners and almost 25 percent of state prisoners were drug offenders. But harsh sentences did not stem the tide of drug offenses, and the high recidivism rate among drug offenders led many officials to conclude that the existing approach to the drug problem was not working. As Judge Diane Strickland of Virginia stated: "Basically, we have had a revolving door phenomenon where we take an offender, lock him up for whatever appropriate period of time, and have him back out in the community without addressing the underlying source of his criminal behavior. . . . We have to come up with something else that we can do for these folks if we're going to try and deter their criminal behavior."[105]

The drug court movement emerged out of dissatisfaction with prevailing approaches to drug crime. The first drug court was established in 1989 in Dade County (Miami), Florida, an area hit hard by drug crime. Among those spearheading this initiative was Janet Reno, Florida's state attorney at that time. After President Bill Clinton appointed Reno as attorney general, the Department of Justice—with strong bipartisan support in Congress—encouraged establishment of drug courts throughout the nation. By 2004, more than 1,100 drug courts were in operation, and hundreds more were in the planning stage. Indeed, some proponents of the drug court concept, such as Chief Judge Judith Kaye of New York, have recommended extending the approach throughout state court systems.[106]

What Is Distinctive about Drug Courts?   Drug courts are distinctive both in their aims and in the means by which they seek to achieve those aims. Drug courts incorporate treatment for substance abuse directly into the judicial process. Offenders typically enter the drug court program before trial, often almost immediately after arrest. They are assigned to a drug treatment program and told when to meet with the judge, who will monitor their progress. Court appearances can occur as often as several times a week or as infrequently as once a month. Offenders undergo drug testing on a regular basis, and positive test results or missed treatment or court appearances can result in immediate sanctions; one drug court judge referred to the jail as "my motel." But the focus of the drug court is less on determining guilt or dispensing punishment than on curing offenders of their substance dependency and reorienting their lives. This ambitious goal may keep offenders under court supervision for an extended period. To graduate from Delaware's drug court, for example, an offender must have four months of total abstinence, hold a steady job, maintain a stable residence, participate in twelve-step meetings, have developed a support network, and have successfully completed a drug treatment program.[107]

Underlying drug courts' program of continuing supervision and treatment is the notion of "therapeutic justice."[108] Traditionally, doing justice entailed determining in an adversarial proceeding whether defendants were guilty or innocent and, if they were guilty, prescribing appropriate punishments. However, in drug courts "the way [justice is] redefined is . . . you have people who have a disease called alcoholism and/or addiction. And what is just is getting them well rather than punishing them for their disease."[109] This redefinition of justice has important consequences. Gone is the emphasis on guilt or innocence: the "focus is on the participant's recovery and law-abiding behavior— not on the merits of the pending case."[110] Gone, too, is the adversarial character of the process, because all courtroom participants are expected to collaborate as a "team" in a treatment regimen for the drug court's "client." This of course requires a substantial change in orientation and responsibilities, particularly for defense attorneys. Gone, too, is the emphasis on the presumption of innocence and various trial rights; in drug court offenders must forego their right to a speedy trial, admit their drug use rather than proclaim their innocence, and submit to regular drug testing so that their progress can be monitored. Also gone is the aim of assigning a punishment commensurate with the offense; instead the aim is to redirect the offender's life. The supervision of offenders by the drug court continues until they have successfully completed their treatment programs. Finally, gone is the role of the judge as impartial arbiter. Instead, judges have broad and ongoing interaction with offenders that may extend to oversight over various aspects of their lives (see Box 6-4).

Evaluating Drug Courts   According to their advocates, drug courts rehabilitate participants and reduce recidivism among drug offenders, thus reducing court caseloads and providing a cost-effective alternative to incarceration. Initially, drug courts reported dramatic decreases in recidivism, but more recent independent studies have tempered claims of success. Still, the most comprehensive review of research on drug courts concluded that drug use and other criminal behavior were substantially reduced while offenders were under the intense supervision of the drug court. The study also found that graduates of drug courts tended to have lower recidivism rates than those who did not participate in the program, although reduction in recidivism from such participation was not dramatic.[111] Nevertheless, these results have led advocates of drug courts to maintain that the question has shifted from whether to institute drug courts to how to run them effectively.

Despite the popularity of drug courts, not everyone supports the concept. Some critics view the drug court's departures from the traditional judicial process as deeply problematic.[112] These critics charge that the language of treatment disguises how punitive drug courts actually are. Drug court judges exercise broad discretion over offenders without significant checks on their authority; thus, judges can impose jail time for drug relapses and determine how long offenders remain under court supervision. For example, those guilty of drug possession typically spend far longer under judicial supervision than they would have spent in jail if convicted. Moreover, those who fail the drug court program remain subject to prosecution for their original offenses.

Critics also contend that drug courts may augment the reach of government power. For one thing, some minor offenders whose cases would not be prosecuted are referred to the drug court. As Judge Morris Hoffman of the Denver criminal court observed: "The very presence of drug court, with its significantly increased capacity for processing cases, has caused the police to make arrests in, and prosecutors to file, the kinds of ten- and twenty-dollar hand-to-hand drug cases which the system would not have bothered with before."[113] For another thing, offenders in drug courts lack the safeguards that come from limited judicial authority, adversarial proceedings, and vigorous representation by counsel. Most important, whereas the aim of criminal law is limited (determination of guilt or innocence and imposition of appropriate punishment), the aim of the drug court is comprehensive (changing fundamentally the lifestyle of the drug user).

BOX
6-4   *Scenes from Drug Courts*

According to Judge Peggy Hora of the Hayward (California) drug court, "We are the judges that get to color outside the lines. . . . The way we relate to the people in drug court is totally different from the traditional jurisprudential role." A few snapshots of what transpires in drug courts show the difference:

- Judge Hora presenting a drug court participant with a graduation balloon to celebrate her passing her GED test.
- Judge Stephanie Duncan-Peters of the Washington, D.C., drug court, roaming her courtroom, microphone in hand, engaging individual offenders about their progress since their last appearance in her court.
- Judge Stanley Goldstein of the Miami drug court, addressing a drug court participant who had relapsed and used drugs: "Any problem you got, you come to me. I'm your Daddy."
- Judge Robert Fogan of the Fort Lauderdale (Florida) drug court, giving offenders a certificate, a T-shirt, and a hug when they graduate from the court's treatment program.

Source: James L. Nolan Jr., *Reinventing Justice: The American Drug Court Movement* (Princeton, NJ: Princeton University Press, 2001), pp. 5–11, 102, 191.

CONCLUSIONS

While the federal Bill of Rights imposes basic requirements for the administration of justice in the United States, the primary responsibility rests with state and local governments. This decentralization of authority has encouraged the development of a rich diversity of institutions, laws, and practices for dealing with criminal justice issues. This diversity is reflected in the legal standards defining criminal justice policy—from the rules regulating pretrial release to the tests for determining responsibility for one's criminal acts and the laws governing the sentencing of criminals. If anything, there is even greater diversity in the discretionary practices—such as prosecutorial dismissal of charges and plea bargaining—that have developed in the absence of legal standards, or at times, in opposition to them. This diversity suggests that it is probably inaccurate to speak of *the* American criminal justice system. There are almost as many systems as there are states and localities.

Yet states and localities develop their distinct approaches in confronting a set of common policy problems. For example, both Supreme Court rulings and notions of fundamental fairness demand that indigent defendants be represented by counsel. The policy question is whether to opt for a public defender program, an assigned counsel system, or some other alternative. Similarly, some mechanism must be devised for distinguishing between cases that merit prosecution and cases that do not. The policy question here is whether this judgment should rest with the prosecutor, the judge at the preliminary hearing, or some other official.

Although some issues in the administration of criminal justice do not excite great controversy, others—including some involving the courts—generate intense conflict. Often these conflicts pit defenders of court practices against political conservatives, who charge that American courts have undermined public safety by showing excessive concern for the rights of criminals and by treating them too leniently. Since the 1970s, these conservatives have won a number of victories in their campaign to reduce the discretion of judges and mandate harsher treatment for offenders. For example, in some jurisdictions, defendants may now be held in "preventive detention" pending trial; have illegally seized evidence used against them, if it was seized in good faith; find it more difficult to mount an insanity defense; and face a mandatory or determinate sentence upon conviction.

The conflict can be seen as a dispute not only about the substance of policy but also about who will set it. Legislators have enacted statutes on several matters—from pretrial release to sentencing—in an effort to reassert control over criminal justice policy. On occasion, executive officials also have sought to determine basic policy. The ban on plea bargaining by Alaska's attorney general is an obvious example. Judges and prosecutors have often opposed these efforts, viewing them as infringements on their prerogatives or as upsetting established modes of operation. At times the opposition has been direct, as when prosecutors and judges in Michigan effectively gutted the state's mandatory-sentencing law. More frequently, judges and prosecutors have sought despite the new requirements to exercise discretion to achieve what they view as desirable outcomes.

Whether justice is better promoted by the faithful application of legal standards established by the legislature or by negotiated settlements is, of course, a hotly disputed topic. It is a question that arises not only in the criminal justice context but also in the civil justice realm, to which the discussion now turns.

NOTES

1. James Eisenstein and Herbert Jacob, *Felony Justice: An Organizational Analysis of Criminal Courts* (Boston: Little, Brown, 1977), p. 131.

2. See Samuel Walker, *Taming the System: The Control of Discretion in Criminal Justice, 1950–1990* (New York: Oxford University Press, 1993).

3. Eisenstein and Jacob, *Felony Justice,* p. 47.

4. *Gideon v. Wainwright,* 372 U.S. 335 (1963).

5. *Argersinger v. Hamlin,* 407 U.S. 25 (1972).

6. *Report to the Nation on Crime and Justice,* 2d ed. (Washington, DC: U.S. Department of Justice, Bureau of Justice Statistics, 1988), pp. 74–75.

7. Quoted in Jonathan Casper, *American Criminal Justice: The Defendant's Perspective* (Englewood Cliffs, NJ: Prentice Hall, 1972), p. 101.

8. David W. Neubauer, *Judicial Process: Law, Courts, and Politics in the United States* (Pacific Grove, CA: Brooks/Cole Publishing, 1991), p. 127.

9. Malcolm M. Feeley, *The Process Is the Punishment: Handling Cases in a Lower Criminal Court* (New York: Russell Sage Foundation, 1979), pp. 30–31. See also Eisenstein and Jacob, *Felony Justice,* p. 285.

10. *Report to the Nation on Crime and Justice,* pp. 11–12, 34–35.

11. See www.fbi.gov/; see also Hans Zeisel, *The Limits of Law Enforcement* (Chicago: University of Chicago Press, 1982), p. 98, fig. 23.

12. Vera Institute of Justice, *Felony Arrests,* rev. ed. (New York: Longman, 1981), p. 5, fig. 2; and Zeisel, *Limits of Law Enforcement,* p. 97.

13. *Report to the Nation on Crime and Justice,* p. 69; and Vera Institute, *Felony Arrests,* pp. 4–5.

14. Zeisel, *Limits of Law Enforcement,* p. 32, fig. 9.

15. James Q. Wilson, *Thinking about Crime* (New York: Basic Books, 1975), p. xii.

16. Brian Forst, Judith Lucianovic, and Sarah J. Cox, *What Happens after Arrest?* (Washington, DC: National Institute of Law Enforcement and Criminal Justice, 1977), pp. 62–68, and Vera Institute, *Felony Arrests,* pp. 6–22 and passim.

17. Zeisel, *Limits of Law Enforcement,* p. 114, and, more generally, pp. 111–112, table 2.

18. Wayne H. Thomas Jr., *Bail Reform in America* (Berkeley: University of California Press, 1976), pp. 40–41.

19. On the bail reform movement, see ibid., and Roy B. Flemming, *Punishment before Trial: An Organizational Perspective on Felony Bail Processes* (New York: Longman, 1982). On the effects of pretrial confinement on case outcomes, see John Goldkamp, "The Effects of Detention on Judicial Decisions: A Closer Look," *Justice System Journal* 5 (spring 1980): 234–257, and Eisenstein and Jacob, *Felony Justice,* pp. 284–285.

20. *Report to the Nation on Crime and Justice,* pp. 76–77.

21. Thomas, *Bail Reform in America,* and Mary A. Torborg, *Pretrial Release: A National Evaluation of Practices and Outcomes* (Washington, DC: National Institute of Justice, 1981).

22. Donald E. Pryor and Walter F. Smith, "Significant Research Findings concerning Pretrial Release," *Pretrial Issues* 4 (Washington, DC: Pretrial Services Resource Center, February 1982).

23. Ibid., and Torborg, *Pretrial Release.*

24. Elizabeth Gaynes, *Typology of State Laws Which Permit the Consideration of Danger in the Pretrial Release Decision* (Washington, DC: Pretrial Services Resource Center, May 1982), and Barbara Gottlieb, *Public Danger as a Factor in Pretrial Release: A Comparative Analysis of State Laws* (Washington, DC: National Institute of Justice, 1985).

25. John Goldkamp, "Questioning the Practice of Pretrial Detention: Some Empirical Evidence from Philadelphia," *Journal of Criminal Law and Criminology* 74 (1983): 1556–1588.

26. *Report to the Nation on Crime and Justice,* p. 77.

27. Deborah Day Emerson, *Grand Jury Reform: A Review of Key Issues* (Washington, DC: National Institute of Justice, U.S. Department of Justice, 1983), as reported in *Report to the Nation on Crime and Justice,* p. 72.

28. This discussion of the grand jury is based on Leroy D. Clark, *The Grand Jury* (New York: Quadrangle Books, 1975), and Neubauer, *Judicial Process,* pp. 203–205.

29. *Wood v. Georgia,* 370 U.S. 375, 390 (1962).

30. Neubauer, *Judicial Process,* p. 205.

31. Quoted in Lawrence Baum, *American Courts: Process and Policy,* 2d ed. (Boston: Houghton Mifflin, 1990), p. 176.

32. This research is summarized in Neubauer, *Judicial Process,* pp. 201–203.

33. David Neubauer, *Criminal Justice in Middle America* (Morristown, NJ: General Learning Press, 1974).

34. *Report to the Nation on Crime and Justice,* p. 84.

35. Martin A. Levin, *Urban Politics and the Criminal Courts* (Chicago: University of Chicago Press, 1977), p. 2.

36. Quoted in Milton Heumann, *Plea Bargaining* (Chicago: University of Chicago Press, 1977), p. 60.

37. Zeisel, *Limits of Law Enforcement,* p. 176.

38. See Eisenstein and Jacob, *Felony Justice,* chap. 2; Arthur I. Rosett and Donald R. Cressy, *Justice by Consent: Plea Bargaining in the American Courthouse* (Philadelphia: Lippincott, 1976), chap. 2 and 5; and Susan R. Thomas Buckle and Leonard G. Buckle, *Bargaining for Justice: Case Disposition and Reform in the Criminal Courts* (New York: Praeger, 1977).

39. Eisenstein and Jacob, *Felony Justice,* p. 248.

40. The caseload-pressure hypothesis is put forth by Abraham Blumberg, *Criminal Justice* (Chicago: Quadrangle Books, 1967). For critical discussions of this hypothesis, see Feeley, *The Process Is the Punishment,* chap. 8, and Heumann, *Plea Bargaining,* chap. 3. Heumann also presents statements by judges and criminal lawyers endorsing the caseload-pressure hypothesis.

41. Albert W. Alschuler, "Plea Bargaining and Its History," and Lawrence M. Friedman, "Plea Bargaining in Historical Perspective," *Law and Society Review* 13 (winter 1979): 211–260.

42. The figures, drawn from Raymond Moley, *Politics and Criminal Prosecution* (New York: Minton, Balch, 1929), and from Illinois Association for Criminal Justice, *The Illinois Crime Survey* (Chicago: Illinois Association for Criminal Justice, 1929), are reported in Alschuler, "Plea Bargaining and Its History," pp. 223, 231.

43. Heumann, *Plea Bargaining,* chap. 3, presents data for Connecticut courts.

44. On criminal prosecutions in Los Angeles, see Lynn M. Mather, *Plea Bargaining or Trial?* (Lexington, MA: Lexington Books, 1979); on prosecutions in Baltimore, see Eisenstein and Jacob, *Felony Justice,* chap. 4.

45. Albert W. Alschuler, "The Prosecutor's Role in Plea Bargaining," *University of Chicago Law Review* 36 (fall 1968): 50–112.

46. See Feeley, *The Process Is the Punishment,* and Heumann, *Plea Bargaining.* Of course, their perception of what justice requires may be mistaken, either because their understanding of justice is flawed or because they lack sufficient information to make an informed judgment.

47. Among the volumes that emphasize this "organizational approach" are Eisenstein and Jacob, *Felony Justice*, and Peter F. Nardulli, *The Courtroom Elite: An Organizational Perspective on Criminal Justice* (Cambridge, MA: Ballinger, 1978).

48. Nardulli, *The Courtroom Elite*, p. 68.

49. Major works critical of plea bargaining include Blumberg, *Criminal Justice;* Jonathan D. Casper, *American Criminal Justice: The Defendant's Perspective* (Englewood Cliffs, NJ: Prentice Hall, 1972); and Kenneth Kipnis, "Criminal Justice and the Negotiated Plea," *Ethics* 56 (1976): 93–106.

50. Kipnis, "Criminal Justice and the Negotiated Plea," and Alschuler, "Prosecutor's Role in Plea Bargaining."

51. See, e.g., Ernest van den Haag, *Punishing Criminals* (New York: Basic Books, 1975).

52. Blumberg, *Criminal Justice.*

53. Ibid.

54. For accounts of Alaska's ban on plea bargaining and its effects, see Michael L. Rubinstein and Teresa J. White, "Alaska's Ban on Plea Bargaining," *Law and Society Review* 13 (winter 1979): 367–383; William F. McDonald and James A. Cramer, *Plea Bargaining* (Lexington, MA: Lexington Books, 1980); and Michael L. Rubinstein, Stevens H. Clarke, and Teresa J. White, *Alaska Bans Plea Bargaining* (Washington, DC: National Institute of Justice, U.S. Department of Justice, 1980).

55. Levin, *Urban Politics and Criminal Courts;* and Eisenstein and Jacob, *Felony Justice.*

56. For illustrative material, see Casper, *American Criminal Justice.*

57. Major attempts to determine the effect of mode of disposition on sentencing include Eisenstein and Jacob, *Felony Justice,* chap. 10, and Feeley, *The Process Is the Punishment,* chap. 5.

58. Heumann, *Plea Bargaining,* p. 142.

59. For the views of attorneys and judges, see ibid., pp. 67, 101, 125, 141.

60. Ibid., pp. 124–126.

61. Ibid., pp. 84–89.

62. See, e.g., van den Haag, *Punishing Criminals.*

63. See, e.g., George Woodworth and Charles A. Pulaski, "Comparative Review of Death Sentences: An Empirical Review of Death Sentences," *Journal of Criminal Law and Criminology* 74 (1983): 661–753.

64. Yale Kamisar, "The Exclusionary Rule in Historical Perspective: The Struggle to Make the Fourth Amendment 'More than an Empty Blessing,'" *Judicature* 62 (February 1979): 337–350.

65. See, e.g., Abraham Goldstein, *The Insanity Defense* (New Haven, CT: Yale University Press, 1967), and Helen Silving, *Essays on Mental Incapacity and Criminal Conduct* (Springfield, IL: Charles C. Thomas, 1967).

66. For a critique of claims that sentencing is "lenient," see Stuart A. Scheingold, *The Politics of Law and Order* (New York: Longman, 1984), pp. 151–153. For a critique of claims that sentencing is discriminatory, see James Eisenstein and Herbert Jacob, *Felony Justice: An Organizational Analysis of the Criminal Courts* (Boston: Little, Brown, 1977), p. 284; John Hagan, "Extra-Legal Attributes and Criminal Sentencing: An Assessment of the Sociological Viewpoint," *Law and Society Review* 8 (spring 1984): 357–383; and, more generally, William Wilbanks, *The Myth of a Racist Criminal Justice System* (Pacific Grove, CA: Brooks/Cole Publishing, 1987). For the argument that sentencing reforms unduly restrict judicial discretion, see Michael Tonry, *Sentencing Matters* (New York: Oxford University Press, 1996); Chris Clarkson and Rod Morgan, *The Politics of Sentencing Reform* (New York: Oxford University Press, 1995); and Kate Stith and Jose A. Cabranes, *Fear of Judging: Sentencing Guidelines in the Federal Courts* (Chicago: University of Chicago Press, 1998).

67. *Silverthorne Lumber Co. v. United States,* 251 U.S. 385 (1920).

68. See, e.g., *State v. Sheridan,* 96 N.W. 730 (Iowa 1903).

69. *Weeks v. United States,* 232 U.S. 383 (1914).

70. *Wolf v. Colorado,* 388 U.S. 25 (1949).

71. *Mapp v. Ohio,* 367 U.S. 643 (1961).

72. See, e.g., *United States v. Leon,* 468 U.S. 897 (1984), and *Massachusetts v. Sheppard,* 468 U.S. 981 (1984).

73. *People v. Defore,* 150 N.E. 585 (1926).

74. Bradley C. Canon, "Is the Exclusionary Rule in Failing Health? Some New Data and a Plea against a Precipitous Conclusion," *Kentucky Law Journal* 62 (1983–84): 681–730.

75. E. Dallin Oaks, "Studying the Exclusionary Rule in Search and Seizure," *University of Chicago Law Review* 37 (1970): 665–757; and James E. Spiotto, "Search and Seizure: An Empirical Study of the Exclusionary Rule and Its Alternatives," *Journal of Legal Studies* 2 (1973): 243–278.

76. National Institute of Justice, *Criminal Justice Research Report—The Effects of the Exclusionary Rule: A Study in California* (Washington, DC: Department of Justice, National Institute of Justice, 1982). For a thought-provoking examination of these and other studies of the effects of the exclusionary rule, see Thomas Y. Davies, "A Hard Look at What We Know (and Still Need to Learn) about the 'Costs' of the Exclusionary Rule: The NIJ Study and Other Studies of 'Lost' Arrests," *American Bar Foundation Research Journal* 1983 (summer): 611–689.

77. Peter F. Nardulli, "The Societal Cost of the Exclusionary Rule: An Empirical Assessment," *American Bar Foundation Research Journal* 1983 (summer): 595, table 2; 597, table 7.

78. Ibid., p. 601, table 12.

79. Ibid., p. 603, table 13.

80. The Attorney General's Task Force on Violent Crime, *Final Report* (Washington, DC: Department of Justice, 1981), *Recommendations,* 40, 55–56. For Supreme Court rulings recognizing a "good faith" exception, see note 72 above.

81. Schlesinger, *Exclusionary Injustice,* pp. 77–84.

82. Jonathan D. Casper, Kennette Benedict, and Jo L. Perry, "The Tort Remedy in Search and Seizure Cases: A Case Study in Juror Decision Making," *American Bar Foundation Research Journal* 13 (spring 1988): 279–303.

83. *M'Naghten's Case,* 10 Clark & Fin. 200, 8 Eng. Rep. 718, 722 (1843).

84. American Law Institute, *Modern Penal Code,* sec. 4.01 (1962).

85. Goldstein, *The Insanity Defense,* p. 87.

86. For general surveys of developments in the aftermath of the Hinckley acquittal, see Ingo Keilitz, "Researching and Reforming the Insanity Defense," *Rutgers Law Review* 39 (winter/spring 1987): 283–322, and Rita J. Simon and David E. Aaronson, *The Insanity Defense: A Critical Assessment of Law and Policy in the Post-Hinckley Era* (New York: Praeger, 1988).

87. Joseph H. Rodriguez, Laura M. LeWinn, and Michael L. Perlin, "The Insanity Defense under Siege: State Legislative Assaults and Legal Rejoinders," *Rutgers Law Journal* 14 (winter 1983): 397–430, and, more generally, Richard A. Pasewark and Hugh McGinley, "Insanity Plea: National Survey of Frequency and Success," *Journal of Psychiatry and Law* 13 (spring/summer 1985): 101–108.

88. Keilitz, "Researching and Reforming the Insanity Defense."

89. Gare A. Smith and James A. Hall, "Evaluating Michigan's Guilty But Mentally Ill Verdicts: An Empirical Study," *Journal of Law Reform* 16 (1982): 77–114.

90. Robert P. Bogenberger, Richard A. Pasewark, Howard Gudeman, and Stephen L. Beiber, "Follow-up of Insanity Acquittees in Hawaii," *International Journal of Law and Psychiatry* 10 (1987): 283–295.

91. Cornelia Stockman, "The Insanity Defense Reform Act in New York State, 1980–1983," *International Journal of Law and Psychiatry* 7 (1984): 367–384, and Jeffrey L. Rogers, Richard A. Pasewark, and Stephen L. Bieber, "Insanity Plea: Predicting Not Guilty by Reason of Insanity Adjudications," *Bulletin of the American Academy of Psychiatry and Law* 16 (1988): 35–52.

92. Grant T. Harris, Marnie E. Rice, and Catherine A. Cormier, "Length of Detention in Matched Groups of Insanity Acquittees and Convicted Offenders," *International Journal of Law and Psychiatry* 14 (1991): 223–236; Mark Pogrebin, Robert Regoli, and Ken Perry, "Not Guilty by Reason of Insanity: A Research Note," *International Journal of Law and Psychiatry* 8 (1986): 237–241; and Rodriguez, LeWinn, and Perlin, "The Insanity Defense under Siege."

93. On the centrality of rehabilitation in penological policy, see Francis A. Allen, *The Decline of the Rehabilitative Ideal* (New Haven, CT: Yale University Press, 1981).

94. On the problems of rehabilitation as a penological approach, see Stuart A. Scheingold, *The Politics of Law and Order* (New York: Longman, 1984), pp. 183–185, and Douglas Lipton, Robert Martinson, and Judith Wilks, *The Effectiveness of Correctional Treatment: A Survey of Treatment Evaluation Studies* (New York: Praeger, 1975).

95. A useful overview on mandatory sentencing, and on sentencing reform more generally, is Sandra Shane-DuBow, Alice P. Brown, and Erik Olsen, *Sentencing Reform in the United States: History, Content, and Effect* (Washington, DC: U.S. Government Printing Office, 1985).

96. On the so-called three-strikes approach to dealing with recidivist criminals, see Tonry, *Sentencing Matters*, and Franklin E. Zimring and Gordon Hawkins, *Incapacitation: Penal Confinement and the Restraint of Crime* (New York: Oxford University Press, 1995).

97. *Blakely v. Washington*, No. 02-1632 (2004). On the effects of *Blakely*, see "Blakely Roils Waters of Federal Sentencing," *The Third Branch* 8 (August 2004): 1–4.*United States v. Booker*, No. 04–104.

98. On the effects of mandatory sentencing, see Milton Heumann and Colin Loftin, "Mandatory Sentencing and the Abolition of Plea Bargaining: The Michigan Felony Firearm Statute," *Law and Society Review* 13 (winter, 1979): 393–430; James A. Beha II, "'And Nobody Can Get You Out': The Impact of a Mandatory Prison Sentence for the Illegal Carrying of a Firearm on the Use of Firearms and on the Administration of Criminal Justice in Boston," *Boston University Law Review* 57 (1977): 96–146 (part 1), 289–333 (part 2); and, more generally, *Sentencing Reform Impacts* (Washington, DC: U.S. Department of Justice, National Institute of Justice, 1987), chap. 3.

99. Quoted in Walker, *Taming the System*, p. 125.

100. See *Sentencing Reform Impacts*, chap. 5–6, and Tamasak Wicharaya, *Simple Theory, Hard Reality: The Impact of Sentencing Reforms on Courts, Prisons, and Crime* (Albany: State University of New York Press, 1995).

101. Stith and Cabranes, *Fear of Judging*, p. 63, table 1.

102. Quoted in ibid., p. 83.

103. Ibid., p. 145.

104. The account of drug courts primarily draws upon James L. Nolan Jr., *Reinventing Justice: The American Drug Court Movement* (Princeton, NJ: Princeton University Press, 2001); Richard Boldt, "Rehabilitative Punishment and the Drug Treatment Court Movement," *Washington University Law Quarterly* 76 (1998): 1205–1306; and Peggy Fulton Hora, William G. Schma, and John T. A. Rosenthal, "Therapeutic Jurisprudence and the Drug Treatment Court Movement: Revolutionizing the Criminal Justice System's Response to Drug Abuse and Crime in America," *Notre Dame Law Review* 74 (January 1999): 439–538.

105. Quoted in Nolan, *Reinventing Justice*, p. 45.

106. For information on the number and location of drug courts, see the Web site of the National Association of Drug Court Professionals at www.ndci.org/. Chief Justice Kaye's comment is quoted in John Feinblatt, Greg Berman, and Derek Denclka, "Judicial Innovation at the Crossroads: The Future of Problem-Solving Courts," *The Court Manager* 15 (2000): 28.

107. Richard S. Gebelein, "The Rebirth of Rehabilitation: Promise and Perils of Drug Courts," *Sentencing and Corrections: Issues for the Twenty-first Century* 6 (May 2000): 3.

108. The most comprehensive and sympathetic account of therapeutic jurisprudence is Hora, Schma, and Rosenthal, "Therapeutic Jurisprudence." This paragraph relies on that source.

109. Quoted in Nolan, *Reinventing Justice,* p. 192.

110. Hora, Schma, and Rosenthal, p. 469.

111. Steven Belenko, "Research on Drug Courts: A Critical Review 2001 Update," National Center on Addiction and Substance Abuse, Columbia University.

112. This and the succeeding paragraph rely on Nolan, *Reinventing Justice,* chap. 8.

113. Morris Hoffman, "The Drug Court Scandal," *North Carolina Law Review* 78 (June 2000): 1502.

CHAPTER 7

CIVIL JUSTICE AND THE COURTS

"What happened to Kerry was not an act of God; it was an act of Dow."[1] That at least was Michael Ryan's explanation of why, four years after he had returned from military service in Vietnam, his daughter was born with multiple birth defects. Like many other soldiers serving in Vietnam, Ryan had been exposed to Agent Orange, a chemical defoliant sprayed by U.S. troops on fields and forests to destroy enemy crops and cover. And like them, he was convinced that Agent Orange caused death or debilitating illness in those exposed to the chemical and led to birth defects among their offspring. Ryan, together with other Vietnam veterans, blamed their problems on the chemical companies (e.g., Dow Chemical) that had produced Agent Orange and demanded justice.

Having a sense of injury and injustice is not, however, the same as proving liability in a court of law. Monsanto, Dow, and other producers of Agent Orange consistently denied that it had any toxic effects. Because the cancers suffered by veterans and the birth defects among their children were not distinctive, it would be difficult to prove that they were linked to Agent Orange rather than other causes. The legal effort to establish such a link would ultimately involve almost 1,500 law firms, representing more than 2.4 million Vietnam veterans and their families. Against them would be arrayed seven corporate defendants, who together spent roughly $100 million in preparation for the Agent Orange trial.

The litigation began in 1978 when Paul Reutershan, a Vietnam veteran dying of cancer, filed suit against Dow and two other chemical manufacturers. Although Reutershan died before the year ended, other Agent Orange suits followed in several jurisdictions. Early in 1979, Victor Yannacone, an attorney, filed an amended version of the Reutershan complaint as a class-action suit. His suit sought damages "in the range of $4 billion to $40 billion" as a trust fund for "all those so unfortunate as to have been and now to be situated at risk, not only during this generation but during generations to come."[2] A panel of federal judges authorized the formation of a class, which would include those

216

allegedly at risk because of Agent Orange. It then consolidated several cases as *In re Agent Orange Product Liability Litigation* for hearing by a federal district court in New York.

Before trial could commence, however, several crucial preliminary legal issues had to be addressed. Were the defendants immune from suit, as they claimed, because they had produced Agent Orange at the request of the government? Should the judge apply state or federal law in deciding the case? In addition to developing legal arguments on these and other questions, the plaintiffs' lawyers had to establish a causal connection between Agent Orange and the disabilities suffered by veterans and their offspring. This was particularly difficult because, as one of their lawyers put it: "Our clients could not help us prove our case. After all, they had not been hit by a truck, victimized by a doctor, or injured by a drug or other consumer product. They didn't know what had happened to them or when it happened. They only knew that something had gone wrong."[3] Thus, to prove their case, the plaintiffs were forced to rely on laboratory studies, epidemiological evidence, and information culled from the files of the defendant companies.

Aggravating these difficulties was the disparity in resources between the parties in the litigation. As Judge George Pratt observed early in the case, the plaintiffs "have limited resources with which to press their claims and [their] plight becomes more desperate and depressing as time goes on," whereas the defendants "have ample resources for counsel and expert witnesses to defend them and . . . probably gain significantly . . . from every delay that they can produce."[4] This problem led to the formation of a huge consortium of interested lawyers to bear the expenses of preparing the case. Even then, the plaintiffs' lawyers often found themselves overmatched.

After five years with little progress, the litigation shifted into high gear with the assignment in October 1983 of Judge Jack Weinstein to succeed Judge Pratt, who had been elevated to the court of appeals. Determined to move the case to resolution, Judge Weinstein established a trial date of May 7, 1984. His action spurred feverish—but largely unsuccessful—efforts by the plaintiffs' attorneys to develop evidence clearly linking Agent Orange to their clients' afflictions. The prospect of a trial also moved the two sides toward settlement because of uncertainty about its outcome and the calamitous consequences of losing for either side.

On Saturday, May 5, two days before the trial was to begin, Judge Weinstein convened all the attorneys to discuss a settlement, instructing them to "bring their toothbrushes" and to be prepared to stay all night Saturday and Sunday if necessary. His intervention succeeded. At 3 A.M. on May 7, just hours before jury selection was to begin, the weary negotiators reached a compromise settlement, under which the chemical companies refused to admit responsibility but agreed to pay the veterans $180 million. The largest class-action suit to that point in U.S. history was over.

The Agent Orange litigation highlights three key aspects of civil justice in the United States.

1. Resolution by negotiation.   Despite the intense preparations for trial, the Agent Orange case was eventually resolved through negotiations between counsel for the plaintiffs and counsel for the defendants. This is characteristic of the vast majority of civil cases, which are settled rather than adjudicated. Indeed, although not all judges are as active as Judge Weinstein in promoting settlement, most courts have adopted procedures that promote fact-finding before trial in order to encourage the settlement of cases. The negotiations in civil cases occur "in the shadow of the law"—that is, with the understanding that either party can demand a trial if a satisfactory agreement cannot be reached.[5] Thus, the process of civil justice parallels the process of criminal justice in the United States in important respects: the encouragement of negotiated settlements, the prospect of trial should negotiations fail, and the resolution of most cases without trial.

2. Access to justice and the "litigation explosion."   The Agent Orange case also highlights an important dispute about the American system of civil justice. One view is that the basic problem in civil justice is ensuring access to the courts for ordinary citizens. From that perspective, one might view the Agent Orange litigation as something of a triumph. For the most part, the plaintiffs were persons of moderate means who had suffered health problems that they attributed to the negligence of large corporations. Nevertheless, these plaintiffs were able to secure legal counsel, to gain a hearing for their claims in the courts, and to obtain at least some redress for their suffering—in short, to gain access and secure some measure of justice.[6]

Other commentators, however, insist that the main problem confronting the U.S. system of civil justice is excessive litigation.[7] From their perspective, the American propensity to litigate has in recent years produced a "litigation explosion," overburdening the courts and weakening the domestic economy. The Agent Orange case by itself did not cause this problem, though it placed heavy demands on the courts during its six-year duration. It does, however, exemplify a type of case involving mass exposure to serious health risks that has significantly increased the civil caseloads of federal and state courts. Although proponents of this view acknowledge that those who cause injuries should be called to account, they contend that mechanisms outside the courts should be devised for dealing with such problems.

3. The diversity of civil litigation.   No single case or set of cases can mirror the diversity of civil litigation in the United States. The Agent Orange case belongs to the category of tort law—that is, cases involving civil wrongs or injuries for which damages are sought. Tort cases may entail, as in the

Agent Orange litigation, multiple claims by workers or consumers against the actions or products of a limited number of corporations. More often, however, they involve relatively simple suits for damages by one individual against another, seeking compensation for damages or injuries suffered in, for example, an automobile accident. (Tort litigation is discussed in greater detail in Chapter 11.)

Although tort litigation constitutes a highly publicized component of civil caseloads, American courts also address many other sorts of civil cases. Some civil cases involve contractual disputes, either between businesses or, more frequently, between a business (usually attempting to collect a debt) and a consumer. Other civil cases arise out of domestic relationships, involving such matters as divorce, child support, and adoption. Still others involve the legal transfer of property from one party to another, as occurs through the administration of a will or the handling of the estate of someone who died intestate (without a will). Finally, an important category of civil cases involves the legal relationship between governments and citizens. These cases may range from constitutional challenges to governmental actions, such as mandatory drug-testing programs, to governmental suits to compel compliance with environmental regulations, antitrust laws, or other statutes.

This description of the types of civil cases, however, raises questions. Why do some conflicts get transformed into legal disputes and taken to court, while others do not? How do courts deal with civil cases brought before them? And how well is the U.S. system of civil justice operating? Are there ways to make it work better? This chapter seeks to answer those questions.

How Cases Arise

In the United States, under our adversarial system of justice, there cannot be a case without a dispute. However, not every dispute, even if it has a legal dimension, is brought to court for resolution. Figure 7-1 outlines the process by which disputes arise and the various means available for dealing with disputes.

Injuries and Grievances

If cases arise out of disputes, then disputes arise out of grievances, and grievances out of injuries. People suffer injuries—physical, economic, psychic—every day. These injuries do not become grievances, however, unless the injured party believes that she is unjustly deprived by another party of something to which she is entitled. Injuries do not become litigable grievances—that is, grievances one could take to court—unless one is deprived of something to

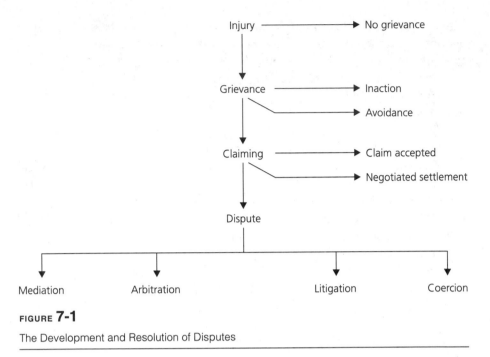

FIGURE **7-1**

The Development and Resolution of Disputes

Source: Richard E. Miller and Austin Sarat, "Grievances, Claims, and Disputes: Assessing the Adversary Culture," *Law and Society Review* 15 (1980–81): 524–565.

which one is legally entitled. A few examples may help clarify this. You have no "grievance" against the government, for example, if it imprisons you for a crime you have committed, because your loss of liberty is deserved. Or suppose your house is destroyed by a tornado. In such a case, you suffered an injury that was undeserved, but you have no "grievance" because no one is responsible for the damage. Finally, suppose you operate a pizzeria, and a competitor cuts into your sales. You certainly have suffered a harm and know who caused it, but there is no litigable "grievance" because you had no legal right to a fixed level of sales or profits.

As these examples suggest, by establishing entitlements and imposing obligations, law defines what constitutes a litigable grievance. This definition may vary from one society to another and may change over time within a society, as the law responds to shifts in public opinion. Some scholars attribute part of the increase in litigation in the United States and elsewhere to legal changes brought about by just such a shift in public opinion.[8] They contend that as advances in science and technology have made it possible to control situations of peril or need, the public has begun to claim a right to be free from unnecessary risk. The law, reflecting this claim, has imposed obligations on government and private parties to deliver goods and services that meet achievable standards of safety and usefulness. It has also made it easy to sue when these obligations are not met; as a result, civil suits have increased.

Responses

Suppose you buy a car that fails to perform to your expectations. You might respond to this problem in various ways.[9] You might do nothing, perhaps justifying your inaction by arguing that everyone gets stuck once in a while ("lumping it"). You might also resolve never to purchase another car from that dealer or that manufacturer. Social scientists call such a change in behavior, designed to reduce or eliminate contact with a disputant, "avoidance."[10] Alternatively, you might go to the dealership and claim that the car should be repaired or that you should be reimbursed for your inconvenience. The dealer might accept your claim, thereby resolving the matter. Or the dealer might make a counteroffer, perhaps to replace defective parts if you pay the labor costs, and a negotiated settlement might be reached. Finally, the dealer may reject your claim, in which case a dispute exists.

What are your options in such circumstances? One possibility is coercion, the threat or use of force to get what you claim is rightfully yours. Revolutions and fights exemplify the use of coercion to resolve disputes. In this example, however, other forms of dispute resolution are more likely. You might seek the intervention of a third party, such as the Better Business Bureau, to help resolve the dispute through mediation. Or you might seek a binding resolution of your dispute outside the courts through arbitration. (These modes of dispute resolution are discussed later in the chapter.) Finally, you might choose litigation, taking your grievance to court.

How do most people deal with their grievances? That depends on the grievance. Surveys indicate that people who believe that they have suffered discrimination are unlikely to take action, whereas those who have suffered physical injuries or damage to their property are likely to press claims.[11] Overall, however, according to a survey of 1,000 randomly selected households nationwide, most resolve their grievances outside the legal system (see Figure 7-2). Three factors largely explain why people are reluctant to take their disputes to court.

1. *Adverse consequences of filing suit.* Many disputants are reluctant to go to court because they fear that escalating the conflict will produce backlash. This is particularly true when the disputants have ongoing relationships that might be jeopardized by a suit. Thus, family members may prefer to settle their disputes out of court; so, too, may neighbors, business partners, and employees involved in disputes on the job. According to one victim of sex discrimination, if she were to sue, "a lot of people might go against me. . . . I wouldn't want to ruin the relationships I do have there."[12]

2. *Costs of litigation.* Disputants also recognize that litigation, with its attorney fees and court costs, is expensive. A trial also may require plaintiffs to miss work, costing them income or even putting their jobs in jeopardy. Added to these monetary costs may be psychic costs. Disputants may be uncomfortable

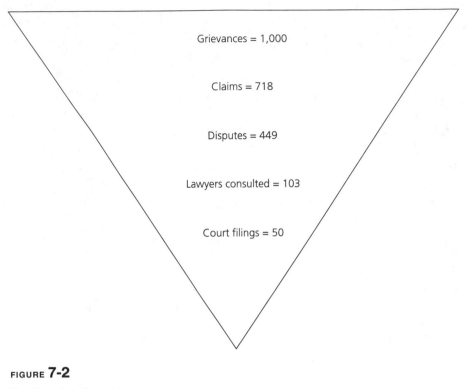

Grievances = 1,000

Claims = 718

Disputes = 449

Lawyers consulted = 103

Court filings = 50

FIGURE **7-2**

The Disputing Pyramid

Source: Richard E. Miller and Austin Sarat, "Grievances, Claims, and Disputes: Assessing the Adversary Culture," *Law and Society Review* 15 (1980–81): 544, fig. 1-A. Figures indicate the general level of disputing per 1,000 grievances. Reprinted by permission of Blackwell Publishing.

consulting a lawyer or anxious about appearing in court. Thus, even if they have a legitimate grievance, disputants may conclude that the costs of going to trial outweigh the expected payoff from a successful suit or that another less costly forum should be used for resolving the dispute.[13]

3. Uncertainty.   Because they do not know the applicable law, potential litigants may be uncertain about their chances of success. They also may be skeptical about whether a single individual can prevail against a company or the government. This uncertainty may deter them from filing suit. As one victim of wage discrimination put it, it would be "me against a large corporation" and thus my "word against a [more powerful] someone else's."[14]

Nevertheless, some disputants are willing to consult lawyers and file suit. When they do, their cases proceed through certain legally established steps from initiation to resolution. It is to these steps, and to the law governing them, that we now turn.

RULES AND PROCESSES

Rules

Civil litigation is governed by three sets of rules. One set of rules establishes the substantive legal standards that judges apply in deciding cases. For example, a statute might define and outlaw racial discrimination, an administrative regulation might set water-quality standards, or the common law might determine when one can collect damages for injuries one has suffered. These standards are examined in Chapters 9 through 12.

A second set of rules (addressed in Chapter 2) governs the jurisdiction of courts and thus guides lawyers on the proper court in which to file a case. Finally, a third set of rules determines the procedures that lawyers must follow in framing and presenting a case from its inception to the exhaustion of all appeals. For most of American history, these procedural rules were established within each state, according to state statutes or rulings announced by state courts. Instead of developing their own procedural rules, each federal court followed the procedures of the state in which it heard cases. Many lawyers complained, however, that this lack of procedural uniformity was confusing, and the American Bar Association campaigned for a standard set of procedural rules for federal litigation. In 1938, in response to these efforts, the Federal Rules of Civil Procedure were adopted. These new rules established a uniform procedure for federal courts that its supporters hailed as "flexible, simple, clear, and efficient."[15] More than half the states have agreed with this assessment, conforming their procedural requirements to the Federal Rules of Civil Procedure.

The Process of Civil Litigation

Because most civil cases are resolved before trial, what occurs during the pretrial phase of litigation is vitally important. The pretrial phase serves to identify the applicable law, define the legal issues, and promote the discovery of factual information pertinent to the resolution of the case. The four major steps during the pretrial phase are: (1) pleadings, (2) discovery, (3) motions, and (4) pretrial conference.[16]

Pleadings   A case begins when the plaintiff—or, more likely, the plaintiff's attorney—files a written complaint with the trial court. Under the Federal Rules of Civil Procedure, which greatly simplified pleadings, a complaint must merely (1) describe the factual basis for the plaintiff's suit, (2) explain why the court has jurisdiction over the case, (3) outline the legal theory on which the complaint relies, and (4) indicate the damages or other relief that the plaintiff seeks. The requirements of the Federal Rules of Civil Procedure are met if the complaint reveals enough information so that the defendant can understand the basis for the suit and respond to the complaint.

Once the plaintiff has filed a complaint, the defendant in the case must be "served" with the complaint—that is, formally notified of the complaint and summoned to appear in court at a particular date and time. Should the defendant fail to appear at the appointed time, the judge may rule in favor of the plaintiff without hearing evidence. This is called a default judgment.

Usually, however, defendants file an answer to the plaintiff's complaint. They may deny some or all of the allegations in the complaint. In the Agent Orange case, for example, the chemical companies denied that their product had caused the health problems suffered by the veterans and their children. Those matters on which the plaintiff and defendant differ then become the basis for the dispute. Alternatively, defendants may admit the truth of the plaintiff's allegation but offer an affirmative defense—that is, they may introduce new facts designed to produce a decision in their favor. A skydiving instructor, for instance, may admit that a student died during a jump but reveal that the student signed a form acknowledging the dangers of skydiving and pledging not to hold the school or instructors responsible for any mishaps. Finally, defendants may respond with a counterclaim, the equivalent of a complaint against the plaintiff. Thus, a driver sued for damages arising out of a traffic accident might file a counterclaim for the damages to her car.

Even if a plaintiff has no intention of taking a dispute to trial, she may have tactical reasons for filing a complaint. She might file a complaint to "engage the authority of the legal system" on her behalf, thereby strengthening her position in the informal resolution of the dispute.[17] Filing a complaint may also signal how seriously the plaintiff views the matter under dispute, thereby inviting the defendant to enter into negotiations to deal with the situation.

Discovery   Discovery involves the pretrial exchange of information between the parties in a lawsuit. Under the Federal Rules of Civil Procedure, every party to a civil action is entitled to the disclosure of all relevant information in the possession of any person.[18] Thus, plaintiffs may demand from defendants (or defendants from plaintiffs) all the information they possess relevant to the subject matter of the case. They may also during discovery question witnesses and others who possess pertinent information. The sole exception to this requirement of full disclosure is for privileged information, such as communications between an attorney and client or between a doctor and patient. The Federal Rules of Civil Procedure permit such broad scope for discovery in order to prevent a party from hiding damaging evidence or an attorney from springing a surprise on an unwary opponent at trial. In so doing, the rules promote verdicts at trial based on the weight of the evidence rather than on courtroom tactics. Full disclosure of facts before trial may also encourage litigants to settle cases. Parties sometimes fail to settle cases because they overestimate the strength of their own position or underestimate that of their opponents. Discovery, however, allows an informed assessment of the strengths and weaknesses of the opposing positions and of the likely outcome of a trial.[19]

Lawyers employ three tools during discovery: depositions, interrogatories, and the production of documents and other physical evidence. A deposition involves oral questioning of a witness under trial-like conditions. Attorneys for both sides question and cross-examine witnesses, and their answers are recorded. This testimony may later be introduced at trial—an alert attorney will pounce on any discrepancies between what a witness says at trial and what he said when he was deposed. An interrogatory consists of a set of written questions directed to a party in a case, to which written answers are prepared and signed under oath. A party to a case may also be required during discovery to produce documents or objects for the other party to inspect, photograph, or copy and to permit access to its premises and its files for these purposes. In addition, the plaintiff in a personal injury case may be required to undergo a physical examination by a physician chosen by the defendant or by the court to substantiate an injury claim. Should a party object to questions or to other requests for information or materials, a judge determines whether the requests are legitimate.

In most cases, the requests for information or materials during discovery are quite limited. However, discovery in complex cases can be time-consuming and expensive. In the first five years of the IBM antitrust case, for example, 64 million pages of records and documents were obtained through discovery.[20] In some instances, "overdiscovery" has led to abuses. According to one judge, "For many lawyers, discovery is a Pavlovian reaction. When the lawsuit is filed . . . the word processor begins to grind out interrogatories and requests for production. Deposition notices drop like autumn leaves."[21]

Plaintiffs may file suit with little basis for their claims, hoping that a "fishing expedition" in the defendant's files during discovery might provide them with the evidence they lack. Attorneys may also multiply requests for information during discovery to drive up the opposing party's expenses or to induce a settlement. Thus, a lawyer for R. J. Reynolds candidly described the strategy behind the tobacco firm's use of depositions in defending a suit: "To paraphrase General Patton, the way we won these cases was not by spending all of Reynolds's money, but by making the other son of a bitch spend all of his."[22] Although the Federal Rules of Civil Procedure permit judges to impose sanctions, including withholding attorneys' fees, on those who abuse discovery, this has not curbed abuses.

Motions   At each stage of the pretrial phase of a case, attorneys for either party can file motions—that is, requests that the judge either issue a legal ruling or take some other action.[23] Under the Federal Rules of Civil Procedure, these motions must be submitted in writing and must specify the legal basis for the motion and the relief or order sought.

Some motions concern procedural matters relating to the conduct of the case. For example, a defendant may file a motion requesting that the plaintiff should be required to amend his complaint to clarify the basis for the suit. Or either party may ask the judge to determine whether certain information is subject to discovery. With other motions a party may seek a resolution of the case in its favor before trial. In the Agent Orange Case, for example, the defendant corporations sought dismissal of the complaint, claiming that they were immune from suit because they were fulfilling a request from the government in producing Agent Orange. Similarly, if the defendant fails to respond to a complaint, the plaintiff may move for a default judgment. Finally, either the plaintiff or the defendant may move for a summary judgment—a binding determination of the case without a trial. However, a judge can grant a motion for summary judgment only if the law is clear and the facts of the case are undisputed, leaving no issue to submit to a jury.

How often are cases resolved through motions rather than settled or adjudicated? The best estimate comes from Herbert Kritzer's intensive study of a sample of more than 1,600 cases in state and federal courts.[24] Kritzer found that 12 percent of the cases were dismissed for technical reasons or dismissed for cause (e.g., failure to state a claim). In another 15 percent, the judge issued a summary judgment, entered a default judgment for the plaintiff, or otherwise decided the case. Thus, although only 7 percent of the sample went to trial, judges contributed to the resolution of an additional 27 percent of civil cases.[25]

Pretrial Conference   The Federal Rules of Civil Procedure authorize (but do not mandate) a conference between the judge and attorneys before a case goes to trial. Most states have followed the federal lead in providing for pretrial conferences. At these conferences, which are usually held after discovery is completed, the judge and the attorneys identify the points of agreement and the issues still in dispute. The attorneys also reveal what witnesses they will call and what evidence they will introduce, thereby facilitating the planning of the trial. In complicated cases a judge may schedule earlier conferences with the attorneys as well to expedite the process of discovery.[26]

Pretrial conferences not only improve the conduct of trials but also promote the settlement of cases. As the Agent Orange litigation shows, judges may actively encourage settlement during pretrial conferences. Some initiate discussion of settlement when lawyers are reluctant to do so out of fear that the suggestion might be interpreted as a sign of weakness. Some also offer attorneys their own assessment of the strengths and weaknesses of the opposing positions and their views on whether settlement offers are reasonable. Lawyers generally applaud aggressive judicial participation in the settlement process. They are more likely to view a settlement as fair if it has received a judicial endorsement, and such an endorsement may help them persuade a recalcitrant client to accept a reasonable settlement offer.[27]

CIVIL CASES AND THEIR OUTCOMES

The Universe of Cases

Federal district courts decide more than 250,000 civil cases each year, and state trial courts decide more than 16 million.[28] The civil caseloads in these courts are extremely diverse. Cases such as the Agent Orange suit and suits against tobacco companies involve hundreds of millions of dollars. Others, such as litigation to collect debts, may involve a few hundred dollars at most. Some cases drag on for years (again, the Agent Orange and tobacco cases are prime examples), while others are quickly settled. Still others—for example, uncontested divorces and adoptions—involve no real dispute but merely require judicial ratification of a settlement worked out between the parties.

Types of Civil Cases   One way to capture the diversity of civil cases is to look at the types of cases that trial courts hear (see Figure 7-3 and Table 7-1). Taken together, the table and figure reveal that, although federal and state trial courts both handle a wide range of civil cases, the mix of civil cases differs considerably. This is hardly surprising: Federal law and state law generally regulate different activities. For example, there is no federal divorce law and no state immigration law. Much of the civil litigation in federal courts involves the federal government as either plaintiff or respondent. Governmental actions and litigation priorities influence the character and extent of that litigation.

Take, for example, recovery and enforcement cases, which involve the United States as plaintiff seeking to recover overpayments of veterans' benefits and student loans in default. In 1980, such cases comprised less than 10 percent of case filings in federal district courts. During the early 1980s, however, the Reagan administration made recovery of money owed to the federal government a priority. As a result the number of these suits increased dramatically, and by 1985, they constituted almost one-quarter of all federal civil cases. When a new president with new priorities was inaugurated, the number of recovery and enforcement cases declined precipitously—by more than 33 percent from 1989 to 1990.[29]

Federal legislation also affects the types of private case commenced in federal district courts. A good example is diversity of citizenship cases, which involve suits between citizens of different states. In 1989, Congress raised the amount that must be at stake for diversity cases to be tried in federal court from $10,000 to $50,000. As a result, from 1989 to 1990, diversity cases dropped 15 percent.[30]

Types of Parties   One may also look at civil cases in terms of the parties involved in the cases. One legal scholar, Marc Galanter, has suggested dividing the parties in civil cases into *one-shotters* (OS) and *repeat players* (RP).[31] One-shotters are litigants who have only occasional recourse to the courts

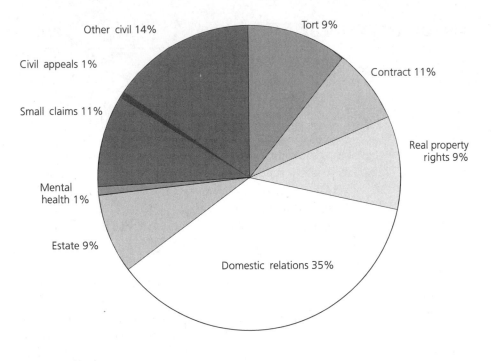

The figure includes data from 27 courts

FIGURE **7-3**

Types of Cases in State Trial Courts of General Jurisdiction

Source: *State Court Caseload Statistics: Annual Report 1992* (Williamsburg, VA: National Center for State Courts, 1994), p. 15, chart 1.17. Used by permission.

(e.g., spouses in divorce actions and taxpayers in tax cases). In contrast, repeat players are engaged in many similar litigations over time (e.g., collection agencies in debt cases and the Internal Revenue Service in tax cases). One-shotters may be either plaintiffs or defendants, as may repeat players. Table 7-2 categorizes various types of litigation based on the parties in the case. Let us look at each category.[32]

OS versus OS   Much of this litigation merely involves judicial ratification of settlements previously agreed to by the parties. For example, more than 90 percent of divorces—by far the most numerous of these cases—are uncontested. When the cases involve real disputes, however, conflict can be intense because the parties often have close personal ties. Spite, resentment, or revenge also may fuel the disputes.

RP versus OS   Many repeat players have legal relationships with large numbers of one-shotters. Owners of apartment complexes, for example, enter into

TABLE 7-1

TYPES OF CASES IN FEDERAL DISTRICT COURTS, 2002

Contract Actions		**38,535**
Insurance	8,258	
Marine	2,381	
Recovery of overpayments and enforcement of judgments	8,646	
Other	18,092	
Real Property Actions		**7,642**
Foreclosures	4,985	
Other	2,657	
Tort Actions		**48,549**
Product liability	31,068	
Other personal injury	17,481	
Actions under Statutes		**106,535**
Antitrust	709	
Bankruptcy	2,895	
Civil rights	40,549	
Environmental matters	1,749	
Forfeiture and penalty	2,843	
Labor laws	15,862	
Prisoner petitions	8,400	
Securities, commodities, and exchanges	3,595	
Social security laws	17,059	
Tax suits	1,126	
Other	13,013	
TOTAL CIVIL CASES		**256,858**

Source: Web site of the federal judiciary: www.uscourts.gov/caseload2003/.

contracts with large numbers of tenants, and finance companies attempt to collect debts from many consumers. These repeat players file suits as part of their normal course of business, using the law to enforce contractual obligations. These cases make up a large part of civil litigation, though many cases are settled before trial.

OS versus RP   It is relatively rare for a one-shotter to sue a repeat player. The various factors discussed earlier—the adverse personal consequences of suing, the costs of litigation, and uncertainty about its outcome—deter most

<table>
<tr><td>TABLE 7-2</td><td colspan="2">COMBINATIONS OF PARTIES AND LITIGATION</td></tr>
</table>

INITIATOR OR CLAIMANT

	One-Shotter	Repeat Player
One-Shotter	Parent v. Parent (custody) Spouse v. Spouse (divorce) Family v. Family Member (insanity commitment) Family v. Family Member (inheritance) Neighbor v. Neighbor Partner v. Partner **OS vs OS** **I**	Prosecutor v. Accused Finance Co. v. Debtor Landlord v. Tenant Internal Revenue Service v. Taxpayer Condemnor v. Property Owner **RP vs OS** **II**
Repeat Player	Welfare Client v. Agency Auto Dealer v. Manufacturer Injury Victim v. Insurance Company Tenant v. Landlord Bankrupt Consumer v. Creditors Defamed v. Publisher **OS vs RP** **III**	Union v. Company Movie Distributor v. Censorship Board Developer v. Suburban Municipality Purchaser v. Supplier Regulatory Agency v. Firms of Regulated Industry **RP vs RP** **IV**

(left margin label: **DEFENDANT**)

Source: Marc Galanter, "Why the 'Haves' Come Out Ahead: Speculations on the Limits of Legal Changes," *Law and Society Review* 9 (Fall 1974), p. 107, fig. 1. Reprinted by permission of Blackwell Publishing.

one-shotters from filing suit. The sole exceptions in this category are personal injury cases. Because attorneys take such cases on a contingent basis—that is, their fee is a percentage of the plaintiff's award—one-shotters need not bear the financial costs of litigation. They are therefore more likely to sue.

RP versus RP   Many repeat players interact frequently with other repeat players. Examples include unions and companies, regulators and regulated firms, and builders and suburbs. To avoid jeopardizing these ongoing, mutually beneficial relationships, repeat players tend to develop mechanisms outside the courts to resolve their disputes.

There are, however, two exceptions to this pattern of low litigation rates. First, some repeat players—for example, the American Civil Liberties Union and the Sierra Club—are committed to furthering particular ends and may be quite willing to reject compromise solutions and take disputes to court. Second, government also tends to be quite heavily involved in litigation with other repeat players, as both plaintiff and defendant.

Outcomes of Civil Cases

The outcome of a civil case depends largely on the facts of the case, the applicable law, and the presentation of the case by the attorneys or by the parties in the case, if they are not represented by counsel. While the facts differ from case to case, some generalizations can be made about the effects of the law and the type of representation. Once again, Galanter's distinction between one-shotters and repeat players is useful.[33]

OS versus OS   In terms of legal representation, one-shotters typically find themselves rather evenly matched. Generally, either both parties have retained counsel or neither has, and neither party is likely to hire an attorney from the elite ranks of the legal profession. Because disparities in the quality of counsel are unlikely to determine the outcome of disputes between one-shotters, the substance of the law may have a decisive effect on the outcome of the case.

The effect of the law—and of changes in the law—on case outcomes are apparent if one looks at the most frequent cases pitting one-shotters against one-shotters, namely, divorce cases.[34] Before 1970, every state required fault-based grounds for divorce, such as adultery or mental cruelty, with the conduct of the parties during the marriage the key determinant of their financial rights and obligations after divorce. Under this law, women fared relatively well in the distribution of marital property and the provision of financial support. In 1970, however, California instituted a system of no-fault divorce under which marriages could be dissolved on the basis of "irreconcilable differences." The California reform, which was soon adopted by other states, also established gender-neutral rules that removed many of the legal and financial protections that the law had provided. Thus, a consequence of instituting no-fault divorce, unanticipated and unintended by reformers, was that "women, and the minor children in their households, typically experience[d] a sharp decline in their standard of living after divorce."[35]

RP versus RP   Because litigation is a normal part of their doing business, repeat players typically retain experienced, specialized counsel. Thus, as in cases involving one-shotters, disputes between repeat players usually involve a rough parity in legal representation. Because repeat players, unlike one-shotters, expect to litigate, they tend to take steps to ensure that the applicable law is favorable to their interests. They may seek to influence the law that government creates. Business and labor, for example, lobby hard on legislation that is like to affect labor relations. If the applicable law arises out of private agreements, then repeat players employ their legal expertise and negotiating skills to fashion favorable contracts. They also attempt to promote a body of judicial precedent favorable to their interests. Thus, in litigation, repeat players are concerned not merely with the outcome of individual cases but also with their long-term legal advantage. Repeat players who succeed in securing favorable legislation, contracts, and judicial interpretations can expect to advance their interests through litigation.

RP versus OS, and OS versus RP   Repeat players enjoy significant advantages in their disputes with one-shotters. Expecting some conflicts in their transactions with one-shotters, repeat players can structure the law at the outset to place themselves at an advantage. As Galanter observes, "it is the RP who writes the form contract, requires the security deposit, and the like," and one-shotters seldom seek to renegotiate the requirements.[36] Moreover, repeat players do not share the one-shotters' concerns about litigating: They understand the process and have sufficient experience to calculate their chances of success. Unlike one-shotters, repeat players usually have hired or retained lawyers, and so their start-up costs for litigating are minimal. Because of this ongoing relationship, the repeat players' lawyers tend to be specialists in the field, whereas those chosen by one-shotters often are not.

The different objectives pursued by one-shotters and repeat players may also work to the repeat players' advantage. As plaintiffs, one-shotters are concerned with having their claims vindicated, and, as defendants, with avoiding or minimizing liability. Repeat players, in contrast, are concerned not only with the present case but also with promoting a favorable outcome in future cases. They therefore will be inclined to settle cases that might establish unfavorable precedents and to adjudicate those that will yield favorable ones. As a result, over time repeat players can create a body of law that serves their interests.

Are things really as dismal for one-shotters as Galanter's analysis suggests? Yes and no. Suits by repeat players against one-shotters constitute the largest category of litigation, and several studies suggest that repeat players generally prevail, often by default judgments.[37] (Of course, in many of these cases—for example, creditor–debtor cases—they prevail because one-shotters have failed to meet their clear legal obligations.) One-shotters, however, have enjoyed considerable success as plaintiffs in product liability cases, in which they are suing manufacturers for injuries suffered as a result of alleged product defects.[38] These cases diverge in important respects from other disputes between one-shotters and repeat players. Expert legal representation for one-shotters tends to be readily available. Plaintiffs' lawyers in product liability cases are legal specialists who take cases on a contingent-fee basis. In addition, this segment of the bar shares the repeat players' interest in the long-term development of product liability law and acts to secure a body of law favorable to their clients'—and their own—interests. In sum, aggressive attorneys representing one-shotters and their interests may help equalize the prospects of repeat players and one-shotters involved in a dispute.

A LITIGATION CRISIS?

The Indictment

In recent years, the U.S. civil justice system has come under sustained attack. Consider the indictment: Americans have developed "a mad romance . . . with the civil litigation process."[39] However outrageous the claim, there is a litigant willing to press it and a court to hear it (see Box 7-1). And encouraging this propensity to litigate differences and file frivolous suits is the world's largest legal profession. Not surprisingly, then, "[o]ur society has become the most litigious society in the world. No other nation is even close."[40] Further, "[t]his massive, mushrooming litigation has caused horrendous ruptures and dislocations at a flabbergasting cost to the nation."[41] Litigants themselves bear some of the costs. With overloaded courts, justice is slower and more expensive than ever. The nation's economy also suffers. "Like a plague of locusts, U.S. lawyers with their clients have descended upon America and are suing the country out of business."[42] Only the nation's economic competitors benefit as energies and resources are diverted from "research and development" to "document production and depositions."[43] Fundamental reform of the civil justice system is essential.

If this harsh assessment is accurate, then one could hardly oppose the call for reform. But is it accurate? Let us first consider the basic premise of the indictment, namely, that the United States is today an excessively litigious society.

Is the United States a Litigious Society?

One way to answer the question is to compare litigation rates in the United States with those in other nations. Contrary to the claims of alarmists, such a comparison suggests that the United States is not exceptional. Some countries—most notably, Japan—have litigation rates far lower than those in the United States (see Box 7-2). But several others—among them, Australia, Denmark, England, and Israel—have roughly comparable litigation rates, and many of these countries have likewise experienced a rapid growth in litigation in recent decades.[44]

One might also consider whether Americans are particularly prone to resolving their disputes by taking them to court. In 2002, civil filings in state courts per 100,000 population ranged from 1,167 in Tennessee to 15,157 in Maryland. However, the surveys of potential legal problems noted previously suggest that Americans are reluctant to litigate and generally do not transform

BOX
7-1

Outrageous Suits?

- A man sues a former girlfriend, trying to force her to pay for his time and expenses on a date she did not keep.
- A class-action suit is filed against General Motors, on behalf of "all persons everywhere now alive and all future unborn generations," seeking $6 trillion in damages for pollution.
- After breaking her finger in a school softball game, a high-school student sues her gym teacher and the city, alleging that the teacher not only failed to instruct her on how to catch a ball but also failed to warn her of the dangers of the sport.
- A group of Washington Redskins fans sue to have a court overturn a controversial referee's call that cost the Redskins a win in a football game.
- The Italian Historical Society of America sues the U.S. Post Office, asking a federal court to bar the issuing of a stamp celebrating Alexander Graham Bell on the grounds that the telephone actually had been invented by Antonio Meucci.
- A woman sues the state of California after being told that she did not win the state lottery, because her ball popped out of the winning slot after momentarily entering it.

Of course, filing a suit and collecting damages are two different things. Courts refused to rule for the plaintiffs in all but the last case. The jury in that case awarded the disappointed lottery player the $3 million jackpot, plus $400,000 for her emotional trauma.

Sources: The first case is described in Lawrence Friedman, *The Republic of Choice: Law, Authority, and Culture* (Cambridge, MA: Harvard University Press, 1990), p. 16; the next four, in Jethro K. Lieberman, *The Litigious Society* (New York: Basic Books, 1981), pp. 4–5; and the final case in Walter K. Olson, *The Litigation Explosion: What Happened When America Unleashed the Lawsuit* (New York: Truman Talley Books, 1991), p. 170.

their disputes into litigation. Americans' willingness to litigate varies from issue to issue. The only comparative study of the propensity to sue concludes that Americans tend to sue in cases of personal injury somewhat more often than Britons or Canadians (but not more often than Australians).[45] This evidence hardly supports the notion of a populace involved in "a mad romance with the civil litigation process."

Finally, one might consider whether Americans are more litigious now than in the past. Certainly, the level of litigation in the United States has risen over

Why Don't the Japanese Sue?

If the United States is seen as a litigious society, then Japan has just the opposite reputation. In 1986, for example, Japan's per capita litigation rate was only one-tenth that of California. This disparity is particularly striking because Japan shares with the United States many characteristics that presumably promote litigation, such as an advanced economy and an urbanized population. Why don't the Japanese sue?

One explanation for the disparity is cultural differences. Traditional Japanese values, it is argued, are oriented toward consensus, avoiding conflict, and subsuming personal concerns in the interest of the group. If the reluctance to litigate has derived from traditional Confucian beliefs, then one would expect litigation rates to rise as the modernization of Japanese society undermined those beliefs. In fact, litigation rates in Japan today are *lower* than in the past. Something in addition to cultural factors must be involved.

Even as Japanese society changes, litigation rates remain low because the government has designed policies to discourage litigation. The Japanese government has restricted the size of the legal profession, thereby reducing access to legal services. The total number of practicing lawyers in Japan is lower than the number of graduates each year from U.S. law schools, and in Japan only 500 new lawyers annually are permitted to pass the bar exam. The rules of Japanese courts, such as the ban on class-action suits, also discourage individuals from pursuing claims. Finally, when disputes do arise, the Japanese government has developed alternative forums to handle them, such as its system of court-annexed mediation and the Traffic Accident Dispute Resolution Center.

The Japanese experience reveals that when disputes arise, the values and expectations of the society can encourage or discourage litigation. But so, too, can governmental policies designed to reduce access, increase delay, and deny relief—or, alternatively, to facilitate legal redress of grievances. Far from being the inevitable product of societal development, litigation reflects the values and institutions of the society.

Sources: Takao Tanase, "The Management of Disputes: Automobile Accident Compensation in Japan," *Law & Society Review* 24 (1990): 651–689; Robert L. Kidder and John A. Hostetler, "Managing Ideologies: Harmony as Ideology in Amish and Japanese Societies," *Law & Society Review* 24 (1990): 895–922; and Lawrence M. Friedman, *Total Justice* (New York: Russell Sage Foundation, 1985).

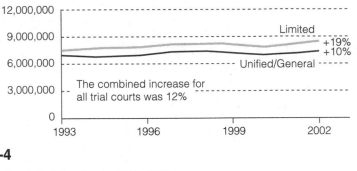

Source: *State Court Caseload Statistics, 2003*, at www.ncsconline.org.

FIGURE 7-4

Total State Court Civil Caseloads, 1993–2002

time (see Figure 7-4). This does not necessarily mean, however, that Americans have become more litigious; because the nation's population has also increased, there are more Americans to file suits. Indeed, from 1900 to 1960, per capita litigation in the United States remained relatively stable.[46] Since that time, however, the increases in litigation have outstripped population growth. Although this seems to support the notion that Americans have become more eager to sue, one should be cautious about drawing that conclusion.

The greatest single source of the increase in civil cases is an increase in divorce and post-divorce proceedings (domestic relations cases). One author wryly notes: "Few of us, I suspect, know many people who filed for divorce because they were enamored of litigation or beguiled by lawyers."[47] In addition, although civil filings rose during the late twentieth and early twenty-first centuries, they did not increase uniformly in all regions of the country and in all areas of the law, as might be expected if Americans had grown more litigious (see Table 7-3). Moreover, historical studies reveal that the growth in litigation in the United States over the course of the twentieth century was episodic and uneven. The "litigation explosion" may thus be merely a short-term phenomenon. Indeed, there is some evidence to support this view. Although the civil litigation rate (excluding domestic relations cases) rose 14 percent in state courts from 1984 to 1999, the rate actually declined almost 7 percent from 1991 to 1999.[48] Finally, historical studies show that current levels of per capita litigation in the United States are not unprecedented. Higher per capita rates existed in colonial times and during part of the nineteenth century.[49]

In sum, despite widely publicized claims to the contrary, the evidence suggests that the United States is not an unusually litigious society. Nonetheless, litigation in the United States may still adversely affect the legal system and the economy, as critics have charged. The economic effects of litigation will

TABLE 7-3	CIVIL FILINGS IN STATE TRIAL COURTS (SELECTED STATES)	
State	**Civil Filings Per 100,000 (All Courts)**	**Caseload Growth 2000–2002 (General Jurisdiction Courts)**
Alabama	4,430	18
Arkansas	4,889	19
California	4,012	3
Hawaii	2,398	−14
Indiana	7,534	14
Kansas	7,263	13
Minnesota	3,080	7
Montana	5,314	8
New Jersey	8,844	6
New Mexico	3,549	8
New York	8,620	1
Texas	2,985	12

Source: Adapted from *Examining the Work of State Courts,2003*, at www.ncsconline.org.

be considered in Chapter 11,when the discussion turns to tort law and product liability claims. The next section considers current efforts to respond to litigation levels and improve the system of civil justice.

IS THERE A BETTER WAY?

Despite their differences, critics of the "litigation explosion" and advocates of greater access to the courts agree that the American system of civil justice must be improved. The general public seems to share their dissatisfaction, viewing litigation as unduly slow, complex, and costly.[50] Other critics of American civil justice complain that formal legal processes hamper courts' ability to address the problems underlying disputes and fashion lasting consensual solutions to those problems.[51]

During the 1970s, legal reformers began to propose that less formal forums be created outside the courts to help solve the problems of heavy caseloads, costly justice, and ineffectiveness in settling disputes. In recent years this movement for "alternative dispute resolution" (or ADR, as it is usually called) has enjoyed considerable success. In 1990, Congress enacted the Administrative Dispute Resolution Act, which requires federal agencies to consider ADR for settling disputes, and in 1998, it enacted the Alternative Dispute Resolution

Act, requiring district courts to establish ADR programs.[52] More than half the states have established their own ADR programs.[53] Corporations and other private institutions have also pioneered their own mechanisms for resolving disputes without recourse to the courts.

Alternatives in Dispute Resolution

Alternative dispute resolution encompasses a wide range of forums and processes. Although considerable differences exist among ADR programs, most involve either *arbitration* or *mediation*.

Arbitration

Voluntary Arbitration   After a period in the major leagues, a baseball player who cannot agree on a salary with his team is eligible to take the dispute to arbitration. The player proposes a salary that he believes is fair and offers arguments and evidence for his position. The team submits a different figure and supports its position. The arbitrator then chooses one of the two figures, and both parties are bound by that decision.

Baseball's system of salary arbitration reveals the basic features of arbitration: A dispute is submitted to a neutral third party, who hears arguments, reviews evidence, and renders a decision. As the example illustrates, most often voluntary arbitration is used to resolve labor disputes. In recent years, however, it has also been employed to settle commercial disputes in various industries, including construction and insurance.[54]

Although the arbitrator plays a quasi-judicial role, voluntary arbitration differs from litigation in crucial respects. First, voluntary arbitration can occur only if both parties have consented, usually by contract, to submit their disputes to arbitration. Baseball's system of salary arbitration, for example, resulted from a collective bargaining agreement between the players' union and the team owners. Second, the arbitrators in voluntary arbitration are selected and paid by the parties. Agreement between the parties determines whether there shall be a single arbitrator or a panel of arbitrators, the scope of their authority, and how they shall be selected. Third, voluntary arbitration proceeds according to ground rules negotiated by the parties. Usually, formal rules of evidence and procedure are dispensed with in arbitration. This procedural informality simplifies and speeds the process. Fourth, voluntary arbitration promotes timely decision making. In simple cases, the arbitrator may render an immediate decision. Even in complex cases arbitrators, because they are not obliged to write opinions, announce their decisions quickly, usually within thirty days of the conclusion of the arbitration hearing.

Court-annexed Arbitration   Court-annexed arbitration might also be called compulsory arbitration.[55] The court assigns selected civil cases, usually those involving relatively small sums of money, to arbitration as a precondition to or substitute for trial. Nevada, for example, requires that all civil actions that arise out of automobile accidents and involve less than $15,000 must be submitted to arbitration.[56] The arbitrator, usually designated by the state, hears arguments and evidence and renders a decision, applying the same legal standards that a judge would apply. If the parties accept the arbitrator's ruling, it is formalized as the court's judgment in the case. If either party objects to the ruling, it can demand a trial of the case; thus, the arbitrator's decision is not binding. In most jurisdictions, however, financial penalties discourage frivolous appeals of arbitrators' rulings. In Colorado, for example, unless the party demanding trial improves its position by more than 10 percent, it must pay up to $1,000 of the costs of the arbitration proceeding.[57]

Since 1952, when the first program was introduced in Pennsylvania, more than half the states and most federal district courts have instituted court-annexed arbitration programs.

Mediation   Mediation attempts to resolve disputes by "assist[ing] the disputants to reach a voluntary settlement of their differences through an agreement that defines their future behavior."[58] In divorce mediation, for example, the agreement may resolve such contentious matters as the division of marital property, child support payments, and visitation rights. In neighborhood disputes, the agreement may specify the actions that each disputant will take or avoid in the future.

Mediators do not render authoritative decisions like arbitrators or judges at trial; they merely facilitate settlements between the disputants. The success of their efforts thus depends on their interpersonal skills and their ability to win the trust and cooperation of the disputants. Advocates of mediation view the lack of coercion as an advantage. Requiring disputants to become actively involved in resolving the dispute ensures that the outcome will be one that is acceptable to both parties.

Mediators promote settlement largely by fostering a productive negotiating climate in which issues are addressed in an orderly fashion, hostility is controlled, and the need for compromise is recognized. They may also play a more active part in the negotiations, obliging the disputants to clarify their objectives, offering suggestions for settlement, and translating the agreements reached into a written document.[59]

In recent years government programs have promoted mediation for resolving disputes between divorcing couples and within neighborhoods. Many states now offer divorce mediation to promote settlements for the division of property, child custody, and visitation rights. California has mandated mediation in all such instances.[60] Although exact figures are unavailable, experts estimated that there were 28,000 divorce mediations in 1980 and more than 34,000 a year later, a rise of almost 25 percent.[61] Similar growth has occurred in the use of mediation to deal with neighborhood disputes. In 1975, there were only 11 neighborhood justice centers nationwide; a decade later, there were 182, and the number has continued to increase.[62] Most of the centers employ mediators to resolve disputes brought by neighborhood residents or referred by police, local courts, or prosecutors' offices.

Does ADR Work?

Legal reformers insist that Alternative Dispute Resolution (ADR) provides fast and inexpensive justice, and the rapid expansion of ADR over the last two decades suggests that their arguments have been persuasive. Nonetheless, ADR has its critics.[63] They observe that some of the claims for ADR seem contradictory: Can ADR really promote greater access to justice and at the same time reduce the demands on the courts? Beyond this, the critics claim that ADR is a class-based reform that shunts the disputes of the average citizen to lesser tribunals while reserving the courts for the concerns and disputes of the elite.[64] Furthermore, they argue that because ADR emphasizes compromise and accommodation, it disarms victims of injustice who insist on the full vindication of their rights. In fact, ADR's emphasis on informal proceedings tends to reinforce unequal power relations by denying to the poor and disadvantaged members of society the due process protections of court proceedings and the equalizing assistance of representation by a lawyer.[65]

These are serious charges. Let us look at the actual effects of ADR, focusing on its consequences for access to justice, the caseloads of the courts, the costs of securing justice, and the quality of justice obtained by those whose disputes are addressed through ADR.

Access to Justice   Many ADR programs have been designed to increase the accessibility of justice, especially for those involved in "minor" disputes. The programs do not charge for services or require lawyers. They may hold hearings at times convenient to all disputants, such as evenings or weekends, and provide multilingual staffs to serve non–English-speaking disputants.[66] Nevertheless, ADR programs have not attracted large numbers of disputants unwilling to bring their disputes to court. The vast majority of cases come to ADR programs on referral from courts or other institutions rather than from disputants directly seeking their services.[67] Thus, ADR programs have not substantially increased access to justice. Whether this will change as ADR programs become institutionalized and better publicized remains to be seen.

Effects on Court Caseloads   Most disputes come to ADR programs on referral, which suggests that the programs relieve caseload pressures on the courts. Many proponents of ADR see this as its prime advantage.[68] Although ADR programs have reduced court caseloads somewhat, their impact has been quite limited. In part, this reflects the small size of most ADR programs. An American Bar Association survey found that 60 percent of ADR programs received fewer than 500 referrals per year, and only 4 percent more than 5,000.[69] Beyond that, the parties using ADR might have settled their disputes before trial if they had not been referred to an ADR program.[70] Finally, ADR programs may not conclusively resolve the cases referred to them. When the disputants cannot reach an agreement in mediation, they may take their dispute to court. When an arbitrator renders a decision in court-annexed arbitration, the losing party has the option of taking the case to court (although relatively few elect to do so).[71] In sum, ADR programs have had only a limited impact on court caseloads.

The Costs of Justice   A major claim of ADR is that it reduces the costs to government of dispensing justice and to disputants of obtaining it. ADR eliminates judges and juries, streamlines procedures, and disposes of disputes more quickly than courts can. Thus, one study found that it cost about $76 to process a case through arbitration and $175 to hear a case.[72] Disputants benefit not only from the greater efficiency of ADR proceedings but also, in most instances, from the opportunity to pursue their claims without incurring the cost of a lawyer. However, insofar as cases referred to ADR that would have settled rather than gone to trial, the financial advantages are limited.

The Quality of Justice   The absence of judges, lawyers, and jurors, however, raises a serious question: Are disputants under ADR receiving "second-class justice"? Critics contend that government uses ADR to get rid of working-class citizens and their disputes rather than give them the serious consideration they deserve. Indeed, studies of mediation programs that deal with neighborhood problems have found that complainants come disproportionately from the lower-middle class.[73] However, not all ADR programs share this class character. Divorce-mediation programs draw disputants from all social classes, as do court-annexed arbitration programs.[74]

Critics also contend that government gives first-class treatment to business cases, while palming off interpersonal disputes to ADR. Undoubtedly, courts are eager to avoid involvement in interpersonal disputes, which court personnel often refer to as "junk cases," complaining that they "don't belong here."[75] Yet their reluctance to deal with interpersonal disputes derives, at least in part, from the recognition that courts are ill-equipped to resolve such disputes. Moreover, ADR may respond to the desire for more harmonious relationships within the society. The real question is whether mediation and arbitration do a better job in resolving disputes.

Legal scholars have attempted to answer the question by surveying disputants' views about the fairness of the process and outcomes under ADR.[76] Their surveys reveal widespread satisfaction with how disputes were handled and resolved. The responses are particularly striking when compared with litigants' evaluations of court processes. In divorce mediation, for example, where participants were involved both with courts and with mediation, 98 percent of those who had success in mediation expressed satisfaction with the process, as did 57 percent of those who had no success, while only 36 percent were satisfied with the court processes.[77] Similar results were obtained when disputants were questioned about how effective judicial rulings and mediation agreements were in promoting long-term solutions to their disputes. Surveys reveal that mediation promotes greater understanding, reduced anger, and improved relationships.

Although these findings suggest the superiority of mediation and arbitration to adjudication, at least for certain types of cases, they do not necessarily demonstrate that cases should be resolved by ADR programs rather than by courts. Most cases that come to the courts are, in fact, settled rather than adjudicated. Judges also engage in mediation to settle cases, as the discussion of the Agent Orange case showed. Thus, even before ADR was widely introduced, the boundaries between litigation and other forms of dispute resolution had blurred.

CONCLUSIONS

"As a litigant," a learned judge once wrote, "I should dread a lawsuit beyond almost anything else short of sickness and death."[78] Nevertheless, Americans file millions of lawsuits each year. This is not because Americans are unusually litigious; the evidence suggests that the United States is not an overly litigious society. But in a complex, populous society like the United States, disputes are bound to arise. Moreover, advances in technology have transformed expectations of justice, making people less willing to accept injuries as fated or as "nobody's fault." Courts afford one mechanism for resolving those disputes and redressing those injuries.

Litigation, however, is only one among a number of options for dealing with grievances. As we have seen, most grievances do not become disputes, and most disputes do not become court cases. Psychological and financial costs and uncertainty discourage potential litigants from filing suit. These costs, however, do not fall evenly on all segments of the population. The differences in the types of civil cases brought to the courts for resolution suggest that the costs weigh more heavily on one-shotters than on repeat players.

Even when litigants do file civil suits, their cases are far more likely to be settled than adjudicated. Indeed, what unites such reforms of the civil justice system as liberalized rules for discovery, pretrial conferences, and the alternative dispute resolution movement is the emphasis on promoting settlement and discouraging trials. Indeed, trials seem an anomaly, occurring only when the various mechanisms designed to produce a consensual solution have failed. In this respect, the system of civil justice in the United States closely resembles the system of criminal justice, with its emphasis on plea bargaining rather than trial. The question remains whether these systems serve the interests of justice.

NOTES

1. Quoted in Peter H. Schuck, *Agent Orange on Trial: Mass Toxic Disasters in the Courts* (Cambridge, MA: Belknap Press, 1986), p. 256. The description of the Agent Orange litigation relies on Schuck's account.

2. Quoted in ibid., p. 45.

3. Quoted in ibid., p. 85.

4. Quoted in ibid., p. 68.

5. Robert Mnookin and Lewis Kornhauser, "Bargaining in the Shadow of the Law: The Case of Divorce," *Yale Law Journal* 88 (1979): 950–977.

6. The argument that it is necessary to increase access to justice is presented in Laura Nader, ed., *No Access to Law: Alternatives to the American Judicial System* (New York: Academic Press, 1980); Mauro Capelletti and D. Garth, "Access to Justice: The Newest Wave in the Worldwide Movement to Make Rights Effective," *Buffalo Law Review* 27 (spring 1978): 181–292; and Daniel McGillis, *Community Dispute Resolution Programs and Public Policy* (Washington, DC: U.S. Department of Justice, National Institute of Justice, 1986), chap. 2.

7. The argument that the United States suffers from too much litigation is presented in Walter K. Olson, *The Litigation Explosion: What Happened When America Unleashed the Lawsuit* (New York: Truman Talley Books, 1991).

8. See Lawrence M. Friedman, *Total Justice* (New York: Russell Sage Foundation, 1985), part 1, and Jethro K. Lieberman, *The Litigious Society* (New York: Basic Books, 1981), chap. 1.

9. This discussion uses a framework developed by William L. F. Felstiner, "Influences of Social Organization on Dispute Processing," *Law and Society Review* 9 (fall 1974): 63–94.

10. William L. F. Felstiner, "Avoidance as Dispute Processing: An Elaboration," *Law and Society Review* 9 (summer 1975): 695.

11. Barbara A. Curran, *The Legal Needs of the Public* (Chicago: American Bar Foundation, 1977), pp. 141–142.

12. Quoted in Kristin Bumiller, *The Civil Rights Society: The Social Construction of Victims* (Baltimore: Johns Hopkins University Press, 1988), p. 90.

13. For a comparative study that documents the importance of costs and alternative forums in deterring civil litigation, see Erhard Blankenburg, "The Infrastructure for Avoiding Civil Litigation: Comparing Cultures of Political Behavior in The Netherlands and West Germany," *Law and Society Review* 28 (1994): 789–808. The use of alternative dispute resolution (ADR) in the United States is discussed later in this chapter.

14. Quoted in Bumiller, *The Civil Rights Society*, p. 52.

15. Charles Alan Wright, *Law of Federal Courts*, 3d ed. (St. Paul, MN: West Publishing, 1976), p. 293.

16. The discussion of the stages in the process of civil litigation draws on Wright, *Law of Federal Courts*, chap. 10; Mary Kay Kane, *Civil Procedure in a Nutshell*, 2d ed. (St. Paul, MN: West Publishing, 1985), chap. 3; William P. McLauchlan, *American Legal*

Processes (New York: John Wiley & Sons, 1977), chap. 3; and David W. Neubauer, *Judicial Process: Law, Courts, and Politics in the United States* (Pacific Grove, CA: Brooks/Cole Publishing, 1991), chap. 11.

17. Sally Engle Merry, *Getting Justice and Getting Even: Legal Consciousness among Working-Class Americans* (Chicago: University of Chicago Press, 1990), p. 87.

18. Wright, *Law of Federal Courts,* p. 398.

19. Richard Posner, "An Economic Approach to Legal Procedure and Judicial Administration," *Journal of Legal Studies* 2 (June 1973): 399–458.

20. Olson, *The Litigation Explosion,* p. 119.

21. Judge William Schwarzer, quoted in Robert E. Litan, "Speeding Up Civil Justice," *Judicature* 73 (October–November 1989): 162.

22. Quoted in Laurie P. Cohen and Alex M. Freedman, "Tobacco Plaintiffs Face a Grilling," *Wall Street Journal,* February 11, 1993, A-6. According to the late Chief Justice Warren Burger, the abuse of discovery has led to "trial by annihilation before the litigants ever reach the courthouse." Warren E. Burger, *Delivery of Justice* (St. Paul, MN: West Publishing, 1990), p. 143.

23. David W. Neubauer, *Judicial Process: Law, Courts, and Politics in the United States,* pp. 285–287.

24. Herbert M. Kritzer, "Adjudication to Settlement: Shading in the Gray," *Judicature* 70 (October–November 1986): 161–165.

25. Kritzer, "Adjudication to Settlement," p. 164, table 3.

26. This discussion of pretrial conferences draws on Wright, *Law of Federal Courts,* pp. 444–447, and Kane, *Civil Procedure in a Nutshell,* pp. 149–154.

27. Wayne D. Brazil, *Settling Civil Suits: Litigators' Views about Appropriate Roles and Effective Techniques for Federal Judges* (Chicago: American Bar Association Press, 1985), pp. 45–46 and passim. For data on civil cases in federal district courts, see the Web site of the federal judiciary at www.uscourts.gov. For data on civil cases in state trial courts, see the Web site of the National Center for State Courts at www.ncsconline.dni.org.

29. See the Web site of the federal judiciary at www.uscourts.gov.

30. Ibid.

31. Marc Galanter, "Why the 'Haves' Come Out Ahead: Speculations on the Limits of Legal Change," *Law and Society Review* 9 (fall 1974): 97–107 and passim.

32. Ibid.

33. Ibid.

34. This analysis follows Lenore J. Weitzman, *The Divorce Revolution* (New York: Free Press, 1985). Subsequent studies have tempered Weitzman's conclusions. See, e.g., Herbert Jacob, *Silent Revolution: The Transformation of Divorce Law in the United States* (Chicago: University of Chicago Press, 1988), and Stephen D. Sugarman and Herma Hill Kay, eds., *Divorce Reform at the Crossroads* (New Haven, CT: Yale University Press, 1990).

35. Weitzman, *The Divorce Revolution,* p. x.

36. Galanter, "Why the 'Haves' Come Out Ahead," p. 98.

37. See generally Craig McEwen and Richard Maiman, "Small Claims Mediation in Maine: An Empirical Assessment," *Maine Law Review* 33 (1981): 237–268; Austin Sarat, "Alternatives in Dispute Processing: Litigation in a Small Claims Court," *Law and Society Review* 10 (spring 1976): 339–376; and Barbara Yngvesson and Patricia Hennessey, "Small Claims, Complex Disputes: A Review of the Small Claims Literature," *Law and Society Review* 9 (winter 1975): 219–274. For a cautionary perspective on those findings, see Neil Vidmar, "The Small Claims Court: A Reconceptualization of Disputes and an Empirical Investigation," *Law and Society Review* 18 (1984): 515–550.

38. Robert Roper and Joanne Martin, "Jury Verdicts and the 'Crisis' in Civil Justice: Some Findings from an Empirical Study," *Justice System Journal* 11 (winter 1986): 321–348.

39. Quoted in Marc Galanter, "The Day after the Litigation Explosion," *Maryland Law Review* 46 (1986): 3.

40. Quoted in Richard D. Catenacci, "Hyperlexis or Hyperbole: Subdividing the Landscape of Disputes and Defusing the Litigation Explosion," *Review of Litigation* 8 (fall 1989): 320.

41. Quoted in Galanter, "Day After the Litigation Explosion," p. 3.

42. Quoted in ibid., p. 4.

43. Quoted in Gregory Brian Butler and Brian David Miller, "Fiddling While Rome Burns: A Response to Dr. Hensler," *Judicature* 75 (February–March 1992): 251.

44. Marc Galanter, "Reading the Landscape of Disputes: What We Know and Don't Know (And Think We Know) about Our Allegedly Contentious and Litigious Society," *UCLA Law Review* 31 (1983): 54–59; and Marc Galanter, "Law Abounding: Legalization around the North Atlantic," *Modern Law Review* 55 (January 1992): 1–25.

45. Herbert M. Kritzer, "Propensity to Sue in England and the United States: Blaming and Claiming in Tort Suits," *Journal of Law and Society* 18 (winter 1991): 400–427. Data on civil filings in American state courts are drawn from *State Court Caseload Statistics, 1999–2000,* available at the Web site of the National Center for State Courts: www.ncsconline.org.

46. David W. Neubauer, "Are We Approaching Judicial Gridlock? A Critical Review of the Literature," *Justice System Journal* 11 (winter 1986): 365.

47. Galanter, "Day After the Litigation Explosion," p. 10.

48. Stephen Daniels, "Ladders and Bushes: The Problem of Caseloads and Studying Court Activities over Time," *American Bar Foundation Research Journal* (1984): 751–796, and Wayne V. McIntosh, *The Appeal of Civil Law: A Political-Economic Analysis of Litigation* (Urbana: University of Illinois Press, 1990), chap. 7. Data on civil filings in American state courts are drawn from *State Court Caseload Statistics, 1999–2000,* available at the Web site of the National Center for State Courts: www.ncsconline.org.

49. Galanter, "Day After the Litigation Explosion," p. 5, and McIntosh, *Appeal of Civil Law,* esp. p. 166, table 7.4.

50. For public opinion data on courts and their operations, see the findings of the 1999 National Conference on Public Trust and Confidence in the Justice System at www.ncsc.dni.us/PTC.

51. A representative exposition of this viewpoint is Stephen B. Goldberg, Eric D. Green, and Frank E. A. Sander, *Dispute Resolution* (Boston: Little Brown & Co., 1985). Not all commentators share this assessment; see, e.g., Christine B. Harrington, *Shadow Justice: The Ideology and Institutionalization of Alternatives to Court* (Westport, CT: Greenwood Press, 1985), chap. 3.

52. Karen V. W. Stone, *Private Justice: The Law of Alternative Dispute Resolution* (New York: Foundation Press, 2000), p. 5.

53. Standing Committee on Dispute Resolution, American Bar Association, *Legislation on Dispute Resolution* (Washington, DC: American Bar Association, 1990), and Stone, *Private Justice,* p. 799.

54. This discussion of arbitration draws on John W. Cooley, "Arbitration vs. Mediation—Explaining the Differences," *Judicature* 69 (February–March 1986): 263–269, and Susan M. Leeson and Bryan M. Johnston, *Ending It* (Cincinnati, OH: Anderson Publishing, 1988), chap. 3.

55. This analysis draws on the treatment of court-annexed arbitration in Leeson and Johnston, *Ending It,* chap. 4; Deborah Hensler, "What We Know and Don't Know about

Court Administered Arbitration," *Judicature* 69 (February–March 1986): 270–278; and
Note, "Court-Annexed Arbitration: The Verdict Is Still Out," *Review of Litigation* 8 (fall
1989): 327–346.

56. Standing Committee on Dispute Resolution, *Legislation on Dispute Resolution,*
p. 75.

57. Colorado Mandatory Arbitration Act, reprinted in *Legislation on Dispute Resolution,* p. 80.

58. Cooley, "Arbitration vs. Mediation—Explaining the Differences," p. 266, and
Leeson and Johnston, *Ending It,* chap. 6.

59. Kenneth Kressel, *The Process of Divorce: How Professionals and Couples Negotiate Settlements* (New York: Basic Books, 1985), pp. 179–180.

60. Ibid., p. 182.

61. Ibid.

62. McGillis, *Community Dispute Resolution Programs and Public Policy,* p. 7.

63. Major works critical of alternative dispute resolution include Richard Abel, *The Politics of Informal Justice* (Orlando, FL: Academic Press, 1982); Jerold Auerbach, *Justice without Law* (New York: Oxford University Press, 1984); Harrington, *Shadow Justice;* and
Lisa Lerman, "Mediation of Wife Abuse Cases: The Adverse Impact on Women," *Harvard Women's Law Journal* 7 (1984): 57–113.

64. Abel, *Politics of Informal Justice.*

65. Owen M. Fiss, "Against Settlement," *Yale Law Journal* 93 (May 1984):
1073–1090, and Penelope E. Bryan, "Killing Us Softly: Divorce Mediation and the Politics
of Power," *Buffalo Law Review* 40 (May 1992): 443–523.

66. McGillis, *Community Dispute Resolution Programs and Public Policy,* p. 87.

67. Merry, *Getting Justice and Getting Even,* pp. 182–188.

68. Harrington, *Shadow Justice,* chap. 1.

69. McGillis, *Community Dispute Resolution Programs and Public Policy,* p. 77.

70. See Deborah R. Hensler, "Our Courts, Ourselves: How the Alternative Dispute
Resolution Movement Is Re-Shaping Our Legal System," *Penn State Law Review* (summer 2003): 165–196.

71. Hensler, "What We Know and Don't Know about Court Administered Arbitration," p. 275.

72. Ibid., p. 274.

73. See the excellent summary of these studies in Merry, *Getting Justice and Getting Even,* pp. 182–188.

74. See Kressel, *The Process of Divorce,* and Hensler, "What We Know and Don't Know
about Court Administered Arbitration," p. 275.

75. Merry, *Getting Justice and Getting Even,* p. 14.

76. These paragraphs rely on the summary of survey data in McGillis, *Community Dispute Resolution Programs and Public Policy,* pp. 61–67. For a dissenting interpretation, see Harrington, *Shadow Justice,* chap. 5.

77. McGillis, *Community Dispute Resolution Programs and Public Policy,* p. 63.

78. Learned Hand, "The Deficiencies of Trials to Reach the Heart of the Matter,"
in Association of the Bar of the City of New York, *Lectures on Legal Topics* (New York:
Macmillan, 1926), p. 105.

CHAPTER 8

JUDICIAL DECISION MAKING

Consider the following two accounts of a ruling by the U.S. Supreme Court.

In *Stanford v. Kentucky* (1989), the Supreme Court upheld the death sentences imposed on two murderers who had committed their crimes before reaching their eighteenth birthdays.[1] Speaking for a five-member Court majority, Justice Antonin Scalia argued that the Eighth Amendment's ban on cruel and unusual punishments did not preclude imposition of the death penalty on those who were juveniles when they committed their offenses. Scalia asserted that the understanding of cruel and unusual punishments at the time the Bill of Rights was ratified offered no support for the claim that the sentences violated constitutional guarantees. Rather, under the common law at the time of the Founding, one could be tried as an adult when one was fourteen years old. Thus, those who adopted the Bill of Rights did not view it as cruel or unusual to treat teenagers as adults in the criminal justice process.

Nor did the Supreme Court's prior rulings require invalidation of the offenders' death sentences. While these precedents established that the Eighth Amendment was to be interpreted in light of the "evolving standards of decency that mark the progress of a maturing society," they also recognized that the statutes enacted by the people's representatives provided the most important evidence of the society's standards of decency.[2] Surveying those statutes, Scalia found that most states permitted capital punishment for sixteen- or seventeen-year-old offenders. He therefore concluded that there was neither a historical nor a modern consensus rejecting capital punishment for juveniles who murder. Consequently, speaking for the Court majority, he upheld the death sentences.

★ ★ ★ ★

In *Stanford v. Kentucky* (1989), the Supreme Court's five-member conservative majority upheld the imposition of death sentences on two murderers who had committed their crimes while still juveniles. The Court's ruling marked yet another defeat for those mounting constitutional challenges to capital punishment in the states. It also continued the tough-minded approach to the rights of defendants that has characterized the Court since the elevation of William Rehnquist to Chief Justice.

President Ronald Reagan deserves much of the credit—or blame—for the Court's increasingly conservative stance in criminal justice cases. Reagan had vowed to appoint conservatives to the Court, and he apparently succeeded. As in many previous cases, all four of Reagan's appointees (all of them Republicans) voted against the defendants' claims. Joining the four to establish the majority was Justice Byron White, who has often provided the crucial fifth vote on criminal justice issues. The decision in *Stanford,* together with other recent conservative rulings, suggest that President Reagan has indeed reversed the orientation of the Supreme Court.

These two accounts present strikingly different explanations of why the justices rejected the constitutional challenge to the death sentences in *Stanford v. Kentucky.* The first account analyzes the legal reasoning that the Supreme Court offered in support of its decision. Thus, it explains the Court's ruling in terms of its interpretation of the original intent of the Eighth Amendment, the Court's precedents, and the approach the Court traditionally employs to determine the "standards of decency" prevailing in the society. The second account, in contrast, altogether ignores those legal factors. Instead, it emphasizes the political orientation of the justices, the political agenda of the president who appointed them, and interpersonal dynamics on the Supreme Court.

These accounts illustrate two distinct approaches to understanding judicial decision making. The first approach, which I shall call the *legal perspective,* distinguishes judicial decision making from the decision making of other political actors such as legislators and executives. According to this perspective, judicial decision making is distinctive because judges are expected to decide cases according to law rather than on the basis of personal predilection or public opinion and because they must justify their rulings through a process of legal reasoning.

The second approach, which might be called the *political perspective,* insists that judicial decision making closely resembles decision making by other political actors. According to this perspective, extralegal factors are decisive in judicial decision making: the attitudes of the judges, their conceptions of how they should behave, and the institutional context in which they operate. Although judges must justify their rulings on the basis of law, law merely provides the justification for judicial decisions; it does not constrain judicial choice.

This chapter describes and compares these two perspectives on judicial decision making. It focuses primarily on decision making in appellate courts because those courts—in contrast with trial courts—are primarily concerned with analyzing legal questions and usually present their analyses in written opinions.

THE LEGAL PERSPECTIVE

The Phases of Judicial Decision Making

According to the legal perspective, judicial decision making involves two phases, discovery and justification. "Discovery" involves the judge's initial determination of how a case should be resolved; "justification" involves the elaboration of the legal bases for the decision in a written opinion.[3] These two phases are interrelated. In the discovery phase the judge may be said to "intuit" the proper resolution of the case—that is, to arrive at the resolution without proceeding through a step-by-step reasoning process. This judicial intuition differs from the intuitive judgment of the average citizen because the judge's intuition is a professional judgment. More specifically, a judge's intuition is informed by his or her legal training and experience on the bench. Thus, one may say that the legal bases for resolving the case play a role in the discovery phase as well as in the justification phase of judicial decision making.[4]

In the justification phase the judge presents the bases for his or her decision in a written opinion. Because judges do not reach their decisions by a process of formal reasoning, the opinions that judges write do not describe the thinking processes by which they arrive at their decisions. Nevertheless, the requirement that judges publicly justify their rulings is crucial to judicial decision making. The requirement forces judges to examine whether there are persuasive legal bases supporting the decision they have intuited. If there are, they explains those bases in the written opinion. If there are not, they must modify their initial position to bring it in line with the weight of legal authority.

The Tools of Judicial Decision Making

To decide cases, judges must determine the applicable law and its meaning, and then apply the law to the facts of the case. This inquiry may lead them to consult a variety of legal or extralegal materials. Three resources are particularly important.

The Legal Text   Judicial decision making begins with the text of the applicable constitution, statute, or administrative regulation. (In cases involving the common law, of course, there is no text because there is no legal enactment to interpret.) The text itself is the fundamental authority, because the judge's function is to give effect to the law enacted by the constitution maker or lawmaker. In addition, the words used in an enactment constitute the best guide to its meaning. It is with this in mind that Justice Felix Frankfurter offered his famous three-step guide to statutory interpretation: (1) Read the statute; (2) read the statute; (3) read the statute![5]

If the meaning of an enactment is clear on its face, then judges need search no further and may merely apply it in the case before them. Legal commentators refer to this as the "plain meaning rule."[6] Often, however, the meaning of an enactment is not immediately obvious; indeed, litigation arises precisely because it is possible to disagree about the meaning of the law. Judges must then analyze the language of the enactment more closely. Consider, for example, the Mann Act—also known as the White Slave Traffic Act—enacted by Congress in 1910. The Mann Act made it a felony to "transport or cause to be transported . . . in interstate commerce . . . any woman or girl for the purpose of prostitution or debauchery, or for any other immoral purpose." While the meaning of "prostitution" is plain, the same cannot be said for the other terms of the Act, "debauchery" and "any other immoral purpose." Suppose a robber paid for a woman's airline ticket so that she could join him in robbing a bank. Assuming bank robbery is immoral, has he violated the Mann Act?

Looking merely at the text of the Mann Act, a judge would answer that the robber had not violated the law. To understand why, one must look at how judges interpret legal texts. They begin with the presumption that the enactment is a coherent effort to accomplish some purpose.[7] Thus, determining the general purpose of a statute or other enactment is crucial to clarifying the meaning of its various parts. In our hypothetical case, for example, the language of the Mann Act ("prostitution" and "debauchery") suggests that it was designed to prevent the transportation of women for the purpose of sexual misconduct. The law did not, then, forbid the transportation of women for bank robbery. Judges also read the words in a legal enactment in context, not just for their dictionary meaning. Justice Oliver Wendell Holmes explained why context is so crucial to interpretation: "A word is not a crystal, transparent and unchanged, it is the skin of a living thought and may vary greatly in color and content, according to the circumstances and the time in which it is used."[8] This context may serve to give specificity to the general language in an enactment. Thus, in the context of the Mann Act, the meaning of "any immoral purpose" is clarified by its appearance in juxtaposition to other language ("prostitution" and "debauchery") dealing with sexual immorality.

As our example illustrates, recurrence to the legal text means more than simply reading the words. The judge examines the text as an integrated whole, determining the purpose of the enactment (which may not be immediately apparent), comparing and reconciling its various provisions, and clarifying its general language through analysis of the context in which the phrases appear. If this analysis does not suffice to answer the legal questions, the judge may turn to other legal materials.

Legislative History   In their interpretive quest, judges may also consult the "legislative history" of the enactment—that is, materials generated in the course of adopting a statute or constitutional provision.[9] To determine the meaning of a statute, a judge may trace its evolution through the records of committee hearings, committee reports summarizing the legislation and its purposes, and statements of legislators during floor debates. In interpreting provisions of the U.S. Constitution, a judge may consult James Madison's *Notes* on the debates at the Constitutional Convention, the debates in the conventions called to ratify the proposed constitution, the *Federalist Papers,* and other commentary contemporaneous with the ratification process.[10] By mining the legislative history of an enactment, a judge may better determine the purposes of the enactment and how its authors believed it should be interpreted.

Legal scholars have long debated the desirability of relying on legislative history. Courts in Great Britain have steadfastly refused to consider legislative materials relating to a statute's passage to determine Parliament's intent.[11] At least in recent years, however, courts in the United States have been quite willing to look to legislative history, particularly for interpreting statutes.[12] Proponents believe that legislative history helps judges resolve ambiguities and interpret enactments in line with the intentions of those who adopted them. For example, a judge interpreting the Mann Act could consult the congressional debates surrounding its adoption to determine how its sponsors understood the terms "debauchery" and "other immoral purposes." Even more important, by consulting legislative history, a judge could ensure that his or her interpretation of the law's purposes coincides with the intentions of the legislators. This is crucial because the legislature's power to enact law necessarily entails the power to prescribe the authoritative meaning of the law that it enacts.[13]

Those who, like Justice Antonin Scalia, oppose the use of legislative history deny that one can ascribe an intention to groups such as legislative bodies or constitutional conventions.[14] They note that statutes and constitutional provisions are the product of group deliberations. Many of those who vote for a measure never state their view of what it means or how it should be interpreted. Those who do speak may do so primarily to influence the judicial interpretation of the provision.[15] There is no reason to assume, however, that the views of those who speak during legislative debates are representative. Legislators may have quite different understandings of the enactments they adopt.[16] Opponents argue that, given the unreliability of legislative history, judges should ignore it in favor of analysis of the enactment and judicial rulings interpreting it.

Precedent   A precedent is an earlier judicial decision that might be used as a basis for deciding a current case. In a hierarchical legal system, lower court judges are obliged to decide cases in line with the precedents established by higher courts. For example, a ruling by the Minnesota Supreme Court on a matter of Minnesota state law is authoritative and binding on judges in the state's trial courts. A ruling by a court of similar rank, however, does not constitute authoritative precedent, in the sense that it need not be followed. For example, a federal court of appeals may interpret a federal law in a particular way, but another federal court of appeals is not obliged to accept the first court's interpretation of the law. Nor, in the United States, is a court legally obliged to adhere to its own previous decisions. The Supreme Court, for example, may overrule its earlier decisions interpreting the Constitution or federal statutes.

Of course, even when precedents are not authoritative, they may still be persuasive. Thus, a federal court of appeals may, after learning how another appeals court has interpreted a federal law, decide that the interpretation was correct and adopt it. Or the Supreme Court may conclude that its earlier rulings interpreting, say, the Eighth Amendment's ban on cruel and unusual punishments were correct and use them to justify its ruling in a current case. Similarly, judges in Alabama or Oregon may seek guidance in the rulings of judges from other states in interpreting the common law.

The system of case law in the United States and Great Britain relies heavily on the doctrine of precedent, or stare decisis, which states that cases should be decided today as they were decided in the past. Indeed, from 1898 to 1966, the House of Lords, the highest court in Great Britain, subscribed to a strict doctrine of precedent, holding itself absolutely bound by its earlier decisions.[17] Although courts in the United States have never embraced this extreme position, they have recognized that strong arguments support judicial adherence to precedent and that departures from precedent therefore require justification.

The doctrine of precedent is particularly important in resolving cases at common law because there is no legal text or legislative history on which to base decisions. However, stare decisis also operates in statutory interpretation and, to a lesser extent, in constitutional adjudication. Box 8-1, which surveys the range of opinion on the use of precedent in judicial decision making, reveals the four reasons that are usually offered for adherence to precedent.[18]

1. Predictability.   Adherence to precedent assures a certainty about results that would otherwise be difficult to obtain. This certainty enables people to predict the legal consequences of their actions and to act accordingly. For example, I am more willing to enter into a contract if I can be sure that the law will support me if the other party violates the contract. And I can have that assurance if the law currently upholds contractual obligations and judges adhere to precedent in contract law.

2. Reliance.   Just as people rely on promises in ordering their affairs, so also do they rely on judicial decisions' authoritatively establishing the meaning of the law and gauge their behavior accordingly. A departure from precedent, then, is analogous to breaking a promise. "Having induced people to act in a certain manner, the legal system could only be blameworthy if it subsequently sought to punish or in any other way thwart the previously announced consequences of action."[19] Simply put, the legal system should give effect to the expectations that it has itself engendered.

3. Equality.   Equality before the law (uniformity of treatment) is an essential element in a just legal system.[20] The doctrine of precedent obliges judges to decide similar cases in the same way. By doing so, it reduces the discretion of judges, thereby ensuring that extraneous factors (e.g., the race, religion, gender, or social status of the parties) do not infect the process of decision.

4. Efficiency.   The doctrine of stare decisis provides judges with a quick and easy basis for justifying their rulings and thus, relieves them of the burden of returning to first principles in each case. Instead of having to "reinvent the wheel," judges can turn to the experience and wisdom of earlier judges. This in turn promotes the timely disposition of cases.

As Box 8-1 indicates, the arguments for stare decisis can be countered by arguments against strict adherence to precedent. Moreover, adherence to precedent is not as easy as it may initially appear. To understand why, we must examine the process of judicial reasoning.

Legal Reasoning as Deductive Reasoning

In 1984, Gregory Johnson was convicted of violating a Texas law prohibiting flag desecration after he burned an American flag as part of a political protest. He appealed his conviction to the U.S. Supreme Court, contending that the Texas statute impinged on his First Amendment right of freedom of speech.[21] Assume that you are a Supreme Court justice confronted with this claim. How do you go about deciding? Should Johnson's conviction be upheld? Or should the Texas law be struck down as unconstitutional?

One possible approach is deductive reasoning. According to the deductive model of judicial decision making, depicted in Figure 8-1, you, acting as a justice, would first analyze the facts of the case to determine the legal category into which the case might best fit. In *Texas v. Johnson,* for example, the category would be First Amendment cases, and, more particularly, cases involving "symbolic speech" (expressive conduct). Next, you would identify the legal rule or standard that governed that category of cases. In constitutional cases, such as our example, you might find that legal rule in the Constitution itself or, more likely, in earlier rulings interpreting the applicable provision. By applying the rule to the facts of the case, you would then determine whether, according to the rule, the Texas law is constitutional or whether Johnson's expressive conduct was protected by the Constitution. Finally, on the basis of this analysis, you would arrive at your decision.

Is the deductive model an accurate depiction of how judges decide cases? The answer is both yes and no. The more settled the legal rule, the more likely it is that judicial decision making will resemble the deductive model. In many cases judges can resolve the dispute straightforwardly on the basis of settled law. Indeed, Justice Benjamin Cardozo estimated that 90 percent of the cases that come before courts are "predestined" in that they could only be decided in one way.[22]

If judicial decision making were always so simple, a computer with all the pertinent legal rules stored in its memory could fill the position of a judge. More to the point, judges who knew the law would always agree on how cases should

---

BOX
8-1

Perspectives on Precedents

"Precedents only prove what was done, but not what was well done." (Thomas Hobbes, English philosopher)

"It is better that the law should be certain than that every judge should speculate upon improvements in it." (Lord Eldon, English jurist)

"The question whether the doctrine of stare decisis should be adhered to . . . is always a choice between relative evils. When it appears that the evil resulting from a continuation of the accepted rule must be productive of greater mischief to the community than can possibly ensue from disregarding the previous adjudications on the subject, courts have frequently and wisely departed from precedent." (Chief Justice Arthur Vanderbilt, New Jersey Supreme Court)

"The force of precedent in the law is heightened by an additional factor: that curious, almost universal sense of justice which urges that all men are properly to be treated alike in like circumstances." (Karl Llewellyn, law professor)

---

be decided. In fact, they often disagree. The justices of the U.S. Supreme Court, for example, decide less than one-third of their cases unanimously.

Why is the deductive model not a fully adequate description of judicial decision making? For legal reasoning to follow the deductive model, there must be a single legal rule for the judge to apply in deciding the case. But there may be cases for which there is no controlling precedent or established legal rule, when, for instance, a judge interprets a recently enacted statute, addresses a novel constitutional claim, or confronts an unprecedented situation at common law. For other cases, there may be more than one category or rule that seems applicable. In fact, the issue in dispute may be which rule should be applied. Thus, the deductive model of judicial decision making cannot explain how judges deal with novel issues or choose between competing rules. Finally, the deductive model portrays the law as static, with judges consistently applying existing legal standards. In actuality, however, judicial decisions may change the law by overruling precedents or announcing new legal standards. The deductive model may explain legal stability, but it cannot account for legal change. It cannot explain why judges depart from precedent or when they should do so.

"This search for a static security—in the law or elsewhere—is misguided. The fact is that security can only be achieved through constant change, through the wise discarding of old ideas that have outlived their usefulness, and through the adapting of others to current facts." (Justice William O. Douglas, U.S. Supreme Court)

"The labors of judges would be increased almost to the breaking point if every past decision could be reopened in every case, and one could not lay one's own course of bricks on the secure foundation of the courses laid by others who had gone before him." (Chief Justice Benjamin Cardozo, New York Court of Appeals)

"It is revolting to have no better reason for a rule of law than that so it was laid down in the time of Henry IV. It is still more revolting if the grounds upon which it was laid down have vanished long since, and the rule simply persist from blind imitation of the past." (Justice Oliver Wendell Holmes, then on the Massachusetts Supreme Judicial Court and later on the U.S. Supreme Court)

Sources: Thomas Hobbes, *A Dialogue Between a Philosopher and a Student of the Common Laws of England*, ed. Joseph Cropsey (Chicago: University of Chicago Press, 1971), p. 129; Lord Eldon: *Sheddon v. Goodrich*, 8 Ves. 497; Arthur Vanderbilt: *Fox v. Snow*, 76 A.2d 877 (N.J. 1950); Karl Llewellyn, "Case Law," *Encyclopedia of the Social Sciences* (New York: Macmillan, 1930), 3:249; William O. Douglas, "Stare Decisis," *Columbia Law Review* 49 (1949): 735; Benjamin Cardozo, *The Nature of the Judicial Process* (New Haven, CT: Yale University Press, 1921), pp. 149–150; Oliver Wendell Holmes, "The Path of the Law," *Harvard Law Review* 10 (1897): 439.

Legal Reasoning as Reasoning by Example

The deficiencies of the deductive model led a group of legal scholars, known as the Legal Realists, to propose alternative explanations of judicial decision making.[23] One influential Legal Realist, Edward Levi, has suggested that legal reasoning is best understood as reasoning by example and analogy rather than as deductive reasoning.[24] Figure 8-2 illustrates Levi's theory.

Levi's Theory To explain Levi's theory, let us return to our example of *Texas v. Johnson*, the flag-burning case.[25] According to Levi, a justice deciding that case would examine how the Supreme Court had previously dealt with expressive conduct that violated state or federal statutes. Presumably, the judge would discover that the Court had ruled in some instances that the First Amendment protected the expressive conduct and in other instances that it did not.[26] The judge would then consider whether the facts in the flag-burning case more closely resembled those in the cases in which the Court had vindicated the expressive conduct or in which it had refused to do so. Presumably, if the

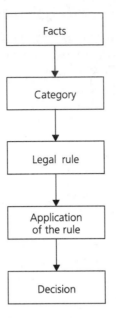

FIGURE **8-1**

The Deductive Model of Judicial Decision Making

Johnson case more closely resembled those instances in which the Court had ruled that the expressive conduct was constitutionally protected and struck down the statutes regulating it, the judge would rule in favor of Johnson. If it more closely resembled those instances in which the Court had denied constitutional protection to the expressive conduct and upheld the laws regulating it, then the judge would rule in favor of Texas.

As Levi recognized, however, the issue is not that simple. Both sets of earlier cases—those upholding and those striking down laws regulating expressive conduct—presumably resemble the flag-burning case in some respects and differ from it in others. A judge must therefore determine which similarities and which differences are decisive. According to Levi, this judicial determination of similarity and difference is the key step in the legal process.

To make this determination, the judge not only decides the case but also devises the legal rule by which the decision is justified. Assuming that the judge ruled in favor of the flag burner, the opinion would announce a legal rule that reconciled the ruling with previous decisions protecting expressive conduct. It would also explain why the present case differed from those in which the Court had ruled against First Amendment claims. Put differently, whereas the deductive model suggests that judges decide by applying known rules to diverse facts, Levi insists that "the rules arise out of *a process which, while comparing fact situations, creates the rules and then applies them.*"[27]

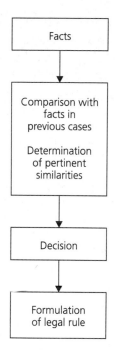

Source: Based on Edward H. Levi, *An Introduction to Legal Reasoning* (Chicago: University of Chicago Press, 1949), chap. 8

Applying Levi's Theory: The Right to Privacy   Levi's theory offers a dynamic model of the process of judicial decision making. The Supreme Court's rulings on the right to privacy can serve as an illustration.

The Court first recognized a constitutional right to privacy in *Griswold v. Connecticut* (1965).[28] At issue in *Griswold* was a Connecticut law that forbade the use of contraceptives and made it a criminal offense for anyone to give birth control information. Although the Constitution does not expressly deal with contraception, Justice William O. Douglas, speaking for the Court, ruled that the Connecticut law violated the constitutional right to privacy, which he found implicit in various other guarantees of the Bill of Rights. The statute, Douglas emphasized, invaded the "intimate relation of husband and wife," and its enforcement would require police to search the bedrooms of married couples for evidence of contraceptive use.[29] Thus, in recognizing the constitutional right to privacy, Douglas portrayed it as inhering in a particular relationship (marriage).

Seven years later, in *Eisenstadt v. Baird* (1972), the contraception issue again came before the Court.[30] Arrested for violating a Massachusetts law that forbade the distribution of contraceptives to unmarried people, William Baird claimed that the law violated the constitutional right to privacy recognized in *Griswold*.

Clearly, there were similarities between the two cases. Both involved laws that forbade the distribution and use of contraceptives to prevent procreation. There were also differences, however. The Massachusetts law did not interfere with marital relations, because it only restricted distribution to unmarried people, and its enforcement did not require police to invade the bedroom. The justices thus had to decide whether the situations in the two cases were fundamentally similar, in which case they would invalidate the Massachusetts law on the basis of their precedent in *Griswold,* or different, in which case they could uphold it.

The Supreme Court in *Eisenstadt* struck down the Massachusetts law as a violation of the constitutional right to privacy. Speaking for the Court, Justice William Brennan noted, "If the right to privacy means anything, it is the right of the individual, married or single, to be free from unwarranted governmental intrusion into matters so fundamentally affecting a person as the decision whether to bear or beget a child."[31]

Although the Court in *Eisenstadt* based its decision on the right to privacy, the quotation indicates that the Court's definition of the right—what Levi refers to as the rule or legal standard—had changed. No longer did the Court view the right to privacy as rooted in certain legally sanctioned relationships, such as marriage (the position it had taken in *Griswold*). Instead, it argued that the right to privacy belonged to the individual. In addition, the Court expanded the right from a safeguard against unreasonable invasions of the marital bedroom into a right to choose whether to procreate.

One year later, the Supreme Court in *Roe v. Wade* confronted a constitutional challenge to state laws restricting abortion.[32] Those who were attacking the laws argued that the restrictions on abortion resembled the restrictions on contraception invalidated in *Griswold* and *Eisenstadt* because they intruded on a woman's decision whether to bear a child and therefore violated her constitutional right to privacy. Those who defended the laws insisted that even if the right to privacy includes the choice whether to procreate, that choice had been made when the woman became pregnant. They further argued that the state's valid interest in the life of the fetus and in the safety of medical procedures for abortion distinguished this situation from those on which the Court had already ruled. They thus concluded that the Court's rulings in *Griswold* and *Eisenstadt* did not require invalidation of the Texas law.

The Supreme Court in *Roe,* however, disagreed. The right to privacy, it held, extended to "activities relating to marriage, procreation, contraception, family relationships, and child rearing and education."[33] This view represented an elaboration—or extension—of the Court's position in *Eisenstadt*. Having established a realm of freedom from unwarranted governmental regulation, the Court held that "a woman's decision whether or not to terminate her pregnancy" fit within this realm and therefore was protected by the right to privacy.[34]

Thirteen years later, the Supreme Court in *Bowers v. Hardwick* (1986) addressed the question of whether the right to privacy extended to consensual homosexual activity.[35] In challenging a Georgia statute that prohibited sodomy, Michael Hardwick noted that the Court's previous privacy rulings—*Griswold, Eisenstadt,* and *Roe*—had all struck down governmental regulations affecting sexual relations. He argued that the Georgia statute resembled the laws struck down in earlier cases in that it likewise regulated choices associated with the realm of sexual intimacy and thus represented an unconstitutional invasion of the right to privacy. A five-member majority on the Court, however, rejected Hardwick's portrayal of the Court's earlier cases. Those cases, Justice Byron White argued for the Court, all involved a connection to "family, marriage, or procreation," a connection absent in the present case. Because the situation in *Bowers* differed in this crucial respect from those in earlier cases, the Court concluded that those cases did not require the extension of the right to privacy to protect homosexual activity. It therefore held that Georgia's sodomy statute was constitutional.

This interpretation of the right to privacy did not last—seventeen years after their ruling in *Bowers*, the justices reversed course in *Lawrence v. Texas* (2003).[36] In striking down a Texas law that outlawed same-sex anal intercourse, a six-member majority concluded that the Court had misinterpreted the situation in *Bowers*. The laws in *Lawrence* and in *Bowers* "touch[ed] upon the most private human conduct, sexual behavior, and in the most private of places, the home." The Court maintained that the right to privacy protected a realm of personal autonomy in such matters and thus viewed the conduct in *Lawrence* as basically similar to the conduct protected in other right-to-privacy cases.

Implications

This survey of the Supreme Court's privacy rulings illustrates one way that legal change occurs in a system of precedent. Judges may not apply precedent in the mechanical fashion the deductive model suggests. Rather, they may reason by example and thus expand or narrow the reach of earlier decisions. In *Eisenstadt* and *Roe*, for example, the Court discovered similarities to *Griswold* that led it to extend the right to privacy to new situations. In contrast, the Court found that the situation in *Bowers* was fundamentally different from that in previous cases and concluded that the right to privacy did not prevent legal regulation of homosexual activity. Only when the Court in *Lawrence* reconceptualized its understanding of the facts did it reach a different conclusion.

If judicial decision making does not proceed by deductive reasoning, can't judges manipulate precedents and other legal materials in order to decide cases on the basis of their personal values? Unfortunately, there is no simple answer to this question. One check on judges is that they must explain and justify their rulings in written opinions. The opinions are subject to public scrutiny and criticism, which imposes some limitation on judges. In addition, judges operate within constraints imposed by the craft of judging and the traditions of the law. Among these constraints is the notion that judges should decide according to

BOX
8-2
Judicial Perspectives on Personal Values and Decision Making

"One who belongs to the most vilified and persecuted minority in history is not likely to be insensitive to the freedoms guaranteed by our Constitution. Were my purely personal attitude relevant, I should wholeheartedly associate myself with the general libertarian views in the Court's opinion, representing as they do the thought and action of a lifetime. But as judges we are neither Jew nor Gentile, neither Catholic nor agnostic. . . . As a member of this Court, I am not justified in writing my private notions of policy into the Constitution, no matter how deeply I may cherish them or how mischievous I may deem their disregard." (Justice Felix Frankfurter, dissenting in *West Virginia Board of Education v. Barnette* [1943])

"The language of the judicial decision is mainly the language of logic. . . . Behind the logical form lies a judgment as to the relative worth and importance of competing legislative grounds, often an inarticulate and unconscious judgment, it is true, and yet the very root and nerve of the whole proceeding." (Justice Oliver Wendell Holmes, at that time a member of the Massachusetts Supreme Judicial Court [1897])

"Since 1879 Connecticut has had on its books a law which forbids the use of contraceptives by anyone. I think this is an uncommonly silly law. . . . But

law, even though it may conflict with their personal views. Box 8-2 suggests that judges take this responsibility seriously. However, it also suggests that how judges interpret the law may be affected by their backgrounds, their experience, and their personal values. This recognition leads us to the political perspective on judicial decision making.

THE POLITICAL PERSPECTIVE

The political perspective on judicial decision making begins with the phenomenon of dissenting opinions on multimember courts. In more than two-thirds of the cases decided by the U.S. Supreme Court in recent years, one or more justices dissented.[37] Although dissent rates are lower on federal courts of we are not asked in this case to say whether we think the law is unwise, or even asinine. We are asked to hold that it violates the United States Constitution. And this I cannot do." (Justice Potter Stewart, dissenting in *Griswold v. Connecticut* [1965])

"Here, indeed, is the point of contact between the legislator's work and [the judge's]. The choice of methods, the appraisement of values, must in the end be guided by like considerations for the one as for the other. . . . [Y]et the judge, even when he is free, is still not wholly free. . . . He is to exercise a discretion informed by tradition, methodized by analogy, disciplined by system, and subordinated to 'the primordial necessity of order in social life'." (Justice Benjamin Cardozo, then of the New York Court of Appeals [1921])

"Cases such as these provide for me an excruciating agony of the spirit. I yield to no one in the depth of my distaste, antipathy, and, indeed, abhorrence, for the death penalty. . . . Were I a legislator, I would vote against the death penalty. . . . I do not sit on these cases, however, as a legislator. . . . Although personally I may rejoice at the Court's result, I find it difficult to accept or justify as a matter of history, of law, or of constitutional pronouncement." (Justice Harry Blackmun, dissenting in *Furman v. Georgia* [1972])

Sources: The quotations from extrajudicial writings are from Oliver Wendell Holmes, "The Path of the Law," *Harvard Law Review* 10 (1897): 444, and from Benjamin A. Cardozo, *The Nature of the Judicial Process* (New Haven, CT: Yale University Press, 1921), p. 141.

appeals and state appellate courts than on the Supreme Court, the judges in the other appellate courts also disagree on how a sizable proportion of their cases should be resolved.[38] According to the political perspective, these disagreements cannot be attributed to legal factors. When a multimember court decides a case, all the judges are construing the same enactments, interpreting the same precedents, and applying the same law to the same set of facts. Thus, differences in the law or in the facts cannot explain differences in judgment.

Differences in judgment occur, according to the political perspective, because the law does not really determine the outcome of most cases. Rarely is the law so clear and definite that only a single position is legally defensible. Rather, in most cases the plaintiff and the defendant can each make a substantial legal argument for ruling in their favor. This is particularly true when, as true for the U.S. Supreme Court and many state supreme courts, the justices

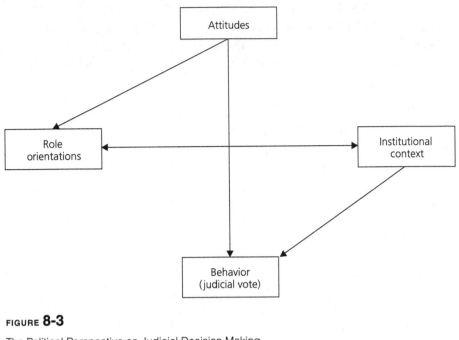

FIGURE **8-3**

The Political Perspective on Judicial Decision Making

Source: Based on the analysis in James L. Gibson, "From Simplicity to Complexity: The Development of Theory in the Study of Judicial Behavior," *Political Behavior* 5 (1983): 7–49.

have discretion to exclude legally unambiguous cases from their docket. In such circumstances, judges must choose among possible outcomes, and their choices reflect the judges' personal political views. The judges' views, then, and not the law, ultimately determine how cases are resolved.

Judicial decision making, however, involves more than judges reading their policy preferences into the law. As James Gibson has observed, "[j]udges' decisions are a function of what they prefer to do, tempered by what they think they ought to do, but constrained by what they perceive is feasible to do."[39] The attitudes of judges determine what they want to do; their role conceptions—their conceptions of proper judicial behavior—affect what the judges believe they ought to do; and public opinion and the institutional context in which they operate circumscribe what judges find it feasible to do.[40] As Figure 8-3 suggests, these factors are often interrelated.

Attitudes

As discussed in Chapter 3, judicial selection is a political process. Presidents typically nominate active members of their political party for federal judgeships and inquire into potential nominees' legal and political views, especially before filling vacancies on the Supreme Court. Politics also affects judicial selection in the states. Partisan election systems, of course, reward loyal and active party members. Political considerations also affect gubernatorial appointments, even when governors are choosing judges under the process of "merit selection." Not surprisingly, given the extensive political backgrounds of those who become judges, they tend to bring to the bench consistent and long-established political views.

The Development of Attitudes   What factors shape the attitudes, the values and beliefs, of judges? Assuming, as the political perspective does, that judicial decision making closely resembles all other political decision making, it follows that the same factors that influence political behavior generally should also influence, either directly or indirectly, how judges decide cases. The formation of politically relevant attitudes begins in early childhood.[41] Many studies have documented the influence of factors such as family background, religion, and socioeconomic status on the development of individuals' political beliefs and behavior.[42]

Judges' values and beliefs, like those of other citizens, may also be influenced by significant political events and nationwide changes in the pattern of opinion. For one generation, the crucial event was the Great Depression; for another, the Vietnam War; for the present generation, perhaps it will be the attack on the World Trade Center. As Justice Benjamin Cardozo has put it, "The great tides and currents which engulf the rest of men do not turn aside in their course and pass the judges by."[43]

The established social practices and patterns of opinion within a particular region may likewise influence judicial attitudes. The values and beliefs of those growing up in the South before the Civil War, for example, were inevitably affected by the institution of slavery, although reactions to that system varied among individuals. More recently, scholars have documented differences in political culture among the various states, differences in patterns of thought and behavior that presumably affect all within those states.[44] Given the political character of judicial selection, one would expect only those who supported the reigning values in the state to attain positions as judges.

According to "Mr. Dooley," a political commentator of the early twentieth century, "the judges follow the election returns."[45] Although Dooley's remark exaggerates the influence of immediate political factors on judicial decisions, it points to an important truth. The legal safeguards of judicial independence do not altogether shield judges from the political environment. They, like everyone else, follow the news and are aware of societal developments and trends in public opinion, including reactions to their decisions. While one would not expect judges to tailor their rulings to conform to public opinion, the political environment may nonetheless influence judicial decision making.

The Effects of Attitudes on Decisions   Do judges' personal attitudes influence the outcome of cases? Despite judges' efforts to banish personal views from their decisions (see Box 8-2), many studies suggest that judges' attitudes do affect their votes. What is particularly significant is that the judges' votes

TABLE
8-1
THE VOTING BEHAVIOR OF SUPREME COURT JUSTICES, 1953–1999

Justice	Appointing President	Percentage Liberal in Civil Liberties Cases
Brennan	Eisenhower	79.5
White	Kennedy	42.4
Marshall	Johnson	81.4
Blackmun	Nixon	52.3
Rehnquist	Nixon	21.8
Stevens	Ford	64.2
O'Connor	Reagan	35.5
Scalia	Reagan	29.6
Souter	Bush	59.9
Thomas	Bush	25.7
Breyer	Clinton	61.1
Ginsburg	Clinton	64.4

Source: Adapted from Jeffrey A. Segal and Harold J. Spaeth, *The Supreme Court and the Attitudinal Model*, 2d ed. (Cambridge, MA: Cambridge University Press, 2002), table 8.2. Reprinted with permission of Cambridge University Press.

often follow clear patterns, dividing along what might be considered liberal and conservative lines. The U.S. Supreme Court furnishes a prime example.

As Table 8-1 shows, when Supreme Court justices disagreed in civil liberties cases, some justices (e.g., William Brennan and Thurgood Marshall) consistently took the liberal position, voting in favor of those who claimed that their rights had been violated. Other justices (e.g., Antonin Scalia and William Rehnquist) regularly adopted the conservative position, voting to uphold challenged laws or governmental actions. The findings might seem to suggest that the law is nothing but an elaborate charade, designed to fool a credulous public, while freeing judges to pursue their own policy goals. The connection between judges' attitudes and their votes is in fact subtler than this account suggests. When the appropriate legal outcome in a case is clear, decisions are unanimous, regardless of the judges' attitudes. But when the appropriate legal outcome is not immediately clear, when appellate judges are confronted with persuasive legal arguments on both sides of an issue, they must determine which arguments are stronger. According to the political perspective, the judges' attitudes inevitably affect this determination by influencing the judges' perception of the issues in the case and their judgment about the strength of the competing legal arguments. The judges are not engaged in duplicity; they simply cannot altogether escape who they are. According to Jeffrey Segal and Harold Spaeth, "Rehnquist votes the way he does because he is extremely conservative; Marshall voted the way he did because he was extremely liberal."[46]

If political attitudes affect the votes of judges on the U.S. Supreme Court, presumably they should on other courts as well. This is difficult to confirm directly, however, because state and federal judges do not readily grant interviews to discuss their political views. Researchers have therefore approached the issue indirectly, often by looking for connections between judges' party affiliations and their voting behavior. This research assumes that because Republicans and Democrats have different political perspectives, party membership will be a good indicator of judges' attitudes: Republican judges will be more conservative, and Democratic judges more liberal. Therefore, if judges' attitudes decisively influence their votes, one should be able to predict the overall pattern of their votes by knowing the judge's party affiliation.

Does party affiliation help predict how judges vote? The most comprehensive survey of research on the issue concludes that there are strong connections between judges' political affiliations and their voting behavior.[47] The connection holds true regardless of whether the courts are federal or state, trial or appellate. Nonetheless, one must be cautious about attributing judicial decisions solely to judges' political attitudes. The connection between affiliation and voting behavior is not universal: the divisions on some courts surveyed bore no relation to the judges' partisan affiliations. In addition, the strength of the connection between party and judicial voting varied from issue to issue and over time, sometimes on the same court.

Other studies have examined connections between judges' social backgrounds or other attributes (e.g., their state of birth, gender, and race) and their voting behavior on the bench. Underlying these studies is the assumption that the judges' backgrounds and attributes shape their attitudes, which in turn affect their decisions.[48] For example, some studies have found that judges who had previous experience as prosecutors are likely to be judicial conservatives.[49] The connection between background characteristics and a judge's voting behavior tends, however, to vary from study to study.[50] In addition, some attributes that one might expect to be important, such as race or gender, have surprisingly little documented effect on a judge's behavior on the bench.[51]

If one cannot consistently predict judges' voting behavior from their social backgrounds, the reason may lie in the influence of other factors on judicial decision making. Among the most important of these are judicial role orientations.

Judicial Role Orientations

As the quotations in Box 8-2 show, judges generally believe that they should submerge their personal beliefs, however deeply felt, and decide cases in accordance with the law. They also hold many other beliefs about what is appropriate and inappropriate judicial behavior. To some extent, the judge's beliefs mirror societal views about the responsibilities of a judge. But the judge's views are elaborated and refined during professional training in law school, through work as a practicing attorney, and through involvement with other members of the legal profession. Once judges are on the bench, their beliefs are further influenced by their experiences as a judge and by the expectations of those with whom they interact, especially their fellow judges.[52]

The process of socialization to the norms of a profession is, of course, not unique to judges. Teachers, doctors, insurance agents, and others all undergo a similar process of learning the norms of conduct for their professions. Beliefs about the sorts of behavior appropriate for judges are referred to as judicial role orientations.[53]

Judicial role orientations operate as self-imposed obligations, restricting the actions that a judge will undertake. They are important because they can affect judicial decisions. For example, role orientations may prevent judges from voting in line with their personal beliefs. As Box 8-2 shows, in *Furman v. Georgia* Justice Harry Blackmun voted to uphold the constitutionality of the death penalty even though he abhorred capital punishment on moral grounds. Similarly, Felix Frankfurter voted to uphold state laws requiring students to salute the American flag, despite his opposition to such laws. In both instance, the justices voted as they did because of their conceptions of appropriate judicial behavior—in particular, their belief that a judge's personal convictions should not affect his vote.

As these examples illustrate, judicial role orientations usually do not require that a judge must vote for a particular outcome. Rather, they affect how judges go about making their decisions. More specifically, role orientations indicate the factors that judges can legitimately consider and how much weight they should give those factors in making their decisions.

The influence of judicial role orientations can be seen in the way that judges treat precedent. If judicial attitudes alone determined judicial decisions, then judges would uphold precedents that supported outcomes they favored and overrule those precedents that produced disagreeable results. In actuality, however, some judges believe that they should adhere to the court's previous rulings, even if they might decide the case differently in the absence of precedent.[54] Thus, when Sandra Day O'Connor was appointed to the Supreme Court by President Ronald Reagan, it was assumed that she shared the president's conservative philosophy and would vote accordingly. However, when the justices had the opportunity to overrule *Roe v. Wade,* the Court's controversial abortion decision, in *Planned Parenthood of Southeastern Pennsylvania v. Casey* (1992), O'Connor refused to do so, citing the necessity to respect precedent.[55] Similarly, despite the Bush administration's urgings in an amicus curiae brief, Justice David Souter disappointed the president who appointed him by voting to strike down religious invocations at graduation ceremonies as a violation of the Establishment Clause.[56] He, too, justified his position as having been compelled by long-established Court precedents.

Although role orientations affect judicial decisions, their exact impact is difficult to determine. There is no consensus about what constitutes proper judicial behavior. Rather, the norms of appropriate conduct vary somewhat from court to court and within courts over time. The practice of filing dissenting opinions provides one example. The norms of judicial behavior on some courts discourage public expressions of dissent, whereas on other courts judges are free to dissent whenever they disagree with the court majority. And whereas dissent was once frowned upon on the U.S. Supreme Court, today dissenting opinions are filed in most cases.[57]

In addition, despite broad areas of agreement (e.g., judges should not engage in partisan politics while on the bench), sitting judges may have quite different conceptions of the judicial role.[58] Some judges subscribe to a philosophy of judicial restraint, which limits the factors that they can validly consider in reaching a decision and the circumstances in which they can legitimately overrule a precedent or strike down a legislative enactment. Other judges embrace the philosophy of judicial activism, which places less emphasis on the doctrine of stare decisis and on deference to legislative judgment. Appropriate judicial behavior, then, depends on the judge's choice of a particular role orientation. Conceivably, a judge's choice among possible role orientations may be influenced by the judge's attitudes and political values. Thus, during the 1960s and 1970s, liberal judges also tended to be activists.[59] Since the mid-1980s, however, judicial conservatives have been interested in reversing many of the rulings of their liberal predecessors, and thus, one finds some conservative judges, such as Justices Clarence Thomas and Antonin Scalia, exhibiting an activist role orientation.[60]

Institutional Factors

Because the decisions of appellate courts are group decisions, interactions among judges also influence judicial decision making. By itself, the vote of a single judge cannot determine the outcome of a case. Thus, judges who wish to ensure that a case is decided in line with their views must convince other judges to endorse their position.[61]

As noted in Chapter 7, the norms of appropriate judicial behavior limit the means that a judge may use to gain acceptance of her position. Whatever efficacy force or intimidation may have in international conflicts, judges cannot use such tactics to achieve their goals. They cannot, like a legislator, trade a vote in one case to gain votes for their position in another. Nor can they promise political support for those who vote with them or threaten political ruin for those who oppose them.

Perhaps the most potent weapon available to a judge is legal expertise—and the ability to bring that expertise to bear in a well-crafted judicial opinion.[62] According to a federal court of appeals judge, "Some judges are simply better than others. Some know more, think better. It would be strange if among nine

---

BOX
8-3

Judicial Attacks

Because appellate courts are small groups in which judges must work together over a long period, one might expect that judges would refrain from harshly criticizing the rulings and opinions of their colleagues. As these excerpts from the opinions of Supreme Court justices reveal, however, judges are quite willing to attack the views of colleagues who disagree with them in a case:

"Nothing in the letter or the spirit of the Constitution or in the precedents squares with the heavy-handed and one-sided action that is so precipitously taken by the court in the name of fulfilling its constitutional responsibilities." (Justice John Marshall Harlan, dissenting in *Miranda v. Arizona* [1966])

"Not in my memory has a plurality gone about its business in such a deceptive fashion. At every level of its review, from its effort to read the real meaning out of the Missouri statute, to its intended evisceration of precedents and its deafening silence about the constitutional protection it would jettison, the plurality obscures the portent of its analysis." (Justice Harry Blackmun, dissenting in *Webster v. Reproductive Health Services* [1989])

---

men all had the same ability. Some simply have more respect than others."[63] The importance of legal expertise is hardly surprising. Committed to deciding cases in accordance with the law, judges are receptive to legal arguments from their colleagues. If those arguments are compelling, they can be persuaded to switch their votes. As Justice Robert Jackson once admitted: "I myself have changed my opinion after reading the opinions of the other members of this Court. And I am as stubborn as most."[64] Of course, the arguments that judges find compelling may to some extent depend on their attitudes and their role conceptions, and a justice seeking to entice a colleague to join his opinion is likely to frame his argument accordingly. Also, judges are more likely to be persuaded by colleagues who generally share their perspective on legal issues.

If judges may persuade their colleagues to vote with them by the strength of their arguments, they may also threaten to write an opinion attacking the position

"Once we depart from the text of the Constitution, just where . . . do we stop? The most amazing feature of the Court's opinion is that it does not even purport to give an answer. . . . Evidently, the governing standard is to be what might be called the unfettered wisdom of a majority of this Court, revealed to an obedient people on a case-by-case basis." (Justice Antonin Scalia, dissenting in *Morrison v. Olson* [1988])

"A number of Justices just short of a majority of the majority that promulgates today's passionate dialectics joined in answering them in [a decision just four years prior]. The distinction attempted between that case and this is trivial, almost to the point of cynicism. . . . Today's judgment will be more interesting to students of psychology and of the judicial processes than to students of constitutional law." (Justice Robert Jackson, dissenting in *Zorach v. Clauson* [1952])

"A few citations to 'research in psychology' that have no particular bearing upon the precise issue here cannot disguise the fact that the Court has gone beyond the realm where judges know what they are doing. The Court's argument . . . is, not to put too fine a point on it, incoherent." (Justice Antonin Scalia, dissenting in *Lee v. Weisman* [1992])

"One wonders whether the majority still believes that race discrimination—or, more accurately, race discrimination against nonwhites—is a problem in our society, or even remembers that it ever was." (Justice Harry Blackmun, dissenting in *Wards Cove Packing Co. v. Atonio* [1989])

taken by those who reject their arguments. The effectiveness of this threat generally depends on the judge's ability to present a persuasive legal argument. As Box 8-3 reveals, judges do not shrink from making stinging attacks on the reasoning of their colleagues or the coherence of their views. Surprisingly, these attacks rarely interfere with working relationships among the justices.

An appellate court is in reality a small group working together over a prolonged period of time: for the judges, it is "a little like being married in a system of arranged marriage with no divorce."[65] Thus, it is not surprising that personal relations with fellow judges also play a role in judicial decision making; agreeable and considerate judges are apt to gain a better reception for their arguments than their more contentious colleagues. Ultimately, though, judges typically come to the bench with firmly established views, and their fellow judges have few weapons beyond legal argument to induce them to changes their minds. Group interaction therefore has only a limited effect on how judges vote.

ANALYZING THE TWO PERSPECTIVES

This chapter described two perspectives on judicial decision making. The legal perspective views judicial decision making as a process of reasoning based on legal principles and judicial precedents. These principles and precedents prescribe a particular outcome in many cases. Even when there is a realm of choice for the judge, law circumscribes the range of choice and guides its exercise. Thus, the law is the most important determinant of judicial decisions.

The political perspective views judicial decision making as a process in which extralegal factors, such as the judges' attitudes and role orientations, are the primary influences on judicial decisions. According to this view, judges' attitudes and orientations color how they view the law and the facts in a case and thereby determine the decisions they reach.

Which of these accounts of judicial decision making is more accurate? Unfortunately, the question has no clear-cut answer. Perhaps the best account of judicial decision making incorporates both legal and extralegal factors. It seems reasonable to assume that judges take their oath to dispense equal justice under law seriously. Thus, when the law is clear, judges can be expected to follow it. As the Legal Realists showed, however, often the law is not clear, and the judge must choose between two plausible legal arguments. Though judges recognize that they must choose the stronger legal argument, their perception of the facts of the case and the strength of the competing arguments is influenced by their experience and beliefs. Their choices, then, cannot be divorced from their attitudes.

Nevertheless, judges are members of the legal profession, and their beliefs have been formed by their legal training. They therefore recognize an obligation not to read their own beliefs into the law. Indeed, their understanding of their responsibilities as judges—their role orientation—encourages them to guard against it. Even though judges' efforts to banish personal views from their decisions are unlikely to be fully effective, they do have some effect. Thus, in the words of Justice Felix Frankfurter:

> The judicial process demands that a judge move within the framework of relevant legal rules and the covenanted modes of thought for ascertaining them. He must think dispassionately and submerge personal feeling on every aspect of a case. There is a good deal of shallow talk that the judicial robe does not change the man within it. It does. The fact is that on the whole judges do lay aside private views in discharging their judicial functions. This is achieved through training, professional habits, self-discipline, and that fortunate alchemy by which men are loyal to the obligations with which they are entrusted.[66]

NOTES

1. *Stanford v. Kentucky,* 492 U.S. 361 (1989).

2. The Supreme Court's recognition of "evolving standards of human decency" as the basis for interpreting the Eighth Amendment stems from *Trop v. Dulles,* 356 U.S. 86 (1958).

3. This distinction is drawn from Richard A. Wasserstrom, *The Judicial Decision: Toward a Theory of Legal Justification* (Stanford, CA: Stanford University Press, 1961), pp. 26–27.

4. Joseph C. Hutcheson Jr., "The Judgment Intuitive: The Function of the 'Hunch' in Judicial Decision," Cornell *Law Quarterly* 14 (1929): 274.

5. Felix Frankfurter, "Some Reflections on the Reading of Statutes," *Columbia Law Review* 47 (1947): 527.

6. As the U.S. Supreme Court put it in *Lake County v. Rollins,* 130 U.S. 662, 670 (1889): "If the words convey a definite meaning, which involves no absurdity, nor any contradiction of other parts of the instrument, then that meaning apparent on the face of the instrument, must be accepted."

7. See Reed Dickerson, *The Interpretation and Application of Statutes* (Boston: Little, Brown, 1975), chap. 8.

8. *Towne v. Eisner,* 245 U.S. 418, 425 (1925).

9. For a discussion of the uses and abuses of legislative history, see Dickerson, *The Interpretation and Application of Statutes,* chap. 10.

10. The usefulness and limitations of these materials are surveyed in James H. Hutson, "The Creation of the Constitution: The Integrity of the Documentary Record," *Texas Law Review* 65 (November 1986): 1–40.

11. Dickerson, *The Interpretation and Application of Statutes,* pp. 161–162.

12. Ibid., chap. 10, and Antonin Scalia, *A Matter of Interpretation: Federal Courts and the Law* (Princeton, NJ: Princeton University Press, 1997).

13. This argument has also been used to justify interpretation of the U.S. Constitution in line with the intentions of the Founders. See Edwin Meese, "Toward a Jurisprudence of Original Intention," *Benchmark* 2 (1986): 1–10.

14. Scalia, *A Matter of Interpretation.* See also Paul Brest, "The Misconceived Quest for the Original Understanding," *Boston University Law Review* 60 (March 1980): 204–238.

15. As Justice Robert Jackson put it in *Schwegmann Bros. v. Calvert Distillers Corp.,* 341 U.S. 385, 395 (1951): "[T]o select casual statements from floor debates, not always distinguished for candor or accuracy, as a basis for making up our minds what law Congress intended to enact is to substitute ourselves for the Congress in one of its important functions." More generally, see Dickerson, *The Interpretation and Application of Statutes,* pp. 156–157.

16. See Lief H. Carter, *Reason in Law* (Boston: Little, Brown, 1979), pp. 71–72, and Brest, "The Misconceived Quest for the Original Understanding."

17. William L. Reynolds, *Judicial Process in a Nutshell* (St. Paul, MN: West Publishing, 1980), p. 168.

18. These arguments are summarized and critiqued in Wasserstrom, *The Judicial Decision,* chap. 4.

19. Ibid., p. 68.

20. As Karl Llewellyn put it: "The force of precedent in law is heightened by an additional factor: that curious, almost universal sense of justice which urges that all men are properly to be treated alike in like circumstances." "Case Law," *Encyclopedia of the Social Sciences* (New York: Macmillan, 1930), 3: 249.

21. *Texas v. Johnson,* 491 U.S. 397 (1989).

22. Benjamin Cardozo, *The Nature of the Judicial Process* (New Haven, CT: Yale University Press, 1921), p. 149.

23. For an excellent overview of Legal Realist thought, see Wilfrid E. Rumble Jr., *American Legal Realism: Skepticism, Reform, and the Judicial Process* (Ithaca, NY: Cornell University Press, 1968).

24. Edward H. Levi, *An Introduction to Legal Reasoning* (Chicago: University of Chicago Press, 1949).

25. 491 U.S. 397 (1989). Levi does not discuss this recent case in his volume.

26. Compare, e.g., *Cohen v. California,* 403 U.S. 15 (1971), with *United States v. O'Brien,* 391 U.S. 367 (1968).

27. Levi, *An Introduction to Legal Reasoning,* p. 4.

28. *Griswold v. Connecticut,* 381 U.S. 479 (1965).

29. 381 U.S. 479, 486.

30. *Eisenstadt v. Baird,* 405 U.S. 438 (1972).

31. 405 U.S. 438, 453.

32. *Roe v. Wade,* 410 U.S. 113 (1973).

33. 410 U.S. 113, 153.

34. Ibid.

35. *Bowers v. Hardwick,* 478 U.S. 186 (1986).

36. *Lawrence v. Texas,* 539 U.S. 558 (2003).

37. Thomas G. Walker, Lee Epstein, and William J. Dixon, "On the Mysterious Demise of Consensual Norms in the United States Supreme Court," *Journal of Politics* 50 (May 1988): 361–389. Year-by-year data on dissent rates, as well as voting blocs on the Supreme Court, can be found each year in the November issue of the *Harvard Law Review.*

38. Ashlyn Kuersten and Donald R. Songer, *Decisions on the U.S. Courts of Appeals* (New York: Garland, 2000), and Henry Glick and George Pruet Jr., "Dissent in State Supreme Courts: Patterns and Correlates of Conflict," in *Judicial Conflict and Consensus: Behavioral Studies of American Appellate Courts,* eds. Sheldon Goldman and Charles M. Lamb (Lexington: University of Kentucky Press, 1986).

39. James L. Gibson, "From Simplicity to Complexity: The Development of Theory in the Study of Judicial Behavior," *Political Behavior* 5 (1983): 9.

40. Ibid. This chapter employs a modified version of Gibson's framework for analysis.

41. See Robert D. Hess and Judith V. Torney, *The Development of Political Attitudes in Children* (Chicago: Aldine, 1967), and David Easton and Jack Dennis, *Children in the Political System: Origins of Political Legitimacy* (Chicago: University of Chicago Press, 1980).

42. See Allan M. Winkler, "Public Opinion," in *The Encyclopedia of American Political History,* ed. Jack Greene (New York: Charles Scribner's Sons, 1988), and Lloyd Free and Hadley Cantril, *The Political Beliefs of Americans* (New York: Simon & Schuster, 1968).

43. Cardozo, *The Nature of the Judicial Process,* p. 168.

44. Daniel J. Elazar, *American Federalism: A View from the States,* 3d ed. (New York: Harper & Row, 1984).

45. Finley Peter Dunne, *The World of Mr. Dooley,* ed. Louis Filler (New York: Collier Books, 1962), p. 89.

46. Jeffrey A. Segal and Harold J. Spaeth, *The Supreme Court and the Attitudinal Model* (New York: Cambridge University Press, 1993), p. 65.

47. Daniel R. Pinello, "Linking Party to Judicial Ideology in American Courts: A Meta-analysis," *Justice System Journal* 20 (1999): 219–254.

48. Gibson, "From Simplicity to Complexity," pp. 23–26.

49. See, e.g., C. Neal Tate, "Personal Attribute Models of the Voting Behavior of U.S. Supreme Court Justices: Liberalism in Civil Liberties and Economic Decisions, 1946–1978," *American Political Science Review* 69 (June 1975): 355–367.

50. See the discussions in Joel B. Grossman, "Social Backgrounds and Judicial Decision-Making: Notes for a Theory," *Journal of Politics* 29 (May 1967): 334–351, and Walter Murphy and Joseph Tanenhaus, *The Study of Public Law* (New York: Random House, 1972), pp. 107–109.

51. Gibson, "From Simplicity to Complexity," pp. 21–22.

52. James L. Gibson, "Judges' Role Orientations, Attitudes, and Decisions: An Interactive Model," *American Political Science Review* 73 (September 1978): 918.

53. Ibid.

54. Some scholars have concluded that, in general, precedent imposes little constraint on judicial decision making. See Harold J. Spaeth and Jeffrey A. Segal, *Majority Rule or Minority Will: Adherence to Precedence on the U.S. Supreme Court* (New York: Cambridge University Press, 1999).

55. *Planned Parenthood of Southeastern Pennsylvania v. Casey,* 502 U.S. 1056 (1992).

56. *Lee v. Weisman,* 505 U.S. 577 (1992).

57. See Walker, Epstein, and Dixon, "On the Mysterious Demise of Consensual Norms."

58. See Glick, *Supreme Courts in State Politics,* chap. 2; John T. Wold, "Political Orientations, Social Backgrounds, and the Role Perceptions of State Supreme Court Judges," *Western Political Quarterly* 27 (1974): 239–248; and Gibson, "Judges' Role Orientations, Attitudes, and Decisions."

59. See James L. Gibson, "Decision Making in Appellate Courts," in Gates and Johnson, *American Courts: A Critical Assessment,* p. 264, table 10-2.

60. Ibid. See also Justice Scalia's opinions ignoring stare decisis and urging new directions for the Court in *Webster v. Reproductive Health Services,* 488 U.S. 1003 (1989); *R.A.V. v. City of St. Paul,* 505 U.S. 377 (1992); and *Planned Parenthood of Southeastern Pennsylvania v. Casey,* 502 U.S. 1056 (1992).

61. Of course, other judges may independently come to the same conclusion.

62. This analysis follows that of Walter F. Murphy, *Elements of Judicial Strategy* (Chicago: University of Chicago Press, 1964), chap. 3.

63. Howard, *Courts of Appeal in the Federal Judicial System,* p. 230.

64. Quoted in Alan Westin, *The Anatomy of a Constitutional Law Case* (New York: Macmillan, 1958), pp. 123–124.

65. Richard A. Posner, *The Federal Courts: Challenge and Reform* (Cambridge, MA: Harvard University Press, 1996), p. 355.

66. *Public Utilities Commission v. Pollack,* 343 U.S. 451, 466 (1959).

JUDICIAL POLICYMAKING

JUDICIAL POLICYMAKING: AN INTRODUCTION   277

FEDERAL COURT POLICYMAKING   304

STATE COURT POLICYMAKING   337

JUDICIAL POLICYMAKING: AN INTRODUCTION

Throughout American history, judges have been accused of deciding cases based on their own policy preferences rather than in accordance with the law. During the first third of the twentieth century, it was political liberals who leveled the charge of judicial usurpation. The justices of the U.S. Supreme Court, they claimed, based their rulings on a particular economic theory (laissez-faire capitalism) rather than on the Constitution. From the 1950s through the 1970s, it was conservatives' turn to express outrage. They denounced the Supreme Court's rulings on pornography, abortion, school prayer, and the rights of defendants as elements of a liberal social agenda with little or no constitutional basis. Most recently, it has again been liberals who have attacked the Supreme Court, charging that its decisions reflect nothing more than the justices' political conservatism.[1]

One need not accept all these charges as accurate. Critics often see a dereliction of judicial duty in every decision with which they disagree. Nevertheless, the criticisms of judicial rulings sound a common theme: The task of the judge is to "say what the law is," not to make law.[2] Policymaking is the responsibility of the other branches of government, so judges who engage in policymaking are usurping power and behaving improperly.

But viewed from another perspective, judicial policymaking is neither exceptional nor suspect. Courts "say what the law is" in the course of deciding cases, and deciding cases inevitably enmeshes them in public policy. Their rulings may announce authoritative legal standards that define public policy within the jurisdiction they serve. In some cases their rulings may influence political action and stimulate or retard societal change, regardless of whether judges decide the cases properly and whether their rulings uphold or strike down governmental actions. The cases of *Grutter v. Bollinger* (2003) and *Gratz v. Bollinger* (2003) illustrate the point.[3]

In *Grutter,* the U.S. Supreme Court upheld an affirmative-action program for admission to the University of Michigan Law School, but in *Gratz,* it struck down a quite different affirmative-action program affecting the admission of undergraduates at the same university. Taken together, the Court's decisions clarified what sorts of affirmative-action programs would survive constitutional scrutiny and what sorts would not. As a result, the University of Michigan retained its criteria for admission to its law school but revised its criteria for undergraduate admissions. The Court's rulings also provided guidance to other colleges and universities seeking to utilize affirmative action in admitting students. Had the Court ruled differently in either of those cases, either upholding or invalidating both programs, this would have had policy consequences as well. Invalidation of both programs might have led some institutions to abandon their affirmative-action programs, or it might have encouraged efforts to seek alternative means of ensuring diversity in their student populations. Conversely, upholding both programs might have stimulated opponents of affirmative action to push for legislation outlawing affirmative action in public colleges and universities in their states. It might also have encouraged advocates of affirmative action to pressure schools without affirmative-action programs to institute them, because the Court had ruled that they were constitutionally permissible.

These examples show that judges cannot altogether avoid policymaking. But it does not prove that critics of judicial policymaking are mistaken. Rather, the two perspectives on judicial policymaking can be viewed as complementary. Whereas one view emphasizes that judicial rulings inevitably have policy consequences, the other view cautions that judicial rulings rooted solely in the policy views of the judges are inappropriate. Before examining how one distinguishes appropriate from inappropriate judicial policymaking, let us look more closely at the character and types of judicial policymaking, which are summarized in Table 9-1.

THE OCCASIONS OF JUDICIAL POLICYMAKING

Judicial Review and Constitutional Policymaking

Constitutions specify the scope of governmental powers, divide those powers among the various branches of government, and confer rights that government cannot violate. When a government exceeds the powers granted to it, when a branch of government exercises powers conferred on another branch, or when a government infringes on constitutionally protected rights, its actions are unconstitutional. Those who are injured by the government's unconstitutional actions may challenge them in the courts and call on judges to invalidate those actions. The power of the courts to determine whether the government's actions are consistent with the Constitution and to invalidate those that are not is known as *judicial review*.

TABLE
9.1

TYPES OF JUDICIAL POLICYMAKING

Type of Policymaking	Definition	Major Policymakers	Legal Basis	Eras of Greatest Policymaking
Constitutional	Judicial review of governmental action to determine its consistency with constitutional requirements	U.S. Supreme Court; state supreme courts	Federal Constitution, state constitution	For federal courts, since the late nineteenth century; for state courts, 1880–1930s and 1970s to the present
Remedial	Establishment and implementation of requirements to eliminate constitutional violations or meet constitutional requirements	Federal district courts	Use of equity power to achieve constitutionally mandated situation	Since the late 1950s (*Brown v. Board of Education*)
Statutory interpretation	Interpretation and application of legislative enactments	Federal courts of appeals; state appellate courts	Federal legislation, state legislation	Since the increase in legislation in the late nineteenth and early twentieth centuries
Oversight of administrative activity	Review of administrative activity to ensure that it is consistent with constitutional, statutory, or agency requirements	Federal courts of appeals; state appellate courts	Federal or state constitution; federal or state legislation; agency rules or other requirements	Since the growth of regulatory agencies, beginning in the early twentieth century, with major increases during the New Deal (1930s) and Great Society (1960s)
Common-law	Judicial enunciation and application of legal standards in the absence of legislation or administrative law	State appellate courts	Judicial precedents, societal standards	During the first half of the nineteenth century and in tort law since World War II
Cumulative	Judicial development of policy through the exercise of discretion in resolving a large number of similar cases	State trial courts	Established practices within the court or jurisdiction	No particular period

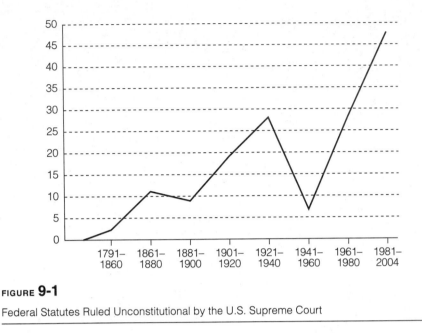

FIGURE **9-1**

Federal Statutes Ruled Unconstitutional by the U.S. Supreme Court

Since the U.S. Supreme Court's first use of the power of judicial review to strike down a congressional statute in *Marbury v. Madison* (1803),[4] judicial review has furnished a prime basis for judicial involvement in policymaking. Courts exercise the power of judicial review in ruling on the constitutionality of federal or state legislation. As Figures 9-1 and 9-2 reveal, the U.S. Supreme Court has struck down more than 140 federal statutes and more than 1,100 state laws. Other governmental actions are likewise subject to constitutional scrutiny. In the celebrated case of *United States v. Nixon* (1973), for example, the Supreme Court ruled that President Richard Nixon could not withhold tapes of White House conversations from a federal district court that was seeking them for use in a criminal prosecution.[5] More frequently, it is lower-level officials, such as police officers, whose actions are challenged as unconstitutional—the Supreme Court decides about twenty cases each year involving the rights of suspects in criminal cases.[6]

The U.S. Supreme Court's constitutional rulings establish binding precedent for all courts in the United States, and the effects of the rulings are felt nationwide. Federal and state courts have the power to consider whether governmental actions coincide with federal constitutional requirements. The rulings of these courts, although they affect only a limited geographic area, may also involve important policy matters. In *James v. Wallace* (1974), for example, a federal district court ruled that confinement in certain Alabama prisons, which were plagued by overcrowding, violence, and grossly inadequate health care, violated the constitutional ban on cruel and unusual punishments.[7] To

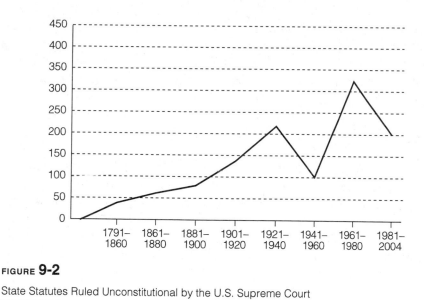

FIGURE **9-2**

State Statutes Ruled Unconstitutional by the U.S. Supreme Court

---

remedy the constitutional violation, Judge Frank Johnson ordered extensive reforms in the prison, requiring substantially increased state expenditures, and established his own guidelines for prison operations.[8] State courts' authority to consider constitutional violations under their state constitutions, as well as under the federal Constitution, may furnish an additional basis for judicial intervention. In 1999, for example, the Michigan Supreme Court invalidated the governor's executive orders transferring control over the state's educational systems from a board of education to a superintendent, and in 2003, the Massachusetts Supreme Judicial Court ruled that the state could not refuse marriage licenses to same-sex couples.[9]

When courts rule on constitutional questions, they operate within clear constraints. Because the power of judicial review is the power to enforce constitutional norms, the federal Constitution or its state counterpart must furnish the basis for judicial decisions.[10] Judges are expected not to substitute their own personal policy views for those of other governmental bodies or validate governmental actions that violate the constitutional norms. Moreover, in reaching their decisions, judges do not act in a vacuum. Only rarely do they consider a constitutional provision without seeking guidance from previous judicial decisions (precedents) interpreting the same provision. Both the force of precedent and the need to justify decisions as constitutionally based serve to guide and confine judges in their exercise of judicial review.

But as Chapter 8 made clear, constitutional interpretation is not a merely mechanical process. Judges do not—and could not—merely "lay the article of the Constitution which is involved beside the statute which is challenged and decide whether the latter squares with the former."[11] Most of the federal constitutional provisions that have generated extensive litigation are phrased in general terms. Examples include the Fourth Amendment's ban on "unreasonable searches and seizures," the Fifth and Fourteenth Amendments' requirement of "due process of law," and the Fourteenth Amendment's guarantee of "the equal protection of the laws." The generality of these phrases requires judges to look beyond the text of the Constitution to determine their meaning.

One source judges may look to is judicial precedents. Although judges can rely on earlier decisions interpreting a constitutional provision, the decisions do not altogether resolve the problem. In some instances, the validity of the Court's earlier rulings may be precisely what is at issue. A famous example is *Brown v. Board of Education* (1954), challenging the constitutionality of legally mandated racial segregation in public schools.[12] If the Supreme Court had decided to follow precedent, it would have upheld the practice of racial segregation based on its earlier decision in *Plessy v. Ferguson* (1896), which permitted states to maintain "separate but equal" facilities.[13] The ultimate touchstone of constitutionality, however, is the Constitution itself, not the precedents of the Supreme Court. Thus, judges may, as they did in *Brown*, depart from precedent when they conclude that previous cases were wrongly decided.

Finally, even when the meaning of a constitutional provision is clear, its application in the specific case may be problematic. In *Chaplin and Drysdale, Chartered v. United States* (1989), for instance, all nine Supreme Court justices recognized that the Sixth Amendment guarantees criminal defendants a right to be represented by counsel at trial.[14] The justices disagreed sharply, however, about whether the federal government could confiscate assets allegedly acquired through drug trafficking when the defendant planned to use them to pay his legal fees. As these examples show, constitutional interpretation involves the exercise of judgment, and reasonable judges, equally devoted to the Constitution, can arrive at quite different understandings of the document.

Remedial Policymaking

As the earlier reference to *James v. Wallace* suggests, judicial involvement in constitutional cases may extend beyond determining whether the Constitution has been violated. Once a constitutional violation is discovered, it must be remedied. "Remedial policymaking" refers to the judicial imposition of requirements on officials to eliminate unconstitutional conditions or practices.

In most cases, judges only need to order officials to stop their unconstitutional conduct and to refrain from it in the future. Thus, in *Reed v. Reed* (1971), its first major ruling on gender discrimination, the Supreme Court ruled that Idaho (and other states) could no longer give an automatic preference to men over women as administrators of estates, and this sufficed to dispose of the problem.[15] When government fails to meet its constitutional obligations, judges may also direct that specific remedial actions must be undertaken. Abraham Chayes describes what is distinctive about such judicial involvement:

> [The judge's decree] seeks to adjust future behavior, not to compensate for past wrong. It is deliberately fashioned rather than logically deduced from the nature of the legal harm suffered. It provides for a complex, on-going regime of performance rather than a simple, one-shot, one-way transfer. . . . [I]t prolongs and deepens, rather than terminates, the court's involvement with the dispute.[16]

As Chayes suggests, remedial policymaking can involve judges in prolonged and detailed supervision of public facilities. Judge Johnson's ruling in *Jones v. Wallace*, for example, required that the prison hire a nutrition consultant and even prescribed the maximum number of inmates per toilet.[17] Such judicial intervention can occur even if courts do not assume immediate policymaking responsibility. In *Brown v. Board of Education* [*Brown* II] (1955), the Supreme Court required school districts to take affirmative steps to eliminate racial segregation in their public school systems.[18] The Court, however, left it up to the various school districts to determine how best to implement this requirement. Federal district court judges could intervene only if districts failed to meet their constitutional responsibility to desegregate their schools. Nevertheless, the refusal of many states and communities to comply with *Brown* compelled federal judges to devise and impose their own school desegregation plans.[19] Sometimes, courts rule that an unconstitutional situation exists but refrain from announcing a remedy. For example, in *Robinson v. Cahill* (1972), the New Jersey Supreme Court ruled that the state's system of school finance violated the New Jersey Constitution but left it to the governor and legislature to devise a replacement.[20] While this approach puts an issue on the political agenda and gives the other branches of government an opportunity to act, it succeeds only if the political authorities are willing to meet their constitutional responsibilities.

Although the federal or state constitution might provide the basis for invalidating government actions, it offers little guidance as to how best to remedy unconstitutional practices or their effects. Consequently, as Chayes notes, judges seeking to remedy constitutional violations necessarily exercise considerable discretion. To determine whether a judge has acted appropriately, one must consider the effectiveness of the judge's approach and whether it intrudes excessively on the powers of other branches of government.[21]

Statutory Interpretation and Judicial Policymaking

Although constitutional cases receive the most attention, they constitute a miniscule portion of court caseloads. Typically, judges are involved in enforcing legislative mandates rather than in invalidating them. The judge deciding a criminal case must determine what the defendant has done and whether those actions violate the criminal law. Judges in civil cases often must apply statutes in reaching their decisions. Thus, the responsibility to "say what the law is" frequently requires the judge to determine the meaning of legislative enactments and how they apply in specific cases.

This responsibility appears to provide little occasion for judicial policymaking. Most disputes are of interest only to the litigants themselves. Even when a dispute has broader significance, the legislature has supplied the standard for resolving it by enacting the statute. Because statutes are designed to serve particular purposes, they can—at least in theory—state precisely the aims to be achieved and the means for their achievement. Thus, in cases involving statutory interpretation, the courts' function may appear to be distinctly subsidiary: to determine what the law means and to decide cases in line with that meaning.

As Chapter 8 suggested, this picture is too simple.[22] Litigants often differ about the meaning of a statute or its application, and thus, deciding the case obliges the judge to choose between competing interpretations of the law proposed by the parties to the case. Frequently, the judge's choice, which is necessary to resolve the specific dispute, can have much wider effects. Indeed, one critic of judicial policymaking has charged that judges have all too often "embark[ed] on ambitious ventures of judicial reform in the name of statutory construction."[23] To understand how the judicial responsibility to interpret the law enmeshes judges in policymaking, one must identify those factors that lead to conflicts over the interpretation of statutes.

Disputes about the meaning of a statute may arise if its provisions are unclear or appear to conflict with one another. Sometimes, this lack of clarity may be inadvertent, the result of poor draftsmanship or inconsistent amendments added during legislative consideration of the measure. Sometimes, however, statutory ambiguity may reflect the technical complexity of the subject matter—or what Justice Felix Frankfurter once referred to as "the intrinsic difficulties of the language."[24] And sometimes unclear statutes may result from legislative efforts to avoid controversial policy choices by settling on broad and general terms that reflect an "agreement on language but not on substance."[25] For example, Title VII of the Civil Rights Act of 1964 outlaws discrimination in employment on the basis of race, color, religion, sex, or national origin but fails to define discrimination. Thus, the legislation's supporters were able to avoid divisive issues, such as whether discrimination must be intentional and whether affirmative action is permissible under the statute.[26] The resolution of these difficult questions was left to the courts, which were obliged to give meaning to the ambiguous provisions in the course of resolving legal disputes.

Disputes may also arise over whether a law applies to a situation that was not contemplated by those who enacted the legislation. *Mortenson v. United States* provides a classic example.[27] Mr. and Mrs. Mortenson operated a (legal) house of prostitution in Grand Island, Nebraska. When they traveled to Salt Lake City to visit Mrs. Mortenson's parents, they took two of their employees along for the trip. After the vacation, they drove back to Nebraska, where their employees resumed their work. The Mortensons were subsequently prosecuted under the Mann Act, a federal statute that (as Chapter 8 indicated) forbade transporting women across state lines "for the purpose of prostitution or debauchery, or for any other immoral purpose."[28] Clearly, the authors of the Act never imagined the Mortensons' situation; they were primarily concerned with preventing the coercion of young women into prostitution. Nevertheless, the government argued that when the Mortensons brought their employees back to work, they were, in fact, transporting them across state lines for the purpose of prostitution. Eventually, the U.S. Supreme Court by a 5–4 vote overturned the Mortensons' conviction.

Social and technological changes may also produce situations that not even the most farsighted legislator could have anticipated. *Diamond v. Chakrabarty* (1980) illustrates how such changes may provide occasions for judicial policymaking.[29] Chakrabarty had created a living microorganism under laboratory conditions and applied for a patent for his invention. Not surprisingly, when Congress enacted the current patent law in 1952, it never considered whether living organisms could be patented, and nothing in the law directly permitted or forbade the patenting of living organisms. The Supreme Court was therefore called on to determine whether the broad language of the patent law, reflecting an intention to reward ingenuity and invention, extended to the creation of such organisms. As the Court recognized, its decision could significantly influence whether genetic research was "accelerated by the hope of reward or slowed by the want of incentive."[30] In ruling in favor of Chakrabarty and permitting the patenting of microorganisms, the Court made important policy, but it did so in the course of fulfilling its responsibility to interpret and apply the law.

Disputes may also arise over how a statute affects earlier legislation. Although the legal principles governing such situations are clear, their application can produce disputes that require judicial intervention. One principle is that if a new congressional or state statute is inconsistent with an existing one, then the more recent enactment supersedes the earlier one. Unless, however, the legislature clearly indicates its intention to supersede an earlier enactment, or unless two laws directly conflict, courts may be asked to determine whether the laws are, in fact, inconsistent. Another principle is that congressional legislation "preempts" (supersedes) inconsistent state legislation. But Congress rarely indicates how its enactments relate to existing state legislation. Thus, when Congress enters a field dominated by state legislation, courts often must determine whether the state law has been preempted. Similarly, when states legislate in an area in which congressional legislation exists, litigation often results. For example, when California enacted a statute outlawing "record piracy" (unauthorized duplication of recordings), several persons challenged their convictions under the Act by claiming that it was preempted by the federal copyright law.[31] They lost.

Oversight of Administrative Activity and Judicial Policymaking

Over the course of the twentieth century, the size of the federal and state governments and the scope of their activities increased dramatically. A major expansion in administrative policymaking has accompanied this unprecedented growth in government. Administrative agencies "legislate" through their power to issue regulations that further define legislative mandates and have the force of law. Agencies "adjudicate" through their power to determine whether persons or organizations have violated law or regulations. And, through their power to award or withhold authorizations and licenses and to establish and enforce eligibility requirements for government benefit programs, agencies control the distribution of important economic goods. Challenges from those injured by administrative policymaking have created new opportunities for judicial policymaking.

Just as litigants may challenge the constitutionality of legislative enactments, so also may they challenge the constitutionality of administrative actions. More frequently, when litigants claim that an agency has exceeded its legal authority, the basis for the claim is statutory rather than constitutional. Because an agency can make policy only in pursuance of its statutory mandate, litigants may claim that an agency's action is inconsistent with its mandate. The courts must then determine whether the agency has exceeded its authority or has adopted policies that are consistent with its authorizing legislation. This was the issue when the federal Food and Drug Administration (FDA) issued regulations dealing with the marketing of tobacco products in 1996. Tobacco companies sued, asserting that Congress had never given the FDA authority to regulate tobacco products, and the U.S. Supreme Court agreed, invalidating the agency's regulations.[32]

In other instances, the challenge may be to administrative inaction rather than administrative action. If a law imposes responsibilities on an agency, a litigant may charge that the agency has failed to carry out its responsibilities. The agency's failure may involve total inaction. More frequently, the issue is whether the agency has responded adequately to the legislative mandate. In *Allen v. Wright*, for example, a group of parents sued the Internal Revenue Service, alleging that it had not adopted sufficient standards and procedures to fulfill its obligation to deny tax-exempt status to racially discriminatory private schools.[33] In such cases, judges must also analyze the statutory requirements imposed on governmental agencies.

Even if an agency has statutory authorization for its actions, litigants may challenge the processes by which the agency arrived at its policy. This is a particularly fertile basis for litigation. The Administrative Procedure Act, enacted by Congress in 1946, specifies the basic procedures that federal agencies must follow in their rulemaking. Subsequent statutes have multiplied procedural requirements, and many agencies have supplemented these statutory requirements with their own rules of procedure. Although judges have sometimes been reluctant to challenge agencies' policy determinations, recognizing that they lack the technical expertise to evaluate agency assessments, they have been much more willing to intervene to ensure procedural regularity. Judicial rulings on procedural issues can often have important policy consequences by requiring agencies to delay or reconsider their actions. Take, for example, the requirement under the National Environmental Protection Act that all agencies prepare an environmental impact statement for any proposal for legislation or "major federal action."[34] Environmental groups have used this requirement as a weapon to delay or seek modifications in projects they oppose by filing suits that challenge the failure to file the statements or the adequacy of those that were filed.[35]

As administrative policymaking has expanded, so has judicial intervention designed to ensure that agencies observe the substantive and procedural requirements imposed on them. This intervention has inevitably enmeshed courts in policy disputes and led them to issue rulings that have had a major impact on public policy.

The Common Law and Judicial Policymaking

As we have seen, constitutions, statutes, and administrative regulations can furnish legal standards for judges to apply when they decide cases. In the United States, the scope of these laws, although vast, is hardly comprehensive. Thus, when a dispute arises regarding, say, whether A is liable for injuries that B has suffered, a judge typically cannot look to the other branches of government for applicable legal standards. Instead, the judge must, in the course of resolving the dispute, establish the law that will govern it. As previously noted, this body of judge-made law, which developed to resolve legal conflicts in the absence of legislative or executive enactments, is termed the common law.

Through their decisions enunciating the common law, the courts clearly make policy. Nevertheless, several factors serve to channel and control this policymaking. Judges have only limited discretion when they devise common-law legal policy. They are not free simply to incorporate their own policy preferences into law. Rather, common law, as the term itself implies, is to reflect the values and practices of the community. As noted in Chapter 1, during the thirteenth and fourteenth centuries, when the common law originated in England, judges drew their standards directly from the common practices of the society. As the body of judicial decisions elaborating these societal standards grew, recourse to legal precedent gradually replaced the direct invocation of community standards. Today, courts generally rely on precedent to decide common-law cases. This reliance on precedent, fortified by the doctrine of *stare decisis*, ensures continuity in the law and limits the range of judicia discretion.

The common-law principles that a court announces have only a limited authority. When a state supreme court announces a principle of common law, it does so in the course of deciding a particular case. When subsequent cases arise that appear similar to the initial case, the court must decide whether to extend, modify, or abandon the principle it initially announced. Thus, the common law is established not so much by an individual decision as by an accumulation of decisions dealing with a particular area of the law. Although a state court's decision may constitute authoritative precedent within the state, its acceptance beyond the state's borders depends not on the authority of the court but on the persuasiveness of the arguments supporting the decision, particularly when a court departs from established principles of the common law and charts a new direction. Although the common law is dynamic rather than static, decisive breaks with past decisions are rare. Change in the common law tends to be incremental, a gradual case-by-case modification of legal standards in response to shifts in the character and values of the society. At each step of the process, the movement can be halted or reversed if it appears to be heading in the wrong direction.

Ultimately, these constraints channel rather than prevent judicial policymaking: Courts inevitably make policy in their interpretation and development of the common law. Nor is this necessarily undesirable. The legal principles that were appropriate for the largely agrarian nation of the eighteenth century could hardly serve the legal needs of the twenty-first century. Social and technological changes have created new problems that require the courts to extend or modify common-law principles. New social relationships have developed that must be taken into account in applying common-law principles. New aspirations have emerged, and the law must be sufficiently flexible to permit their fulfillment.

In sum, the courts' responsibility to resolve disputes in the absence of legal enactments obliges them to make law. Although no single court or decision establishes policy, legal standards emerge from the multiplicity of common-law rulings that judges are called on to make. Although change is typically gradual and may in some instances only be discernible in retrospect, the common law must be dynamic to serve the needs of a changing society. These changes in the common law generally grow out of changes in the broader society. At the same time, the courts' decisions can also encourage or retard societal trends. Common-law policymaking thus both reflects and affects American society.

Cumulative Policymaking

Although some cases raise important policy issues, most court cases involve more mundane disputes that are of concern only to the disputants. No new legal principles emerge from these cases, and the societal impact of individual judicial decisions is minimal. However, one should not distinguish too sharply between the few decisions that announce new policy and those decisions that make up the bulk of court business. For although the relatively routine cases, taken individually, may be relatively insignificant, they may in the aggregate embody important policy choices.

Judges often exercise considerable discretion in resolving these more mundane disputes. Ordinarily, judges decide cases by applying the law. At times, however, the society's sense of justice cannot readily be reduced to precise legal standards. In such circumstances the legislature may merely announce a general standard and rely on judges to use their discretion to do justice on a case-by-case basis. The state's policy thus is not defined by legislative mandate but rather emerges from the totality of judicial decisions, a process known as cumulative policymaking.

Sentencing in criminal cases illustrates this sort of cumulative policymaking. Until the imposition of sentencing guidelines (see Chapter 6), criminal law in the United States tended to define the minimum and maximum penalties for various offenses—for example, five to ten years for armed robbery—but allowed the judge considerable discretion in sentencing within those guidelines. Although the sentence meted out to an individual offender does not establish policy, the overall pattern of sentencing in criminal cases does constitute important policymaking, because it reveals how the society regards various crimes. The lower sentences for possession of marijuana during the late 1960s, for example, indicated a change in societal standards even before state legislatures acted to reduce penalties. In addition, a comparison of the sentences meted out to members of various racial and economic groups provides one indication of the society's commitment to equal justice. Charges of racial bias in sentencing and complaints about judges who are "soft on crime," whether justified or not, indicate that cumulative policymaking can be highly controversial.

A second example of cumulative policymaking is child custody awards in contested divorce cases.[36] When parents cannot agree on a custody arrangement, trial court judges determine which parent shall retain custody or whether joint custody shall be awarded. Although the judge's award is to serve the "best interests of the child," this vague standard affords considerable latitude for the exercise of judicial discretion.[37] Once again, the decision in individual cases may be of concern chiefly to the contending parties. The cumulative effect of those decisions, however, defines how the society weighs the various factors that might be considered in determining the child's "best interest." During the early twentieth century, for example, judges—rhapsodizing that "there is but a twilight zone between a mother's love and an atmosphere of heaven"—consistently supported maternal claims for custody.[38] In recent decades, however, fathers have become more willing to seek custody and more successful in obtaining it. As this change suggests, cumulative policymaking can both respond to and influence developments occurring in the broader society.

Cumulative policymaking thus occurs when a series of decisions in essentially similar cases in effect defines policy in a given area. Although legislation or rulings by appellate courts may circumscribe the range of judicial choice, trial judges often retain considerable leeway in deciding individual cases. When they exercise this discretion, judges rarely announce broad policy standards. Indeed, they may give little consideration to the broader policy that their decisions create. Nonetheless, the results of their decisions define the policy of the state.

THE INCIDENCE OF JUDICIAL POLICYMAKING

The Level of Judicial Policymaking

Although judicial policymaking is not a recent phenomenon, judges are more involved in policymaking today than in the past. What accounts for this? It may be that today's judges are more willing, even eager, to participate in policymaking than were judges in earlier eras.[39] Recognizing this, groups may also be more willing to use the courts to advance their policy objectives.[40] Perhaps the primary reason for increased judicial policymaking, however, is simply that there is now more law and more litigation.

At one time, many state constitutions mandated that the state legislature meet only every other year and limited the length of legislative sessions. Today, most state legislatures meet annually, for a longer period, and enact more laws.[41] Except when its members are campaigning for reelection, Congress is almost continually in session. Perhaps the biggest change, however, involves administrative rulemaking. The creation of regulatory agencies during the twentieth century has produced an explosion of federal rules and regulations.[42] In 1936, for example, the Code of Federal Regulations, which includes all regulations issued by federal agencies, numbered 2,619 pages. Today, these regulations stretch over more than 67,000 pages.[43] Because the increase in law creates new rights and responsibilities, it stimulates litigation. Many of these cases, however, do not involve judicial policymaking. Judges merely enforce preexisting legal standards, and the outcomes of the cases are of consequence only to the litigants. Many other cases create new opportunities for—and indeed, may oblige judges to engage in—judicial policymaking.

Historical Shifts in Judicial Policymaking

Changes have occurred over time not only in the level but also in the character of judicial policymaking (see Table 9-1).

Constitutional Policymaking   The twentieth century was the main era for constitutional policymaking in the United States. The Supreme Court invalidated only two federal statutes and 34 state statutes before 1860.[44] During the late nineteenth century, however, state and federal courts became more active in overturning legislative enactments, and this activism peaked in the late twentieth century. As Figures 9-1 and 9-2 show, more than one-third of the congressional and state statutes declared unconstitutional have been invalidated by the U.S. Supreme Court since 1960. Over the past three decades, state courts have also shown a renewed willingness to strike down statutes that violate state declarations of rights, a phenomenon explored in Chapter 11.

Remedial Policymaking   The imposition of detailed plans of action to remedy constitutional violations began in the 1950s with the effort to implement *Brown v. Board of Education,* the Supreme Court's school desegregation decision, and has continued as courts have become more involved in supervising the operations of such governmental institutions as prisons and school systems.[45]

Statutory Policymaking   As already noted, federal and state legislation increased dramatically during the twentieth century. As the amount of legislation increased, so did the volume of litigation over its interpretation and the level of statutory policymaking by judges. Equally important was a change in the character of legislation. During the nineteenth century, federal statutes primarily involved the distribution of benefits to citizens (the Homestead Act, which made public lands available to settlers, is a prime example), and such legislation rarely provoked disputes. Statutes enacted during the twentieth century, however, substantially expanded the scope of federal and state regulation of private conduct, and this in turn prompted challenges by those who were affected by the regulatory legislation. Often these disputes about the interpretation and application of regulatory statutes would wind up in the courts.[46]

Oversight of Administrative Agencies   Although some state regulatory agencies were created during the nineteenth century, most federal administrative agencies were established in bursts of creative energy during the Progressive Era (roughly 1900–1920), the New Deal (1932–1940), and the Great Society period (roughly 1963–1970).[47] The establishment of new agencies prompted increased administrative activity and expanded judicial involvement in the oversight of that activity.

Common-Law Policymaking   During the nation's first century, when most American law was enunciated by courts rather than enacted by legislatures, common-law policymaking was the most important judicial policymaking.[48] From 1800 to 1870, U.S. courts introduced important innovations in the common law. Judges adapted English common-law doctrines to the more democratic and egalitarian society found in the United States. They also eased and encouraged the transition from an agrarian society to a more industrialized one.[49]

During the twentieth century, the scope of the common law contracted as statutes and administrative regulations replaced common law in such fields as employer–employee relations. However, since World War II, state appellate courts have introduced revolutionary changes in tort law, the law governing liability for injuries that one has caused. Some of these changes are discussed in Chapter 11.

Cumulative Policymaking   Cumulative policymaking has taken place throughout the nation's history.

The Agenda of Judicial Policymaking

As American society changes, so do the sorts of issue that come before the courts, and the focus of judicial policymaking shifts in turn. The changing agenda of the U.S. Supreme Court illustrates the point. During the nineteenth century, relatively few cases coming before the Court involved constitutional issues, whereas today a large proportion do. Even more important are the changes in the sorts of constitutional issue the Court addresses. Before the Civil War, constitutional cases usually involved disputes about the respective spheres of the national and state governments. After the Civil War, industrialization and the growth of large corporations prompted governmental efforts to deal with those developments, and the Court's constitutional agenda focused on the scope of federal and state power to regulate economic enterprises. Since the late 1930s, when the Court recognized broad federal and state authority to regulate economic matters, it has been most involved in delineating the scope of constitutional rights.[50]

The policymaking agendas of other courts also reflect societal changes. For example, a study of the dockets of state supreme courts over a 100-year period documents a shift from commercial to noncommercial cases and concludes that the courts "seem to be less concerned with the stabilization and protection of property rights, more concerned with the individual and the downtrodden, and more willing to consider rulings that promote social change."[51] A similar study of federal courts of appeals concludes that criminal cases and cases involving the federal government has risen dramatically, confirming the importance of legislation in stimulating litigation. Whereas private economic disputes dominated the dockets of courts of appeals early in the twentieth century, such disputes constituted a much smaller proportion of the courts' caseload by the late twentieth century.[52]

Assessing Judicial Policymaking

Criteria for Evaluation

Most people evaluate judicial policymaking on the basis of results. They praise judicial policies that they favor and condemn those they dislike without distinguishing between courts and other political institutions. They react to the substance of the policy, not its legal basis. Thus, if they are pro-life, they applaud Supreme Court rulings that restrict abortion. If they are politically conservative, they deplore lenient sentences for offenders.

This section, however, focuses on two other criteria for evaluating judicial policymaking: legitimacy and capacity (policy effectiveness). To determine whether a judicial decision that enunciates policy is legitimate, we must ask: Is the issue one that judges may properly address, and is there an adequate legal basis for the court's position? Note that our answer might not coincide with our policy views. We might condemn as illegitimate a judicial ruling that advances a policy we favor; alternatively, we may acknowledge another judicial ruling as legitimate, even while deploring the specific policy announced by the court.

To assess judicial policymaking in terms of judicial capacity or policy effectiveness, we ask a different question: Has the policy announced by the court succeeded in achieving its goals? Applying this criterion, we evaluate court-ordered busing by examining whether it, in fact, promoted racial integration in schools (see Chapter 10). Or we evaluate the exclusionary rule by analyzing whether it, in fact, deters police misconduct (see Chapter 6). Let us turn first to the issue of judicial policymaking capacity.

Judicial Capacity and Policy Effectiveness[53]

Every governmental institution has its own characteristic approach to defining and dealing with policy issues. The particular approach reflects the background and expertise of the policymakers, the way they make their policy decisions, and the resources they command to ensure that their policies are carried out. Some commentators have concluded that, compared to other governmental bodies, courts are relatively ill-equipped to devise and implement policy. Donald Horowitz, the most well-known of these critics, identifies several problems with judicial policymaking.[54]

Timeliness of Addressing Problems   Timing is important in successful policymaking. If a problem is addressed too early, without adequate understanding of its dimensions or the range of possible solutions, remedial efforts are unlikely to succeed and may merely produce other problems. Conversely, if a problem is addressed too late, it may be more difficult to solve.

Courts do not control when they will confront policy issues because they do not control their own agendas. Rather, they must passively await the decision of litigants to bring policy issues before them for resolution. With the exception of the U.S. Supreme Court (and to a lesser extent, some state high courts), they cannot decline to hear properly brought cases, even if the cases raise policy issues that are not ripe for resolution. In sum, although timing may be essential to effective policymaking, it is largely a matter of chance whether courts will address problems at the time most conducive to their successful resolution.

Adequacy of Information   The wisdom of policy choices often depends on the quality of the information that policymakers receive and the uses to which they put it. According to Horowitz, courts are less likely than other institutions to obtain relevant information and use it effectively.

Courts announce broad policy—for example, the inadmissibility of illegally seized evidence—in the course of deciding specific cases. This poses no difficulty if the case is representative of all possible situations that the court's ruling will affect. According to Horowitz, this rarely happens; rather, courts make policy without information about many situations that their policy will affect, and the result of such ill-informed policymaking is likely to be bad policy.

In addition, because courts must decide issues on the basis of law, the information they receive in legal briefs and oral argument tends to focus on legal considerations rather than on the desirability of a policy or the likely consequences of alternative approaches to a problem. Even if such information were conveyed, judges could hardly refuse to recognize a constitutional or legal right because of doubts about its desirability. Whereas other policymakers tend to view policy issues in terms of ranges of alternatives and costs and benefits, courts necessarily view the issues in terms of legal rights and legal duties.

Furthermore, courts confront policy issues only in adversarial proceedings, with the issues framed as disputes between two specific parties. Although other groups and interests may be affected by the court's decision, they have no legal standing to present their views and concerns and may not even know about the litigation. Even when the parties do not monopolize the transmission of information (e.g., when other groups submit amicus curiae briefs), the input the court receives is typically less rich and complete than that available to a legislature or administrative agency considering a policy issue. For example, rules of evidence may keep relevant information from the court. Whereas other governmental bodies can seek out additional information on their own (through legislative hearings or commission studies on a problem), courts must rely on the information they receive through legal briefs and oral argument. Even if that information is inadequate, courts cannot decline to decide or postpone their decision.

Finally, because judges in general jurisdiction courts decide cases in a variety of fields, they approach cases that involve issues of public policy as generalists rather than as experts. In theory, this allows them to bring a fresh perspective to problems. But it also means that they lack the background that specialization in a particular field brings. Judges typically lack the ability to understand and make use of sophisticated information that is relevant to policy even when it is made available to them. Confronted with expert testimony, they lack the skills necessary to evaluate the experts' claims or, if the experts disagree, to choose among conflicting views. Whether the issue is the carcinogenic effects of Agent Orange, the environmental consequences of opening public lands to private development, or the deterrent effects of capital punishment, judges confront technical problems as amateurs.

Flexibility of Response   The more flexibility policymakers have in devising solutions to problems, the more likely they are to solve them. According to Horowitz, courts have far fewer options than do other policymakers. Because courts must decide cases on the basis of law, they cannot impose a compromise solution on disputants, no matter how desirable. Further, if persons possess a right, they possess it regardless of cost, and thus cost-benefit analysis, the prime approach to contemporary policymaking, plays little role in judicial policymaking. Finally, courts have fewer means of remedying illegal situations than do other governmental institutions. They can forbid, permit, or require actions, but they can neither tax nor spend (although their orders may require expenditures by other branches). They can neither create new agencies to administer their directives nor appoint officials to oversee their implementation.

Monitoring the Effects of Decisions   Once a policy is established, policymakers must monitor its implementation to ensure that the policy is carried out (compliance) and that it has its desired effects. This policy review also allows policymakers to modify their policies when earlier approaches have proven ineffective in achieving the desired results.

According to Horowitz, courts cannot effectively monitor the effects of their decisions or respond to those effects as easily as can other policymakers. Instead of overseeing the consequences of their decisions, judges typically turn to other cases once they have announced a decision. When the target population for a decision is large—for example, police officers who interrogate suspects—judges have no way to monitor compliance with their ruling. Even when the target population is relatively small, courts often do not know whether their decisions are being carried out unless affected groups bring instances of noncompliance to their attention in a new lawsuit.

A further problem plagues judicial efforts to ensure that their policies have the desired effect. Because the American legal system emphasizes adherence to precedent, courts are generally reluctant to overrule earlier decisions, particularly recent ones. Thus, courts cannot readily change course when confronted with evidence that their policy directives have failed to achieve their desired results. Even when they can determine the consequences of their decisions, respect for precedent renders judges less able than other policy-makers to benefit from that information.

Evaluating Horowitz's Critique   Not all observers agree with Horowitz that courts are particularly ill-equipped to devise policy.[55] The recent prolifer-ation of remedial policymaking, they claim, shows that Horowitz underesti-mates courts' ability to devise new approaches to deal with unfamiliar problems. Beyond that, they insist that courts fare badly in Horowitz's analysis because he unfairly compares the actual operation of courts to an idealized pic-ture of legislatures and administrative agencies. Legislators—just like judges—are generalists, confronting a wide array of issues with incomplete information. Like judges also, they do not control their own agendas but instead must address those issues on which the public demands action. Just like judicial issues, legislative issues frequently arise because of a single incident. For example, reform of election procedures emerged as an issue following the controversy over the outcome of the 2000 presidential election. In addition, legislators and administrators, just like judges, have difficulty supervising the operation of their policies; the Savings and Loan debacle of the early 1990s, for instance, illustrates the ineffectiveness of legislative and administrative over-sight. Finally, as *Brown v. Board of Education* and the Alabama prison litiga-tion demonstrated, the choice is often not between the courts' or some other institution's addressing a problem but between judicial intervention and gov-ernmental inaction.

Some commentators also insist that insofar as judges do have a distinctive approach to policymaking, this may prove an advantage rather than a disad-vantage. The emphasis on reasoned justification in judicial decision making, for example, may promote more thoughtful policy pronouncements. Further-more, judges—especially federal judges—enjoy an independence from parti-san pressures and the importunings of special interests. Their relative insulation may enable them to pursue policies that serve the public interest rather than short-term political advantage.[56]

Finally, insofar as Horowitz's critique is accurate, it applies primarily to sit-uations in which a judge announces broad policy in a single case. As we have seen, not all judicial policymaking fits that pattern. Common-law policymaking and cumulative policymaking generally involve an incremental, case-by-case approach. Judges usually do not announce broad policy in the course of statu-tory policymaking or judicial oversight of administrative activity. Horowitz's critique therefore seems particularly applicable to constitutional policymaking and remedial policymaking.

Legitimacy

Even if judges cannot altogether avoid policymaking, this does not mean that all judicial policymaking is legitimate. Judges may announce decisions that have no basis in law but merely reflect their personal policy views. Or their rulings may clearly invade the powers and prerogatives of the other branches of government. In such circumstances, few people would deny that the rulings were illegitimate. However, people may well disagree about what constitutes an adequate legal basis for a decision or what the judiciary's proper role is in governing a democratic society. Indeed, throughout the nation's history, the scope of judicial authority has prompted fierce debate.

In recent years the debate has been framed in terms of "judicial activism" versus "judicial restraint." Unfortunately, these terms obscure as much as they clarify. The term "judicial activism" has frequently been used to criticize judicial rulings, although some scholars and judges have applauded such activism, particularly when it results in a broad definition of individual rights.[57] Thus, characterizing a decision as activist or restrained does not necessarily resolve whether it is legitimate or not.

In addition, the meaning of the terms themselves is far from clear. In an effort to replace polemics with precision, political scientist Bradley Canon identified several criteria for comparing activist and "restraintist" decisions (see Box 9-1).[58]

Useful though Canon's list may be for clarifying the various understandings of activism and restraint, it also underscores the limitations and confusions in the contemporary debate over judicial activism and restraint. Most obviously, as Canon himself acknowledges, the criteria for activism and restraint apply best to constitutional policymaking. By definition, statutory and cumulative policymaking do not overturn legislation. Common-law policymaking does not preclude policymaking by other branches of government.

Even if one limits one's attention to constitutional policymaking, the distinction between activism and restraint is not altogether satisfactory. Whereas some judicial decisions might be characterized as clearly activist and others as clearly restraintist, many decisions may be activist in some aspects and restrained in others. When the U.S. Supreme Court reversed course in 1937 and began to uphold New Deal legislation, its rulings were activist in that they overruled precedent, but restrained in that they upheld congressional legislation.[59] Similarly, the Court in *Brown v. Board of Education* rejected the prevailing standard of "separate but equal" and overturned laws in several states but arguably did so to bring the interpretation of the Equal Protection Clause in line with the clear implications of its language.[60] Thus, depending on the criteria one employs, one could characterize those rulings as either activist or restrained.

BOX
9-1

Dimensions of Judicial Activism
and Restraint

1. Majoritarianism.   Activist decisions negate policies adopted through democratic processes; "restraintist" decisions uphold them.

2. Interpretive stability.   Activist decisions modify or overrule earlier court decisions, doctrines, or interpretations; restraintist decisions leave them intact.

3. Interpretive fidelity.   Activist decisions interpret constitutional provisions in a manner that diverges from the clear intentions of their drafters or the clear implications of the language used; restraintist decisions adhere to the text and the original understanding of provisions.

4. Substance–democratic process distinction.   Activist decisions make substantive policy; restraintist decisions merely preserve the democratic process.

5. Specificity of policy.   Activist decisions announce detailed policy directives; restraintist policy leaves discretion to other agencies or individuals.

6. Availability of an alternative policymaker.   Activist decisions supersede serious consideration of the same problem by other governmental agencies; restraintist decisions promote it.

Source: Adapted from Bradley C. Canon, "A Framework for the Analysis of Judicial Activism," in *Supreme Court Activism and Restraint*, eds. Stephen C. Halpern and Charles M. Lamb (Lexington, MA: Lexington Books, 1982), pp. 386–387. Used by permission.

The main problem with discussions of judicial activism and restraint, however, is that they distract attention from the primary question in assessing the legitimacy of judicial policymaking: whether the court's rulings are legally defensible. Put differently, the most important criterion for judging the legitimacy of judicial decisions and judicial policymaking is what Canon has termed "interpretive fidelity." Judicial policymaking is legitimate, whether or not it overturns congressional statutes and judicial precedents, if the court's ruling is consistent with the text and intention of the provision being interpreted. Conversely, a judicial decision is illegitimate if it follows precedent or upholds legislation when fidelity to the Constitution demands their invalidation. Of course, acceptance of interpretive fidelity as the primary criterion does not eliminate disputes. Judges disagree, often vehemently, about how to interpret constitutional provisions and other legal texts. Commentators constantly debate whether courts have adequately justified their rulings. Chapter 8 suggested why such disagreements may occur, even among those committed to the disinterested interpretation of the law.

CONCLUSIONS

This chapter has attempted to dispel several myths about judicial policymaking. One myth is that judicial policymaking necessarily involves a judicial usurpation of power. At times this may be the case, but generally judicial policymaking is the unavoidable result of judges' fulfilling their responsibility to decide cases in accordance with the law. In the course of making a decision, judges interpret constitutions and statutes, oversee the actions of administrative agencies, and elaborate the common law. The decisions they render have policy consequences, often regardless of how they rule, and thus judges are unavoidably involved in public policy development.

A second myth is that the growth of judicial policymaking reflects an effort by activist judges to exercise power. Although there may be individual judges who have abused their positions, more seems to be involved than the character of the judges. After all, more than a decade of judicial appointments by Presidents Reagan and Bush, both of whom expressed fervent opposition to judicial activism, did not eliminate judicial policymaking. Rather, government expansion and an ever-growing body of law are primarily responsible for judicial policymaking, not the composition of the judiciary.

A third myth is that judicial policymaking is necessarily undemocratic because the will of the judge prevails over the will of the populace. In actuality, much judicial policymaking does not place courts at odds with the popular will. In statutory policymaking and judicial oversight of administrative agencies, judges are presumably giving effect to, rather than overriding, the will of the legislature. In common-law policymaking they are acting in the absence of legislation, and in cumulative policymaking they are exercising discretion within bounds set by the legislature. Constitutional policymaking sometimes places judges at odds with legislatures, but often the judges invalidate actions of officials—for example, police officers—who are themselves not directly accountable to the public. Finally, in remedial policymaking judges sometimes displace other policymakers but typically do so only when those policymakers have failed to act to meet constitutional requirements.

Judicial policymaking is not, of course, beyond criticism. Judges at times exceed their legitimate powers, render unwise decisions, or announce policies that fail to achieve their objectives. To understand and assess judicial policymaking, however, one must look closely at how judges reach their decisions and at the effects their decisions actually have. Thus, Chapter 10 examines in detail federal court policymaking on two important issues, school desegregation and abortion, and Chapter 11 looks at state court policymaking involving school finance and product liability.

NOTES

1. See generally, David M. O'Brien, *Storm Center: The Supreme Court in American Politics,* 5th ed. (New York: Norton, 1999); Alpheus Mason, *The Supreme Court from Taft to Burger,* 3d ed. (Baton Rouge: Louisiana State University Press, 1979); Lawrence Tribe, *God Save This Honorable Court* (New York: Random House, 1985); Christopher Wolfe, *The Rise of Modern Judicial Review* (New York: Basic Books, 1986); and Tinsley E. Yarbrough, *The Rehnquist Court and the Constitution* (New York: Oxford University Press, 2000).

2. The quotation is from Chief Justice John Marshall's opinion for the Court in *Marbury v. Madison,* 5 U.S. (1 Cranch) 137, 173 (1803), the first case in which the U.S. Supreme Court struck down a congressional statute as unconstitutional.

3. *Gratz v. Bollinger,* 539 U.S. 244 (2003), and *Grutter v. Bollinger,* 539 U.S. 306 (2003).

4. *Marbury v. Madison,* 5 U.S. (1 Cranch) 137 (1803). There are a few instances of state exercise of judicial review before 1800. See Sylvia Snowiss, *Judicial Review and the Law of the Constitution* (New Haven, CT: Yale University Press, 1990).

5. *United States v. Nixon,* 418 U.S. 683 (1974).

6. For annual data on the work of the Supreme Court, see the November issue of the *Harvard Law Review.*

7. *James v. Wallace,* 382 F.Supp. 1177 (M.D. Ala. 1974); *James v. Wallace,* 406 F.Supp. 318 (M.D. Ala. 1976).

8. For an account of Judge Frank Johnson's involvement, see Tinsley E. Yarbrough, *Judge Frank Johnson and Human Rights in Alabama* (Tuscaloosa: University of Alabama Press, 1981); and Jethro K. Lieberman, *The Litigious Society* (New York: Basic Books, 1981), chap. 5.

9. *Straus v. Governor,* 592 N.W.2d 53 (Mich. 1999), and *Goodridge v. Department of Public Health,* SJC-08860 (Mass. 2003).

10. This is more complicated than it sounds. For representative efforts by constitutional theorists to address the issue, see Sotirios Barber, *On What the Constitution Means* (Baltimore: Johns Hopkins University Press, 1984); Robert Bork, *The Tempting of America: The Political Seduction of the Law* (New York: Free Press, 1990); John Hart Ely, *Democracy and Distrust: A Theory of Judicial Review* (Cambridge, MA: Harvard University Press, 1980); Gary Jacobsohn, *The Supreme Court and the Decline of Constitutional Aspiration* (Totowa, NJ: Rowman and Littlefield, 1986); and Keith E. Whittington, *Constitutional Interpretation: Textual Meaning, Original Intent, and Judicial Review* (Lawrence: University Press of Kansas, 1999).

11. The quotation is from Justice Owen Roberts's opinion for the Court in *United States v. Butler,* 297 U.S. 1 (1936).

12. *Brown v. Board of Education,* 347 U.S. 483 (1954).

13. *Plessy v. Ferguson,* 163 U.S. 537 (1896).

14. *Chaplin and Drysdale, Chartered v. United States,* 491 U.S. 617 (1989).

15. *Reed v. Reed*, 404 U.S. 71 (1971).

16. Abram Chayes, "The Role of the Judge in Public Law Litigation," *Harvard Law Review* 89 (1976): 1298.

17. *James v. Wallace*, 406 F.Supp. 318 (M.D. Ala. 1976).

18. *Brown v. Board of Education [Brown II]*, 349 U.S. 294 (1955).

19. The role of federal judges in desegregation efforts is discussed in Chapter 10.

20. *Robinson v. Cahill [Robinson I]*, 303 A.2d 273 (N.J. 1973), and *Robinson v. Cahill [Robinson II]*, 339 A.2d 193 (N.J. 1975). See the discussion of school finance in Chapter 11.

21. For discussion of these limits, see Gary L. McDowell, *Equity and the Constitution: The Supreme Court, Equitable Relief, and Public Policy* (Chicago: University of Chicago Press, 1982).

22. A useful summary of the problems involved in statutory interpretation is found in Cass Sunstein, *After the Rights Revolution* (Cambridge, MA: Harvard University Press, 1990), chap. 4. For quite different approaches to solving these problems, see Antonin Scalia, *A Matter of Interpretation: Federal Courts and the Law* (Princeton, NJ: Princeton University Press, 1997), and William N. Eskridge Jr., *Dynamic Statutory Interpretation* (Cambridge: Harvard University Press, 1994).

23. Donald L. Horowitz, *The Courts and Social Policy* (Washington, DC: Brookings, 1977), p. 13.

24. Felix Frankfurter, "Some Reflections on the Reading of Statutes," *Record of the Association of the Bar of the City of New York* 2 (1947), reprinted in Walter F. Murphy, C. Herman Pritchett, and Lee Epstein, *Courts, Judges, and Politics*, 5th ed. (New York: McGraw-Hill, 2001), p.489.

25. Quotation attributed to the director of the House legislative counsel's office, quoted in Sol M. Linowitz with Martin Mayer, *The Betrayed Profession: Lawyering at the End of the Twentieth Century* (New York: Charles Scribner's Sons, 1994), p. 224.

26. Important cases spawned by this failure to define discrimination include: *Griggs v. Duke Power Co.*, 401 U.S. 424 (1970); *United Steelworkers of America v. Weber*, 443 U.S. 193 (1979); and *Wards Cove Packing Co. v. Atonio*, 490 U.S. 642 (1989). Congress ultimately overruled *Wards Cove*, together with several other rulings, in the Civil Rights Act of 1991.

27. 322 U.S. 369 (1944).

28. 18 U.S.C.A. sec. 398.

29. *Diamond v. Chakrabarty*, 447 U.S. 303 (1980).

30. Ibid., at 317.

31. *Goldstein v. California*, 412 U.S. 546 (1973).

32. *Food and Drug Administration v. Brown & Williamson Tobacco Corp.*, 529 U.S. 120 (2000). For an overview of litigation against the tobacco industry, see Martha A. Derthick, *Up in Smoke: From Legislation to Litigation in Tobacco Politics* (Washington, D.C.: CQ Press, 2002).

33. *Allen v. Wright*, 468 U.S. 737 (1984).

34. According to sec. 102 (2)(C) of the Act, the environmental impact statement must address (1) the environmental impact of the act; (2) any adverse environmental effects that cannot be avoided should the proposal be implemented; (3) alternatives to the proposed action; (4) the relation between local short-term uses of man's environment and the maintenance of long-term productivity; and (5) any irreversible and irretrievable commitments of resources that would be involved in the proposed action should it be implemented.

35. See, e.g., *Environmental Defense Fund, Inc. v. Corps of Engineers*, 470 F.2d 289 (8th Cir. 1973). For a more general perspective, see Martin Shapiro, *Who Guards the Guardians? Judicial Control of Administration* (Athens: University of Georgia Press, 1988), especially chap. 3.

36. See generally, G. Alan Tarr and Mary Cornelia Porter, "Gender Equality and Judicial Federalism: The Role of State Appellate Courts," *Hastings Constitutional Law Quarterly* 9 (summer 1982): 942–950.

37. Ibid., pp. 963–969, table E.

38. *Tuter v. Tuter,* 120 S.W.2d 203, 205 (Mo. Ct. App. 1938).

39. In part, this reflects and further promotes the support for judicial activism within the academic and legal communities. For a summary of the arguments for judicial activism, see Christopher Wolfe, *Judicial Activism: Bulwark of Freedom or Precarious Security* (Pacific Grove, CA: Brooks/Cole Publishing, 1991).

40. This phenomenon is not limited to the United States—see Charles R. Epps, *The Rights Revolution: Lawyers, Activists, and Supreme Courts in Comparative Perspective* (Chicago: University of Chicago Press, 1998).

41. See Rich Jones, "The State Legislatures," *Book of the States, 1992–93* (Lexington, KY: Council of State Governments, 1992), pp. 128–129.

42. For the history of the creation of such agencies, see James Q. Wilson, "The Rise of the Bureaucratic State," *The Public Interest* 41 (fall 1975): 77–103, and Richard Harris and Sidney Milkis, *The Politics of Regulatory Change: A Tale of Two Agencies,* 2d ed. (New York: Oxford University Press, 1996).

43. George C. Greanias and Duane Windsor, "Is Judicial Restraint Possible in an Administrative Society?" *Judicature* 64 (April 1981): 402, and Kerwin, *Rulemaking,* p. 24.

44. For a listing of federal and state statutes declared unconstitutional by the U.S. Supreme Court, see the Constitution of the United States of America: Analysis and Interpretation at www.gpoaccess.gov/constitution.

45. *Brown v. Board of Education* [*Brown* II], 349 U.S. 294 (1955). For a detailed analysis of remedial policymaking, see Malcolm M. Feeley and Edward L. Rubin, *Judicial Policy Making and the Modern State: How the Courts Reformed America's Prisons* (New York: Cambridge University Press, 1998).

46. On the changing character of federal legislation, see Theodore J. Lowi and Benjamin Ginsberg, *American Government: Freedom and Power* (New York: W. W. Norton, 1990), p. 70, table 3.1.

47. Wilson, "The Rise of the Bureaucratic State."

48. William E. Nelson, *Americanization of the Common Law* (Cambridge, MA: Harvard University Press, 1975).

49. Morton J. Horwitz, *The Transformation of American Law, 1780–1860* (Cambridge, MA: Harvard University Press, 1977).

50. For an overview of changes in the Supreme Court's agenda over time, see O'Brien, *Storm Center,* pp. 225–234.

51. Robert A. Kagan, Bliss Cartwright, Lawrence M. Friedman, and Stanton Wheeler, "The Business of State Supreme Courts, 1870–1970," *Stanford Law Review* 30 (November 1977): 155.

52. Lawrence Baum, Sheldon Goldman, and Austin Sarat, "The Evolution of Litigation in the Federal Courts of Appeals, 1895–1975," *Law and Society Review* 16 (1981–82): 291–309.

53. This account relies on G. Alan Tarr and Russell S. Harrison, "Legitimacy and Capacity in State Supreme Court Policymaking: The New Jersey Court and Exclusionary Zoning," *Rutgers Law Journal* 15 (spring 1984): 542–547.

54. Horowitz, *The Courts and Social Policy.*

55. See Ralph Cavanagh and Austin Sarat, "Thinking about Courts: Toward and Beyond a Jurisprudence of Judicial Competence," *Law and Society Review* 14 (winter 1980): 371–420, and Stephen L. Wasby, "Arrogation of Power or Accountability: Judicial Imperialism Revisited," *Judicature* 65 (October 1981): 208–219.

56. See, e.g., Michael J. Perry, *The Constitution, the Courts, and Human Rights* (New York: Yale University Press, 1982); and Arthur S. Miller, "In Defense of Judicial Activism," in *Supreme Court Activism and Restraint*, eds. Stephen C. Halpern and Charles M. Lamb (Lexington, MA: Lexington Books, 1982).

57. See, e.g., Perry, *The Constitution, the Courts, and Human Rights;* Ronald Dworkin, *Taking Rights Seriously* (Cambridge, MA: Harvard University Press, 1977); and John Hart Ely, *Democracy and Distrust: A Theory of Judicial Review* (Cambridge, MA: Harvard University Press, 1980).

58. Bradley C. Canon, "A Framework for the Analysis of Judicial Activism," in Halpern and Lamb, *Supreme Court Activism and Restraint.*

59. *National Labor Relations Board v. Jones and Laughlin Steel Corporation,* 301 U.S. 1 (1937), overturning such rulings as *United States v. E. C. Knight Company,* 156 U.S. 1 (1895) and *Carter v. Carter Coal Company,* 298 U.S. 298 (1936).

60. *Brown v. Board of Education,* 347 U.S. 483 (1954), overturning *Plessy v. Ferguson,* 163 U.S. 537 (1896).

FEDERAL COURT POLICYMAKING

This chapter focuses on two controversial issues confronted by federal courts during the last half of the twentieth century: school desegregation and abortion. Certainly, no account of federal court policymaking can pretend to be comprehensive, given the variety of policy issues that federal courts address. But the rulings on school desegregation and abortion, as well as the reactions to them, illustrate crucial features of federal court policymaking. The chapter considers (1) the process by which these policy issues were transformed into legal disputes and brought before the courts for resolution, (2) how federal court policy on these issues has developed, (3) the interplay between judicial rulings and the political process, and (4) how effective the federal courts have been in achieving their policy objectives.

SCHOOL DESEGREGATION

Brown v. Board of Education is one of the most celebrated rulings ever announced by the U.S. Supreme Court.[1] Before *Brown,* the Supreme Court's record on racial injustice was best exemplified by the infamous Dred Scott case and by *Plessy v. Ferguson* (1896), in which the Court upheld racial segregation under the doctrine of "separate but equal."[2] In *Brown,* the Court repudiated its dismal past and enshrined racial equality as a fundamental constitutional principle. Proclamation of this principle, however, did not dispel disagreement about its meaning or ensure its acceptance. This section examines the Supreme Court's constitutional policymaking on school desegregation and the remedial policymaking of lower federal courts charged with implementing *Brown.* Table 10-1 provides a chronology of the Supreme Court's most important desegregation rulings.

TABLE 10-1   MAJOR SUPREME COURT RULINGS ON SCHOOL DESEGREGATION

Case	Ruling
Brown v. Board of Education [*Brown* I] (1954)	Declared that state-mandated racial segregation in public schools violated the Equal Protection Clause.
Brown v. Board of Education [*Brown* II] (1955)	Required local school districts to dismantle their dual school systems with "all deliberate speed."
Green v. County School Board of New Kent County (1968)	Required local school districts to devise school desegregation plans that would *immediately* promote integration.
Swann v. Charlotte-Mecklenburg Board of Education (1970)	Upheld a variety of remedies—including busing, school pairing and redrawing attendance zones—as means to promote school desegregation.
Keyes v. School District No. 1, Denver, Colorado (1973)	Held that the use of racial considerations in drawing attendance boundaries, assigning teachers, and locating new school violated *Brown* and justified imposition of a desegregation plan.
Milliken v. Bradley [*Milliken* I] (1974)	Ruled that lower courts could not order interdistrict busing without evidence that suburban districts had acted to promote racial segregation in schools.
Milliken v. Bradley [*Milliken* II]	Ruled that a district court could order a state to pay for educational programs to repair the educational harms inflicted by segregation in a district whose racial composition precluded substantial desegregation.
Oklahoma City v. Dowell (1991)	Ruled that once a school district complied with a court imposed desegregation decree and eliminated vestiges of past discrimination, it had dismantled its dual school system and was no longer obliged to maintain mandatory busing and racial balance plans.
Missouri v. Jenkins (1995)	Ruled that *Milliken* II remedies should be limited in time and extent and defined restoration of local control as a primary goal in desegregation cases.

The Road to Brown

Brown represented the culmination of a litigation campaign designed to overturn the system of racial segregation endorsed in *Plessy v. Ferguson.*[3] The Legal Defense Fund of the National Association for the Advancement of Colored People (NAACP) spearheaded the fight against segregation under the direction of Charles Houston and later Thurgood Marshall. During the early 1930s, when the NAACP began its campaign, *Plessy* was firmly established, precluding a frontal assault on the "separate but equal" doctrine. But Houston believed that a long-term strategy of undermining segregation could succeed. The Legal Defense Fund began by bringing before the courts particularly egregious denials of equality—not only to combat particular injustices but also to mobilize support for the NAACP's fight for racial equality and to inform the judiciary about the evils of segregation.

Public education was particular concern. The Southern states had eagerly accepted *Plessy*'s invitation to institute racial separation, requiring white and black students to attend separate schools, but then had ignored *Plessy*'s requirement of equality.[4] In the 1920s, for example, Georgia spent eight times as much on white students as it did on African American students, and Mississippi five times as much.[5] The Legal Defense Fund enjoyed particular success in challenging segregation in graduate and professional schools. Because fewer students were involved, challenges to segregation at the graduate level aroused less controversy. More important, denials of equality at that level were easier to document. Because all states operated elementary and secondary schools for African Americans, a successful constitutional challenge required a detailed demonstration of inequalities between the white and black schools. In contrast, many states did not offer graduate programs for African American students, and thus, their refusal to admit qualified black applicants to existing programs violated the requirement of equality. During the two decades before *Brown*, the U.S. Supreme Court upheld several of the Legal Defense Fund's challenges to educational inequalities in graduate and professional schools.[6] These victories paved the way for the direct attack on racial segregation in *Brown*.

In retrospect, the series of cases leading to *Brown* resemble a carefully plotted campaign, with central direction of the course and pace of litigation.[7] Indeed, many other groups—for example, women's groups and environmental groups—have looked to these cases for a model of how to pursue policy ends through the courts.[8] In actuality, however, the Legal Defense Fund's campaign was less systematic than hindsight may suggest. Although the aim of eliminating racial subordination did not change, the Legal Defense Fund litigated cases in a variety of fields, often attacking targets of opportunity rather than following a long-term plan. As favorable precedents accumulated in school cases, the Legal Defense Fund did decide to concentrate more attention on school desegregation. Mark Tushnet has observed that "[i]f the military metaphor referring to a litigation campaign is helpful, the campaign was conducted on a terrain that repeatedly required changes in maneuvers."[9]

Brown *I and* Brown *II*

In 1952, the Supreme Court granted certiorari to consider a direct challenge to racial segregation in the public schools of Topeka, Kansas. Similar cases from Delaware, South Carolina, and Virginia were consolidated with *Brown* on appeal.[10] The Court also heard argument in a fifth case, *Bolling v. Sharpe*, which dealt with segregation in the public schools in Washington, D.C.[11] The appointment of a new chief justice, the reargument of the cases before the reconstituted Court, and intra-court negotiations to secure unanimity among the justices all delayed a decision in the cases.[12] Finally, on May 17, 1954, the Court announced its rulings. Speaking for the Court, Chief Justice Earl Warren found that African American children were psychologically injured by being forced to attend separate schools. He therefore concluded that "in the field of education the doctrine of 'separate but equal' has no place."[13]

The Court in *Brown* offered two somewhat incompatible explanations for its claim of psychological harm. On the one hand, it suggested that the harm to African American students came from state-enforced segregation, which communicated a message of black inferiority; thus, replacing racial criteria with color-blind criteria for school attendance would suffice to remedy the injury. On the other hand, the Court also argued that African American students were injured by lack of contact with their white peers. From this perspective, eliminating racial criteria would not suffice; rather, racial integration of the schools was necessary because only integrated education could be equal education.[14]

The Court did not resolve this ambiguity in *Brown* I, as the decision came to be called, because it postponed consideration of how to implement its ruling until its next term. The justices recognized that, given the "wide applicability" of its ruling and the "great variety of local conditions," implementation would be no easy task. At the time of the ruling, seventeen Southern and border states, plus the District of Columbia, mandated racial segregation in their elementary and secondary schools. Four other states—Arizona, Kansas, New Mexico, and Wyoming—permitted segregation by local option. Altogether, more than 70 percent of African American children in the United States attended schools in these twenty-one states and the District of Columbia.[15]

In *Brown* II, the Court conducted more than thirteen hours of oral argument, permitting all interested parties to state their views on how to dismantle the system of segregated education. Arguing for the NAACP, Thurgood Marshall pressed for an immediate start to desegregation. In contrast, counsel for the Southern states, seeking "a gradualism with infinity as the deadline," warned of dire consequences if the Court required immediate desegregation.[16]

On its face, the Court's decree in *Brown* II seems to have sided with the NAACP. The justices reaffirmed their commitment to *Brown* I and insisted that "the vitality of these constitutional principles cannot be allowed to yield simply because of disagreement with them."[17] They imposed on local school districts the responsibility for solving problems associated with the implementation of *Brown* and admitting students on a nondiscriminatory basis "with all deliberate speed." Finally, the Court authorized federal district courts to oversee the process of desegregation and to use their equity powers to ensure compliance if local officials deviated from the mandate of *Brown*.

Nevertheless, *Brown* II posed problems. The Court failed to clarify whether *Brown* required racial integration of previously segregated schools or merely the assignment of children to schools on a nonracial basis. Equally important, the Court's ruling could be read as permitting, even condoning, delay. By exaggerating the administrative problems that might be encountered in desegregation, *Brown* II seemed to be telling Southern school districts that they could delay desegregation. The absence of deadlines for starting or completing desegregation, as well as the language of "all deliberate speed," conveyed the same message. Indeed, *Brown* II seemed to encourage proponents of segregation to create local problems to justify delay. Small wonder, then, that Southern officials were elated. A Southern attorney explained: "We couldn't ask for anything better than to have our local, native Mississippi district judges consider [the integration problem]. . . . Our local judges know the local situation, and it may be 100 years before it's feasible."[18] NAACP officials, meanwhile, considered *Brown* II "a great mistake."[19]

The Response to Brown, *1954–1964*

For the most part, desegregation proceeded without excessive controversy or resistance in the Northern and border states. Districts that had maintained dual school systems complied in good faith with *Brown's* requirements.[20] Topeka, Kansas, for example, the city that produced the *Brown* case, introduced a desegregation plan in 1955, assigning all students to their neighborhood schools.[21] The school board of Washington, D.C., prepared a desegregation plan even before *Bolling v. Sharpe* was decided and adopted the plan only eight days after the decision.[22] By 1961, more than half the black students in the border states were attending school with whites, and this proportion increased in succeeding years.[23] In sum, *Brown* succeeded in eliminating dual school systems in those Northern and border states that had required or permitted them.

The South was another story. In some areas efforts to implement *Brown* met with defiance. In Little Rock, Arkansas, Governor Orval Faubus deliberately provoked a violent confrontation over the desegregation of Central High School. Only after President Dwight Eisenhower dispatched federal troops to protect the black students who were to attend Central from hostile mobs—and after the Supreme Court sternly denied the school board's request to postpone desegregation—did a fragile peace return.[24] The Virginia legislature empowered the governor to seize and close any school threatened with racial integration and forbade the use of state funds for any integrated schools. In fact, the public schools in Prince Edward County, Virginia, closed for four years, while white students attended "private" schools supported by tuition grants from the state. Eventually, the Supreme Court halted the charade and authorized the district court to reopen the public schools on a desegregated basis and require funding for them.[25] Meanwhile, several Southern states launched campaigns of legal harassment against the NAACP and other civil rights organizations. These efforts, along with the violence and intimidation practiced by the Ku Klux Klan and the White Citizens' Councils, put advocates of desegregation on the defensive. Despite the rigid segregation in Mississippi, for instance, no desegregation suits were filed in the state until 1961.[26] As Richard Kluger put it, an "exorcism is seldom a pretty spectacle."[27]

Not all Southern resistance was overtly illegal. Opponents of *Brown* appealed to public opinion, seeking to inflame hostility toward the Supreme Court and desegregation. The most influential of these appeals was the "Southern Manifesto," which denounced *Brown* as an abuse of judicial authority and pledged to overturn it "by all lawful means." More than 100 Southern senators and representatives signed the manifesto. School boards masked their intransigence in inaction, offering ingenious justifications for delay instead of desegregation plans. State legislatures meanwhile enacted laws designed to fortify segregation and discourage desegregation. A Louisiana law, for example, denied promotion or graduation to any student of a desegregated school, and a Georgia law deprived police officers of their retirement and disability benefits if they failed to enforce the state's segregation laws. From 1954 to 1957 alone, Southern states enacted more than 130 new laws and constitutional amendments designed to preserve segregation.[28] Commentators wryly noted that in Southern school desegregation there was far more deliberation than speed.

Faced with obstructionism by Southern political officials, civil rights groups sought relief from the federal district courts. However, these courts often could not—or did not—help. Some Southern district court judges, reflecting the political milieu in which they served, sought to contain rather than enforce *Brown*. Thus, Judge Davidson, whose rulings in a Dallas desegregation case were reversed six times, lamented that the "white man has a right to maintain his racial integrity, and it can't be done so easily in integrated schools."[29] Even those judges committed to upholding *Brown* found it difficult to know what to do. The Supreme Court's mandate in *Brown* II was ambiguous at best, yet the Court refused to hear cases in which it might clarify its position. In the absence of guidance from the Court, some federal judges used their discretion to narrow the effect of *Brown*, maintaining that it merely required the use of race-neutral criteria for assigning pupils.[30] Thus, school districts met their constitutional obligations even if their schools remained almost completely segregated. Other judges were "content with [desegregation at] the pace of an extraordinarily arthritic snail."[31] Those judges who recognized that *Brown* required real desegregation often found themselves stymied by ingenious efforts to preserve racial separation. They would no sooner invalidate one law as inconsistent with *Brown* than the state legislature would pass another, mirroring the Southern saying, "as long as we can legislate, we can segregate."[32]

Figure 10-1 dramatically illustrates the failure of school desegregation in the South in the decade following *Brown*. As late as 1963, less than 1 percent of black students in the South were attending school with white children. Even in localities where the Supreme Court had intervened directly, the results were

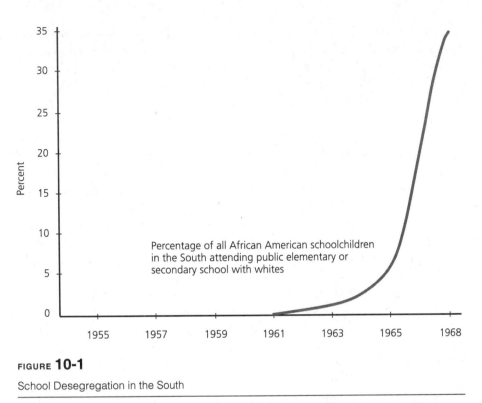

FIGURE **10-1**

School Desegregation in the South

Source: Gerald Rosenberg, *The Hollow Hope: Can Courts Bring about Social Change?* (Chicago: University of Chicago Press, 1991), p. 179, fig. 6.1. Copyright © 1991 by The University of Chicago Press. Reprinted with permission.

discouraging. For example, in 1963, only 69 of the 7,700 students at the supposedly desegregated, "formerly" white junior and senior high schools in Little Rock were black.[33] In the South, at least, *Brown's* tenth anniversary offered no cause for celebration.[34]

School Desegregation, 1964–1971

While Figure 10-1 reveals that school segregation continued in the South through 1964, it also documents a dramatic shift in attendance patterns in the second decade after *Brown*. In 1964, only 1.2 percent of African American students in the South attended school with whites; by 1973, 91.3 percent did. What accounts for this remarkable shift? First, after 1964, Congress and the federal executive branch joined with the Court in promoting school desegregation. Second, the Supreme Court forcefully intervened, clarifying what constituted a violation of *Brown* and what measures lower courts might impose to remedy violations.

Congress's enactment of the Civil Rights Act of 1964 "represented a gathering and coalescence of the [national] will on the whole question of Southern school segregation."[35] Title II of the Act authorized the Department of Justice to sue "for the orderly achievement of desegregation in public education." This relieved the NAACP of much of the burden and expense of litigating desegregation and effectively undercut the Southern strategy of deterring desegregation suits by attacking civil rights organizations. Title VI of the Act prohibited the dispersal of federal funds to units of government, including school districts, that practiced racial discrimination. This provision became important with the passage of the Elementary and Secondary Education Act (ESEA) in 1965. ESEA established a program of federal financial aid to school districts, and, given the poverty in many Southern states, their districts stood to benefit from the aid program. However, if a school district refused to desegregate, its federal funds could be cut off. Thus, if the Civil Rights Act proffered the stick of federal enforcement, ESEA offered the carrot of federal inducements. By 1969, federal funds made up between 11 and 21 percent of state budgets for public schools in the Southern states.[36] Southern school districts, therefore, could no longer afford to defy court orders to desegregate without jeopardizing the flow of federal dollars on which they had become dependent. One expert concludes: "the change [in Southern resistance to desegregation] would have been impossible without the lure of money from the Elementary and Secondary Education Act."[37]

In 1968, the Supreme Court also clarified what compliance with *Brown* entailed. The Court's way was prepared by rulings of the Fifth Circuit Court of Appeals and by guidelines developed by the Department of Health, Education, and Welfare (HEW) to implement the Civil Rights Act of 1964. In a series of cases in the mid-1960s, Judge John Minor Wisdom argued that compliance with *Brown* entailed more than the elimination of racial criteria in assigning students. States had not only to cease segregating but also to start integrating their schools.[38] The HEW guidelines sounded a similar theme, measuring desegregation by the number of blacks and whites in school together. In *Green v. County School Board* (1968), the Supreme Court endorsed this understanding of *Brown* by invalidating a "freedom-of-choice" plan under which students could choose which school they would attend.[39] This "freedom" was illusory, the Court held, because pressure might be applied to discourage black students from selecting the white school. More important, the Court rejected "freedom-of-choice" because it failed to produce meaningful integration. Implicit in this ruling were two assumptions. First, without state segregation laws, racial integration would have occurred; second, the responsibility of previously segregated school systems was to achieve the level of integration that would have existed in the absence of segregation. By portraying *Brown* as requiring racial integration, the Court ensured that racial balance would thereafter be a crucial element in its decisions.

The Court's new forcefulness can also be seen in the measures it endorsed for remedying violations of *Brown*. In *Green,* the Court bluntly stated that the time for "deliberate speed" had passed, that desegregation must be immediate.[40] In *Swann v. Charlotte-Mecklenburg Board of Education* (1971), the Court specifically endorsed a variety of remedial measures that some district court judges had used to promote desegregation.[41] Among these were the alteration of student attendance zones and the busing of students to achieve integration. Although the Court cautioned that busing could not "risk the health of the children or significantly impinge on the educational process," the main effect of *Swann* was to fortify district court judges in their aggressive efforts "to eliminate from the public schools all vestiges of state-imposed segregation."[42] The effects of the efforts of Congress and the Court were apparent almost immediately: by 1972, public schools in the South and border states were the least segregated in the country.

The Courts and School Desegregation, 1971–2004

The Changing Context of School Desegregation   During the late 1960s and the 1970s, school desegregation litigation entered a new phase. Plaintiffs expanded the scope of desegregation efforts, challenging racial segregation in Northern urban districts as well as in the South. The decision to confront Northern school segregation seemed logical. With the massive emigration of African Americans from the South in the decades after World War II, a large and increasing percentage of black schoolchildren lived in Northern urban areas, and many of these children found themselves in single-race schools.

Several factors complicated desegregation litigation in the North. Southern school districts had forthrightly maintained segregated systems, but most Northern cities never expressly mandated separate schools for blacks and whites. Because *Brown* outlawed only *intentional* school segregation, the mere fact of segregated schools did not violate the Constitution. Proving constitutional violations therefore was more difficult than it had been in Southern school cases. Some Northern districts did pursue blatantly policies. In Dayton, Ohio, for example, African American teachers were forbidden to teach white students.[43] In most cases, however, Northern school officials had contrived to promote racial segregation through a series of undramatic and—on their face—race-neutral policy choices. In Denver, for example, the school board gerrymandered school attendance zones to maintain racially homogeneous schools and set up mobile classrooms at black schools rather than transfer the overflow of students to underutilized white schools.[44] In Boston, the school board established feeder patterns that ensured that students from white elementary schools would attend white middle schools and constructed new schools with sizes and locations designed to maintain racial separation.[45] Plaintiffs in Northern desegregation suits had to prove that such actions, which on their face were racially neutral, were intended to promote segregation rather than serve other valid purposes and therefore violated the mandate of *Brown*.

Even if they could prove intentional segregation, plaintiffs—and the courts providing relief—faced a further hurdle. To a considerable extent, patterns of racial segregation in Northern schools mirrored long-standing residential segregation. This complicated efforts to prove that school segregation resulted from official discrimination rather than from private housing choices. Even if official discrimination contributed to school segregation, it was difficult to define its precise effect. Because *Brown* only permitted district judges to eliminate the effects of intentional segregation, the scope of the district court's remedy had to coincide with the scope of the constitutional violation.

Designing an effective remedy for segregation was also problematic. Given the degree of residential segregation in Northern cities, judges could not achieve substantial integration merely by assigning students to their neighborhood schools. Even busing students to other schools within a school district might not produce substantial integration. School districts in Northern cities did not encompass the entire metropolitan area. Rather, suburban school districts, whose student population was primarily white, typically ringed urban school districts whose student population was heavily nonwhite. This configuration posed an obstacle to meaningful integration. It also ensured a ready "escape" for families reluctant to send their children to predominantly nonwhite schools. If enough families exited the school district, that too could frustrate judicial efforts to achieve desegregation.

Judicial Rulings and Popular Responses   At the outset of the 1970s, the Supreme Court adopted an aggressive approach to school desegregation. In *Swann* it upheld a federal district court's desegregation plan that ordered busing for more than 13,000 students.[46] While denying that the Constitution required "any particular degree of racial balance and mixing," the Court endorsed reliance on the racial composition of the whole school district in determining the scope of constitutional violations.[47] The decision rescued plaintiffs from the task of proving the effect of discriminatory policies. The Court simply assumed that in the absence of state-imposed segregation, the proportion of black and white students in specific schools would generally coincide with their distribution in the school district as a whole.

In its first Northern desegregation case, *Keyes v. School District No. 1, Denver, Colorado* (1973), the Court upheld the federal district court's finding that the school board's various efforts to maintain racially homogeneous schools violated *Brown*.[48] The Court also eased the burden of proof on plaintiffs who sought to prove intentional segregation. If the plaintiff could prove intentional segregation in one part of the school system, the justices held, then the burden of proof shifted to the school board to show that segregation in other parts of the school system did not result from official action. Because proving this was virtually impossible, *Keyes* in effect permitted districtwide desegregation remedies, including busing, based on violations occurring in only one part of the district.

The public response to this sort of aggressive judicial intervention was overwhelmingly negative. Congress cut off federal funds for busing in 1972 and in 1978 forbade HEW to terminate federal funds to school districts when compliance with desegregation would require busing. More than 200 members of Congress supported a constitutional amendment to outlaw busing for racial balance.[49] In some Northern communities, the response recalled the violence in Little Rock. In Pontiac, Michigan, arsonists firebombed ten school buses, and at South Boston High, after a white student was stabbed, an angry mob trapped 135 black students in the school for four hours, until a police decoy operation extricated them.[50] In many cities, court-ordered busing prompted "white flight" to private schools or to the suburbs. In Memphis, Tennessee, 35 percent of white students left the public school system during the first year of busing, and in New Castle County, Delaware, white enrollment following busing declined 50 percent.[51] Instead of promoting racial integration, busing in these communities accelerated the transition to a virtually all-black school system.

In the face of such widespread opposition, the Supreme Court retreated. In *Milliken v. Bradley* [*Milliken* I] (1974), the Court curtailed the power of district court judges to remedy segregation.[52] The judge in *Milliken* had ordered busing between Detroit and surrounding suburban school districts to relieve segregation in the city's schools. By a 5–4 vote, the Court reversed the lower court, holding that because the suburban districts had not participated in the segregation of the Detroit schools, they were not obliged to participate in efforts to desegregate them. By prohibiting interdistrict busing except when suburban districts had connived to segregate inner-city schools, the Court effectively undercut efforts to integrate Northern urban school districts. In the wake of *Milliken* I, some district courts turned from reassigning students to mandating programs of educational improvements as the remedy for constitutional violations. However, the Supreme Court indicated in *Missouri v. Jenkins* [*Jenkins* III] (1995) that there were limits to the fiscal burdens that judges could impose on school districts and that the remedial programs they devised had to be tied to undoing the effects of unlawful segregation.[53]

Dayton Board of Education v. Brinkman [*Dayton* I] (1977) increased the plaintiffs' burden of proof in desegregation cases and further curtailed the remedial powers of lower court judges.[54] No longer, the Court held, would discrimination in one part of a school district create a presumption of systemwide discrimination as it had in *Keyes*. Instead, the Court held that "isolated" violations did not justify systemwide desegregation plans. The justices cautioned that judicial remedies must not go beyond redressing the "incremental segregative effect" of the district's constitutional violations.[55]

Finally, in *Pasadena Board of Education v. Spangler* (1976) and *Freeman v. Pitts* (1992), the Court suggested that the time for judicial supervision of school desegregation was coming to a close.[56] The Court held that once a school district had met its duty to desegregate, school authorities did not have to continue to adjust attendance zones to promote integration. Even if shifts in the district's population promoted the resegregation of schools, the mandate of *Brown* was to eliminate the effects of intentional segregation, not to guarantee integrated schools. Between 1980 and 2000, twenty-five large urban districts, North and South, were judged to have complied with desegregation decrees and remedied the effects of past discrimination and were thus released from federal judicial supervision.

The Legacy of Brown

As noted, in 1954, twenty-one states and the District of Columbia, enrolling more than 70 percent of African American students in the United States, either required racial segregation in their schools or permitted it by local option. *Brown* succeeded in desegregating public schools in Northern and border states that had maintained dual school systems, but a decade after *Brown* 99 percent of African American students in the South still attended segregated schools. Congressional intervention prompted the desegregation of Southern schools in the late 1960s and early 1970s, so that by 1972, 91 percent of African American students in the South were attending integrated schools.[57]

In the late 1960s, plaintiffs began to file suits designed to promote racial integration in education nationwide. As a result, by 1991, more than half of all public-school students were attending school in districts that had formal desegregation plans.[58] Nevertheless, because of changing demographics, white flight, and the Supreme Court's rejection of interdistrict busing, these efforts did not result in a significant decline in racial segregation.[59] Demographic shifts effectively resegregated school districts in several urban areas, leading many civil rights advocates to shift their emphasis from racial integration to improving the quality of education for African American students.[60] By 2004, the percentage of black schoolchildren attending majority white public schools was lower than at anytime since 1968. Although one hesitates to call the Court's intervention a failure, it is clear that *Brown* and succeeding cases did not guarantee racial integration in public education.

ABORTION

More than the normal contingent of reporters was on hand for the final day of the Supreme Court's 1991–1992 term. A large crowd of demonstrators and spectators had also gathered outside the Supreme Court, anticipating—or dreading—the

TABLE
10-2 **MAJOR SUPREME COURT RULINGS ON ABORTION**

Case	Holding
Roe v. Wade; Doe v. Bolton (1972)	Recognized a woman's constitutional right to terminate her pregnancy, struck down state laws restricting abortion, and established a framework for determining the validity of state regulations of abortion.
Planned Parenthood of Central Missouri v. Danforth (1976)	Struck down state requirements of spousal and, for minors, parental consent for abortions; invalidated various regulations of medical procedures for abortion.
Harris v. McRae (1980)	Upheld congressional legislation banning the use of federal Medicaid funds for abortions, unless abortion was necessary to preserve the life of the mother or in cases of rape or incest.
Akron v. Akron Center for Reproductive Health (1983)	Invalidated a requirement that abortions after the first trimester be performed in a hospital; reaffirmed the Court's ruling in Roe.
Webster v. Reproductive Health Services (1989)	Upheld a prohibition on abortions by state employees or in state facilities, except to save the life of the mother, and a requirement of viability tests for fetuses more than 20 weeks old.
Planned Parenthood of of Southeastern Pennsylvania v. Casey (1992)	Reaffirmed the abortion right announced in Roe; upheld requirements that certain information be furnished to women 24 hours before an abortion, that minors obtain parental consent for an (1992) abortion (with the possibility of judicial approval as an alternative), and that medical facilities performing abortions file medical information with the state; invalidated a spousal notification requirement.
Stenberg v. Carhart (2000)	Struck down a state law banning "partial birth" abortion unless necessary to save the life of the mother.

Court's ruling in *Planned Parenthood of Southeastern Pennsylvania v. Casey*.[61] At issue in *Casey* was the constitutionality of a Pennsylvania law that restricted the availability of abortion by imposing various requirements on women who were seeking abortions and on the facilities providing them (see Table 10-2). Many Court watchers believed that those restrictions interfered with the right of women to terminate their pregnancies, a right that the Court had recognized twenty years earlier in *Roe v. Wade*.[62] They thus expected that *Casey* would provide the vehicle for the Court to overrule *Roe*.

The Court's decision in *Casey*, however, defied expectations, pleasing neither pro-life nor pro-choice groups. On the one hand, the Court apparently circumscribed the constitutional right announced in *Roe*, with a coalition of five justices upholding all the provisions of the Pennsylvania statute except the requirement that a woman notify her spouse before obtaining an abortion. On the other hand, a different coalition of five justices expressly reaffirmed *Roe* and the abortion right recognized in that case. What was clear was that the justices were bitterly divided on the abortion issue. Four justices—Rehnquist, Scalia, Thomas, and White—insisted that the Pennsylvania statute was constitutional and that *Roe* should be overruled. Two justices—Blackmun and Stevens—maintained that *Roe* should be affirmed and the Pennsylvania law struck down in its entirety. The three remaining justices—O'Connor, Kennedy, and Souter—cast the decisive votes in the case. While upholding most provisions of the Pennsylvania law, they refused—largely on the basis of *stare decisis*—to repudiate *Roe*. Although Justice Scalia and Chief Justice Rehnquist attacked the three justices' interpretation of history and *stare decisis* in scathing terms, *Casey* confirmed that *Roe* would remain part of American law for the foreseeable future.[63]

 Casey was hardly the first major confrontation over abortion on the Supreme Court. Abortion had stirred controversy ever since it emerged as a legal issue in the 1960s. Let us look more closely at the emergence of abortion as an issue and at judicial decisions dealing with it.

Abortion Becomes a Legal Issue

Like most important policy issues that make their way to the Supreme Court, abortion did not emerge as a constitutional issue by happenstance or through the dogged efforts of a single person. Although there was never a fully orchestrated plan to test the constitutionality of restrictions on abortion, a loose network of groups committed to liberalizing state abortion laws had formed in the decade before *Roe*. Thus, *Roe v. Wade*, like *Brown v. Board of Education*, is best understood as the culmination of a broader campaign to promote legal change.[64]

 In the early 1960s, the laws in most states permitted abortion only in limited circumstances, such as to save the life of the mother. These laws, which dated from the late nineteenth century, effectively restricted legal abortions—only 8,000 were performed nationwide in 1966. However, the laws did not eliminate abortions—the same year, an estimated 1 million illegal abortions were performed.[65]

 Beginning in the 1950s, support for state restrictions on abortion began to erode. Physicians at medical conferences questioned the restrictions as an infringement on their exercise of medical judgment. Of even greater significance was the publication in 1962 of a model penal law by the American Law Institute (ALI) that permitted abortion when pregnancy was the result of rape or incest, when its continuation threatened the physical or mental health of the mother, or when there was a risk of birth defects. During the early 1960s, reports about the fertility drug Thalidomide and an outbreak of German measles, both of which caused birth defects, brought the issue of abortion before the general public. When the California State Board of Medical Examiners brought disciplinary charges against two prominent physicians who had

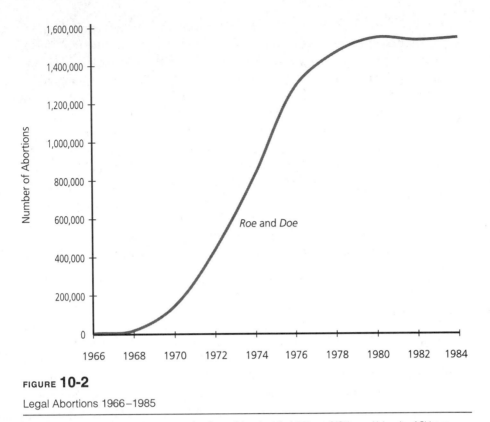

FIGURE 10-2

Legal Abortions 1966–1985

Source: Gerald Rosenberg, *The Hollow Hope: Can Courts Bring about Social Change?* (Chicago: University of Chicago Press, 1991), p. 179, table 6.1. Copyright © 1991 by The University of Chicago Press. Reprinted with permission.

performed abortions on women with German measles, the state's medical profession rallied behind the doctors and urged the California legislature to liberalize the state's abortion law.

As abortion became a more salient issue and as opinion on abortion shifted, groups such as the National Association for Repeal of Abortion Laws (NARAL) formed to campaign for more permissive abortion policies. In the seven years before *Roe* (1966–1972), these groups enjoyed considerable success. Fourteen states enacted more liberal abortion laws, generally modeled on the ALI guidelines, and four states—Alaska, Hawaii, New York, and Washington—repealed their existing laws, making abortion an unrestricted medical procedure.[66] As Figure 10-2 shows, passage of these laws dramatically increased the number of legal abortions performed in the United States. Nevertheless, because the reform laws still placed restrictions on abortion, large numbers of illegal abortions continued to be performed, even in states that had modified their laws.[67] Abortion advocates concluded that even the ALI-style laws did not ensure adequate access to abortion.

While pursuing legislative reform, abortion advocates also contemplated taking the issue to the courts. The Supreme Court's ruling in *Brown v. Board of Education* had convinced liberal reformers that judicial rulings could inaugurate far-reaching social changes.[68] In addition, judicial resolution of the abortion issue had significant advantages. Whereas legislative reform required a state-by-state effort, a single Supreme Court ruling could establish policy nationwide. Moreover, once the Supreme Court recognized a constitutional right to choose whether to terminate a pregnancy, it would require a constitutional amendment or a shift on the Court to overturn the ruling. Finally, a judicial ruling would provide a firmer foundation for legalized abortion, establishing it as a woman's right rather than merely a matter of physicians' interests or health concerns.

If the potential rewards of litigation were great, so too were the risks. Because a pregnant woman challenging a state abortion law would no longer be pregnant by the time her case reached the Supreme Court, the Court might avoid the issue on technical grounds, much as it had refused to hear an early challenge to Connecticut's ban on the sale and use of contraceptives.[69] Even worse (from the pro-choice perspective), the Court might uphold state abortion laws, dealing the reformers a major setback. Advocates of abortion reform, therefore, faced two problems. First, they had to find an appropriate plaintiff to challenge a state abortion law. (As Box 10-1 indicates, the discovery of "Jane Roe" occurred largely by chance.) Second, they had to develop persuasive arguments for the unconstitutionality of state abortion laws. This was a complicated task because the Constitution does not expressly deal with the right to terminate a pregnancy and the states had for more than a century had laws on the books restricting abortion. Abortion reformers therefore devoted considerable energy to legal research, hoping to influence legal thinking on the abortion issue. The Association for the Study of Abortion, for example, funded the research for an article by law professor Cyril Means on the history of the abortion right. This legal research paid dividends when the Supreme Court cited the article seven times in support of its ruling in *Roe v. Wade*.[70] When the Supreme Court agreed to hear constitutional challenges to the abortion laws in Texas and Georgia, groups within the abortion rights movement worked together to write the legal briefs and prepare the attorneys for oral argument.[71]

Roe v. Wade

In *Roe v. Wade*, the Supreme Court invalidated Texas's traditional abortion statute, and in the companion case of *Doe v. Bolton*, it struck down Georgia's reformed (ALI-style) abortion law.[72] Speaking for a seven-member majority, Justice Harry Blackmun concluded that the right to privacy, initially recognized in *Griswold v. Connecticut*[73] eight years earlier, "is broad enough to encompass a woman's decision whether or not to terminate her pregnancy."[74]

BOX
10-1

Who Is Jane Roe?

When *Roe v. Wade* was argued before the U.S. Supreme Court, the plaintiff's attorneys used a pseudonym, "Jane Roe," to protect her from the social stigma of acknowledging that she was pregnant but unmarried. But eight years after the ruling, Norma McCorvey disclosed that she was "Jane Roe." At the time the case was initiated, Norma McCorvey—or "Pixie," as she was called by her carnival coworkers—was 21. Married at age 16, divorced, and the mother of a five-year-old daughter, McCorvey felt that she could not care for another child. She claimed—falsely, she later admitted—that her pregnancy was the result of rape, hoping that would enable her to get an abortion. But Texas's law outlawed abortions except to save the life of the mother, and McCorvey could not find a physician to perform an illegal abortion. She resigned herself to having the baby and giving it up for adoption. When she spoke to a lawyer about this, he referred her to Linda Coffee and Sarah Weddington, two lawyers who were eager to challenge the Texas abortion statute. After discussing the matter with them, McCorvey agreed to serve as plaintiff in the case.

How did *Roe v. Wade* affect Norma McCorvey? It did not enable her to get an abortion. Her child was born and given up for adoption before the Supreme Court ever heard her case. Although she was at the time ecstatic about the Court's ruling ("It makes me feel like I'm on top of Mount Everest"), she played little role in the litigation and did not even attend the oral argument before the Supreme Court. Indeed, when told

This right, the Court cautioned, was not absolute. During the first trimester (first twelve weeks) of pregnancy, a woman—in conjunction with her physician—could decide whether to terminate her pregnancy without state interference. During the second trimester, states could regulate the abortion procedure, but only to safeguard maternal health. During the third trimester, which coincides with the viability of the fetus (i.e., its ability to survive outside the womb), states could regulate or even ban abortion, except when it was necessary to preserve the life or health of the mother.

Roe and *Doe* had implications far beyond Texas and Georgia. Thirty-one states had abortion laws like Texas's, thirteen had reformed laws like Georgia's, and two banned all abortions. Presumably, the Court's rulings required those states to abandon their abortion laws. Only the four states that had repealed their abortion laws were unaffected. The opinion of the Court also enunciated that her case was being appealed to the Court, she reacted: "My God, all those people are so important. They don't have time to listen to some little old Texas girl who got in trouble."

McCorvey's disclosure that she was "Jane Roe" thrust her into the spotlight, and she became actively involved in abortion politics, speaking at pro-choice rallies and working as marketing director at an abortion clinic in Dallas. Then, in 1995, she underwent a change of heart. She quit her job at the clinic and was baptized by Reverend Flip Benham, national director of the antiabortion group Operation Rescue. In a radio interview after the conversion, she declared, "I'm pro-life. I think I have always been pro-life, I just didn't know it." In 1998, she joined the Catholic Church and currently spearheads a pro-life ministry. She filed suit petitioning that *Roe v. Wade* be reversed, but a federal court of appeals ruled against her in 2004.

As Norma McCorvey's story illustrates, the people whose cases reach the Supreme Court may be quite ordinary people. But the litigation is not ordinary litigation. Except in criminal cases, the litigants have often "disappeared" by the time the Court hears their cases. This is hardly surprising, for the Supreme Court does not review cases to correct injustices to particular individuals but to decide legal issues of national importance. Thus, what is at stake is not so much the fate of the litigants—indeed, in McCorvey's case, the ruling in *Roe* had no immediate effect on her situation—but the legal principles that will govern the nation.

Sources: McCorvey's quotations and basic information about her background are drawn from Marian Faux, *Roe v. Wade* (New York: Macmillan, 1988), and Norma McCorvey with Andy Meisler, *I Am Roe: My Life, Roe v. Wade, and Freedom of Choice* (New York: HarperCollins, 1994). Information on McCorvey's pro-choice activities and her conversion to a pro-life stance are drawn from "Woman behind the Symbols in Abortion Debate," *New York Times*, May 9, 1989, A18; and www.roenomore.org.

unusually detailed guidelines that governed how states could regulate abortion in the future. The clarity of the Court's guidelines stands in sharp contrast to the vague "all deliberate speed" formula in *Brown v. Board of Education*. After *Roe*, states for the most part knew what sorts of regulations of abortion would survive judicial scrutiny. The very detail of the guidelines, however, particularly in the absence of clear support in the text of the Constitution, opened the Court to criticism that it was legislating rather than judging.[75]

The Response to Roe

The general public's immediate response to *Roe* was rather muted; former President Lyndon Johnson died on the day that *Roe* was decided, and his death, not the Court's decision, captured the day's headlines.[76] The groups most interested in the litigation reacted in predictable fashion. Lawrence Lader, chairman of the NARAL, hailed the Court's ruling as "a thunderbolt" and "even more conclusive than any of us had dared to hope."[77] John Cardinal Krol, president of the National Catholic Conference, charged the Court with opening the door to "the greatest slaughter of innocent life in the history of mankind."[78]

The Pro-life Offensive   When a supporter went to the pro-choice headquarters in New York after *Roe* was decided, she found it shut tight, with a sign posted that they had won and that everyone had gone home.[79] In a sense this typified the response of pro-choice groups to *Roe*. They assumed that *Roe* had ended the battle, and they relied on the courts to repel any efforts to restrict a woman's right to terminate her pregnancy. But for pro-life advocates, the battle had just begun. *Roe* galvanized pro-life forces, sparking a grassroots movement committed to overturning the Court's ruling and opposing the spread of abortion.[80] The pro-life forces sought to influence public opinion through picketing, demonstrations, and pray-ins, tactics learned from the civil rights movement. More radical pro-life groups, such as Operation Rescue, attempted to prevent abortions, descending en masse on abortion clinics and forcibly blocking access to staff and patients. Most important, however, pro-life groups put pressure on public officials to oppose and limit abortion. If they had lost in the judicial arena, they sought in other arenas to reverse or limit the Court's ruling.

The most direct way to overturn a Supreme Court ruling is by constitutional amendment; indeed, five amendments have been adopted, in whole or in part, to overturn Supreme Court decisions.[81] Pro-life forces, however, have failed to persuade Congress to support an antiabortion amendment. Although 275 antiabortion amendments were proposed in Congress from 1973 to 1985, only one received committee approval and reached the floor of the House, where it failed to win a simple majority vote.[82] Senator Jesse Helms of North Carolina introduced a Human Life Bill that would have defined human life as beginning at conception, but it too found little support. The only success pro-life forces enjoyed in Congress was the enactment of the Hyde Amendment, which barred the use of Medicaid funds for abortions except to save the life of the mother. When this legislation was challenged, the Supreme Court backed away from a confrontation with Congress, ruling the Hyde Amendment constitutional by a 5–4 vote.[83]

Pro-life forces fared better with the executive branch during the presidencies of Ronald Reagan and George H. Bush (1981–1993). Presidents Reagan and Bush initiated administrative actions designed to discourage abortion, such as banning the use of foreign aid money to support abortions, prohibiting the use of fetal tissue in medical research, and banning counseling or referring for abortion at federally funded clinics. Although this last directive—labeled the "gag rule" by critics—was challenged in the courts, in *Rust v. Sullivan* (1991), the Supreme Court sustained the ban.[84] Perhaps most important, the Reagan and Bush administrations sought to undermine *Roe v. Wade* in the courts by appointing judges who were opposed to abortion and by filing amicus curiae briefs urging the Supreme Court to overrule *Roe*.

The election of President Clinton marked a setback for pro-life forces. Clinton campaigned on a pro-choice platform and promised to appoint judges solicitous of abortion rights. Early in his administration, he issued executive orders lifting the "gag rule" at federally funded clinics, removing antiabortion restrictions on foreign aid, and otherwise reversing pro-life policies of previous administrations. He also vetoed a ban on a controversial procedure used in late-term abortions, labeled by abortion opponents as "partial birth" abortion.

The pendulum swung back in a pro-life direction with the election of George W. Bush in 2000. President Bush supported and signed congressional legislation outlawing "partial birth" abortions, although lower federal courts struck down the law in 2004. He also limited federal funding for stem cell research and in his judicial appointments sought judges who were pro-life.

The reaction of state legislatures to *Roe* varied enormously. While some states sought to bring their laws in line with *Roe*, others attempted to impede access to abortion. Some states blatantly defied the Court's ruling. North Dakota and Rhode Island, for example, enacted laws banning abortion except to save the life of the mother. Other states, while not challenging *Roe* directly, adopted legislation that sought to exploit "loopholes" in the decision. The laws—requiring spousal and parental consent, mandatory waiting periods, hospitalization, and elaborate statistical reporting—served three purposes. First, they discouraged abortions by increasing the expense or difficulty of obtaining an abortion. Second, they drained the time and resources of the pro-choice groups that challenged the laws and of the courts that had to hear those challenges. Third, they provided opportunities for opponents of abortion to urge the Supreme Court to reconsider its ruling in *Roe*.[85]

Abortion Rulings after *Roe* In contrast with the field of school desegregation, where the Supreme Court virtually withdrew for a decade after announcing its landmark ruling in *Brown*, the Court remained actively involved with abortion policy. In the two decades after *Roe*, the justices ruled on twenty-one abortion cases.[86] From 1973 to 1986, the Court consistently reaffirmed its basic holding and closely policed state efforts to curtail the right recognized in *Roe*. Thus, it invalidated requirements for spousal and parental consent, counseling, and hospitalization, and various regulations of abortion procedures.[87] Only governmental refusals to fund abortions and a requirement that parents must be notified before a minor could receive an abortion survived the Court's scrutiny.[88] After 1986, however, the Court's composition changed, and so did its rulings (see Table 10-2). From 1986 to 1992, four members of the *Roe* majority retired, and Presidents Reagan and Bush replaced them with justices much less sympathetic to *Roe*. These changes brought a reversal of roles for pro-life and pro-choice groups. Opponents of abortion, sensing victory, turned their attention to the courts and appealed cases to the newly constituted Court in the hope that the justices would seize the opportunity to reverse *Roe*. Pro-choice groups, meanwhile, turned to the political arena, mobilizing support for pro-choice candidates and urging Congress to enact legislation safeguarding abortion rights.

In *Webster v. Reproductive Health Services* (1989) and in *Planned Parenthood of Southeastern Pennsylvania v. Casey* (1992), the justices did discard the trimester framework used by Justice Blackmun in *Roe*. They also upheld a number of state regulations that limited the availability of abortion, including some that they had struck down in earlier cases (e.g., a mandatory waiting period before an abortion). Nevertheless, five votes could not be obtained for overruling *Roe*. In his dissent in *Webster,* Justice Harry Blackmun, who wrote the opinion of the Court in *Roe,* warned that "the signs are evident and very ominous, and a chill wind blows."[89] With the election of President Clinton, who pledged during his campaign to fill vacancies on the Court with judges who were supportive of abortion rights, and the appointment of Ruth Bader Ginsburg and Stephen Breyer to the Supreme Court, *Roe* won at least a temporary reprieve. Indeed, in *Stenberg v. Carhart* (2000) the Court struck down a state law banning "partial birth" abortions unless necessary to save the life of the mother. Although the election of George W. Bush in 2000 and his reelection in 2004 placed the White House once again in the hands of pro-life forces, he did not have the opportunity to appoint justices during his first term of office.

The Effects of Roe

Though they agree on little else, both pro-life and pro-choice groups believe that *Roe v. Wade* inaugurated an abortion revolution. According to Justice Blackmun, who wrote the Court's opinion in *Roe*, the aim was to secure "the fundamental constitutional right of women to decide whether to terminate a pregnancy."[90] Yet given the questions raised about judicial policymaking capacity, did *Roe* in fact ensure that women could secure legal abortions?

Figure 10-2, which depicts the incidence of legal abortions in the United States between 1966 and 1985, permits several observations. First, as noted earlier, the trend toward the availability of legal abortions began before *Roe,* following the enactment of reform statutes in some states and the repeal of abortion laws in others. Second, although *Roe* did not initiate the trend toward increased access to abortion services, it certainly continued the trend. The rate of increase in legal abortions actually declined slightly after *Roe*. Still, there is no way to know whether legal abortions would have increased as much without the Court's ruling. Third, by 1980, the level of legal abortions in the United States had stabilized, and it has declined since 1990—according to the Centers for Disease Control, from 1.4 million legal abortions in 1990 to 862,000 in

1999.[91] Whether the decline is the result of the efforts of abortion opponents, through the Hyde Amendment and various state laws, to decrease access to abortion or an indication of changes in social mores is difficult to tell. A study by the Centers for Disease Control found that approximately 94 percent of women who would have been eligible for Medicaid funding before the Hyde Amendment were able to obtain some kind of funding for their abortions.[92] Similarly, bans on abortions in public hospitals or by public employees did not reduce abortion levels. Private clinics, responding to market demand, have filled the gap.[93]

If the Court's aim in *Roe* was to settle the issue of abortion, however, it failed to do so. Before *Roe,* abortion reform was proceeding in various states with a minimum of fanfare and only moderate political conflict. *Roe,* however, changed that. The decision became a rallying point for pro-choice and pro-life forces alike. It increased the visibility of abortion, nationalized the issue, and intensified the conflict over it. One must wonder whether, as in Western Europe, abortion would have become more widely available with less conflict if the Court had not intervened.[94]

Brown, Roe, AND BEYOND

The federal courts' policymaking on school desegregation and abortion illustrates how political issues come before the federal courts for resolution, how judicial policies change over time, how those affected by judicial policies may respond to them, and why judicial policies achieve or fail to achieve their objectives.

The Development of Legal Issues

Both *Brown* and *Roe* resulted from campaigns to change public policy through the courts. These campaigns resembled each other in some respects. Although the reform groups sought to dictate the focus and timing of litigation, they also had to respond to unexpected opportunities, such as the discovery of a suitable plaintiff in *Roe,* and to fortuitous developments, such as the accumulation of favorable precedents in the graduate school cases litigated before *Brown.* The two campaigns, however, also reveal the different uses that groups seeking legal reform may make of litigation. Realizing that Southern school districts would not voluntarily desegregate their schools, the NAACP relied exclusively on litigation to achieve this goal. In contrast, abortion reformers used litigation not as an alternative to political action but as an additional weapon in their effort to liberalize abortion laws. In fact, abortion reformers enjoyed considerable success in the legislative arena before challenging restrictions on abortion in the courts.

Most constitutional policymaking by the federal courts involves group sponsorship of litigation, as in *Brown* and *Roe*. Groups may also pursue their political or ideological aims in cases involving statutory interpretation or the oversight of administrative activity. They may seek to use the courts to build on victories won in the political arena or to reverse the losses they suffered there. The phenomenon of group sponsorship is hardly surprising, given the costs of litigation and the lack of financial incentives for individual plaintiffs. The main exception to group sponsorship involves defendants in criminal cases who claim that their rights were violated, as they have a strong personal stake in the outcome of their cases.

Policy Change

The Supreme Court's rulings on school desegregation and abortion reveal the various ways that judicial policies may change over time. Sometimes the changes are dramatic, occurring through landmark rulings such as *Brown* that overrule previous decisions and announce a fundamental shift in direction. More frequently, however, changes in judicial policies are gradual or incremental. A court may explicitly modify its position in the light of changing circumstances, as the Supreme Court did in dispensing with "all deliberate speed" and demanding immediate desegregation in the late 1960s after gaining the support of Congress and the presidency in its desegregation efforts. A court may also expand a legal principle by applying it to a new situation, as the Supreme Court did in *Roe v. Wade,* extending the right to privacy to encompass the right to terminate a pregnancy. In addition, a court may signal a change in policy by narrowing a legal principle announced in previous cases or by refusing to apply it to new situations. The Supreme Court's rejection of interdistrict busing in *Milliken v. Bradley* is a prime example. Finally, a court may subtly modify policy by undermining precedents even as it claims to be adhering to them. The Supreme Court's refusal to overrule *Roe v. Wade* while upholding regulations inconsistent with it in *Planned Parenthood of Southeastern Pennsylvania v. Casey* is a case in point.

What causes changes in judicial policy? Some changes result from changes in judicial personnel. When judges are replaced by others with different legal and political views, the judicial decisions will reflect those differences. However, personnel changes on the courts, unlike those in other branches, rarely produce dramatic shifts in policy. As Chapter 8 indicated, the authority of precedent, judicial role conceptions, and other legal constraints may all limit the speed and scope of policy change. (The Supreme Court's unwillingness to overrule *Roe v. Wade* out of respect for *stare decisis* is an example).

Policy changes may also result from judicial dissatisfaction with the results of previous judicial policies. For instance, in *Green v. County School Board of New Kent County* the Court had thirteen years' experience with Southern efforts to delay compliance with *Brown* or evade it through programs that produced minimal desegregation. The prolonged failure to comply convinced the justices to set more specific standards for the implementation of *Brown's* mandates, requiring immediate elimination of dual school systems and asserting that districts' plans were to be judged by the level of integration they produced.

In formulating new judicial policies, judges may rely on counsel for the contending parties or on amicus curiae briefs for guidance. Thus, both Thurgood Marshall for the NAACP and the attorneys for the Southern states influenced the desegregation guidelines established in *Brown* II. Judges may also borrow from the experience of other courts that have addressed similar problems in the past. The Supreme Court drew on the rulings of appeals courts in clarifying the meaning of desegregation and the experience of district courts in determining measures that might be undertaken to implement *Brown.*

Finally, judicial policies may also be shaped to some extent by the political environment in which judges operate. Some commentators have suggested, for example, that the Supreme Court's rulings in *Brown* and *Roe* followed rather than led shifts in public opinion.[95] The Supreme Court's willingness to accord the South a period of adjustment through the mechanism of "all deliberate speed" also suggests a sensitivity to political environment, as does *Milliken v. Bradley,* in which the Court curtailed aggressive district court intervention in the face of widespread public opposition.

Legal Obligation

A judicial ruling imposes legal obligations on the parties to the case and on lower court judges, who must apply the legal principles enunciated by the court in future cases. Judicial rulings also have legal implications for a broader "target population" that is in the same situation as the parties to the case. The size of this target population depends on the breadth of the legal principles a court announces, which in turn depends to a considerable extent on the breadth of the enactment the court is interpreting. Constitutional provisions, for example, tend to be more broadly applicable than statutes or administrative regulations. To some extent, however, courts themselves may determine the legal implications of their rulings by choosing the legal principles on which they will base their decisions. For example, before *Brown,* the Supreme Court tied its rulings in school cases to the particular facts of the cases, so that they primarily affected the parties in the cases. In *Brown,* however, the Court held that state-mandated segregation in education was unconstitutional, thus expanding the target population to include all states and localities that had established segregated school systems.

What legal obligations are imposed on a target population by a judicial ruling? Unfortunately, there is no consensus. Some legal scholars insist that a judicial ruling announces legal standards that are authoritative throughout the jurisdiction served by the court. Thus, a district court's ruling invalidating a practice requires all those within the district to refrain from the practice; a Supreme Court ruling has the same effect nationwide.[96] Other legal scholars maintain that what is authoritative is the court's ruling in the case, not the legal principles on which it was based. Thus, one may dispute those legal principles and engage in practices which, if legally challenged, would furnish the court with an opportunity to reconsider the principles it had announced.[97] Other legal scholars distinguish between settled and unsettled law, arguing that one may engage in actions inconsistent with the legal principles announced in a case only until those principles have become firmly established.[98] Under this standard, any racial discrimination in education would violate a legal principle established in *Brown* and confirmed in succeeding cases.

In most cases, those who are affected by judicial rulings comply with them. *Brown* and *Roe*, however, reveal that the mere existence of legal obligations does not guarantee compliance.

Communication Problems   Lower court judges or members of the target population may not comply with judicial mandates if they are unclear about what actions are required. For example, after *Brown* II, many district court judges were unsure about whether school districts had to integrate their schools or merely cease using racial criteria in student assignment. They also were unclear about the remedial measures they could employ if districts failed to meet their obligations under *Brown*. The Court's lack of clarity in *Brown*, along with its refusal to hear subsequent school cases and resolve ambiguities, increased the discretion of district court judges and officials dealing with school desegregation. Many used the opportunity to confine the effects of *Brown*.

In contrast, clear mandates, such as those enunciated in the Supreme Court's early abortion rulings, reduce discretion and encourage actions in line with the Court's aims. In *Roe v. Wade* the Court announced detailed legal standards, and during the next decade it further elaborated their implications in reviewing post-*Roe* legislation. Similarly, in *Swann v. Charlotte-Mecklenburg Board of Education*, the Supreme Court clarified what compliance with *Brown* required and specifically endorsed various remedial measures employed by district courts to implement *Brown*. Nevertheless, the effects of a clear initial mandate can be undermined by subsequent rulings that are inconsistent with it or that suggest a change in policy direction. The Supreme Court's rulings on abortion since 1987, which raised questions about the continuing authority of *Roe*'s guidelines, illustrate this phenomenon.

Finally, a target population cannot comply with a ruling unless that ruling is transmitted to it. Beyond officially promulgating their decisions, courts have no control over the transmission of their mandates. Usually this poses no problem; those who are affected by a judicial ruling are aware of the court's action. But this is not always the case, particularly when the target population is large. For example, when the Supreme Court announces a ruling affecting the power of police officers to conduct searches or interrogations, not all officers may hear of the ruling.[99] Similarly, many taxpayers may be unaware of Tax Court rulings that affect their tax liability.

Even if members of the target population are aware of a judicial ruling, they may misunderstand it. For example, some school officials erroneously interpreted the Supreme Court's invalidation of prayer in the public schools as merely forbidding coercion of students who did not wish to pray.[100] Such misinterpretations may occur because of ambiguities in the judicial ruling. Even if a ruling is clear, it may be simplified or distorted in the course of transmission. Most police officers, for example, get their information about rulings on police practices from nonjudicial sources, such as local officials, police training sessions, and the mass media. They can comply with the rulings only if those sources faithfully and accurately convey what the court has said.[101]

Noncompliance   Usually, people conform to the legal requirements announced in judicial decisions. Indeed, the effectiveness of judicial policy prescriptions largely depends on voluntary compliance. At times, however, the parties to a case, lower court judges, or members of the target population may refuse to undertake or refrain from actions as required by judicial rulings. Several state legislatures, for example, either ignored *Roe v. Wade* or enacted laws clearly inconsistent with its mandates. Most Southern school districts did not desegregate their schools in the decade after *Brown* II, and some district court judges abetted their noncompliance by refusing to enforce *Brown*. Even those district court judges who sought to implement *Brown* often found themselves outmaneuvered. Only the intervention of Congress, which enacted the 1964 Civil Rights Act and the Elementary and Secondary Education Act, and the executive branch, which enforced those laws, produced compliance in the South.

The federal judiciary's difficulties in implementing *Brown* underscore its limited power to compel compliance, particularly when opposition is widespread. As Alexander Hamilton noted in *The Federalist Papers*, the judiciary does not control "either the sword or the purse" and must "ultimately depend upon the aid of the executive arm even for the efficacy of its judgments."[102] When the executive and legislative branches support the federal judiciary, compliance with judicial mandates is likely. Thus, when the power of the sword and of the purse were brought to bear on Southern school districts after 1964, noncompliance rapidly ended. But when the other branches of the national government maintain neutrality or oppose judicial policies, the federal courts' ability to ensure compliance declines dramatically.[103]

Policy Effectiveness

All judicial policymaking faces the question, Did the court achieve its objective? The answer may not always be easy. It may be difficult, for instance, to determine the court's objective. If the aim in *Brown v. Board of Education* and succeeding cases was to eliminate official support for racial segregation, then the Court clearly succeeded; overt discrimination in education has virtually disappeared. If the Court's aim, however, was to ensure that children attended integrated schools, then the Court did not completely succeed. Today, most urban school districts, North and South, are racially homogeneous. In addition, some districts in which racial integration existed have, with population shifts, moved toward resegregation. If the Court's objective in *Brown* was to guarantee a good education to all students without regard to race, then again the Court has had only limited success. Indeed, as Chapter 11 will show, reformers interested in improving education for the disadvantaged have in recent years focused their attention more on school finance than on desegregation.

Disentangling whether judicial decisions or other factors produced particular effects may also be difficult. Take, for example, the phenomenon of white flight—that is, the movement of white families (and schoolchildren) from urban to suburban school districts. Opponents of court-ordered busing charged that it produced white flight and that judicial policies aimed at promoting integration were counterproductive, leading instead to racial isolation for minority students in urban school districts.[104] Other commentators, however, denied that court-ordered busing precipitated the white exodus from the cities and urban school districts. The population shift, they maintained, was a national phenomenon, not limited to municipalities with court-ordered busing, and busing itself did not accelerate the process.[105]

Similarly, when the goals of judicial policy are achieved, one cannot always assume that judicial decisions produced the effects. The late 1960s, for example, witnessed a rapid and sweeping desegregation of Southern schools, as required by *Brown*. As we have seen, however, congressional legislation and executive enforcement had more to do with the change than *Brown* did.

Even when judicial decisions achieve their objectives, other factors that neither the judges nor those who brought suit anticipated may play a key role. In *Roe v. Wade,* for instance, the Supreme Court attempted to make the option of abortion more widely available. Increases in legal abortions after 1973 indicate that the Court succeeded, but not in the way abortion reformers—and probably the justices—had expected. The reformers had assumed that hospitals would perform abortions once they were legal. The vast majority of public and private hospitals, however, continued to refuse to perform abortions even after 1973.[106] This created the possibility that the Court would be stymied by the opposition of institutions it had depended on to implement its policy, just as it had been in *Brown*.

Hospitals, it turned out, were not crucial to the success of *Roe*. When they refused to perform abortions, medical clinics were opened to meet the demand for abortions.[107] The alternative institutions developed because there was a financial incentive for providing abortions. Ironically, neither abortion reformers nor the justices foresaw how critical clinics would be. Indeed, the issue of where abortions were to be performed was ignored in the briefs submitted by the parties in *Roe* and was addressed only briefly in Justice Blackmun's opinion for the Court. In that sense, the success of *Roe* was as much the result of chance as of planning.[108]

Ultimately, the effectiveness of judicial policies may depend on the adequacy of the judges' understanding of the social processes that they are trying to influence. As discussed in Chapter 9, critics of judicial policymaking assert that judges lack the expertise and cannot acquire the knowledge necessary for effective policymaking.[109] Although this is not the place to offer conclusions about the validity of this critique, the survey of school desegregation and abortion cases provides useful material for those interested in evaluating the claims against federal judicial policymaking.

NOTES

1. *Brown v. Board of Education*, 347 U.S. 483 (1954). The case is commonly referred to as *Brown* I.

2. *Scott v. Sandford*, 60 U.S. (19 Howard) 393 (1857), and *Plessy v. Ferguson*, 163 U.S. 537 (1896).

3. The discussion of the school desegregation litigation before *Brown* relies on Daniel M. Berman, *It Is So Ordered: The Supreme Court Rules on School Segregation* (New York: Norton, 1966); Richard Kluger, *Simple Justice* (New York: Knopf, 1975); Mark V. Tushnet, *The NAACP's Legal Strategy against Segregated Education, 1925–1950* (Chapel Hill: University of North Carolina Press, 1987); and Stephen Wasby, "Interest Groups in Court: Race Relations Litigation," in *Interest Group Politics*, eds. Allan Cigler and Burdett Loomis (Washington, DC: Congressional Quarterly Press, 1983).

4. The classic account of the development of racial segregation is C. Vann Woodward, *The Strange Career of Jim Crow* (New York: Oxford University Press, 1966).

5. Cited in Tushnet, *The NAACP's Legal Strategy against Segregated Education*, p. 5.

6. Important victories included *Missouri ex rel. Gaines v. Canada*, 305 U.S. 337 (1938); *Sweatt v. Painter*, 339 U.S. 629 (1950); and *McLaurin v. Oklahoma State Regents for Higher Education*, 339 U.S. 637 (1950).

7. This argument follows Tushnet, *The NAACP's Legal Strategy against Segregated Education*, chap. 8.

8. See, e.g., Karen O'Connor, *Women's Organizations' Use of the Courts* (Lexington, MA: Lexington Books, 1980), and Robert Rabin, "Lawyers for Social Change: Perspectives on Public Interest Law," *Stanford Law Review* 28 (January 1970): 207–261.

9. Tushnet, *The NAACP's Legal Strategy against Segregated Education*, pp. 145–146.

10. For a discussion of these cases and their aftermath, see Raymond Wolters, *The Burden of Brown: Thirty Years of School Desegregation* (Knoxville: University of Tennessee Press, 1984).

11. *Bolling v. Sharpe*, 347 U.S. 497 (1954).

12. On the intra-court politics surrounding *Brown*, see Kluger, *Simple Justice*, part 3; S. Sidney Ulmer, "Earl Warren and the *Brown* Decision," *Journal of Politics* 33 (1971): 689–702; and Mark Tushnet with Katya Lezin, "What Really Happened in *Brown v. Board of Education,*" *Columbia Law Review* 91 (December 1991): 1867–1930.

13. *Brown v. Board of Education*, 347 U.S. 483, 495.

14. The analysis follows Robert L. Carter, "A Reassessment of *Brown v. Board,*" and Diane Ravitch, "Desegregation: Varieties of Meanings," both found in *Shades of Brown: New Perspectives on School Desegregation*, ed. Derrick Bell (New York: Teachers College Press, 1980).

15. "Southern states" refers to Alabama, Arkansas, Florida, Georgia, Louisiana, Mississippi, North Carolina, South Carolina, Tennessee, Texas, and Virginia.; "border states," Delaware, Kentucky, Maryland, Missouri, Oklahoma, and West Virginia. The state of the law at the time of *Brown* is drawn from Gerald R. Rosenberg, *The Hollow Hope: Can Courts Bring about Social Change?* (Chicago: University of Chicago Press, 1991), p. 42.

16. J. Harvie Wilkinson, *From Brown to Bakke: The Supreme Court and School Integration, 1954–1968* (New York: Oxford University Press, 1979), pp. 64–77. The account of the aftermath of *Brown* relies on, in addition to Wilkinson's volume, Rosenberg, *The Hollow Hope*, chap. 2–5; Stephen L. Wasby, Anthony A. D'Amato, and Rosemary Metrailer, *Desegregation from Brown to Alexander* (Carbondale: Southern Illinois University Press, 1977); Wolters, *The Burden of Brown;* and David J. Armor, *Forced Justice: School Desegregation and the Law* (New York: Oxford University Press, 1995).

17. *Brown v. Board of Education* [*Brown* II], 349 U.S. 294, 300 (1955).

18. Quoted in Wilkinson, *From Brown to Bakke,* p. 65.

19. Quoted in ibid., p. 66.

20. Ibid., pp. 69–70.

21. Wolters, *The Burden of Brown,* p. 256. Racial segregation was not the only form that racial discrimination took in Topeka's schools; see Wolters, pp. 254–255, and Kluger, *Simple Justice*, pp. 381–382.

22. Wolters, *The Burden of Brown,* p. 12.

23. Rosenberg, *The Hollow Hope,* p. 50, table 2-1.

24. The Supreme Court's ruling was *Cooper v. Aaron*, 358 U.S. 1 (1958). Background on the Little Rock debacle is found in Wilkinson, *From Brown to Bakke,* pp. 88–95.

25. The Supreme Court's ruling was *Griffin v. County School Board*, 375 U.S. 391 (1964). Background on the closing of schools in Prince Edward County is found in Wilkinson, *From Brown to Bakke,* pp. 95–102, and Wolters, *The Burden of Brown,* pp. 65–128.

26. On the war against the NAACP, see Robert H. Birkby and Walter F. Murphy, "Interest Group Conflict in the Judicial Arena: The First Amendment and Group Access to the Courts," *Texas Law Review* 42 (1964): 1018–1048. Pertinent cases include *NAACP v. Alabama*, 357 U.S. 449 (1958), and *Gibson v. Florida Legislative Investigating Committee*, 372 U.S. 539 (1963). On the absence of school desegregation suits in Mississippi, see Jack W. Peltason, *Fifty-Eight Lonely Men* (Urbana: University of Illinois Press, 1971), p. 99.

27. Kluger, *Simple Justice*, p. 748.

28. Rosenberg, *The Hollow Hope*, p. 79.

29. Quoted in Reed Sarrat, *The Ordeal of Desegregation* (New York: Harper, 1966), p. 201.

30. See, e.g., Judge John J. Parker's influential opinion in *Briggs v. Elliott*, 132 F.Supp. 776, 777 (E.D.S.C. 1955).

31. Walter Gellhorn, "A Decade of Desegregation—Retrospect and Prospect," *Utah Law Review* 9 (1964): 6.

32. Quoted in Harrell R. Rodgers Jr., and Charles S. Bullock III, *Law and Social Change: Civil Rights Laws and Their Consequences* (New York: McGraw-Hill, 1972), p. 72.

33. Rosenberg, *The Hollow Hope*, p. 84.

34. Wilkinson, *From Brown to Bakke*, p. 102.

35. Ibid., p. 108.

36. These data are drawn from Rosenberg, *The Hollow Hope*, p. 98.

37. Gary Orfield, *The Reconstruction of Southern Education* (New York: Wiley, 1969), p. 228.

38. This analysis follows Wilkinson, *From Brown to Bakke*, pp. 108–118. The pertinent Fifth Circuit cases are *Singleton v. Jackson Municipal Separate School District* I, 348 F.2d 729 (5th Cir. 1965); *Singleton v. Jackson Municipal Separate School District* II, 355 F.2d 865 (5th Cir. 1966); and *United States v. Jefferson County Board of Education,* 372 F.2d 836 (5th Cir. 1966).

39. *Green v. County School Board,* 391 U.S. 430 (1968).

40. 391 U.S. 430, 439. See also *Alexander v. Holmes County Board of Education,* 396 U.S. 19 (1969).

41. *Swann v. Charlotte-Mecklenburg Board of Education,* 402 U.S. 1 (1971).

42. 402 U.S. 1, 30–31 and 15.

43. Paul R. Dimond, *Beyond Busing: Inside the Challenge to Urban Segregation* (Ann Arbor: University of Michigan Press, 1985), chap. 1 and 6.

44. Wilkinson, *From Brown to Bakke*, p. 197.

45. Ibid., p. 206.

46. *Swann v. Charlotte-Mecklenburg Board of Education,* 402 U.S. 1 (1971).

47. Ibid., at 30–31.

48. *Keyes v. School District No. 1, Denver, Colorado,* 413 U.S. 189 (1973).

49. *Statement of the United States Commission on Civil Rights on School Desegregation* (Washington, DC: U.S. Government Printing Office, 1982); James Bolner and Robert Shanley, *Busing: The Political and Judicial Process* (New York: Praeger, 1974); and Dimond, *Beyond Busing*, pp. 385–386.

50. Wilkinson, *From Brown to Bakke*, pp. 202 and 207.

51. Ibid., p. 180, and Wolters, *The Burden of Brown*, pp. 246–247.

52. *Milliken v. Bradley* [*Milliken* I], 418 U.S. 717 (1974).

53. For district court remedies, see *Milliken v. Bradley* [*Milliken* II], 433 U.S. 267 (1977), and *Missouri v. Jenkins* [*Jenkins* II], 495 U.S. 33 (1990); for the Supreme Court's rejection of district court overreaching, see *Missouri v. Jenkins* [*Jenkins* III], 515 U.S. 70 (1995).

54. *Dayton Board of Education v. Brinkman* [*Dayton* I], 433 U.S. 406 (1977). The *Dayton* litigation is chronicled in Dimond, *Beyond Busing*, chap. 6–8 and 15–16.

55. See, e.g., *Dayton Board of Education v. Brinkman* [*Dayton* II], 443 U.S. 526 (1979), and *Columbus Board of Education v. Penick,* 443 U.S. 499 (1979).

56. *Pasadena City Board of Education v. Spangler,* 427 U.S. 424 (1976); for a more recent ruling curtailing judicial supervision of school districts, see *Freeman v. Pitts,* 503 U.S. 467 (1992). For an overview of the movement away from judicial supervision of school desegregation, see Gary Orfield, Susan Eaton, and the Harvard Project on School Desegregation, *Dismantling Desegregation: The Quiet Reversal of Brown v. Board of Education* (New York: New Press, 1996).

57. See Rosenberg, *The Hollow Hope*, p. 50, table 2.1.

58. Armor, *Forced Justice,* p. 166, table 4.1.

59. See, e.g., Micheal Giles, Douglas Gatlin, and Everett Cataldo, "White Flight and Percent Black: The Tipping Point Reexamined," *Social Science Quarterly* 57 (June 1976): 85–92.

60. See, e.g., Robert L. Carter, "A Reassessment of *Brown v. Board*," and Ronald R. Edmonds, "Effective Education for Minority Pupils: *Brown* Confounded or Confirmed," in Bell, *Shades of Brown.*

61. *Planned Parenthood of Southeastern Pennsylvania v. Casey,* 502 U.S. 1056 (1992).

62. *Roe v. Wade,* 410 U.S. 113 (1972). Indeed, one expert on the Supreme Court claims that the Court's ruling in *Casey* made him "realize how little I understood about judicial behavior." See Lawrence Baum, *The Puzzle of Judicial Behavior* (Ann Arbor: University of Michigan Press, 1997), p. ix.

63. Such criticism is, of course, not unique to this case. See the discussion in Chapter 8.

64. This account of the origins of abortion legislation and of the movement to liberalize state abortion laws relies primarily on Marian Faux, *Roe v. Wade* (New York: Macmillan, 1988); Lawrence Lader, *Abortion II: Making the Revolution* (Boston: Beacon Press, 1973); Eva R. Rubin, *Abortion, Politics, and the Courts,* Rev. ed. (Westport, CT: Greenwood Press, 1987); Gerald R. Rosenberg, *The Hollow Hope,* chap. 6–9; and N. E. H. Hull and Peter C. Hoffer, *Roe v. Wade: The Abortion Rights Controversy in American History* (Lawrence: University Press of Kansas, 2001).

65. Rosenberg, *The Hollow Hope,* p. 180, table 6.1.

66. Rubin, *Abortion, Politics, and the Courts,* p. 164.

67. Faux, *Roe v. Wade,* p. 117.

68. See, e.g., Aryeh Neier, *Only Judgment: The Limits of Litigation in Social Change* (Middletown, CT: Wesleyan University Press, 1982); and Jennifer L. Hochschild, *The New American Dilemma* (New Haven, CT: Yale University Press, 1984).

69. *Poe v. Ullman,* 367 U.S. 497 (1961). For an enlightening discussion of the considerations underlying the Court's initial avoidance of the birth-control case, see Alexander M. Bickel, *The Least Dangerous Branch: The Supreme Court at the Bar of Politics* (Indianapolis, IN: Bobbs-Merrill, 1962), pp. 143–156.

70. The article was Cyril Means, "The Phoenix of Abortional Freedom: Is a Penumbral or Ninth Amendment Right about to Arise from the Nineteenth-Century Legislative Ashes of a Fourteenth-Century Common Law Liberty?" *New York Forum* 17 (fall 1971): 335–410. The sponsorship of abortion reformers is documented in Faux, *Roe v. Wade,* p. 217.

71. See Faux, *Roe v. Wade,* chap. 13.

72. *Roe v. Wade,* 410 U.S. 113 (1973), and *Doe v. Bolton,* 410 U.S. 179 (1973).

73. *Griswold v. Connecticut,* 381 U.S. 479 (1965).

74. *Roe v. Wade,* 410 U.S. 113, 153.

75. Such criticism even came from some scholars who had endorsed previous activist rulings of the Warren Court. See, e.g., John Hart Ely, "The Wages of Crying Wolf: A Comment on *Roe v. Wade,*" *Yale Law Journal* 82 (1973): 920–949.

76. The account of the response to *Roe* draws particularly on Barbara H. Craig and David M. O'Brien, *Abortion and American Politics* (Chatham, NJ: Chatham House, 1993); Rubin, *Abortion, Politics, and the Court;* Rosenberg, *The Hollow Hope;* and Raymond Tatalovich, "Abortion: Prochoice versus Prolife," in *Social Regulatory Policy: Moral Controversies in American Politics,* eds. Raymond Tatalovich and Byron W. Daynes (Boulder, CO: Westview Press, 1988).

77. Lader, *Abortion II,* frontispiece.

78. Quoted in Faux, *Roe v. Wade,* p. 305.

79. Michele McKeegan, *Abortion Politics: Mutiny in the Ranks of the Right* (New York: Free Press, 1992), p. 130.

80. On the pro-life movement and abortion politics, see Raymond Tatalovich and Byron W. Daynes, *The Politics of Abortion: A Study of Community Conflict in Public Policy Making* (New York: Praeger, 1981); Frederick S. Jaffe, Barbara L. Lindheim, and

Philip R. Lee, *Abortion Politics: Private Morality and Public Policy* (New York: McGraw-Hill, 1981); and William Saletan, *Bearing Right: How the Conservatives Won the Abortion War* (Berkeley: University of California Press, 2003).

81. The Eleventh Amendment overruled *Chisholm v. Georgia,* 2 U.S. 419 (1793); the Fourteenth Amendment, *Scott v. Sandford,* 60 U.S. 393 (1857); the Sixteenth Amendment, *Pollock v. Farmers' Loan & Trust Co.,* 157 U.S. 429 (1895); the Twenty-Fourth Amendment, *Breedlove v. Suttles,* 302 U.S. 277 (1937); and the Twenty-Sixth Amendment, *Oregon v. Mitchell,* 400 U.S. 112 (1970).

82. Tatalovich, "Abortion: Prochoice versus Prolife," p. 200.

83. *Harris v. McRae,* 448 U.S. 297 (1980); 238 members of Congress submitted an *amicus curiae* brief in the case, urging the Court to uphold the Hyde Amendment.

84. *Rust v. Sullivan,* 500 U.S. 173 (1991). For a discussion of the Reagan and Bush administrations' initiatives, albeit from a critical perspective, see McKeegan, *Abortion Politics,* chap. 4–8.

85. Rosenberg, *The Hollow Hope,* pp. 187–188.

86. Early post-*Roe* cases include *Bigelow v. Virginia,* 421 U.S. 809 (1975); *Connecticut v. Mentillo,* 423 U.S. 9 (1975); *Planned Parenthood of Central Missouri v. Danforth,* 428 U.S. 52 (1976); *Beal v. Doe,* 432 U.S. 438 (1977); *Maher v. Roe,* 432 U.S. 464 (1977); *Poelker v. Doe,* 432 U.S. 519 (1977); *Colautti v. Franklin,* 439 U.S. 379 (1979); *Bellotti v. Baird,* 443 U.S. 622 (1979); *Harris v. McRae,* 448 U.S. 297 (1980); *Williams v. Zbaraz,* 448 U.S. 358 (1980); *H.L. v. Matheson,* 450 U.S. 398 (1981); *Akron v. Akron Center for Reproductive Health, Inc.,* 462 U.S. 416 (1983); *Simopoulos v. Virginia,* 462 U.S. 506 (1983); *Planned Parenthood Associated of Kansas City, Missouri v. Ashcroft,* 462 U.S. 476 (1983); and *Thornburgh v. American College of Obstetricians and Gynecologists,* 476 U.S. 747 (1976).

87. See *Planned Parenthood of Central Missouri v. Danforth* (spousal consent and parental consent); *Akron v. Akron Center for Reproductive Health* (counseling and hospitalization requirements); and *Thornburgh v. American College of Obstetricians and Gynecologists* (burdensome medical procedures).

88. See *Harris v. McRae* (ban on Medicaid funding for abortions) and *H.L. v. Matheson* (parental notification requirement).

89. *Webster v. Reproductive Health Services,* 492 U.S. 490 (1989).

90. *Roe v. Wade,* 410 U.S. 113, 153.

91. Figures compiled by the Centers for Disease Control, reported at www.cdc.gov.

92. Rosenberg, *The Hollow Hope,* p. 187.

93. Ibid., p. 190.

94. For an enlightening comparative analysis, see Mary Ann Glendon, *Abortion and Divorce in Western Law* (Cambridge, MA: Harvard University Press, 1987), chap. 1 and 3.

95. On *Roe,* see ibid.; on *Brown,* see Lewis Steel, "Nine Men in Black Who Think White," *New York Times Magazine,* October 13, 1968. More generally, see Rosenberg, *The Hollow Hope,* chap. 5–6.

96. For an analysis of scholarly support for this position, see Gary L. Jacobsohn, *The Supreme Court and the Decline of Constitutional Aspiration* (Totowa, NJ: Rowman & Littlefield, 1986), chap. 7.

97. See ibid., and Sanford Levinson, *Constitutional Faith* (Princeton, NJ: Princeton University Press, 1988).

98. See Jacobsohn, *The Supreme Court and the Decline of Constitutional Aspiration,* chap. 6–7.

99. See, e.g., Neil A. Milner, *The Court and Local Law Enforcement: The Impact of Miranda* (Beverly Hills, CA: Sage Publications, 1971).

100. See William K. Muir Jr., *Prayer in the Public Schools: Law and Attitude Change* (Chicago: University of Chicago Press, 1967), and Richard Johnson, *The Dynamics of Compliance* (Evanston, IL: Northwestern University Press, 1967).

101. On communication problems and judicial impact, see Charles A. Johnson and Bradley C. Canon, *Judicial Policies: Implementation and Impact,* 2d ed. (Washington, DC: Congressional Quarterly Press, 1999), pp. 167–173.

102. Alexander Hamilton, John Jay, and James Madison, *The Federalist Papers,* ed. Clinton Rossiter (New York: New American Library, 1961), no. 78, p. 465.

103. See Rosenberg, *The Hollow Hope,* chap. 1 and passim.

104. For alternative perspectives on the busing issue, see James S. Coleman, Sara D. Kelly, and John Moore, *Recent Trends in School Desegregation* (Washington, DC: Urban Institute, 1975), and Gary Orfield, *Must We Bus? Segregated Schools and National Policy* (Washington, DC: Brookings Institution, 1978).

105. Thomas Pettigrew and Robert L. Green, "School Desegregation in Large Cities: A Critique of the Coleman 'White Flight' Thesis," *Harvard Educational Review* 46 (February 1976): 1–53, and Christine H. Rossell, "School Desegregation and White Flight," *Political Science Quarterly* 90 (winter 1975–76): 673–695.

106. See Rosenberg, *The Hollow Hope,* p. 190, table 6.2. The analysis in this section follows Rosenberg, pp. 189–201.

107. Ibid., p. 197, tables 6.4 and 6.5.

108. Ibid., pp. 200–201.

109. See Donald L. Horowitz, *The Courts and Social Policy* (Washington, DC: Brookings, 1977), and, more generally, the discussion in Chapter 9.

STATE COURT POLICYMAKING

Although rulings such as *Brown v. Board of Education* and *Roe v. Wade* attract national attention, less publicized judicial decisions also enunciate important policy. Many of these rulings come from state courts. Indeed, according to Justice William Brennan, who served on both the U.S. Supreme Court and the New Jersey Supreme Court, "[t]he composite work of the courts in the fifty states probably has greater significance [than that of the U.S. Supreme Court] in measuring how well America attains the ideal of equal justice for all."[1]

This chapter focuses on state courts' constitutional policymaking in dealing with public school finance and with their common-law policymaking on product liability (the legal standards governing suits for damages for injuries caused by defective products). In addition to its intrinsic importance, state court policymaking in these fields reveals basic features of how state courts participate in governing. This chapter also highlights the influence on state judicial policymaking of state courts' relationships with federal courts, with courts in other states, and with the state legislature and other institutions of state government.

SCHOOL FINANCE

Federal courts, not state courts, were initially at the forefront of legal efforts to reform state systems for financing public education. In 1971, Demetrio Rodriguez filed a class-action suit in federal district court, arguing that Texas's school finance system violated the Equal Protection Clause of the federal Constitution. The system that Rodriguez challenged resembled those in most other states. Funding for elementary and secondary schools came primarily from local property taxes.[2] Thus, the level of spending for education varied from school district to school district, depending on the value of taxable property in the district and on the rate at which it was taxed. The interdistrict differences in spending per child could be substantial. At the time of Rodriguez's suit, the Edgewood Independent School District in San Antonio annually spent $356 per pupil, while the neighboring Alamo Heights district spent $564.[3]

According to Rodriguez, the disparities in funding among school districts, produced by this reliance on local property taxes, resulted in unequal and inadequate education for students in property-poor districts.[4] He further asserted that the funding disparities violated the federal Constitution. A federal district court agreed and struck down Texas's school finance system as inconsistent with the Equal Protection Clause of the Fourteenth Amendment. But in *San Antonio Independent School District v. Rodriguez* (1973), the U.S. Supreme Court reversed the district court's decision by a 5–4 vote.[5] The Court majority maintained that the Equal Protection Clause did not require equal expenditures in school districts and that Texas's school finance system was constitutional.

Although *Rodriguez* precluded further challenges under the federal Constitution, it did not end school finance litigation. Over the next three decades, fifteen state supreme courts struck down the school finance system in their state as unconstitutional.[6] Among these was the Texas Supreme Court, which unanimously ruled, sixteen years after *Rodriguez*, that the state's school finance system violated the Texas Constitution.[7] Let us look more closely at the transformation of school finance litigation and its consequences.

The Development of School Finance Litigation

Litigating for Change   For courts to rule on the constitutionality of state systems of school finance, litigants must be willing to raise the issue and offer a legal basis for their claims. *Brown v. Board of Education* was crucial in stimulating school finance litigation, because it focused attention on the detrimental effects of inequalities in education, prompting social commentators and political activists to consider the impact of other forms of educational inequality.[8] *Brown* also signaled the justices' willingness to use the Equal Protection Clause to combat inequalities.[9] It thus encouraged potential litigants to believe that they would have a forum receptive to their claims. Finally, the ruling appeared to show that the Supreme Court could inaugurate major social change, while the slow pace and uncertain results of state-by-state legislative reform of school finance made the judicial path to reform attractive. Not surprisingly school finance reformers pinned their hopes on the U.S. Supreme Court.

But the reformers had miscalculated badly. When *Rodriguez* came to the Supreme Court in the early 1970s, the Court's composition and orientation had changed. Republican President Richard Nixon had appointed four new justices who were more committed to judicial restraint than their predecessors and not interested in egalitarian crusades. In *Rodriguez,* the Nixon appointees supplied four of the five votes needed to uphold Texas's school finance system, ensuring that federal courts would not play a role in school finance reform.

State Courts and State Law   But thirteen days after the Supreme Court announced its decision in *Rodriguez,* the New Jersey Supreme Court in *Robinson v. Cahill* unanimously ruled the state's school finance system unconstitutional.[10] New Jersey's system for financing public education closely resembled Texas's, which—according to the U.S. Supreme Court—met federal constitutional requirements. Thus, the New Jersey justices could not base their ruling on the federal Equal Protection Clause. Instead, they held that New Jersey's school finance system violated the state constitution's requirement that the state provide to all children a "thorough and efficient education."[11]

Robinson transformed the campaign for school finance reform by reminding potential litigants and government officials that state systems of school finance had to satisfy state, as well as federal, constitutional requirements. It showed that the applicable state provisions were not identical to those in the federal Constitution; there was no federal analogue to the "thorough and efficient" clause or to other state constitutional requirements (see Box 11-1). *Robinson* also reminded potential litigants that a favorable ruling on school finance under the state constitution could not be reversed by the U.S. Supreme Court, because state supreme courts are the authoritative interpreters of their state constitutions. Thus, victories won in state court would not turn into defeats in federal court. Finally, *Robinson* demonstrated that state courts might be more sympathetic to school finance challenges than were the federal courts, leading reformers to look to their state constitutions and state courts in challenging school finance systems. As the attorney in Connecticut's school finance case put it, *Robinson* "fired my imagination."[12]

School Finance Litigation in State Courts   After *Robinson,* reformers in several states initiated state constitutional challenges to school finance systems. In the seven years after *Rodriguez,* twelve state supreme courts heard challenges to their states' school finance systems (see Table 11-1).[13] Reformers enjoyed some success, prevailing in half the cases. After 1980, however, interest in school finance litigation waned. From 1981 to 1988, litigants filed only seven suits against school finance programs, and in all but one of those cases the state supreme court upheld the states' programs.[14] From 1989 on, however, reformers have launched a new wave of litigation and enjoyed considerable success.[15] One successful suit was in New Jersey, where the state's supreme court ruled that the "reformed" program established after *Robinson* did not remedy "the constitutional failure of education in poorer urban districts" and mandated greater aid to those districts.[16]

State Constitutional Provisions and School Finance

Many states have distinctive constitutional provisions that are relevant to school finance:

Illinois: The Illinois Constitution states that "[a] fundamental goal for the People of the State is the educational development of all persons to the limits of their capacities" and requires the state to "provide for an efficient system of high quality public educational institutions and services." (art. 10, sec. 1)

Montana: The Montana Constitution requires the state to provide "a system of education which will develop the full educational potential of each person. Equality of educational opportunity is guaranteed to each person of the state." (art. 10, sec. 1)

New Jersey: "The Legislature shall provide for the support of a thorough and efficient system of free public schools." (art. 8, sec. 14)

New Mexico: "Children of Spanish descent in the state of New Mexico . . . shall forever enjoy perfect equality with other children in all public schools." (art. 12, sec. 10)

Texas: "It shall be the duty of the legislature of the state to establish and make suitable provision for the support and maintenance of an efficient system of public free schools." (art. 7, sec. 1)

Wyoming: The Wyoming Constitution mandates a "complete and uniform system of public instruction." (art. 7, sec. 1)

Three decades of school finance litigation confirm that by relying on their state constitutions, state courts could engage in constitutional policymaking independent of the U.S. Supreme Court. Yet in some states the courts upheld school finance programs and in others they invalidated the programs. Given the similarities among the challenged programs, why did state courts disagree about their constitutionality?

TABLE

11-1
TABLE 11-1   SCHOOL FINANCE LITIGATION IN THE STATES

Period	State Law Invalidated	State Law Upheld
One (1973–1980)	New Jersey (1973) California (1976) Connecticut (1977) Washington (1978) Wyoming (1978) West Virginia (1979)	Arizona (1973) Montana (1974) Idaho (1975) Oregon (1976) Pennsylvania (1978) Ohio (1979)
Two (1981–1988)	Arkansas (1983)	Georgia (1981) Colorado (1982) Maryland (1983) New York (1983) Oklahoma (1987) South Carolina (1988)
Three (1989–2000)	Kentucky (1989) Montana (1989) Texas (1989) New Jersey (1990) Massachusetts (1993) Tennessee (1993) Ohio (1997) Vermont (1997)	Wisconsin (1989) Minnesota (1993) Kansas (1994) Rhode Island (1995) Illinois (1996) Arizona (1994)

Differences in state law do not account for the disparate rulings, as state courts have reached opposite results interpreting virtually identical constitutional provisions. These conflicting interpretations of similar provisions may reflect differences in judges' conceptions of the judicial role (discussed in Chapter 9). Some state judges, stressing the importance of judicial restraint, upheld school finance programs because they believed it proper to defer to the state legislature. Thus, New York's supreme court noted that it was "particularly appropriate for . . . the legislative body (reflective of and responsive as it is to the public will)" to make decisions about the allocation of public funds.[17] Other judges, rejecting judicial activism, feared that their "unwise and unwarranted entry into the controversial area of public school financing" would transform their court into a "super-legislature," and embroil it "in a turbulent field of social, economic, and political policy."[18]

Even some judges who invalidated state school finance programs insisted that judicial restraint guided their actions, asserting that their intrusion into a field traditionally reserved for the legislature was compelled by the state's violation of clear constitutional commands.[19] And troubled by the apparent conflict between fidelity to the state constitution and respect for legislative prerogatives, they tended to leave the design of remedial measures to the legislature. Yet some judges who invalidated state programs forthrightly embraced judicial activism. West Virginia's high court, for example, not only struck down the state's school finance system but also designated eight specific academic areas in which schools were required to develop student capacities.[20]

One might also expect that the justices' political views would explain the different rulings on such a controversial policy issue. But it is not clear that these views exerted much direct influence on decisions. Take, for example, the Texas school finance case. The opinion of the court was written by Justice Oscar Mauzy, a Democrat who had formerly chaired the state senate's education committee.[21] One might easily attribute his vote for the reform of school finance to his background and political perspective. Yet, if political backgrounds and views directly determined votes, one would not expect the other eight members of the Texas Supreme Court—five Democrats and three Republicans—to have joined Mauzy's opinion. The New Jersey Supreme Court's rulings in *Robinson v. Cahill* and in *Abbott v. Burke,* its more recent school finance ruling, also defy explanation in simple partisan terms. Although the justices included both Democrats and Republicans, both decisions were unanimous.[22]

State Courts and State Legislatures   Once a court has identified a constitutional violation, the court must act to remedy it. In many cases, the remedy is straightforward. A court may order officials to cease their unconstitutional conduct or may award damages to those whose constitutional rights were violated. In the school finance cases, however, the remedial task was more complicated. If a court concluded that the existing school finance system violated the state constitution, then the court would have to ensure that a constitutionally adequate system replaced it.

But could state supreme courts meet that responsibility? State judges had no special expertise in education policy. They could not raise revenue to guarantee adequate funding for poorer districts. They were ill-equipped to supervise the implementation of policy. In short, they exhibited the very limitations that had led some scholars to despair of effective judicial policymaking.[23]

State supreme courts dealt with this problem in various ways. The California Supreme Court in *Serrano v. Priest* (1976) held that the state violated the Equal Protection Clause of the California Constitution by allowing school expenditures per student, which depended on property values, to fluctuate from district to district.[24] Given that definition of the constitutional violation, the court merely required the state to ensure that funding per student not depend on the wealth of the school district. The clarity of the court's standard eased compliance by the state legislature, reallocating school funds without involving the court in education policy. Indeed, this ruling, along with Proposition 13—a subsequent anti-tax amendment to the California

Constitution—produced a virtual equality of expenditures per student across the state.[25] Yet the California Supreme Court avoided entanglement in the details of education policymaking only by ignoring the complexities of education policy. The court simply assumed that additional funding in poor districts would necessarily improve education.

A more complex situation confronted those courts that invalidated school finance programs because they failed to provide a "thorough and efficient education" or to meet other requirements established by the education articles of their state constitutions. Such provisions imposed on state governments the obligation to provide a quality education for all students and on courts a duty to ensure that the state met that responsibility. But if the other branches of state government failed to meet their responsibility, would the state supreme court have to intervene with its own education plan?

Aware of their limitations as policymakers, most state supreme courts sought to achieve their educational goals through agenda setting.[26] They did not attempt to devise and impose their own policy, a task for which they were ill-suited. Rather, providing only the broadest of guidelines, they left it to the governor and state legislature to come up with a policy that met constitutional requirements. Thus, the courts' agenda setting reordered the political priorities of the other branches of state government, and invalidation of existing policy forced governors and legislatures to address the issue of school finance. But governors and legislatures were given considerable leeway to devise their own approaches to remedying the constitutional violations identified by the court.[27] Judicial intervention therefore did not foreclose opportunities for legislative policymaking.

Agenda setting was attractive to state courts because it kept them from getting bogged down in the details of education policymaking. But agenda setting also involved them in ongoing oversight of legislative efforts to meet constitutional requirements. For example, in 1971 the New Jersey Supreme Court announced its initial ruling in *Robinson v. Cahill* (*Robinson* I), but it did not issue its final ruling in the case until 1976 (*Robinson* VII).[28]

Judicial agenda setting did not always promote prompt and effective reform of public education. One notable success, however, was in Kentucky, where the governor and state legislature cooperated to produce landmark legislation that overhauled the state's system of public education and imposed the new taxes necessary to support the change.[29] But in many other states the legislative response was slow and begrudging. In retrospect, this was hardly surprising. That state legislatures had not previously initiated reforms on their own testified to the strong interests attached to the existing school finance system. Moreover, school finance reform often got tied up in political maneuvering. In Texas, for example, it took four special legislative sessions and two gubernatorial vetoes before a new school funding plan was enacted.[30] In New Jersey, more than a year passed after *Robinson v. Cahill* without any legislative action because the lame-duck governor lacked the political muscle for effective leadership. It took five years to get school finance reforms enacted and implemented and even then they proved inadequate.[31]

Even when the legislature did act, that did not always resolve matters. Judicial agenda setting gave legislators considerable leeway in determining how to satisfy constitutional requirements. Yet the greater the leeway, the more difficult it was for legislators to determine what the requirements were. What, after all, is "a thorough and efficient education" and how does one determine when it has been achieved? Also, legislators were sometimes loath to take responsibility for court-mandated reforms, particularly if they required tax increases or were otherwise unpopular. Some state legislators thus enacted laws that failed to meet fully the constitutional requirements set by the court or that sought to circumscribe the effects of the court's ruling. In doing so, they were implicitly negotiating with the state supreme court about what sort of policy it would accept.

In such circumstances, the state supreme court was faced with two choices. It could invalidate the new law and provoke a confrontation with the legislature, or it could avoid confrontation by upholding the new law even though it did not fully conform to the court's mandates. State supreme courts followed both courses. Indeed, sometimes a court pursued both courses simultaneously, as did the New Jersey Supreme Court following *Robinson* I. The New Jersey court granted a nine-month extension after its deadline for legislative action ran out, a move that to some indicated a wavering judicial commitment to school finance reform. Four months later, however, the court reversed course and threatened to redistribute school aid itself if the legislature failed to act. But when legislation was enacted that only partially fulfilled the court's mandate, the justices upheld the legislation against constitutional challenges. Then, when the legislature balked at funding the new law, the court set a deadline after which the state was forbidden to operate schools under the old school finance program. The deadline passed, the state's schools closed, and a week later the New Jersey legislature appropriated funds for the implementation of the new law.

Whatever the degree of cooperation between courts and legislatures in school finance reform, the question remains whether state judicial intervention has actually promoted better education for students in poorer districts. Most state rulings on school reform have focused on equalizing funding among school districts, apparently based on the assumption that there is a direct correlation between expenditure levels and educational outcomes. This focus may also reflect how plaintiffs have framed the issue of school reform, emphasizing easily quantifiable funding discrepancies. But whether funding equalization has translated into educational success remains unclear. Political officials and scholars have questioned the courts' emphasis on fiscal factors, insisting that dollars alone do not lead to improved education.[32] So far, there is little systematic evidence documenting how school finance reform has affected student performance.[33]

The Broader Context of State Constitutional Policymaking

The description of school finance litigation emphasized how constitutional policymaking involves state supreme courts and other institutions of state government. State supreme courts' interactions with federal courts and supreme courts in other states, however, are also crucial to state constitutional policymaking.

Federal Courts and State Court Policymaking   The rulings on school finance reveal how state supreme courts engage in independent constitutional policymaking. Through the interpretation of their state constitutions, these courts have a major impact on educational policy in their states, and their rulings are not subject to review or reversal by the U.S. Supreme Court. School finance is only one of several areas in which state courts have relied on state constitutions to protect rights not guaranteed by the federal Constitution. State bills of rights contain various other guarantees that have no parallel in the federal Bill of Rights (see Box 11-2). Even rights protected by the federal Constitution may have a different scope under state constitutions, due to distinctive constitutional language or state constitutional history. For example, whereas inequalities in school funding did not violate the Equal Protection Clause of the federal Constitution, the California Supreme Court held that they violated the equality requirements of the California Constitution. Since the early 1970s, state courts have increasingly looked to state guarantees to develop a body of state civil-liberties law, a phenomenon known as "the new judicial federalism."[34]

Perhaps because state courts have primary responsibility for the administration of criminal justice, initially the main focus of the new judicial federalism was the elaboration of state guarantees of defendants' rights.[35] Some state courts have announced interpretations of state provisions—for example, on search and seizure, double jeopardy, and self-incrimination—that diverge from the U.S. Supreme Court's interpretation of analogous federal guarantees.[36] In other cases state courts have interpreted state provisions that have no federal analogue, such as Oregon's prohibition on "unnecessary rigor" in punishment.[37]

State courts have also announced pioneering rulings outside the criminal justice area. Particularly noteworthy are state rulings on same-sex relationships (see Box 11-3), gender equality, the right to privacy, and the separation of church and state.[38] State judges have even begun to develop their own approaches to

BOX

11-2   *Same-Sex Marriage in Massachusetts*

The contrast in *Goodridge v. Massachusetts Department of Public Health* (2003) could hardly have been more stark. Four justices of the Massachusetts Supreme Judicial Court concluded that the state could not restrict marriage to opposite-sex couples. "The Massachusetts Constitution," Chief Justice Margaret Marshall wrote, "affirms the dignity and equality of all individuals. It forbids the creation of second-class citizens." The three dissenting justices saw the case quite differently: "Today the court has transformed its role as protector of rights into the role of creator of rights."

Yet the Massachusetts justices were not the first to address the claims of same-sex couples. Four years earlier, in *Baker v. State*, the Vermont Supreme Court had held that the state's constitution required that same-sex couples be afforded the same rights and benefits as different-sex married couples. And in *Baehr v. Lewin* (1993), the Hawaii Supreme Court had cast doubt on the constitutionality of a state statute reserving marriage to opposite-sex couples. Both rulings produced immediate reactions. In Vermont the legislature responded to *Baker* by allowing same-sex couples to enter into "civil unions," extending the benefits of marriage to them but not the right to marry. In Hawaii, in contrast, voters approved an amendment to the Hawaii Constitution stating that "the legislature shall have the power to reserve marriage to opposite-sex couples."

The response in Massachusetts resembled the responses in both Vermont and Hawaii. On the one hand, the Massachusetts Senate asked the Supreme Judicial Court for an advisory opinion as to whether recognizing civil unions would satisfy the requirements of *Goodridge*. However, the same four justices who formed the majority in *Goodridge* rejected

areas of law, such as freedom of speech and equal protection, long dominated by the Supreme Court and federal constitutional law.[39]

The development of the new judicial federalism shows both the independent policymaking role played by state courts and the influence of policymaking in federal courts on state courts. From the 1930s to the 1960s, federal courts took a more expansive view of civil liberties than did state courts. This led litigants who sought to protect or expand rights to file their suits in federal court or base their claims in state courts on the federal Constitution. Only this option. On the other hand, the Massachusetts Legislature proposed a constitutional amendment to overrule *Goodridge* but recognize civil unions, though the proposed amendment would require approval by a second session of the legislature, delaying until 2006 its submission to the voters for ratification.

Beyond the borders of Massachusetts, *Goodridge* activated groups opposed to same-sex marriage. With the support of President Bush, members of Congress proposed a constitutional amendment that defined marriage as occurring only between a man and a woman and prohibited interpretation of the federal or state constitutions to "require that marriage or the legal incidents thereof be conferred upon any union other than the union of a man and a woman." However, in both the House of Representatives and the Senate, the proposal failed to secure the two-thirds majority required for a federal constitutional amendment. But at the state level, opponents of same-sex marriage enjoyed greater success. During 2004 thirteen states amended their constitutions to restrict marriage to different-sex couples, joining Alaska, Hawaii, Nebraska, and Nevada which had done so in the aftermath of *Baehr*.

Goodridge and the reactions to it show that controversial judicial rulings rarely settle matters. *Goodridge* contributed to the national debate over same-sex relationships, but it certainly did not end it. Nevertheless, judicial rulings such as *Goodridge* do have important effects. They elevate issues on the public agenda, and they often change the terms of debate. Thus, after *Goodridge* the focus shifted to constitutional amendments as a way to protect traditional understandings of marriage from judicial invalidation. *Goodridge* thus shows a court playing a crucial—but not a dominant—role in the policy process.

Sources: *Goodridge v. Massachusetts Department of Public Health*, 798 N.E.2d 941 (Mass. 2003); *Opinions of the Justices to the Senate*, 802 N.E.2d 565 (Mass. 2004); Mark Strasser, *On Same-Sex Marriage, Civil Unions, and the Rule of Law* (Westport, CT: Praeger, 2002); and Helen Dewar, "House Rejects Same-Sex Marriage Ban," *Washington Post* A27, October 1, 2004.

when the Supreme Court became less receptive, as a result of personnel changes, to their claims, did civil-liberties advocates turn their attention to state courts and state law. School finance litigation exemplifies that pattern. Until *Rodriguez* dashed their hopes, reformers expected their victory would come in the U.S. Supreme Court. Only when they failed there did they begin to seriously consider state provisions dealing with education. Thus, the orientation of the U.S. Supreme Court and litigants' response to that orientation have a major influence on opportunities for state constitutional policymaking.[40]

BOX
11-3

Distinctive State Constitutional Guarantees

State constitutions protect a number of rights not expressly mentioned in the U.S. Constitution, as the following provisions illustrate:

Right to privacy: "The right of individual privacy is essential to the well-being of a free society and shall not be infringed without the showing of a compelling state interest." (Montana Constitution, art. 2, sec. 10)

Ban on public aid to parochial schools: "No public money or property shall be appropriated for or applied to any religious worship, exercise or instruction, or the support of any religious establishment" (Washington Constitution, art. 1, Sec. 11). "All schools maintained or supported wholly or in part by the public funds shall be forever free from sectarian control or influence." (Washington Constitution, art. 9, sec. 4)

Right to a legal remedy: "All courts shall be open, and every person, for an injury done to him in his person, property or reputation, shall have remedy by due course of law." (Connecticut Constitution, art. 1, sec. 10)

Interstate Influences   School finance cases show that state supreme court rulings can have important effects beyond the borders of the state. The New Jersey Supreme Court's ruling in *Robinson v. Cahill,* for example, stimulated litigation in several states by showing the potential for state constitutional challenges to school finance programs. Indeed, the proliferation of groups using litigation to pursue policy reforms virtually ensures that battles won on one front will be refought on others.[41] In mounting their challenges to school finance programs, groups often drew on arguments made by courts in other states. Thus, after the New Jersey court relied on the state constitution's "thorough and efficient education" clause to invalidate the state's system of school finance, reformers in other states with similar constitutional provisions argued that their state supreme courts should adopt the interpretation of the New Jersey court. Therefore, when state supreme courts announced their rulings, their opinions often relied heavily on arguments from school finance rulings in other states.

These precedents were not controlling: Each state supreme court is the authoritative interpreter of its own state constitution. Nevertheless, the positive

Gender equality: "Equality of rights under the law shall not be denied or abridged by the State on account of sex." (Hawaii Constitution, art. 1, sec. 21)

Right to bear arms: "All persons . . . have certain inherent and inalienable rights; among these are . . . the right to keep and bear arms for security or defense of self, family, home, and others, and for lawful common defense, hunting, recreational use, and all other lawful purposes, and such rights shall not be denied or infringed by the state or any subdivision thereof." (Nebraska Constitution, art. 1, sec. 1)

Right to bail: "All persons shall be bailable by sufficient sureties, except for capital offenses where the proof is evident or the presumption great." (Ohio Constitution, art. 1, sec. 9)

Freedom from excessive punishments: "Persons arrested or imprisoned shall not be treated with unnecessary rigor." (Utah Constitution, art. 1, sec. 9)

Right to safe schools: "Such public safety extends to public primary, elementary, junior high, and senior high school campuses, where students and staff have the right to be safe and secure in their persons." (California Constitution, art. 1, sec. 28)

orientation toward precedent in the United States promoted interstate borrowing. This orientation toward precedent created an expectation that judges would consult and give weight to earlier rulings even when they were not strictly controlling. It also encouraged attorneys to rely on out-of-state precedents to bolster their legal arguments. Finally, because state supreme courts confronted common legal problems, they found it useful to determine how other states had handled similar problems.[42]

THE TORT LAW REVOLUTION AND PRODUCTS LIABILITY LAW

Tort law deals with civil wrongs (other than breach of contract) that result in death, personal injury, or property damage, and for which a person can sue to recover damages. Tort law cases range from suits in "fender bender" traffic accidents to cases of medical malpractice to personal injury cases resulting from defective or dangerous consumer products. For the most part, state courts prescribe the rules that govern the resolution of tort law cases through their decisions elaborating the common law.

These rules have changed dramatically since the 1950s. State appellate courts have transformed the standards for determining liability, abolished long-standing immunities from suits, and reduced or eliminated many other barriers that plaintiffs face in recovering damages for injuries they have suffered. Particularly controversial have been state courts' innovations relating to product liability—that is, the responsibility of manufacturers or sellers for injuries suffered by consumers of their products. Some commentators believe that these rulings have enhanced the safety of consumers by raising the costs that businesses pay for accidents, negligence, and poorly designed products. These higher costs, it is assumed, give businesses an incentive to remove dangerous items from the market and to develop safer products. Other commentators argue, however, that the nation's tort law system hinders innovation and reduces the competitiveness of U.S. firms without increasing safety.

This section examines how state judges have established new policy on the obligations of producers to consumers. It documents the policy changes that have occurred, considers the factors that have led state courts to inaugurate these changes, and assesses the claims of proponents and opponents about the effects of the tort law revolution. Finally, this section examines recent developments in the battle between plaintiff and defendant, involving the intersection of tort law and state constitutional law. Box 11-4 contains a glossary of terms pertinent to the debate over products liability law.

The Changing Face of Products Liability Law

The First Regime in Products Liability Law   The first regime in tort law (and hence in products liability law) lasted into the middle of the nineteenth century. During this first regime, people were generally held responsible for any harms their actions may have caused, whether intentional or inadvertent. Underlying this standard was the notion that tort law exists primarily to redress injuries. This standard served to impede change in the society. Because people were responsible for any adverse effects their actions might produce, the prudent course was to refrain from action, particularly from risky actions. Put simply, under the first regime one acted at one's own peril.[43]

The Second Regime in Products Liability Law   The second regime developed during the nineteenth century as state courts adapted the common law to the shift from an agrarian economy to an industrial one. The key question confronting the courts was how to treat accidental injuries caused by risky, although socially useful, activities.[44] For industrial capitalism to flourish, it was widely assumed that entrepreneurs had to be free to take risks and launch new enterprises without the constraint of legal responsibility for every adverse consequence of their actions. Society would presumably benefit if producers' freedom of action was maximized, even if this meant that the "quiet citizen must keep out of the way of the exuberantly active one."[45]

One crucial change during the second regime was a reconceptualization of the aims of tort law. State judges during the nineteenth century began to view tort law as primarily concerned with deterring injurious conduct. This switch in orientation from redressing injuries to deterring misconduct had far-reaching consequences. No longer was one responsible for all injuries caused by one's actions. Under the second regime one was liable only if those injuries were foreseeable and if one failed to exercise due care to avoid them. In thus enshrining negligence as the standard for determining liability, state courts imparted a moral dimension to tort law; one was liable only when one's actions were blameworthy. But adoption of the negligence standard also made it more difficult for plaintiffs to secure redress for injuries. They had to prove not only that the defendant's actions injured them but also that the defendant had acted negligently. As Justice Oliver Wendell Holmes summed it up, "the general principle of our law is that loss from accident must lie where it falls, and that principle is not affected by the fact that a human being is the instrument of misfortune."[46]

State courts also limited producers' tort liability by modifying the traditional understanding of whom obligations were owed to. Under the first regime, one's duty of care was universal, extending to all people. Under the second regime, however, contract emerged as the primary basis for establishing obligations. If a producer entered into a contract with a purchaser, then both were in privity of contract, and courts would enforce the obligations established by the contract. But if a producer did not enter into a contract with a purchaser because he did not sell directly to consumers, then the common law generally assumed that the producer had no duties to that purchaser. Moreover, producers could reduce the risk of products liability suits by disclaiming responsibility in sales contracts for injuries that their products might cause.

State courts developed other legal doctrines—the fellow servant rule, assumption of risk, and contributory negligence—that served to immunize producers from liability. Perhaps the most important of these was the contributory negligence doctrine, under which plaintiffs were barred from redress if their own negligence had contributed, no matter how slightly, to the injury they suffered. Although some state courts devised exceptions that eased the burdens on plaintiffs, the effect of legal developments during the second regime was to restrict the compensatory function of the law of torts.[47]

BOX
11-4 **A Products Liability Glossary**

Assumption of risk: The rule that persons accept the risks inherent in situations they willingly enter, such as taking a dangerous job, and therefore cannot claim damages if they are injured.

Comparative negligence: The rule that plaintiff's recovery will be reduced in proportion to the degree that his own negligence was responsible for his injury.

Contributory negligence: The rule that plaintiff may not recover damages if he is wholly or partially responsible for his injury.

Design defect: A defect in a product that occurs because the design is not as safe as it should have been, though the product was manufactured as it was designed.

Enterprise liability: Under this standard, liability rests on each member of an industry that produced a product that harmed consumers, with liability usually apportioned according to each member's share of the market for that product.

Failure to warn: The failure of a defendant in a products liability case to have provided adequate warnings or instructions about the use of its product.

Fellow servant rule: The rule that employers were not liable for workers' injuries brought about by the negligence of a fellow worker; they were liable only when they were personally at fault.

Liability under the Second Regime   To clarify the implications of the policies adopted by state courts under the second regime, consider the following scenarios:[48]

- Helen Henningsen was injured when the ten-day-old Plymouth she was driving crashed because of defects in the vehicle's steering system. She sued both the dealer who sold her husband the car and the manufacturer, seeking reimbursement for her medical expenses and the cost of repairs to the car.
- When David Larsen's Chevrolet Corvair collided head-on with another car, the force of the collision thrust the Corvair's steering column into

Manufacturing defect: A defect resulting from a product's not having been manufactured as it had been designed.

Negligence: The defendant's breach of a duty to exercise due care.

Privity of contract: The contractual relationship between buyer and seller that provides a basis for liability for defective products. Traditionally, however, consumers under this doctrine could not sue manufacturers for defective goods unless they had bought the goods directly from the manufacturer.

Punitive damages: In cases in which it is proved that the defendant acted willfully, maliciously, or fraudulently, a plaintiff may be awarded punitive or exemplary damages in addition to compensatory damages to punish the defendant or set an example for similar wrongdoers.

State-of-the-art defense: The defense that permits a defendant in a design defect case to avoid liability if at the time of manufacture no safer design was available; or, in a failure to warn case, if at the time of manufacture there was no way for the defendant to have known of the danger he failed to warn against.

Strict liability: Under this standard, one who sells a product in a defective condition unreasonably dangerous to a consumer is held liable for harm caused by the defect.

Tort: Any civil legal wrong, other than a breach of contract, that results in personal injury, death, or property damage, and for which a person can sue to recover damages.

Larsen's head. He sued General Motors, the manufacturer, claiming that its design was unsafe.

- In the late 1940s, several firms produced and marketed DES (diethyl-stilbestrol), a drug given to pregnant women to prevent miscarriages. In 1971, scientists discovered a link between DES and a form of cancer occurring in the daughters of women who took the drug. Because none of the "DES daughters" could identify which firm manufactured the DES taken by their mothers, they sued all of the manufacturers of the drug.

Under the products liability law that existed in most states from the mid-nineteenth century through the 1950s, the plaintiffs likely would have lost all three cases. In the first scenario, Mrs. Henningsen had not purchased the car; her husband had. Because she had not formed a contract with the Plymouth dealership, it had no contractual obligation to her. Moreover, even if her husband had been driving when the accident occurred, he could not have collected damages for medical expenses because the standard purchase agreement he signed limited the dealer's liability only to replacement of defective parts. Nor could the Henningsens have collected from the car's manufacturer, even if the vehicle was defective when it left the assembly line; neither Henningsen had privity of contract with Plymouth, so the manufacturer had no legal obligations to either of them. Finally, they could not collect from the dealer who sold them the car because the defect did not result from negligence on his part.

In the second scenario, David Larsen, the driver of the Corvair, also would not have collected damages under the second regime. Like the Henningsens, he had no contract with the car's manufacturer and so did not meet the requirement of privity of contract. In addition, the collision that led to his injury did not result from a defect in the manufacture of the car; all Corvairs had the same steering column. Finally, Larsen's injury occurred partly because of driver error, and thus the doctrine of contributory negligence, under which plaintiffs are barred from redress if their actions contributed to an injury, immunized General Motors.

In the final scenario, no company that produced DES would be held liable because none could be proven to have produced the DES that injured the daughters. The plaintiffs would also have had to prove that the companies either knew of or should have foreseen the carcinogenic properties of DES, because under a negligence standard one is liable for injuries one causes only if they are foreseeable and preventable.

The Third Regime in Products Liability Law   Beginning in the late 1950s, a fundamental shift occurred in products liability law as legal doctrines were developed that simplified plaintiffs' efforts to obtain redress for injuries. Indicative of this shift is the fact that, under this third regime (contemporary products liability law), the plaintiffs in all three of the above scenarios were legally entitled to damages for their injuries.

Privity of Contract and Strict Liability   In the first scenario, Mrs. Henningsen was able to recover damages because of the elimination of privity of contract. In *Henningsen v. Bloomfield Motors* (1960), the New Jersey Supreme Court ruled that when manufacturers offer a product for purchase, the product is accompanied by an implied warranty that it is reasonably suitable for use.[49] Those who are injured by defective products may sue for damages even if they have no contractual relations with the manufacturer. The court further held that manufacturers could not use contractual provisions to escape liability for injuries caused by their defective products.

Three years after *Henningsen,* the California Supreme Court went even further, adopting strict liability as the standard in products liability cases.[50] It thus held manufacturers of defective products responsible for any injuries they caused. Strict liability shifted the focus from the conduct of the producer, which was crucial under the negligence standard, to the product itself. All the plaintiff had to prove was that the product was defective and caused the injury.

Once the New Jersey and California supreme courts pioneered these doctrinal changes, other state appellate courts quickly followed their lead. Within a decade and a half, more than two-thirds of the states had embraced strict liability and eliminated the requirement of privity of contract. As Lawrence Baum and Bradley Canon put it, "Never before had such a momentous change in tort law swept the American states so rapidly."[51]

Design Defect and Comparative Negligence   In the second scenario, Larsen's injuries did not result from negligence or errors in the construction of his Corvair; the car was manufactured exactly as it had been designed. Under current products liability law, however, conformity to design specifications is not decisive. State courts have recognized that a defendant may also be liable if the design of the product that caused an injury is defective—that is, if there was a safer alternative design for the product. In Larsen's case, for example, there were ways to design a steering column so that it would not impale the driver's head or chest in a collision. Chevrolet's faulty design unreasonably created dangers and thus, Larsen could sue for damages suffered because of the defect.

Under the tort doctrines of the second regime, Larsen's contributory negligence, his partial responsibility for the crash, would have barred him from recovering for his injuries. In recent years, however, most states have adopted the comparative negligence standard. Under this new standard, a plaintiff's partial responsibility does not preclude recovery for injuries. Instead, the damages received are merely reduced in proportion to the degree that one's own negligence was responsible for one's injury.

It is hard to overestimate the importance of these changes in expanding plaintiffs' opportunities for redress. Adoption of comparative negligence eliminated a major barrier to products liability suits. And as Jethro Lieberman noted, "Strict liability for design defect has become a dominant part of the law governing products because it seems to be the only standard that can reach a large class of injuries left untouched by the earlier doctrines."[52]

Failure to Warn, Enterprise Liability, and Punitive Damages   The third scenario, the DES case, reveals further innovations in products liability law. The drug DES did serve the purpose of preventing miscarriages, and arguably no better design may have been available at the time it was produced.

Nonetheless, DES was dangerous if used for other than its intended purpose, and even when used for its intended purpose it had certain residual hazards. The manufacturers of DES, however, did not warn women of the dangers of the drug. Under modern products liability law their failure to warn made them strictly liable for injuries caused by the drug. The only recognized exception to this warning requirement is if, at the time of manufacture, there was no way the defendant knew or could have known of the dangers that the product posed (the so-called state-of-the-art defense). Some states do not even allow this defense against failure-to-warn claims.[53]

Courts have also permitted recovery even when, as in the DES case, plaintiffs could not identify which company manufactured the product that harmed them. Rather than deny relief, courts established the doctrine of enterprise liability, under which all manufacturers of a product are required to pay damages for injuries it caused. In the DES case the court apportioned liability among the companies that had produced the drug on the basis of their market shares. The doctrine of enterprise liability has proved particularly helpful in assessing liability in so-called toxic torts cases, such as those involving exposure to asbestos or Agent Orange, in which a huge number of plaintiffs have been injured by a generic product.[54]

Finally, when the defendant's conduct was willful, malicious, or fraudulent, courts may award punitive damages as well as compensation for injuries. Punitive damages punish defendants by imposing on them costs greater than the injuries they caused. Punitive damages also warn other potential wrongdoers of the costs of misconduct, possibly deterring such behavior. Because jury imposition of punitive damages can dramatically increase the liability of defendants, punitive damages have become very controversial.

Causes of the Revolution in Products Liability Law   The dramatic transformation of judicial policy from the second to the third regime, like that from the first regime to the second, reflected changes in both social conditions and social philosophy. The industrialization of the American economy in the late nineteenth century led to increased work-related accidents as workers dealt with more dangerous machinery and materials. Consumers benefited from the wider range of products on the market but often lacked the technical expertise to assess the engineering or safety of modern goods. Neither could they individually bargain with mass producers for guarantees that the goods they bought were safe and durable. But when consumers and workers were injured, products liability law during the second regime made it difficult for them to collect damages.[55]

This policy on products liability meshed with laissez-faire economic theory and the philosophy of rugged individualism dominant in the late nineteenth and early twentieth centuries. But over time the prevailing social and legal philosophy changed and, as it did, it affected the perspective on the relationship between producers and consumers. Lawrence Friedman has characterized this new perspective as an expectation of "total justice," a notion that one should obtain redress for any harm one suffers.[56] Jethro Lieberman has described the emergence of a "fiduciary ethic," a sense that individuals have a duty to see that their actions do not harm others.[57] If policy on products liability was to reflect these changing societal conditions and views, it would have to do more than mitigate the harshness of privity of contract and other legal doctrines.[58] The new policy would have to make its primary aim compensating the victims of accidents rather than deterring misconduct.[59]

Although changing conditions and societal views may have provided the impetus for a shift in policy, the shift itself could not have occurred if state judges had not been willing to overrule precedents and enunciate new legal standards.[60] Initially, some judges refused to do so, maintaining that the doctrine of *stare decisis* required them to adhere to established legal principles. As one judge said, "The judicial wastebasket should not be filled with precedents only a few years old."[61] Other judges, also insisting on judicial restraint, argued that policymaking was the province of legislatures, not courts. But some activist state judges concluded that neither respect for precedent nor judicial role constraints prevented them from reforming products liability law. They argued that alteration of policies on products liability could not be a usurpation of legislative authority, because those policies had been established by judges. Furthermore, courts were responsible for the growth of the common law as well as for maintaining legal stability. Thus, the New Jersey Supreme Court forthrightly declared, "The law should be based on current concepts of what is right and just, and the judiciary should be alert to the never ending need for keeping common-law principles abreast of the times."[62]

When activist courts such as the New Jersey and California supreme courts initiated changes in products liability law, they dramatically altered the legal landscape. Legal principles that had appeared to be settled were no longer settled, and movement appeared to be away from previously established positions. Moreover, the rulings of these activist courts appeared to have vindicated the legitimacy of court-initiated policy changes. Finally, although most state appellate courts were reluctant to take a leadership role, they were equally reluctant to defend legal doctrines that had been repudiated by a majority of their sister courts. In sum, by challenging the established doctrines in products liability law, the activist courts created a momentum that carried less adventuresome courts along the path of reform.[63]

The Consequences of Policy Change

According to their proponents, the reforms in products liability policy have ensured safer consumer goods by inducing manufacturers to improve product safety rather than risk costly suits for injuries caused by their products.[64]

Although producers would bear the costs of injuries under the new products liability policy, proponents assumed that this was not a problem because producers could figure those costs into the prices of the goods they sold and could purchase liability insurance to reduce their risks.[65]

But according to critics of the products liability reforms, this is not how the reforms have worked out. The changes in law have transformed "the doers, the makers, and the providers of this world . . . into perpetual prey, pursued and worried at every turn by a hound-like legal profession."[66] In addition, erratic and excessive jury awards have prompted insurance companies to refuse coverage; one company official found the United States "as unpredictable from an underwriter's point of view as a banana republic."[67] And U.S. firms, deterred from innovation by the threat of lawsuits, have found themselves at a competitive disadvantage in the global marketplace. Let us examine these charges.

The Critique of Products Liability Reforms

Innovation and the Range of Goods   Critics claim that changes in products liability policy have deterred entrepreneurial innovation to the detriment of consumers and the nation's place in the world economy.[68] Under a system of strict liability, jurors focus on the defects in products rather than on the care taken in design and production to reduce risks for consumers. The jurors, critics claim, tend to sympathize with accident victims and are predisposed to assume that the new is more dangerous than the familiar. Therefore, they tend to award damages whenever a plaintiff using a new product is injured, even in the face of strong scientific evidence against the plaintiff's claim.[69] And even when defendants ultimately prevail, the costs of defending liability suits can be ruinous. For example, although manufacturers of light aircraft won more than 80 percent of products liability cases brought to trial, liability costs have added an estimated $70,000 to the price of each light airplane.[70]

Faced with the prospect of excessive and at times capricious damage awards, firms may cease production of safe products or withhold new products from the market. A survey of the nation's 500 largest corporations found that 25 percent claimed to have withdrawn products from the market because of liability or insurance problems.[71] Firms may also opt out of particularly risky fields. For example, though in the early 1970s thirteen pharmaceutical companies pursued research in contraception and fertility, by the late 1980s only one did.[72] Other firms may decide to stick with products for which the risks are known, rather than develop new products, even if they believe the new products are safer. Indeed, a firm that develops a safer product opens itself up to suits by plaintiffs who use the advances to argue that there was a design defect in the earlier, less safe version.

As one commentator summed it up, the "risk of lawsuits is so great, and the consequences so potentially disastrous, that the inevitable result is for more caution in product innovation [in the United States] than in other advanced nations."[73] This not only places U.S. firms at a competitive disadvantage with foreign firms but also deprives Americans of new, desirable, and often safer consumer goods.

Unjustifiable Awards and Frivolous Claims   Critics also charge that contemporary products liability law exacerbates the worst tendencies of civil juries. Jurors lack the expertise to evaluate complex technical information, but under the strict-liability standard, cases often turn on testimony by scientific experts about the causes of injuries or defects in product design. Not surprisingly, then, jurors' decisions in products liability cases often are capricious and unpredictable. Critics also allege that jurors tend to be sympathetic to accident victims, hostile to corporations, and eager to impose the costs of accidents on "deep-pocket" defendants rather than on individuals.[74] Judgments under current products liability law reflect those biases, with plaintiffs reaping excessive and undeserved damage awards and defendants saddled with punitive damages.[75] For instance, no plaintiff was awarded a million dollars until 1964 but now million-dollar verdicts are routine.[76]

These unjustified verdicts and excessive awards, critics charge, merely encourage more products liability litigation as plaintiffs seek to cash in and attorneys to earn large contingent fees at the expense of producers.[77] The pro-plaintiff bias of civil juries and the capriciousness of their verdicts also affects the settlement of products liability cases. Fearful of an excessive award if they take a case to trial, defendants may settle cases even when the claims against them lack merit.[78] This too promotes more products liability suits.

Costs and Benefits   What are the costs of this system of products liability? According to the Institute on Civil Justice, the United States spent between $29 and $36 billion on tort litigation in 1985.[79] (Products liability cases are only a part, though an important one, of overall tort litigation.) Accident victims receive only about half of this sum, with the remainder going to attorneys and insurers for administering the claims settlement process.[80] Despite these enormous expenditures, critics charge that Americans are not significantly safer than they were under the second regime.[81] In sum, the policy adopted by state courts has proven to be an extremely costly but ineffective means of promoting consumer safety.

Evaluating the Evidence   Scholars have only recently begun to gather evidence about these claims. This research does not fully support either the proponents or the critics of the products liability policy developed by the courts.

A Products Liability Litigation Explosion?   Critics charge that the changes in products liability policy led to an explosion in litigation against producers. The strongest evidence supporting this claim is the astronomical increase in products

---

BOX

11-5   *A Simple Cup of Coffee*

You may have heard of Stella Liebeck, the "McDonald's coffee lady."
After the coffee she purchased at a McDonald's drive-in window spilled
and burned her when she was attempting to remove its top to add cream
and sugar, she sued McDonald's, and a jury awarded her almost $3 mil-
lion in damages. Comedians had a field day with the incident, while critics charged that the "outrageous" verdict revealed a system of civil justice
that was out of control, with greedy plaintiffs cashing in against "deep
pockets" defendants.

   In fact, however, things were not quite that simple. For one thing,
the injuries that Liebeck suffered were quite severe: The coffee scalded
her groin, thighs, and buttocks, resulting in third-degree burns over
6 percent of her body and requiring a week in the hospital and skin grafts.
And Liebeck initially sought to recover only $20,000, a figure sufficient
for her medical expenses, wages lost by her daughter while nursing her,
and pain and suffering. As the trial date approached without a settlement,
the amount demanded by Liebeck's attorney escalated to $300,000.

---

liability suits in federal courts: fewer than 2,000 in 1974, but more than 31,000 by
2002.[82] But these figures are misleading because much of the increase in products
liability suits was tied to only three products (asbestos, the Dalkon Shield, and
Bendectin), so there was no dramatic across-the-board increase in litigation.[83]

   Neither is there a continuing products liability explosion in state courts,
where the vast majority of products liability cases are heard. What the state
data show is that tort filings rose 39 percent from 1975 to 1999.[84] But the
increase was not steady throughout this period, as accounts of a products liability explosion might lead one to believe. In fact, from 1993–2003, tort cases
declined 5 percent.[85]

A Boon for Plaintiffs?   Critics also charge that the products liability revolution, combined with jury sympathy for plaintiffs and bias against businesses,
resulted in unwarranted victories for plaintiffs and overgenerous awards when
they do prevail. Yet no systematic data support this claim. Critics rely largely
on "horror stories," simply assuming that the cases described are typical
instead of isolated and unrepresentative. Also, the accounts of these cases are
frequently exaggerated or inaccurate (see Box 11-5).

A mediator encouraged McDonald's to settle for $225,000. But McDonald's denied responsibility, and the case went to trial.

The trial went badly for McDonald's. There was uncontradicted testimony that McDonald's served its coffee at an unusually high temperature and that it had refused to warn the public or lower the coffee's temperature, despite more than 700 previous complaints of scalding. The jury found for Liebeck, awarding her $160,000 in compensatory damages ($200,000 minus $40,000 for her 20 percent responsibility for her injuries). To punish McDonald's, the jury also awarded her $2.7 million in punitive damages, the equivalent of two days' worth of coffee sales by the corporation.

Did the accident make Stella Liebeck a millionaire? Not really. The trial judge subsequently reduced the punitive damages to $480,000, using a routine judicial standard that punitive damages should not be more than three times the compensatory damages. On appeal, the New Mexico Supreme Court upheld the reduction of award. Nevertheless, the ruling did have broader effects. In the wake of the jury award, Wendy's restaurants reduced the temperature of their hot chocolate.

Sources: The account of the Liebeck case relies on Judith Acks, William Haltom, and Michael McCann, "Symbolic Stella: On Media Coverage of Personal Injury Litigation and the Production of Legal Knowledge," *Law and Courts* 7 (summer 1997): 5–7, and Jay M. Feinman, *Law 101: Everything You Need to Know about the American Legal System* (New York: Oxford University Press, 2000).

A study by the federal government of tort cases in state courts in the nation's seventy-five largest counties provides the best systematic data available on case outcomes. The study found that plaintiffs prevailed in just over half the cases (52 percent). Plaintiffs won just over a quarter of the time in medical malpractice cases (27 percent). Interestingly, although most tort cases involved jury trials, plaintiffs actually fared better in bench trials, winning 65 percent of the time. In those products liability cases in which plaintiffs prevailed, the median award was $450,000, with damages in almost 40 percent of the cases topping $1,000,000. In less than 3 percent of the cases, however, were punitive damages awarded.[86]

These data offer only limited support for critics' claims. Juries do not overwhelmingly support plaintiffs, and punitive damages are rarely awarded. Yet one should be cautious in drawing conclusions from these data. For one thing, they report only cases that went to trial, not the majority of tort cases settled or dropped prior to trial. In addition, the figures on jury awards may be inflated, because trial judges or appellate courts may subsequently reduce them. A study of verdicts in Cook County (Illinois) and San Francisco County, for example, found that reductions for jury awards of more than $1 million were close to 40 percent.[87] Finally, contrary to critics' claims, interviews with jurors reveal not a bias against business but a suspicion of plaintiffs' motives and actions.[88]

What Effects on Safety and Innovation?   Proponents and critics of the products liability reforms disagree sharply about how reforms have affected product safety. Proponents believe that changes in products liability law and in levels of litigation would prompt producers to devote greater attention to product safety, leading to fewer accidents. The very limited research available, however, has found no relationship between these legal changes and accident rates.[89] Even when acknowledging that factors such as technological change and consumer demands may affect accident rates, there is no concrete evidence vindicating the hopes of products liability reformers.

Aside from these data, the only other evidence is expert opinion. One group of economists that surveyed product safety in various industries and economic sectors concluded that, except in the chemical industry, changes in products liability law had done little to improve product safety.[90] When safety improvements did occur, they resulted primarily from adverse publicity generated by litigation about a product's safety, which reduced consumer demand.[91] The economists also concluded that—again with the exception of the chemical industry—changes in products liability law tended to impede the development and marketing of new products.[92]

Responses to the Products Liability "Crisis"

Concerns about a crisis in products liability, whether warranted or not, prompted legal changes designed to relieve the burden on defendants. Some of these changes originated in state courts. Beginning in the 1980s, several supreme courts modified their policies on products liability.[93] Some courts declined to extend doctrines that benefit plaintiffs to new situations. Thus, they refused to impose strict liability on producers of dangerous but defectless products, such as handguns, alcohol, and swimming pools, or on producers who failed to warn victims of scientifically unknown risks.[94] Other state courts retreated from pro-plaintiff positions. The New Jersey Supreme Court, for example, limited the imposition of enterprise liability solely to asbestos cases.[95] Similarly, the California Supreme Court refused to extend liability to a drug company based, among other things, on the effect that liability would have on drug research and the development of new drugs.[96]

Even more important were so-called tort reform initiatives undertaken by state legislatures. Beginning in the 1980s, legislatures in every state considered legislation to modify or overturn common-law doctrines enunciated by state courts. In one three-year period, forty-eight state legislatures adopted tort reform legislation.[97] Several states established caps on punitive damages or on damages for non-economic injuries such as pain and suffering. Some states discouraged suits through statutes of limitation that required that suits be filed within a set period after an injury was suffered. Others did so through statutes of repose. Utah, for example, barred products liability claims six years after purchase or ten years after the date the product was manufactured. Finally, some states sought to discourage litigation by placing limits on attorneys' contingent fees or by imposing sanctions on attorneys who filed frivolous suits.[98]

With the enactment of these tort reform statutes, the conflict over products liability law entered a new phase. The plaintiffs' bar responded to this legislation by challenging many of these tort reform statutes as unconstitutional. For example, they argued that statutory limits on punitive or non-economic damages violated state constitutional guarantees of jury trial because they limited the discretion of jurors in awarding damages. They also contended that statutes of limitation and statutes of repose violated the "open courts" provisions of state constitutions, which guarantee that the courts be available for the redress of injuries.[99] Their arguments enjoyed considerable success. During the 1980s and 1990s, supreme courts in twenty-six states invalidated more than ninety tort reform statutes.[100] But this hardly resolved matters. State legislatures continued to enact tort reform statutes, seeking to devise legislation that would withstand judicial scrutiny. Meanwhile, proponents of tort reform denounced the courts' rulings, insisting that they were an unwarranted substitution of judicial policy preferences for those of the people's representatives. One suspects that the battle against judicial nullification of civil justice reform has just begun. The hotly contested and heavily financed judicial elections of 2000 in Alabama, Ohio, and Texas (see Chapter 3) make clear that this battle will involve not only legal arguments to state supreme courts but also attempts by both pro-plaintiff and pro-defendant forces to influence the composition of these courts.

CONCLUSIONS

As school finance cases reveal, constitutional policymaking in state courts is influenced by those courts' relations with federal courts, supreme courts of other states, and other institutions of state government. The development of products liability law suggests that federal courts have considerably less influence on common-law policymaking. On occasion federal rulings may guide state legal developments. For example, charitable institutions were immune from tort suits in most states until a ruling in a federal court of appeals led states to reconsider and eliminate the immunity.[101] But overall, federal courts decide such a miniscule proportion of common-law cases that their opportunities for influence are quite limited. Also, state courts have traditionally assumed responsibility for the development of the common law and thus have no reason to look to the federal courts for direction.

Considerably more important is the influence of state courts in other states. In dealing with the common law, there is no legal text—no statute, constitutional provision, or administrative regulation—to interpret. Consequently, precedent, including the rulings of courts in sister states, becomes more important in guiding judicial decisions. Reliance on precedent contributes to stability in the law when the rulings in various states coincide. But when they diverge, state courts' reliance on precedent can, paradoxically, be a force for legal change. Success by a litigant in one state can encourage litigants in other states to raise the same legal issue. When they do, they can point to favorable precedents in other states in arguing for legal change. If a state court consults only its own prior cases, respect for precedent, *stare decisis,* will promote legal continuity. But if a court considers precedents from beyond the state's borders, it may find conflicting interpretations of the common law. When it does, this conflict diminishes the authority of the court's prior rulings because those precedents then represent only one possible interpretation of the common law. Or, from a different perspective, the availability of precedents to support both sides in a case gives judges the opportunity to choose which precedent they will follow. Thus, once some states adopted the strict-liability standard, judges in other states could decide whether to follow their own precedents or join the movement for strict liability.

The development of products liability law during the third regime also reveals that common-law policymaking takes place within the context of state politics. State legislators can by statute overturn legal principles enunciated by judges and redirect the course of common law. For example, during the 1980s, when the products liability rulings of state judges were viewed as tilting the balance too much in favor of plaintiffs, several state legislatures acted to redress the balance. Moreover, state legislatures may affect the course of the common law even without legislating. After all, the potential for legislative intervention may itself act as a constraint on judicial decisions. Still, it would be a mistake to view the relation between state courts and legislators as simply conflictual. Most judicial decisions interpreting the common law provoke no response from legislators. Judicial decisions and legislative responses (or nonresponses) can be viewed as a form of implicit negotiation through which judges and legislators seek to leave their mark on the common law.

NOTES

---

1. William J. Brennan Jr., "State Supreme Court Judge versus United States Supreme Court Justice: A Change in Function and Perspective," *University of Florida Law Review* 19 (1966): 236.

2. See William E. Thro, "To Render Them Safe: The Analysis of State Constitutional Provisions in Public School Finance Reform Litigation," *Virginia Law Review* 75 (1989): 1647. For data on the contributions of federal, state, and local sources to school budgets, see the Web site of the U.S. Department of Education at http://nces.ed.gov/pubs2000/Digest99/Chapter2.html.

3. *San Antonio Independent School District v. Rodriguez*, 411 U.S. 1, 11–13 (1973).

4. See the discussion of this contention in K. Forbis Jordan and Kern Alexander, "Constitutional Methods of Financing Public Schools," in *Constitutional Reform of School Finance*, eds. Kern Alexander and K. Forbis Jordan (Lexington, MA: Lexington Books, 1973).

5. *San Antonio Independent School District v. Rodriguez*, 411 U.S. 1 (1973).

6. These cases include *DuPree v. Alma School District* No. 30, 651 S.W.2d 90 (Ark. 1983); *Serrano v. Priest* [Serrano II], 557 P.2d 929 (Cal. 1976); *Horton v. Meskill,* 376 A.2d 359 (Conn. 1977); *Rose v. Council for Better Education,* 790 S.W.2d 186 (Ky. 1989); *Helena Elementary School District No. 1 v. State,* 769 P.2d 684 (Mont. 1989); *Robinson v. Cahill,* 303 A.2d 273 (N.J. 1973); *Seattle School District No. 1 v. State,* 585 P.2d 71 (Wash. 1978); *Pauley v. Kelly,* 255 S.E.2d 859 (W. Va. 1979); and *Washakie County School District No. 1 v. Herschler,* 606 P.2d 310 (Wyo. 1980).

7. *Edgewood Independent School District v. Kirby* [*Edgewood* I], 777 S.W.2d 391 (Tex. 1989).

8. *Brown v. Board of Education,* 347 U.S. 483 (1954). On the influence of *Brown* on reformers, see John E. Coons, William H. Clune III, and Stephen D. Sugarman, *Private Wealth and Public Education* (Cambridge, MA: Belknap Press, 1970), and Alexander and Jordan, *Constitutional Reform of School Finance.*

9. See, e.g., *Griffin v. Illinois,* 351 U.S. 12 (1958); *Douglas v. California,* 372 U.S. 353 (1963); and *Harper v. Virginia State Board of Elections,* 383 U.S. 663 (1966).

10. *Robinson v. Cahill,* 303 A.2d 273 (N.J. 1973).

11. New Jersey Constitution, art. 8, sec. 14, para. 1.

12. Wesley W. Horton, "Memoirs of a Connecticut School Finance Lawyer," *Connecticut Law Review* 24 (spring 1992): 706.

13. The cases during this period in which plaintiffs' challenges succeeded are listed in note 6 above. Unsuccessful challenges include *Thompson v. Engleking,* 537 P.2d 635 (Idaho 1975); *Milliken v. Green,* 203 N.W.2d 457 (Mich. 1972); *Woodahl v. Straub,* 520 P.2d 776 (Mont. 1974); *Board of Education v. Walter,* 390 N.E.2d 813 (Ohio 1979); *Olsen v. Oregon,* 554 P.2d 139 (Or. 1976); and *Danson v. Casey,* 399 A.2d 476 (Pa. 1978).

14. School finance reformers enjoyed their only success during this period in *Dupree v. Alma School District No. 30,* 651 S.W.2d 90 (Ark. 1983). Unsuccessful challenges include *Lujan v. State Board of Education,* 649 P.2d 1005 (Col. 1982); *Thompson v. McDaniels,* 285 S.E.2d 156 (Ga. 1981); *Hornbeck v. Somerset County Board of Education,* 458 A.2d 758 (Md. 1983); *Board of Education v. Nyquist,* 439 N.E.2d 359 (N.Y. 1982); *Fair School Finance Council of Oklahoma, Inc. v. State,* 746 P.2d 1135 (Okla. 1987); and *Richland County v. Campbell,* 364 S.E.2d 470 (S.C. 1988).

15. Successful challenges to state systems of public school finance from 1989 to 2004 include *Roosevelt Elementary School District v. Bishop,* 877 P.2d 806 (Ariz. 1994); *Rose v. Council for Better Education,* 790 S.W.2d 186 (Ky. 1989); *McDuffy v. Secretary, Executive Office of Education,* 615 N.E.2d 516 (Mass. 1993); *Helena Elementary School District No. 1 v. State,* 760 P.2d 684 (Mont. 1989); *Abbott v. Burke,* 575 A.2d 359 (N.J. 1990); *DeRolph v. State,* 681 N.E.2d 424 (Ohio 1997); *Edgewood Independent School District v. Kirby,* 777 S.W.2d 391 (Tex. 1989); *Tennessee Small School System v. McWherter,* 851 S.W.2d 139 (Tenn. 1993); and *Brigham v. State,* 692 A.2d 384 (Vt. 1997). Unsuccessful challenges to systems of school finance include *Committee for Educational Rights v.*

Edgar, 672 N.E.2d 1178 (Ill. 1996); *Unified School District v. Kansas,* 885 P.2d 1570 (Kan. 1994); *Skeen v. Minnesota,* 505 N.W.2d 299 (Minn. 1993); *Pawtucket v. Sundlum,* 662 A.2d 40 (R.I. 1995); and *Kukor v. Grover,* 436 N.W.2d 568 (Wis. 1989).

16. *Abbott v. Burke,* 575 A.2d 359, 394 (N.J. 1990).

17. *Board of Education v. Nyquist,* 439 N.E.2d 359, 369 (N.Y. 1982).

18. *Thompson v. Engleking,* 537 P.2d 635, 640–641 (Idaho 1975).

19. See, e.g., *Helena Elementary School District No. 1 v. State,* 769 P.2d 684, 689–690 (Mont. 1989).

20. *Pauley v. Kelly,* 255 S.E.2d 859, 877 (W. Va. 1979).

21. Janice C. May, "Financing Public Schools in Texas: A Protracted Imbroglio," *State Constitutional Commentaries and Notes* 2 (fall 1990): 9.

22. The New Jersey Supreme Court has a tradition of unanimity in major cases. See G. Alan Tarr and Mary Cornelia Aldis Porter, *State Supreme Courts in State and Nation* (New Haven, CT: Yale University Press, 1988), chap. 5.

23. Donald L. Horowitz, *The Courts and Social Policy* (Washington, DC: Brookings, 1977). For a detailed discussion of Horowitz's critique of judicial policymaking capacity, see Chapter 9.

24. *Serrano v. Priest,* 557 P.2d 929 (Cal. 1977).

25 Charles S. Benson, "Definitions of Equity in School Finance in Texas, New Jersey, and Kentucky," *Harvard Journal on Legislation* 28 (summer 1991): 405, n. 20.

26. Mary Cornelia Porter and G. Alan Tarr, Introduction to *State Supreme Courts: Policymakers in the Federal System,* eds. Mary Cornelia Porter and G. Alan Tarr (Westport, CT: Greenwood Press, 1982), p. xvii.

27. Ibid.

28. *Robinson v. Cahill* [Robinson I]. 303 A.2d 273 (N.J. 1973), and *Robinson v. Cahill* [Robinson VII], 360 A.2d 400 (N.J. 1976).

29. On school finance reform in Kentucky, see Kern Alexander, "The Common School Ideal and the Limits of Legislative Authority: The Kentucky Case," *Harvard Journal on Legislation* 28 (summer 1991): 341–366, and Bert T. Combs, "Creative Constitutional Law: The Kentucky School Reform Law," *Harvard Journal on Legislation* 28 (summer 1991): 367–378.

30. On school finance reform in Texas, see May, "Financing Public Schools in Texas," and William P. Hobby and Billy D. Walker, "Legislative Reform of the Texas Public School Finance System, 1973–1991," *Harvard Journal on Legislation* 28 (summer 1991): 379–394.

31. On the politics of school finance reform after *Robinson v. Cahill,* see Richard Lehne, *The Quest for Justice: The Politics of School Finance Reform* (New York: Longman, 1978).

32. Debate on the relation between levels of funding and quality of education has been a constant aspect of finance reform efforts. See Eric A. Hanushek, "When School Finance 'Reform' May Not Be Good Policy," *Harvard Journal on Legislation* 28 (summer 1991): 423–456, and Ronald F. Ferguson, "Paying for Public Education: New Evidence on How and Why Money Matters," *Harvard Journal on Legislation* 28 (summer 1991): 465–498. 000. The analysis follows Tarr and Porter, *State Supreme Courts in State and Nation,* p. 217.

33. For an analysis of the effects of school finance litigation in one state, see Russell S. Harrison and G. Alan Tarr, "School Finance and Inequality in New Jersey," in *Constitutional Politics in the States: Contemporary Controversies and Historical Patterns,* ed. G. Alan Tarr (Westport, CT: Greenwood Press, 1996). More generally, see Douglas Reed, *On Equal Terms: The Constitutional Politics of Educational Opportunity* (Princeton, NJ: Princeton University Press, 2001).

34. For an overview of the new judicial federalism, see G. Alan Tarr, "The New Judicial Federalism in Perspective," *Notre Dame Law Review* 72 (May 1997): 1097–1118.

35. See Barry Latzer, *State Constitutions and Criminal Justice* (Westport, CT: Greenwood Press, 1991).

36. Rulings enunciating distinctive state standards include, for search and seizure, *State v. Boland,* 800 P. d 1112 (Wash. 1990); for double jeopardy, *State v. Lachat,* 343 S.E.2d 872 (N.C. 1986); and for self-incrimination, *State v. Mercier,* 509 A.2d 1246 (N.J. 1986).

37. *Sterling v. Cupp,* 625 P.2d 123 (Or. 1981).

38. On privacy, see *In re Quinlan,* 355 A.2d 647 (N.J. 1976); on gender equality, see *Opinion of the Justices to the House of Representatives,* 371 N.E.2d 426 (Mass. 1977), and, more generally, G. Alan Tarr and Mary Cornelia Porter, "Gender Equality and Judicial Federalism: The Role of State Appellate Courts," *Hastings Constitutional Law Quarterly* 9 (summer 1982): 919–973; on church and state, see *Fox v. City of Los Angeles,* 587 P.2d 663 (Cal. 1978), and, more generally, G. Alan Tarr, "Church and State in the States," *Washington Law Review* 64 (January 1989): 73–110.

39. On free speech, see *Robins v. Pruneyard Shopping Center,* 592 P.2d 341 (Cal. 1979); on equal protection of the laws, see *Washakie County School District v. Herschler,* 606 P.2d 310 (Wyo. 1980).

40. See Porter and Tarr, *State Supreme Courts,* pp. xix–xx.

41. Ibid., p. xxi.

42. Tarr and Porter, *State Supreme Courts in State and Nation,* pp. 27–30.

43. This account relies on Jethro Lieberman, *The Litigious Society* (New York: Basic Books, 1981), pp. 34–36.

44. G. Edward White, *Tort Law in America: An Intellectual History* (New York: Oxford University Press, 1985), p. 61.

45. Quoted in Lieberman, *The Litigious Society,* p. 37. On the development of tort law doctrine during the second regime, see, in addition to Lieberman, Morton J. Horwitz, *The Transformation of American Law, 1780–1860* (Cambridge, MA: Harvard University Press, 1977), and White, *Tort Law in America,* chap. 2–4.

46. Quoted in Lieberman, *The Litigious Society,* p. 36. On the various—and at times competing—ends of tort law, see Robert E. Litan, Peter Swire, and Clifford Winston, "The U.S. Liability System: Background and Trends," in *Liability: Perspectives and Policy,* eds. Robert E. Litan and Clifford Winston (Washington, DC: Brookings, 1988), pp. 3–5.

47. White, *Tort Law in America,* pp. 61–62; perhaps the most important case alleviating the harshness of tort law doctrine is *MacPherson v. Buick Motor Co.,* 111 N.E. 1050 (N.Y. 1916).

48. These scenarios are based on actual cases. The first scenario is discussed in Tarr and Porter, *State Supreme Courts in State and Nation,* pp. 225–226. The second and third scenarios are drawn from Peter W. Huber, *Liability: The Legal Revolution and Its Consequences* (New York: Basic Books, 1988), pp. 38 and 81.

49. *Henningsen v. Bloomfield Motors,* 161 A.2d 69 (N.J. 1960).

50. *Greenman v. Yuma Power Products Co.,* 377 P.2d 897 (Cal. 1963).

51. Lawrence Baum and Bradley C. Canon, "State Supreme Courts as Activists: New Doctrines in the Law of Torts," in Porter and Tarr, *State Supreme Courts,* p. 88.

52. Lieberman, *The Litigious Society,* p. 43.

53. For rulings rejecting the state-of-the-art defense, see *Beshada v. Johns-Manville Products Corp.,* 447 A.2d 539 (N.J. 1982), and *Majdic v. Cincinnati Machine Co.,* 537 A.2d 334 (Pa. 1988). For a recent ruling upholding it, see *Bernier v. Raymond Industries,* 539 A.2d 621 (Me. 1988). For commentary on the defense and on state rulings regarding it, see "Defeat for the State-of-the-Art Defense in New Jersey Products Liability: *Beshada v. Johns-Manville Products Corp.,*" *Rutgers Law Journal* 14 (1983): 953–975.

54. The DES case is *Sindell v. Abbott Laboratories,* 607 P.2d 924 (Cal. 1980).

55. This account relies on Lieberman, *The Litigious Society,* pp. 38–40, and White, *Tort Law in America,* chap. 3–4.

56. Lawrence M. Friedman, *Total Justice* (New York: Russell Sage Foundation, 1985), chap. 4.

57. See Lieberman, *The Litigious Society,* chap. 1.

58. See Baum and Canon, "State Supreme Courts as Activists," pp. 87–88.

59. White, *Tort Law in America,* pp. 176–178.

60. The analysis in this paragraph relies on Robert Keeton, *Venturing to Do Justice: Reforming the Private Law* (Cambridge, MA: Harvard University Press, 1969), and Baum and Canon, "State Supreme Courts as Activists," pp. 93–97.

61. *Cochran v. Keeton,* 252 So. 2d 313, 318 (Ala. 1971), quoted in Baum and Canon, "State Supreme Courts as Activists," p. 96. For a more detailed assessment of the Alabama Supreme Court's changing perspective on tort law reform, see Tarr and Porter, *State Supreme Courts in State and Nation,* chap. 3.

62. *Schipper v. Levitt and Sons,* 207 A.2d 314, 325 (N.J. 1965), quoted in Baum and Canon, "State Supreme Courts as Activists," p. 96. For a discussion of the New Jersey Supreme Court's orientation toward modernization of the common law, see Tarr and Porter, *State Supreme Courts in State and Nation,* chap. 5.

63. Tarr and Porter, *State Supreme Courts in State and Nation,* pp. 39–40.

64. Litan, Swire, and Winston, "The U.S. Liability System," p. 3, and Edward J. Kionka, *Torts in a Nutshell: Injuries to Persons and Property* (St. Paul, MN: West Publishing, 1977), pp. 12–13.

65. On the importance of the development of liability insurance to tort law reform, see Baum and Canon, "State Supreme Courts as Activists," p. 86. Judicial recognition of its importance is found in *Henningsen v. Bloomfield Motors,* and *Seely v. White Motor Co.,* 403 P.2d 145 (Cal. 1965).

66. Huber, *Liability,* p. 154.

67. Ibid., p. 141.

68. The critics' account of how changes in products liability policy have affected innovation is drawn from Huber, *Liability,* especially chap. 1 and 10, and from Peter W. Huber and Robert E. Litan, "Overview," in *The Liability Maze: The Impact of Liability Law on Safety and Innovation,* eds. Huber and Litan (Washington, DC: Brookings, 1991).

69. See Peter W. Huber, *Galileo's Revenge: Junk Science in the Courtroom* (New York: Basic Books, 1991).

70. Robert Martin, "General Aviation Manufacturing: An Industry under Siege," in Huber and Litan, *The Liability Maze,* pp. 483–484.

71. Reported in W. Kip Viscusi and Michael J. Moore, "An Industrial Profile of the Links between Product Liability and Innovation," in Huber and Litan, *The Liability Maze,* p. 81.

72. R. H. Weaver, *Impact of Product Liability on the Development of New Medical Technologies* (Chicago: American Medical Association, 1988), p. 9.

73. Michael E. Porter, *The Competitive Advantage of Nations* (New York: Free Press, 1990), p. 649.

74. See generally, Huber, *Liability,* and Walter K. Olson, *The Litigation Explosion: What Happened When America Unleashed the Lawsuit* (New York: Dutton, 1991).

75. See, e.g., Litan, Swire, and Winston, "The U.S. Liability System: Background and Trends," in Litan and Winston, *Liability,* pp. 7–10; and Huber, *Liability,* p. 10.

76. Lieberman, *The Litigious Society,* p. 34.

77. For a summary of pertinent sources, see Stephen Daniels, "The Question of Jury Competence and the Politics of Civil Justice Reform: Symbols, Rhetoric, and Agenda-Building," *Law and Contemporary Problems* 52 (autumn 1989): 269–270.

78. Ibid., pp. 279–280.

79. James S. Kakalik and Nicholas M. Pace, *Costs and Compensation Paid in Tort Litigation* (Santa Monica, CA: Rand Corporation, Institute for Civil Justice, 1986), pp. ix–x.

80. Ibid.

81. See George L. Priest, "Products Liability Law and the Accident Rate," in Litan and Winston, *Liability.*

82. See www.uscourts.gov/caseload2002/tables/.

83. See "Civil Trial Cases and Verdicts in Large Counties, 2001" at www.ojp.usdoj.gov/bjs/pdf/ctcvlc01.pdf. More generally, see Stephen Daniels and Joanne Martin, *Civil Juries and the Politics of Reform* (Evanston, IL: Northwestern University Press, 1995).

84. Deborah R. Hensler, Mary E. Vaiana, James S. Kakalik, and Mark A. Peterson, *Trends in Tort Litigation: The Story behind the Statistics* (Santa Monica, CA: Rand Corporation, Institute for Civil Justice, 1987), p. 19.

85. Audrey Chin and Mark A. Peterson, *Deep Pockets, Empty Pockets: Who Wins in Cook County Jury Trials* (Santa Monica, CA: Rand Corporation, Institute for Civil Justice, 1985), pp. 41–44.

86. See Mark A. Peterson, *Civil Juries in the 1980s: Trends in Jury Trials and Verdicts in California and Cook County, Illinois* (Santa Monica, CA: Rand Corporation, Institute for Civil Justice, 1987).

87. Hensler et al., *Trends in Tort Litigation,* p. 22.

88. Valerie P. Hans and William S. Lofquist, "Jurors' Judgments of Business Liability in Tort Cases: Implications for the Litigation Explosion Debate," *Law and Society Review* 26 (1992): 85–115.

89. See Priest, "Products Liability Law and the Accident Rate," and George L. Priest, "The New Legal Structure of Risk Control," *Daedalus* (fall 1990): 207–227.

90. Huber and Litan, "Overview," *The Liability Maze,* pp. 12–15.

91. Ibid., pp. 10–11.

92. Ibid., pp. 16–18.

93. The analysis in this paragraph relies on Theresa M. Schwartz, "Products Liability Reform by the Judiciary," *Gonzaga Law Review* 27 (1991/92): 303–334; Joseph A. Henderson Jr., *UCLA Law Review* 37 (February 1990): 479–553; and Theodore Eisenberg and James A. Henderson Jr., "Inside the Quiet Revolution in Products Liability," *UCLA Law Review* 39 (April 1992): 731–810.

94. Schwartz, "Products Liability Reform by the Judiciary."

95. *Feldman v. Lederle Laboratories,* 479 A.2d 374 (N.J. 1984), narrowing *Beshada v. Johns-Mansville Products Corporation,* 447 A.2d 539 (N.J. 1982).

96. *Brown v. Superior Court,* 751 P.2d 470 (Cal. 1988).

97. Joseph Sanders and Craig Joyce, "'Off to the Races': The 1980s Tort Crisis and the Law Reform Process," *Houston Law Review* 27 (March 1990): 218–223; see also Robert E. Litan and Clifford Winston, "Policy Options," in Litan and Winston, *Liability,* pp. 230–231, table 8-2.

98. Litan and Winston, "Policy Options," pp. 232–233, table 8-3, and Sanders and Joyce, "Off to the Races," p. 257.

99. Robert S. Peck, "In Defense of Fundamental Principles: The Unconstitutionality of Tort Reform," *Seton Hall Law Review* 31 (2001): 672–682.

100. For a listing of these cases, see Victor E. Schwartz and Leah Lorber, "Judicial Nullification of Civil Justice Reform Violates the Fundamental Federal Constitutional Principle of Separation of Powers: How to Restore the Right Balance," *Rutgers Law Journal* 32 (2002), appendix.

101. *Georgetown College v. Hughes,* 130 F.2d 810 (D.C. Cir. 1942). See, more generally, Bradley C. Canon and Dean Jaros, "The Impact of Changes in Judicial Doctrines: The Abrogation of Charitable Immunity," *Law and Society Review* 13 (1979): 969–986.

For Further Reading

This volume has provided an introduction to the judicial process and judicial policymaking. Those interested in exploring these subjects further may wish to read pertinent judicial decisions. They may also wish to consult the following books, articles, and Internet resources.

Judicial Decisions

United States Reports is the official publication of U.S. Supreme Court decisions. Currently more than 540 volumes, it contains the text of every Supreme Court decision. To find a case, one uses the case's citation. For example, the citation for *Gideon v. Wainwright* (discussed in Chapter 2) is 372 U.S. 335. The "U.S." indicates that the case is found in *U.S. Reports.* The number preceding "U.S." is the volume of *U.S. Reports* in which the case is found, and the number following it is the page number on which the case begins. Thus, *Gideon v. Wainwright* begins on page 335 of volume 372 of *U.S. Reports.* Even before their publication in *U.S. Reports,* recent Court rulings are available on the Internet. The most accessible online site for U.S. Supreme Court decisions is the Cornell Law School Server. This server provides the full text of all Supreme Court decisions since 1890, which can be accessed at www.law.cornell.edu/supct/, with current decisions posted the same day they are released by the Court. Another Web site that provides the texts of Supreme Court decisions, as well as a host of other legal resources, is FindLaw at www.findlaw.com/casecode/supreme.html/. For those particularly interested in current Supreme Court rulings, the Cornell Web site also offers a free e-mail subscription service that provides summaries of Supreme Court rulings on the day that they are announced.

The decisions of lower federal courts and state courts are also published, with a similar citation system for locating particular decisions. The *Federal Reporter* series includes most decisions of the U.S. Courts of Appeals, and the *Federal Supplement* series contains selected decisions of the U.S. District Courts. Some states publish an official reporter series with the text of selected state appellate rulings. These rulings may also be found in the *National Reporter* series, published by West Publishing Company, which groups the decisions of state appellate courts in regional reporters. The *South Eastern Reporter,* for example, contains state appellate rulings from Georgia, North Carolina, South Carolina, Virginia, and West Virginia.

RESOURCES ON THE INTERNET

In recent years, information and materials pertinent to law and courts have proliferated on the Internet. For information about the U.S. Supreme Court, the place to begin is the Court's official Web site at www.supremecourtus.gov/. For oral arguments from historic Supreme Court cases, the Northwestern University site known as the Oyez Project provides recordings digitized from tapes in the National Archives. The site can be accessed at www.oyez.nwu.edu/. A good overview of the Supreme Court's constitutional rulings is found in The Constitution of the United States of America: Analysis and Interpretation at www.gpoaccess.gov/constitution/index.html.

Information on the federal courts can be obtained at the federal courts homepage at www.uscourts.gov. One can find federal appeals court rulings at www.law.vill.edu/Fed-Ct/fedcourt.html. This site also links to the home pages for various federal agencies, such as the Department of Justice, that are involved with the courts and their operations. A prime site for information about state courts is the National Center for State Courts at www.ncsconline.org. Information on state constitutions and on subnational constitutions in other countries is provided by the Center for State Constitutional Studies at Rutgers University-Camden (www-camlaw. rutgers.edu/statecon/) and by the International Association of Subnational Constitutional Law (http://camden-www.rutgers.edu/dept-pages/iascl/). Information on recent legal developments can be found at Findlaw (www.findlaw.com) and at the Common Law site (www.thecommonlaw.com).

Still other Web sites provide information about law schools and legal education, most notably the Law School Admissions Council site at www.lsac.org, the Association of American Law Schools site at www.aals.org, and FindLaw at http://stu.findlaw.com/prelaw/. More general information on the American legal profession can be obtained from the American Bar Association at www.abanet.org. Finally, to find additional legal materials and resources, one can use a search engine such as Yahoo! (www.yahoo.com/). A particularly helpful index of legal resources is found at www.yahoo.com/Government/Law/Legal_Research. Resources specific to particular chapters of the book are indicated below.

CHAPTER 1: COURTS AND LAW

Blackstone, William. *Commentaries on the Law of England.* Chicago: University of Chicago Press, 1979.

David, Rene, and John Brierly. *Major Legal Systems of the World Today.* 2d ed. London: Stevens & Sons, 1978.

Farnsworth, E. Allan. *An Introduction to the Legal System of the United States.* 2d ed. London: Oceana Publications, 1983.

Friedman, Lawrence M. *A History of American Law.* 2d ed. New York: Simon & Schuster, 1983.

Glendon, Mary Ann. *Rights Talk: The Impoverishment of Political Discourse.* New York: Maxwell Macmillan, 1991.

Glendon, Mary Ann, Michael Wallace Gordon, and Christopher Osakwe. *Comparative Legal Traditions.* 2d ed. St. Paul, MN: West, 1994.

Horwitz, Morton J. *The Transformation of American Law, 1760–1860.* Cambridge, MA: Harvard University Press, 1977.

Hurst, J. Willard. *The Growth of American Law: The Law Makers.* Boston: Little, Brown, 1950.

Jacob, Herbert, Erhard Blankenburg, Herbert M. Kritzer, Doris Marie Provine, and Joseph Sanders. *Courts, Law, and Politics in Comparative Perspective.* New Haven, CT: Yale University Press, 1996.

Merryman, John H. *The Civil Law Tradition.* Stanford, CA: Stanford University Press, 1969.

Plucknett, Theodore F. T. *A Concise History of the Common Law.* 5th ed. Boston: Little, Brown, 1956.

Tate, C. Neal, and Torbjorn Vallinder. *The Global Expansion of Judicial Power.* New York: New York University Press, 1995.

Watson, Alan. *The Making of the Civil Law.* Cambridge, MA: Harvard University Press, 1981.

Weiss, Bernard G. *The Spirit of Islamic Law.* Athens: University of Georgia Press, 1998.

Zweigert, Konrad, and Hein Kotz. *Introduction to Comparative Law.* 2d rev. ed. Oxford, UK: Clarendon Press, 1987.

CHAPTER 2: THE FEDERAL AND STATE COURT SYSTEMS

Bator, Paul M., Paul J. Mishkin, David L. Shapiro, and Herbert Wechsler. *Hart and Wechsler's The Federal Courts in the Federal System.* 2d ed. Mineola, NY: Foundation Press, 1980.

Champagne, Anthony, and Judith Haydel, eds. *Judicial Reform in the States.* Lanham, MD: University Press of America, 1993.

Friedman, Lawrence M. *A History of American Law.* 2d ed. New York: Simon & Schuster, 1983.

Gates, John B., and Charles A. Johnson, eds. *The American Courts: A Critical Assessment.* Washington, DC: CQ Press, 1991.

Howard, J. Woodford Jr. *Courts of Appeals in the Federal Judicial System.* Princeton, NJ: Princeton University Press, 1981.

Lewis, Anthony. *Gideon's Trumpet.* New York: Vintage, 1964.

Porter, Mary Cornelia, and G. Alan Tarr, eds. *State Supreme Courts: Policymakers in the Federal System.* Westport, CT: Greenwood Press, 1982.

Posner, Richard A. *The Federal Courts: Challenge and Reform.* Cambridge, MA: Harvard University Press, 1996.

Rehnquist, William H. *The Supreme Court.* 2d ed. New York: Knopf, 2001.

Rowland, C. K., and Robert A. Carp. *Politics and Judgment in Federal District Courts.* Lawrence: University Press of Kansas, 1996.

Solimine, Michael E., and James L. Walker. *Respecting State Courts: The Inevitability of Judicial Federalism.* Westport, CT: Greenwood Press, 1999.

Surrency, Edwin C. *History of the Federal Courts*. 2d ed. Dobbs Ferry, NY: Oceana, 2002.

Tarr, G. Alan, and Mary Cornelia Aldis Porter. *State Supreme Courts in State and Nation*. New Haven, CT: Yale University Press, 1988.

Tobin, Robert W. *Creating the Judicial Branch: The Unfinished Reform*. Williamsburg, VA: National Center for State Courts, 1999.

Chapter 3: Judges

Abraham, Henry J. *Justices, Presidents, and Senators: A History of the U.S. Supreme Court Appointments from Washington to Clinton*. Rev. ed. Lanham, MD: Rowman & Littlefield, 1999.

Barrow, Deborah J., Gary Zuk, and Gerard S. Gryski. *The Federal Judiciary and Institutional Change*. Ann Arbor: University of Michigan Press, 1996.

Coffin, Frank M. *On Appeal: Courts, Lawyering and Judging*. New York: Norton, 1994.

Dubois, Philip L. *From Ballot to Bench: Judicial Elections and the Quest for Accountability*. Austin: University of Texas Press, 1980.

Gerhardt, Michael J. *The Federal Appointments Process: A Constitutional and Historical Analysis*. Durham, NC: Duke University Press, 2003.

Goldman, Sheldon. *Picking Federal Judges: Lower Court Selection from Roosevelt through Reagan*. New Haven, CT: Yale University Press, 1997.

Goldman, Sheldon, Elliot Slotnick, Gerard Gryski, Gary Zuk, and Sara Schiavoni. "W. Bush Remaking the Judiciary: Like Father Like Son?" *Judicature* 86 (May–June 2003): 282–309.

Jeffries, John C. *Justice Lewis F. Powell Jr.* New York: Charles Scribner's Sons, 1994.

Maltese, John Anthony. *The Selling of Supreme Court Nominees*. Baltimore: Johns Hopkins University Press, 1995.

Murphy, Bruce A. *Wild Bill: The Legend and Life of William O. Douglas*. New York: Random House, 2003.

O'Brien, David. *Judicial Roulette*. New York: Priority Press, 1988.

Pinello, Daniel R. *The Impact of Judicial-Selection Method on State-Supreme-Court Policy*. Westport, CT: Greenwood Press, 1995.

Ryan, John Paul, Allan Ashman, Bruce D. Sales, and Sandra Shane-Dubow. *American Trial Judges*. New York: Free Press, 1980.

Scherer, Nancy. *Scoring Points: Politicians, Activists, and the Lower Federal Court Appointment Process*. Stanford, CA: Stanford University Press, 2004.

Sheldon, Charles H., and Linda S. Maule. *Choosing Justice: The Recruitment of State and Federal Judges*. Pullman: Washington State University Press, 1998.

Silverstein, Mark. *Judicious Choices: The New Politics of Supreme Court Confirmations*. New York: Norton, 1994.

Washington, Linn. *Black Judges on Justice: Perspectives from the Bench*. New York: The New Press, 1994.

Watson, Richard A., and Rondal G. Downing. *The Politics of the Bench and the Bar: Judicial Selection under the Missouri Non-Partisan Court Plan*. New York: John Wiley & Sons, 1969.

Yalof, David Alistair. *Pursuit of Justices: Presidential Politics and the Selection of Supreme Court Nominees.* Chicago: University of Chicago Press, 1999.

CHAPTER 4: LAWYERS

Abel, Richard L. *American Lawyers.* New York: Oxford University Press, 1989.

Auerbach, Jerold S. *Unequal Justice: Lawyers and Social Change in Modern America.* New York: Oxford University Press, 1976.

Baer, Judith A. *Women in American Law: The Struggle Toward Equality from the New Deal to the Present.* 2d ed. New York: Holmes & Meier, 1996.

Galanter, Marc, and Thomas Palay. *Tournament of Lawyers: The Transformation of the Big Law Firm.* Chicago: University of Chicago Press, 1991.

Glendon, Mary Ann. *A Nation under Lawyers: How the Crisis in the Legal Profession Is Transforming American Society.* New York: Farrar, Straus & Giroux, 1994.

Hagan, John, and Fiona Kay. *Gender in Practice: A Study of Lawyers' Lives.* New York: Oxford University Press, 1995.

Heinz, John P., and Edward O. Laumann. *Chicago Lawyers: The Social Structure of the Bar.* New York: Russell Sage Foundation and American Bar Association, 1982.

Kelly, Michael J. *Lives of Lawyers: Journeys in the Organizations of Practice.* Ann Arbor: University of Michigan Press, 1994.

Kessler, Mark. *Legal Services for the Poor.* Westport, CT: Greenwood Press, 1987.

Lawrence, Susan E. *The Poor in Court.* Princeton, NJ: Princeton University Press, 1990.

Luban, David. *Lawyers and Justice.* Princeton, NJ: Princeton University Press, 1988.

McGuire, Kevin T. *The Supreme Court Bar: Legal Elites in the Washington Community.* Charlottesville: University Press of Virginia, 1993.

Olson, Susan M. *Clients and Lawyers.* Westport, CT: Greenwood Press, 1984.

Spangler, Eve. *Lawyers for Hire.* New Haven, CT: Yale University Press, 1986.

Stevens, Robert. *Law School.* Chapel Hill: University of North Carolina Press, 1983.

Stewart, James B. *The Partners: Inside America's Most Powerful Law Firms.* New York: Simon & Schuster, 1983.

Turow, Scott. *One L.* New York: Putnam, 1977.

Wice, Paul. *Judges and Lawyers: The Human Side of Justice.* New York: HarperCollins, 1991.

CHAPTER 5: TRIALS AND APPEALS

Abramson, Jeffrey, ed. *Postmortem: The O. J. Simpson Case.* New York: Basic Books, 1996.

———. *We the Jury: The Jury System and the Ideal of Democracy.* New York: Basic Books, 1994.

Adler, Steven. *The Jury: Trial and Error in the American Courtroom.* New York: Random House, 1994.

Baum, Lawrence. *The Supreme Court*. 7th ed. Washington, DC: CQ Press, 2001.

Biskupic, Joan, and Elder Witt. *Guide to the U.S. Supreme Court*. 3d ed. Washington, DC: CQ Press, 1997.

Dickson, Del, ed. *The Supreme Court in Conference*. New York: Oxford University Press, 2001.

Epstein, Lee, Jeffery A. Segal, Harold J. Spaeth, and Thomas G. Walker, eds. *The Supreme Court Compendium: Decisions and Developments*. 3d ed. Washington, DC: CQ Press, 2003.

Goldman, Sheldon, and Charles M. Lamb, eds. *Judicial Conflict and Consensus: Behavioral Studies of American Appellate Courts*. Lexington: University of Kentucky Press, 1986.

Hans, Valerie P., and Neil Vidmar. *Judging the Jury*. New York: Plenum Press, 1986.

Jonakait, Randolph N. *The American Jury System*. New Haven, CT: Yale University Press, 2003.

Kalven, Harry, Jr., and Hans Zeisel. *The American Jury*. Boston: Little, Brown, 1966.

Kassin, Saul M., and Lawrence S. Wrightsman, eds. *The Psychology of Evidence and Trial Procedure*. Beverly Hills, CA: Sage Publications, 1985.

Kloppenberg, Lisa A. *Playing It Safe: How the Supreme Court Sidesteps Hard Cases and Stunts the Development of the Law*. New York: New York University Press, 2001.

Masterson, William A., ed. *Civil Trial Practice: Strategies and Techniques*. New York: Practicing Law Institute, 1986.

O'Brien, David M. *Storm Center: The Supreme Court in American Politics*. 5th ed. New York: Norton, 1999.

Perry, H. W., Jr. *Deciding to Decide: Agenda Setting in the United States Supreme Court*. Cambridge, MA: Harvard University Press, 1991.

Rehnquist, William H. *The Supreme Court*. 2d ed. New York: Knopf, 2001.

Sales, Bruce D., ed. *The Trial Process*. New York: Plenum Press, 1981.

Strier, Franklin. *Reconstructing Justice: An Agenda for Trial Reform*. Westport, CT: Quorum Books, 1994.

Chapter 6: Criminal Justice and the Courts

Boland, Barbara, Catherine H. Conly, Lynn Warner, Ronald Sones, and William Martin. *The Prosecution of Felony Arrests, 1986*. Washington, DC: U.S. Department of Justice, Bureau of Justice Statistics, 1989.

Bureau of Justice Statistics. *Report to the Nation on Crime and Justice*. 2d ed. Washington, DC: U.S. Department of Justice, 1988.

Eisenstein, James, and Herbert Jacob. *Felony Justice: An Organizational Analysis of Criminal Courts*. Boston: Little, Brown, 1977.

Feeley, Malcolm M. *The Process Is the Punishment: Handling Cases in a Lower Criminal Court*. New York: Russell Sage Foundation, 1979.

Fisher, George. *Plea Bargaining's Triumph: A History of Plea Bargaining in America*. Stanford, CA: Stanford University Press, 2003.

Forst, Brian, Judith Lucianovic, and Sarah J. Cox. *What Happens after Arrest?* Washington, DC: National Institute of Law Enforcement and Criminal Justice, 1977.

Friedman, Lawrence M. *Crime and Punishment in American History.* New York: Basic Books, 1993.

Heumann, Milton. *Plea Bargaining.* Chicago: University of Chicago Press, 1978.

Kennedy, Randall. *Race, Crime, and the Law.* New York: Pantheon, 1997.

Levin, Martin A. *Urban Politics and the Criminal Courts.* Chicago: University of Chicago Press, 1977.

Nardulli, Peter F., James Eisenstein, and Roy B. Flemming. *The Tenor of Justice.* Urbana: University of Illinois Press, 1988.

Scheck, Barry, Peter Neufeld, and Jim Dwyer. *Actual Innocence: When Justice Goes Wrong and How to Make It Right.* New York: Signet Books, 2001.

Scheingold, Stuart A. *The Politics of Law and Order.* New York: Longman, 1984.

Simon, Rita J., and David E. Aaronson. *The Insanity Defense: A Critical Assessment of Law and Policy in the Post-Hinckley Era.* New York: Praeger, 1988.

Stith, Kate, and Jose A. Cabranes. *Fear of Judging: Sentencing Guidelines in the Federal Courts.* Chicago: University of Chicago Press, 1998.

Symposium on Plea Bargaining. *Law and Society Review* 13 (winter 1979): 197–657.

Tonry, Michael. *Sentencing Matters.* New York: Oxford University Press, 1996.

CHAPTER 7: CIVIL JUSTICE AND THE COURTS

Abel, Richard, ed. *The Politics of Informal Justice.* Orlando, FL: Academic Press, 1982.

Bumiller, Kristin. *The Civil Rights Society: The Social Construction of Victims.* Baltimore: Johns Hopkins University Press, 1988.

Daniels, Stephen, and Joanne Martin. *Civil Justice and the Politics of Reform.* Evanston, IL: Northwestern University Press and the American Bar Foundation, 1995.

Friedman, Lawrence M. *Total Justice.* New York: Russell Sage Foundation, 1985.

Harr, Jonathan. *A Civil Action.* New York: Random House, 1995.

Harrington, Christine B. *Shadow Justice: The Ideology and Institutionalization of Alternatives to Court.* Westport, CT: Greenwood Press, 1985.

Lieberman, Jethro K. *The Litigious Society.* New York: Basic Books, 1981.

McGillis, Daniel. *Community Dispute Resolution Programs and Public Policy.* Washington, DC: U.S. Department of Justice, National Institute of Justice, 1986.

McIntosh, Wayne V. *The Appeal of Civil Law: A Political-Economic Analysis of Litigation.* Urbana: University of Illinois Press, 1990.

McLauchlan, William P. *American Legal Processes.* New York: John Wiley & Sons, 1977.

Merry, Sally Engle. *Getting Justice and Getting Even: Legal Consciousness among Working-Class Americans.* Chicago: University of Chicago Press, 1990.

Merry, Sally Engle, and Neal Milner, eds. *The Possibility of Popular Justice: A Case Study of Community Mediation in the United States.* Ann Arbor: University of Michigan Press, 1993.

Nader, Laura, ed. *Access to Justice: Alternatives to the American Judicial System*. New York: Academic Press, 1980.

Olson, Walter K. *The Litigation Explosion: What Happened When America Unleashed the Lawsuit*. New York: Truman Talley Books, 1991.

Resnick, Judith. *Processes of the Law: Understanding Courts and Their Alternatives*. New York: Foundation Press, 2004.

Schuck, Peter H. *Agent Orange on Trial: Mass Toxic Disasters in the Courts*. Cambridge, MA: Belknap Press, 1986.

Weitzman, Lenore J. *The Divorce Revolution*. New York: Free Press, 1985.

Chapter 8: Judicial Decision Making

Baum, Lawrence. *The Puzzle of Judicial Behavior*. Ann Arbor: University of Michigan Press, 1997.

Cardozo, Benjamin. *The Nature of the Judicial Process*. New Haven, CT: Yale University Press, 1921.

Carp, Robert A., and C. K. Rowland. *Policymaking and Politics in the Federal District Courts*. Knoxville: University of Tennessee Press, 1983.

Clayton, Cornell W., and Howard Gillman, eds. *Supreme Court Decision-Making: New Institutionalist Approaches*. Chicago: University of Chicago Press, 1999.

Dickerson, Reed. *The Interpretation and Application of Statutes*. Boston: Little, Brown, 1975.

Epstein, Lee, and Jack Knight. *The Choices Justices Make*. Washington, DC: CQ Press, 1998.

Eskridge, William N. *Dynamics of Statutory Interpretation*. Cambridge, MA: Harvard University Press, 1994.

Levi, Edward H. *An Introduction to Legal Reasoning*. Chicago: University of Chicago Press, 1949.

Marshall, Thomas R. *Public Opinion and the Supreme Court*. Boston: Unwin Hyman, 1989.

Murphy, Walter F. *Elements of Judicial Strategy*. Chicago: University of Chicago Press, 1964.

O'Connor, Karen. *Women's Organizations' Use of the Courts*. Lexington, MA: Lexington Books, 1980.

Rumble, Wilfrid E., Jr. *American Legal Realism: Skepticism, Reform, and the Judicial Process*. Ithaca, NY: Cornell University Press, 1968.

Scalia, Antonin. *A Matter of Interpretation: Federal Courts and the Law*. Princeton, NJ: Princeton University Press, 1997.

Schwartz, Bernard. *How the Supreme Court Decides Cases*. New York: Oxford University Press, 1996.

Segal, Jeffrey A., and Harold J. Spaeth. *The Supreme Court and the Attitudinal Model*. 2d ed. Cambridge, MA: Cambridge University Press, 2003.

Vandevelde, Kenneth J. *Thinking Like a Lawyer: An Introduction to Legal Reasoning*. Boulder, CO: Westview Press, 1996.

Wasserstrom, Richard A. *The Judicial Decision: Toward a Theory of Legal Justification.* Stanford, CA: Stanford University Press, 1961.

CHAPTER 9: JUDICIAL POLICYMAKING: AN INTRODUCTION

Epps, Charles R. *The Rights Revolution: Lawyers, Activists, and Supreme Courts in Comparative Perspective.* Chicago: University of Chicago Press, 1998.

Feinman, Jay M. *Law 101: Everything You Need to Know about the American Legal System.* New York: Oxford University Press, 2000.

Halpern, Stephen C., and Charles M. Lamb, eds. *Supreme Court Activism and Restraint.* Lexington, MA: Lexington Books, 1982.

Horowitz, Donald L. *The Courts and Social Policy.* Washington, DC: Brookings, 1977.

Horwitz, Morton J. *The Transformation of American Law, 1780–1860.* Cambridge, MA: Harvard University Press, 1977.

Lieberman, Jethro K. *The Litigious Society.* New York: Basic Books, 1981.

O'Brien, David M. *Storm Center: The Supreme Court in American Politics.* 5th ed. New York: Norton, 1999.

Shapiro, Martin. *Who Guards the Guardians? Judicial Control of Administration.* Athens: University of Georgia Press, 1988.

Tarr, G. Alan. *Judicial Impact and State Supreme Courts.* Lexington, MA: Lexington Books, 1977.

Tate, C. Neal, and Torbjorn Vallinder, eds. *The Global Expansion of Judicial Power.* New York: New York University Press, 1995.

Wolfe, Christopher. *The Rise of Modern Judicial Review.* New York: Basic Books, 1986.

———. *Judicial Activism: Bulwark of Freedom or Precarious Security?* Rev. ed. Lanham, MD: Rowman & Littlefield, 1997.

Yarbrough, Tinsley E. *Judge Frank Johnson and Human Rights in Alabama.* Tuscaloosa: University of Alabama Press, 1981.

CHAPTER 10: FEDERAL COURT POLICYMAKING

Armor, David J. *Forced Justice: School Desegregation and the Law.* New York: Oxford University Press, 1995.

Bell, Derrick. *Silent Covenants: Brown v. Board of Education and the Unfulfilled Hopes for Racial Reform.* New York: Oxford University Press, 2004.

Clotfelter, Charles T. *After Brown: The Rise and Retreat of School Desegregation.* Princeton, NJ: Princeton University Press, 2004.

Craig, Barbara H., and David M. O'Brien. *Abortion and American Politics.* Chatham, NJ: Chatham House, 1993.

Epstein, Lee, and Joseph F. Kobylka. *The Supreme Court and Legal Change: Abortion and the Death Penalty.* Chapel Hill: University of North Carolina Press, 1992.

Faux, Marian. *Roe v. Wade.* New York: Macmillan, 1988.

Garrow, David J. *Liberty and Sexuality: The Right to Privacy and the Making of Roe v. Wade.* New York: Macmillan, 1994.

Glendon, Mary Ann. *Abortion and Divorce in Western Law.* Cambridge, MA: Harvard University Press, 1987.

Hochschild, Jennifer L. *The New American Dilemma.* New Haven, CT: Yale University Press, 1984.

Johnson, Charles A., and Bradley C. Canon. *Judicial Policies: Implementation and Impact.* 2d ed. Washington, DC: CQ Press, 1999.

Keynes, Edward, with Randall K. Miller. *The Court vs. Congress: Prayer, Busing, and Abortion.* Durham, NC: Duke University Press, 1989.

Kluger, Richard. *Simple Justice.* New York: Knopf, 1975.

Orfield, Gary, and Susan E. Eaton. *Dismantling Desegregation: The Quiet Reversal of Brown v. Board of Education.* New York: New Press, 1996.

Peltason, Jack W. *Fifty-Eight Lonely Men: Southern Federal Judges and School Desegregation.* 2d ed. Urbana: University of Illinois Press, 1971.

Rosenberg, Gerald R. *The Hollow Hope: Can Courts Bring about Social Change?* Chicago: University of Chicago Press, 1991.

Rubin, Eva R. *Abortion, Politics, and the Courts.* Westport, CT: Greenwood Press, 1987.

Tatalovich, Raymond. *The Politics of Abortion in the United States and Canada: A Comparison.* Armonk, NY: M. E. Sharpe, 1997.

Tushnet, Mark V. *The NAACP's Legal Strategy against Segregated Education, 1925–1950.* Chapel Hill: University of North Carolina Press, 1987.

Wasby, Stephen L. *Race Relations Litigation in an Age of Complexity.* Charlottesville: University Press of Virginia, 1995.

Wilkinson, J. Harvie. *From Brown to Bakke: The Supreme Court and School Integration, 1954–1968.* New York: Oxford University Press, 1978.

Wolters, Raymond. *The Burden of Brown: Thirty Years of School Desegregation.* Knoxville: University of Tennessee Press, 1984.

Yarbrough, Tinsley E. *The Rehnquist Court and the Constitution.* New York: Oxford University Press, 2000.

CHAPTER 11: STATE COURT POLICYMAKING

Alexander, Kern, and K. Forbis Jordan, eds. *Constitutional Reform of School Finance.* Lexington, MA: Lexington Books, 1973.

Bosworth, Matthew. *Catalyzing Courts: State Supreme Courts and Public School Finance.* Albany: State University of New York Press, 2000.

Daniels, Stephen, and Joanne Martin. *Civil Juries and the Politics of Reform.* Evanston, IL: Northwestern University Press and the American Bar Foundation, 1995.

Friesen, Jennifer. *State Constitutional Law: Litigating Individual Rights, Claims, and Defenses.* 2d ed. Charlottesville, VA: Michie, 1995.

Hensler, Deborah R., Mary E. Vaiana, James S. Kakalik, and Mark A. Peterson. *Trends in Tort Litigation: The Story Behind the Statistics.* Santa Monica, CA: Rand Corporation, Institute for Civil Justice, 1987.

Huber, Peter W. *Liability: The Legal Revolution and Its Consequences.* New York: Basic Books, 1988.

Lehne, Richard. *The Quest for Justice: The Politics of School Finance Reform.* New York: Longman, 1978.

Lieberman, Jethro. *The Litigious Society.* New York: Basic Books, 1981.

Litan, Robert E., and Clifford Winston, eds. *Liability: Perspectives and Policy.* Washington, DC: Brookings, 1988.

Porter, Mary Cornelia, and G. Alan Tarr, eds. *State Supreme Courts: Policymakers in the Federal System.* Westport, CT: Greenwood Press, 1982.

Reed, Douglas S. *On Equal Terms: The Constitutional Politics of Educational Opportunity.* Princeton, NJ: Princeton University Press, 2001.

Special Issue: New Developments in State Constitutional Law. *Publius: The Journal of Federalism* 17 (winter 1987): 1–179.

Symposium: Investing in Our Children's Future: School Finance Reform in the '90s. *Harvard Journal on Legislation* 28 (summer 1991): 293–568.

Symposium: The Future of State Supreme Courts as Institutions in the Law. *Notre Dame Law Review* 72 (May 1997): 1009–1218.

Tarr, G. Alan. *Understanding State Constitutions.* Princeton, NJ: Princeton University Press, 1998.

———, ed. *Constitutional Politics in the States.* Westport, CT: Greenwood Press, 1996.

Tarr, G. Alan, and Mary Cornelia Aldis Porter. *State Supreme Courts in State and Nation.* New Haven, CT: Yale University Press, 1988.

White, G. Edward. *Tort Law in America: An Intellectual History.* New York: Oxford University Press, 1985.

Williams, Robert F. *State Constitutional Law: Cases and Materials.* 3d ed. Charlottesville, VA: Lexis Law Publishing, 1999.

Index

ABA. *See* American Bar Association
Abbott v. Burke, 342
Abortion, 315–325
    as legal issue, 317–319
    major rulings on, 316
    Roe v. Wade and, 17, 84, 157
    *Webster v. Reproductive Health
        Services,* 165
Access to legal services, 117–124
    alternative dispute resolution and, 240
Accountability, judicial, 56–57
Acheson, Eleanor Dean, 77–78
Adams, John, 30
Administrative Dispute Resolution Act of
    1990, 237
Administrative law, 10–11
Administrative oversight, 286–287, 291
Administrative Procedure Act of 1946, 287
Adversarial system, 101
    clients in, 124–126
    securing and confronting witnesses in,
        141–142
    tactics in, 137
Advertising, 115, 121
Affirmative action, 15–17, 111, 277–278
African Americans. *See* Minorities
African law, 5
Agenda setting
    appellate court, 166–167
    state court, 343–344
    Supreme Court, 156–162
Agent Orange litigation, 216–219, 356
*Akron v. Akron Center for Reproductive
    Health,* 316
Alien Terrorist Removal Court, 30–31

Allen v. Wright, 286
Alternative Dispute Resolution Act of
    1998, 237–238
Alternative dispute resolution (ADR),
    237–242
American Bar Association, 111
    on adversary system, 101, 103
    group legal services and, 123
    judicial selection and, 74
    pro bono work and, 124
    procedural rules of, 223
    reform efforts of, 47
    Standing Committee on Federal
        Judiciary, 74, 111
American Civil Liberties Union, 162–163
American Judicature Society, 47
American Jury, The, 153
American Law Institute (ALI), 198–199,
    317
Amicus curiae briefs, 162–163, 327
Apodaca v. Oregon, 152
Appeals, 155–168
    in other appellate courts, 166–168
    process of, 155–156
    U.S. Supreme Court, 156–166
Appellate courts, 28, 39–41
    agenda setting in, 166–167
    appeals process in, 166–168
    decision making in, 167
    information gathering in, 167
    intermediate state, 43, 45
    judges in, 90–92
    judicial selection and, 72–74
    promulgating decisions in, 168
    See also Supreme Court, U.S.

Arbitration, 238–239
Argersinger v. Hamlin, 174
Arrests, 175–178
    Miranda v. Arizona and, 157–158,
        162–163, 165
Assigned counsel systems, 174
Association of American Law
        Schools, 105
Assumption of risk, 351, 352
Attitudes of judges, 262–265
Attorney General's Task Force on Violent
        Crime, 197
Avocats, 104
Awards, excessive, 360–361

Baehr v. Lewin, 346
Bail, 180–181, 349
Baker v. State, 346
Barber, Kathleen, 64–65
Bar exams, 103–104
Barristers, 106–107
Bates v. State Bar of Arizona, 121
Bell, Griffin, 73–74
Bench trials, 142–143
Berrigan, Daniel, 146
Betts v. Brady, 26
Bickel, Alexander, 84
Biden, Joseph, 54
Bird, Rose, 66–67
Black, Hugo, 141, 158
Blackmun, Harry, 79, 84, 324
Blakely v. Washington, 203
Bolling v. Sharpe, 306, 308
Bork, Robert H., 53–55, 71, 74
Bowers v. Hardwick, 258–259
Brady, James, 197
Brennan, William, 41, 79, 81, 83, 164, 337
Breyer, Stephen, 85
Brown v. Board of Education, 16–17,
        283, 304–315
    communication problems with,
        328–329
    desegregation under, 310–315
    effectiveness of, 330–331
    II, 307–308
    judicial activism and, 297
    legacy of, 315
    Marshall and, 98, 125, 305–306
    opinion writing for, 164
    precedent and, 282

responses to, 308–310
    social change and, 319
Bryant, Kobe, 148
Burden of proof, 142
Burger, Warren, 84
Bush, George H. W., 75–77
    abortion and, 322–323
Bush, George W., 71, 72
    abortion and, 323
    judicial selection under, 78–79
    Pickering and, 80–81
Bush v. Gore, 56, 160
Business law, 10

Cabranes, Jose, 204–205
Canon, Bradley, 297–298
Capital punishment, 66–68, 247–248
Cardozo, Benjamin, 195, 253, 263
Carter, Jimmy, 72, 75
Caseloads
    alternative dispute resolution and,
        240–241
    appellate court, 40
    district court, 36, 38
    federal court, 34–35
    plea bargaining and, 187–189
    state court, 41–42
    Supreme Court, 41
Celebrezze, Frank, 63–64
Centers for Disease Control, 325
Certiorari, writ of, 158–159, 160, 161
*Chaplin and Drysdale, Chartered v.
        United States,* 282
Charges, 178–180
Chayes, Abraham, 283
Cheney, Richard, 78
Child custody awards, 289–290
Chisholm v. Georgia, 33
Circuit courts, 29–30
Civil law, 11
    access to legal services and, 119–124
Civil litigation, 216–246
    alternative dispute resolution in,
        237–242
    discovery in, 224–225
    diversity in, 218–219
    how cases arise in, 219–222
    injuries and grievances in, 219–220
    in Japan, 235
    litigation crisis and, 233–237

litigation explosion and, 218
motions in, 225–226
negotiation in, 218
outcomes in, 231–233
parties in, 227–231
pleadings in, 223–224
pretrial conference in, 226
process in, 223–226
responses in, 221–222
rules in, 223
universe of cases in, 227–231
Civil Rights Act of 1964, 284, 310–311
Civil War, 33–34
Clinton, Bill, 71, 72, 77–78, 81
abortion and, 323
Closed-panel plans, 123–124
Closing arguments, 149
Code of Federal Regulations, 290
Coffee, Linda, 320
Coffin, Frank, 90
Commercial law, 10
Common-law systems, 3, 6–7, 8–9
judicial policymaking and, 287–288, 292
Comparative negligence, 352, 355
Comprehensive Crime Control Act of
1984, 200
Conditional release, 181
Constitutional courts, 28
See also Federal courts
Constitutional law, 9–10
Constitutional policymaking, 278–282, 291
state, 343–349
Contingent fees, 122–123
Contraception, 257–258
Contract law, 10
Contract systems, 174
Contributory negligence, 351, 352
Corporate counsel, 115
Corpus Juris Civilis (Justinian), 7
Costs of litigation, 221–222, 233, 359
alternative dispute resolution and, 241
Court-annexed arbitration, 238–239
Court of Chancery, 12–13
Court of Military Appeals, 30
Courts, 25–52
civil justice and, 216–246
criminal justice and, 172–215
drug, 205–208
dual system of, 26
equity and, 12–13

federal, 28–41
misconceptions about, 13–17
public policy and, 15–17
state, 41–49
uncertainty and, 13–15
Crimes, 175–178
Criminal justice, 172–215
bail and pretrial release in, 180–181
charges and dismissals in, 178–180
crimes and arrest in, 175–178
defense attorneys in, 174
drug courts in, 205–208
exclusionary rule and, 193–197
grand juries in, 181–183
insanity defense and, 197–200
plea bargaining in, 183–192
policy issues in, 192–208
preliminary hearings in, 181–183
process of, 175–183
prosecutors in, 173
sentencing and, 201–205
Criminal law, 11
access to legal services and, 118–119
government attorneys in, 116–117
trial by jury and, 141
Cumulative policymaking, 289–290, 292

Darrow, Clarence, 146
Dartmouth College v. Woodward, 163
Daschle, Tom, 81
Dayton Board of Education v. Brinkman,
314
Death penalty, 66–68, 247–248
Decision Quest, 145
Deductive reasoning, 253–254
Default judgments, 224
Defense attorneys, 174
plea bargaining and, 183–187
De novo trials, 45
Deposit bail, 180
Depositions, 225
Dershowitz, Alan, 136
DES (diethylstilbestrol), 353, 354,
355–356
Desegregation, 16–17, 98, 125, 282
federal courts on, 304–315
Design defects, 352, 355
Deukmejian, George, 67
Diamond v. Chakrabarty, 285
Dimitrius, Jo-Ellen, 145

Discovery, 224–225, 248–249
Discuss list, 159–160
Dismissals, 178–180
District attorneys, 173
District courts, 36–39
    judicial selection and, 72–74
    types of cases in, 229
Diversity of citizenship cases, 227
Divorce, 231, 241–242
    judicial policymaking and, 289–290
Doe v. Bolton, 319
Douglas, William O., 158, 164, 257
Drug courts, 205–208
Due process, 282
Duncan-Peters, Stephanie, 208
Duncan v. Louisiana, 141

École Nationale de la Magistrature, 86
Eisenhower, Dwight, 79, 81, 83, 308
Eisenstadt v. Baird, 257–258
Eisenstein, James, 187
Elementary and Secondary Education
        Act (ESEA) of 1965, 311
Elite law firms, 113–114
En banc panels, 41, 45
Enterprise liability, 352, 355–356
Equal protection, 282
Equity, 12–13
Escobedo v. Illinois, 157–158
Ethics, 99–101, 111
    plea bargaining and, 191–192
    pro bono work and, 124
Evidence
    exclusionary rule and, 193–197
    reasonable doubt and, 178
Exclusionary rule, 193–197

Failure to warn, 352, 355–356
Family law, 10
Far Eastern law, 5
Faubus, Orval, 308
Federal Bureau of Investigation (FBI),
        175, 177
Federal courts, 28–41
    appellate, 39–41
    caseloads and, 34–35
    civil cases in, 227–231
    Congress and, 34
    development of, 28–31
    district, 36–39
    intercourt relations and, 40

judges in, 71–79
jurisdiction of, 31–35
policymaking by, 304–336
size of judiciary in, 71–72
state court policymaking and, 345–346
structure of, 28
Supreme Court, 41
types of cases in, 229
Federalism
    courts and, 26, 28–29
    jurisdiction and, 32–35
Federalist Papers (Hamilton), 71, 250, 329
Federal Judicial Center, 88
"Federal question" cases, 33
Federal Reporter, 168
Federal Rules of Civil Procedure, 223–226
Federal Sentencing Guidelines, 202–205
Feeley, Malcolm, 175, 185
Fellow servant rule, 351, 352
Fifth Amendment, 142, 181
Flag burning cases, 253, 255–256
Flag-salute cases, 157
Flexibility of response, 295
Fogan, Robert, 208
Food and Drug Administration (FDA),
        286
Foreign Intelligence Surveillance Court,
        30
Fortas, Abraham, 88
Frankfurter, Felix, 88, 140, 159, 164
    on judicial decision making, 270
    on statutory interpretation, 284
Freedman's Bureau, 119–120
Freedom-of-choice plans, 311–312
Freeman v. Pitts, 315
Friedman, Lawrence, 357
Furman v. Georgia, 266

Galanter, Marc, 227, 232
Gender equality, 349
Gibson, James, 262
Gideon v. Wainwright, 25–26, 27,
        118–119, 141, 174
Ginsburg, Ruth Bader, 85
Goldfarb v. Virginia State Bar, 121
Goldstein, Stanley, 208
Good faith exception, 195, 197
*Goodridge v. Massachusetts Department
        of Public Health,* 346–347
Government attorneys, 116–117
Grand juries, 181–183

Gratz v. Bollinger, 277–278
Gray, Horace, 158
Great Society period, 291
*Green v. County School Board of New
	Kent County,* 311–312, 326–327
Grievances, 219–220
	responses to, 221–222
Griswold v. Connecticut, 257, 319
Gross, Avrum, 190
Group legal services (GLS), 123–124
Grutter v. Bollinger, 111, 277–278
Guilty but mentally ill, 200

Habeas Corpus Act of 1867, 33–34
Hall, Melinda Gann, 62
Hamilton, Alexander, 71, 329
Harlan, John Marshall, 88, 163
Harris v. McRae, 316
Harvard Law School, 104–105, 106
Heinz, John, 117
Helms, Jesse, 322
Henningsen, Helen, 352, 354
Henningsen v. Bloomfield Motors, 354–355
Hinckley, John, Jr., 197–198
Hindu law, 5
Hoffman, Morris, 207
Holmes, Oliver Wendell, 13, 84, 158, 250,
	351
Homosexual activity, 258–259
	same-sex marriage and, 346–347
Hora, Peggy, 208
Horowitz, Donald, 293–296
Houston, Charles, 305–306
Hughes, Charles Evans, 164
Human Life Bill, 322
Hung juries, 151

Impeachment, 56, 78
Indictment, 182
Indigent defendants, 118–119, 141
	Escobedo v. Illinois, 157–158
	Gideon v. Wainwright, 25–26, 27,
		118–119, 141
In forma pauperis petitions, 156
Initial appearances, 178–179
Injuries, 219–220
Inquisitorial systems, 102–103
*In re Agent Orange Product Liability
	Litigation,* 216–219
Insanity defense, 197–200
Internal Revenue Service, 30

Interrogations, 193–197
Interrogatories, 225
Interstate influences, 348–349
Islamic law, 5
Ives v. South Buffalo Railway, 34

Jackson, Robert, 268
Jacob, Herbert, 187
James v. Wallace, 280–281
Japan, litigation rates in, 235
Jefferson, Thomas, 30, 56
Jeffords, Jim, 78
Johnson, Lyndon, 88, 120
Johnson v. Louisiana, 152
Johnson v. Zerbst, 141
Jones v. Wallace, 283
Judges, 53–96
	advocacy and arbitration by, 86–88
	appellate, 90–92
	attitudes of, 262–265
	in bench trials, 142–143
	decision making by, 247–273
	federal, 71–79
	in France, 86, 87
	importance of, 55
	independence vs. accountability of,
		56–57
	instructions to juries by, 149–150
	plea bargaining and, 186–187
	presidential appointment of, 71–79
	in pretrial conferences, 226
	qualifications of, 55, 58
	representativeness of, 57
	selection of, 55, 57–69, 71–86
	state, 57–71
	Supreme Court, 79–86
	trial, 88–90
	work of, 86–92
Judicial activism, 267, 297–299, 341–342
Judicial decision making, 247–273
	deductive reasoning in, 253–254
	implications of, 259–260
	institutional factors in, 267–270
	judicial roles and, 265–267
	legal perspective on, 248–261
	legislative history in, 250–251
	personal values and, 260–261
	phases of, 248–249
	political perspective on, 248, 260–270
	precedent in, 251–253
	tools of, 249–253

Judicial independence, 56–57
Judicial policymaking, 277–303
    administrative oversight and, 286–287,
        291
    agenda of, 292
    common law and, 287–288, 292
    cumulative, 289–290, 292
    development of legal issues and,
        325–326
    evaluating, 293–299
    historical shifts in, 291–292
    incidence of, 290–292
    judicial review and, 278–282, 291
    legal obligation and, 327–329
    legitimacy of, 297–299
    levels of, 290
    occasions of, 278–290
    policy change and, 326–327
    policy effectiveness and, 330–331
    remedial, 282–283, 291
    state court, 337–364
    statutory interpretation and, 283–286,
        291
Judicial restraint, 267, 297–299
Judicial review, 278–282
Judicial selection, 57–69
    under Carter, 75
    under Clinton, 77–78
    effects of systems for, 68–69
    federal, 71–79
    in France, 86, 87
    under George W. Bush, 78–79
    gubernatorial appointment, 60
    legislative election, 60
    merit-based, 59–60, 65–68
    modes of, 57–61
    nonpartisan elections, 60
    partisan elections, 60
    politics of elections in, 61–65
    under Reagan and Bush, 75–77
    senatorial courtesy and, 72–74
    Supreme Court, 79–86
Judiciary Act of 1789, 29, 33
Juries, 150–155
    decision making in, 151–152
    evaluating, 152–155
    grand, 181–183
    historical changes in, 150–151
    hung, 151
    instructions to, 149–150
    mock, 146

nullification of, 151, 153–154
    right to trial by, 140–141
    selection of, 143–147
    shadow, 146
    size of, 151–152
Jurisdiction, 31–35
Justification phase, 248–249
Justinian, 7

Kavanaugh, Brett, 78
Kaye, Judith, 206
Kennedy, Anthony, 54–55
Kennedy, Robert, 73
Kennedy, Ted, 53–54
*Keyes v. School District No. 1, Denver,
    Colorado,* 313–314
Kluger, Richard, 309
Koerner, Gustave, 104
Kritzer, Herbert, 226
Krol, John Cardinal, 322
Ku Klux Klan, 308–309

Lader, Lawrence, 321–322
Langdell, Christopher Columbus,
    104–105
Larsen, David, 352–353, 354, 355
Laumann, Edward, 117
Law, 9–13
    criminal and civil, 11
    disputes about, 139
    equity and, 12–13
    misconceptions about, 13–17
    private and public, 9–11
    public policy and, 15–17
    substantive and procedural, 12
    uncertainty and, 13–15
Law clerks, 158–159
Lawrence v. Texas, 259
Law School Admission Test (LSAT),
    102–103
Lawyers, 97–131
    access to services of, 117–124
    advertising by, 115, 121–122
    clients and, 124–126
    contingent fees and, 122–123
    criticisms of, 1–2, 99–101
    defense, 174
    demographics of, 109–111
    divided legal profession and, 117
    education of, 102–107
    ethics and, 99–101

in Great Britain, 106–107
indigent defendants and, 25–26, 27, 118–119, 141, 157–158
inquisitorial systems and, 102–103
in jury selection, 144–147
legal profession and, 102–111
minorities as, 109, 111
monopoly of, 122
number of, 107–108
organization of legal profession and, 111
in other countries, 104
practices of, 112–117
prosecutors, 173
right to counsel and, 141
tactics of, 137
women as, 105, 109
Lee v. Weisman, 13–14
Legal aid, 119–121
Legal briefs, 162–163
Legal clinics, 115, 121–122
Legal Defense Fund, 305–306
Legal expertise, 267–270
Legal obligations of policy changes, 327–329
Legal perspective, 248–261
Legal practices, 112–117
Legal Realists, 255–259, 270
Legal reasoning
  deductive, 253–254
  by example, 255–259
Legal Services Corporation (LSC), 116, 120–121, 122
  lawyer/client relationship and, 126
Legal Services Program (LSP), 120
Legal systems, 3–9
  civil-law, 7–9
  common-law, 3, 6–7, 8–9
Legal text, 249–250
Legislative courts, 28
  See also Federal courts
Legislative history, 250–251
Legitimacy, of judicial policymaking, 297–299
Levi, Edward, 255–259
Liebeck, Stella, 360–361
Lieberman, Jethro, 357
Litigation explosion, 218, 233–237
  alternative dispute resolution and, 237–242
  product liability, 359–362

Madison, James, 29, 250
Majoritarianism, 298
Mandatory minimum sentences, 201
Mann Act, 249–250
Manufacturing defects, 353
Mapp v. Ohio, 194
Marbury v. Madison, 280
Marriage, same-sex, 346–347
Marshall, Margaret, 346–347
Marshall, Thurgood, 83, 97–99
  Brown v. Board of Education and, 305–306, 307
Master jury lists, 143–144
McCorvey, Norma, 320–321
  See also Roe v. Wade
McReynolds, James, 166
Mediation, 239–240
Merit selection, 59–60, 65–68
Milliken v. Bradley, 314, 326
Minorities
  affirmative action and, 15–17, 111
  civil rights cases and, 38
  desegregation and, 16–17, 98, 125, 304–315
  in district courts, 38
  judicial representativeness and, 57, 69–71
  jury selection and, 144–145
  as lawyers, 109, 111
  in the Supreme Court, 83
Miranda v. Arizona, 157–158, 162–163, 165
Missouri Plan, 59–60
Missouri v. Jenkins, 314
M'Naghten test, 198–200
Model Code of Judicial Conduct, 111
Model Penal Code, 198–199, 317
Mortenson v. United States, 284–285
Motions, 225–226

Napoleonic Code, 8
Nardulli, Peter, 189
National Association for Repeal of Abortion Laws (NARAL), 318
National Association for the Advancement of Colored People (NAACP), 305–306
  Marshall and, 97–98
National Environmental Protection Act, 287
National Institute of Justice, 196

National Judicial College, 88
National Reporter, 168
Negligence, 353
Neubauer, David, 183
New Deal, 291
New England School of Law, 105
Nixon, Richard, 83–84, 84
Not guilty by reason of insanity (NGRI), 200
Nullification, jury, 151

O'Connor, Sandra Day, 83, 84–85, 165, 203–204, 266
Omnibus Budget Act of 1996, 120
Omnibus Judgeship Act of 1978, 72
O'Neill, Joy, 136
One-shotters (OS), 227–233
Opening statements, 147
Open-panel plans, 123–124
Oral argument, 163

Pasadena Board of Education v. Spangler, 315
Peel, Robert, 198
Penn, William, 150–151
Pickering, Charles, 80–81
Plain meaning rule, 249–250
Planned Parenthood of Central Missouri v. Danforth, 316
Planned Parenthood of Southeastern Pennsylvania v. Casey, 266, 316–317, 324
Plea bargaining, 183–192
    criticisms of, 189–190
    cross-cultural comparison of, 184–185
    evaluating, 191–192
    process of, 183–187
    reasons for, 187–189
Pleadings, 223–224
Plessy v. Ferguson, 282, 304, 305–306
Police misconduct, 193–197
Policymaking
    federal court, 304–336
    judicial, 277–303
    in product liability, 349–363
    state court, 337–370
Political parties
    judicial decision making and, 263–265
    judicial selection and, 61–65
    Supreme Court justices and, 81, 83

Political perspective, 248
    attitudes and, 262–265
Portia Law School, 105
Pound, Roscoe, 6
Powell, Lewis, 53, 83, 97, 98–99, 159
Pratt, George, 217
Precedent
    in common-law systems, 6
    efficiency and, 253
    equality and, 252
    in judicial decision making, 251–253
    perspectives on, 254–255
    predictability and, 252
    reliance on, 252
Preliminary hearings, 181–183
Presidential appointments, 71–79
    obstacles to, 84–86
    selection criteria and, 80–84
Pretrial conferences, 226
Pretrial release, 180–181
Privacy, right to, 257–259, 348
Private law, 9–11
Privity of contract, 353, 354–355
Pro bono work, 124
Procedural law, 12
Product liability law, 350–363
    changes in, 350–357
    consequences of policy changes in, 357–362
    responses to, 362–363
Progressive Era, 291
Prosecutors, 173
Public defenders, 118–119, 174
Public law, 9–11
Public policy, 15–17
Punitive damages, 353, 355–356

Reagan, Ronald, 53
    abortion and, 322–323
    Hinckley and, 197–198
    judicial appointments by, 75–77, 84–85
Reasoning by example, 255–259
Recess appointments, 80–81
Reed v. Reed, 282–283
Regents of the University of California v. Bakke, 15–16
Rehabilitation, 201, 206–207
    See also Sentencing
Rehnquist, William, 83, 84, 163, 164
    voting patterns of, 264–265

Rein, Catherine, 115
Release on recognizance, 181
Remedial policymaking, 282–283, 291
Reno, Janet, 205
Repeat players (RP), 227–233
Representativeness, judicial, 57, 69
Republican Party of Minnesota v. White,
    62
Resnick, Alice, 63
Reutershan, Paul, 216
Rights, legal
    to counsel, 25–26, 118–119, 141
    privacy, 257–259, 348
    state guarantees of, 348–349
    trial by jury, 140–141
    in trials, 140–142
Right to treatment, 126
Robert, Bill, 66–67
Robinson v. Cahill, 283, 339, 342, 343,
    344
Roe v. Wade, 17, 84, 319–325
    effectiveness of, 330–331
    effects of, 324–325
    overruling, 157, 165, 266
    privacy rights and, 258
    responses to, 321–324
Role orientations, 265–267
Roman law, 7–8
Roosevelt, Franklin, 83
Roosevelt, Theodore, 83, 84
Rule of Four, 159–160
Russell, Charles, 87
Rust v. Sullivan, 322–323
Ryan, Michael, 216

Same-sex marriage, 346–347
*San Antonio Independent School District
    v. Rodriguez,* 337–339
Scalia, Antonin, 83, 163, 165, 251
School financing, 283, 337–349
    development of litigation on, 338–345
    interstate influences and, 348–349
Searches, illegal, 193–197, 282
Segal, Jeffrey, 265
Segregation, 16–17, 98, 125, 282
    federal courts on, 304–315
Senatorial courtesy, 72–74
Sentencing, 201–205
    discrimination in, 193
    judicial policymaking and, 289

plea bargaining and, 183–187
    reforms in, 201–204
Sentencing Reform Act of 1984, 202
Serrano v. Priest, 342–343
Simpson, O. J., 2, 135, 145, 146
Smith, William French, 197
Socialist law, 4
Socialization, 266
Sofaer, Abraham, 100
Solicitors, 106–107
Solo practices, 114–115
Souter, David, 84, 266
Southeastern Reporter, 168
Southern Manifesto, 309
Spaeth, Harold, 265
Specter, Arlen, 54
Speedy Trial Act of 1974, 141
Spence, Gerry, 146
Standing Committee on Federal
    Judiciary, 74, 111
Stanford v. Kentucky, 247–248
Stare decisis, 6, 253
    judicial policymaking and, 287–288
    See also Precedent
State courts, 41–48
    caseloads in, 41–42
    civil cases in, 227–231
    development of, 46–48
    judges in, 57–71
    policymaking in, 337–370
    state legislatures and, 342–345
    structure of, 43–45
    trial, 45
State-of-the-art defense, 353
Statutory interpretation, 283–286, 291
Stenberg v. Carhart, 316, 324
Stevens, John Paul, 159
Stith, Kate, 204–205
Strickland, Diane, 205
Strict liability, 353, 354–355
Substantive law, 12
Supreme Court, U.S., 41
    on abortion, 315–325
    on affirmative action, 15–17, 111,
        277–278
    agenda setting in, 156–162
    on capital punishment, 247–248
    case selection in, 158–162
    constitutional law and, 9–10
    as court of last resort, 28

Supreme Court U.S. (*Continued*)
  criteria for judicial selection to, 80–84
  decision making in, 163–165
  on flag burning, 253, 255–256
  on gender discrimination, 282–283
  information gathering in, 162–163
  intercourt relations and, 40
  judicial policymaking agenda of, 292
  judicial selection for, 79–86
  jurisdiction of, 34–35
  law clerks in, 158–159
  obstacles to presidential influence in,
      84–86
  opinion writing, 164–165
  policy change and, 326–327
  on privacy, 257–259
  process in, 156–166
  promulgating decisions in, 165–166
  rejection of nominees to, 85
  on school financing, 283
  on segregation, 16–17, 98, 125, 282,
      304–315
  on sentencing guidelines, 203–204
  voting behavior of, 264–265
Supreme Courts, state, 43, 44, 339,
    342–343
*Swann v. Charlotte-Mecklenburg Board
    of Education,* 312, 328

Tax Court, 30
Texas v. Johnson, 253, 255–256
Text, legal, 249–250
Therapeutic justice, 206–207
Thomas, Clarence, 71, 85
Timeliness, 293–294
Tocqueville, Alexis de, 156
Tort law, 10, 218–219, 349–363
  products liability law and, 350–363
Trials, 135–171
  access to legal services and, 117–124
  appeals, 155–168
  bench vs. jury, 142–143
  defendant's case in, 148–149
  as disputes, 138–139
  diversity of, 140
  fact-finding in, 138–139
  judges in, 88–90
  by jury, 140–141, 142–155
  process in, 142–150

prosecution's case in, 147–148
  rights in, 140–142
True bills, 182
Truman, Harry, 84
Tushnet, Mark, 306

Uncertainty
  in civil justice, 222
  courts/law and, 13–15
Uniform Crime Reports (UCR), 175, 177
United States Reports, 166
United States v. Booker, 203–204
United States v. Nixon, 84, 164, 280
Unsecured bail, 180

Venire, 144
Vinson, Donald, 145
Voir dire, 144, 145–146
Voluntary arbitration, 238
Von Bulow, Klaus, 135–136
Von Bulow, Sunny, 135–136

War on drugs, 205–208
War on Poverty, 120
Warren, Earl, 160
Wealth, influence of, 100
Webster, Daniel, 163
Webster v. Reproductive Health Services,
    165, 316, 324
Weddington, Sarah, 320
Weeks v. United States, 194
Weinstein, Jack, 217–218
White, Byron, 141, 259
White, Penny, 67
White Slave Traffic Act of 1910,
    249–250
Williams v. Florida, 152
William the Conqueror, 3
Wilson, James Q., 178
Wisdom, John Minor, 311
Witnesses
  defendant's case and, 148–149
  prosecution's case and, 147–148
  securing and confronting, 141–142
Wolf v. Colorado, 194
Writ of certiorari, 158–159, 160, 161

Yale Law School, 106
Yannacone, Victor, 216